XML Development with Java™ 2

Michael C. Daconta

Albert J. Saganich Jr.

D1455926

SAMS

201 West 103rd St., Indianapolis, Indiana, 46290 USA

XML Development with Java™ 2

Copyright ©2000 by Sams Publishing

International Standard Book Number: 0-672-31653-6

Library of Congress Catalog Card Number: 99-63647

Printed in the United States of America

First Printing: October 2000

02 01 00   4 3 2 1

Trademarks

All terms mentioned in this book that are known to be trademarks or service marks have been appropriately capitalized. Sams Publishing cannot attest to the accuracy of this information. Use of a term in this book should not be regarded as affecting the validity of any trademark or service mark.

Warning and Disclaimer

Every effort has been made to make this book as complete and as accurate as possible, but no warranty or fitness is implied. The information provided is on an "as is" basis. The authors and the publisher shall have neither liability or responsibility to any person or entity with respect to any loss or damages arising from the information contained in this book or from the use of the CD or programs accompanying it.

ASSOCIATE PUBLISHER
Michael Stephens

ACQUISITIONS EDITOR
Steve Anglin

DEVELOPMENT EDITORS
Gus A. Miklos
Mark Renfrow

MANAGING EDITOR
Matt Purcell

PROJECT EDITOR
George E. Nedeff

COPY EDITORS
Michael Dietsch
Pat Kinyon

INDEXER
Diane Brenner

PROOFREADER
Matt Wynalda

TECHNICAL EDITOR
Piroz Mohseni

SOFTWARE DEVELOPMENT SPECIALIST
Dan Scherf

INTERIOR DESIGN
Gary Adair
Anne Jones

COVER DESIGN
Anne Jones

PRODUCTION
Darin Crone

Overview

Contents

3   The Document Object Model (DOM)   91

About the Authors

Michael C. Daconta is the Director of Web and Technology Services for McDonald Bradley, Inc., where he develops advanced systems with Java, JavaScript, and XML. Additionally, Mr. Daconta teaches introductory and advanced courses in numerous Web technologies. He is a Sun-certified Java programmer who has been developing software for 16 years. He co-authored *Java Pitfalls* and *Java 2 and JavaScript for C and C++ Programmers* and authored *C++ Pointers and Dynamic Memory Management*.

Albert J. Saganich Jr. is a principal technologist with BEA Systems Inc., where he develops, trains, and mentors on Java, XML, and related Internet technologies. Al is currently responsible for developing and maintaining the BEA WebLogic Server training curriculum and presents training materials whenever he can. He has been involved with software development for almost 15 years and has co-authored *Java 2 and JavaScript for C and C++ Programmers* (with Mike Daconta) as well as *The Microsoft Visual J++ SourceBook* (with Jay Cross). In his spare time Al writes articles on Java, C++, and XML, trains in the martial arts, and rides dirt bikes with his children.

Dedications

This book is dedicated to the men and women of the World Wide Web Consortium (W3C) and the whole XML community. Their tireless efforts have created the foundation of our technological future. Without their accomplishments, this work would not exist. As Sir Isaac Newton said, "If I have seen further, it is because I have stood on the shoulders of giants." Thank you.

—Michael Daconta

This book is also dedicated to my friend of many years, Brian Dilley, who recently died of cancer. Brian was a wonderful person, a great father, and a dedicated husband, and he is greatly missed.

—Al Saganich

Acknowledgments

Whenever I sit down to write acknowledgements I feel like George Bailey in *It's a Wonderful Life,* when, at the end of the movie, he is overwhelmed with gratitude for the multitude of friends in his life. I am lucky to have the supportive family and friends that I do. Here is a brief thank you.

Thanks to my dear wife Lynne and my children CJ, Gregory, and Samantha. There are no words to express the wonderfully bizarre rituals of raising a family, except maybe "Go team!" Thanks to the rest of my family—my father and "Grandma T," Shirley and Buddy, my mother, and the "Arizona gang."

Thanks to a great co-author, Al Saganich, for another heroic effort. Thanks to Steve Anglin at Sams Publishing for his patience and willingness to get it right.

Thanks to my new friends at McDonald Bradley: Sharon McDonald, Ken Bartee, Danny Proko, Charlie Sowell, and Gayle Levin. The warm McDonald Bradley culture is the perfect environment for innovation, camaraderie and software excellence. Thanks to my MDITDS colleagues for their hard work on a tough, forward-looking project: Sandy Whittington, Janice Pryor, Ruben Wise, Don Bolser, Joel Gladding, and Larry Thimm.

Finally, thanks to my readers. Your dedication to poring through source code and struggling through complex explanations inspires me to keep pushing hard to make it better. Thanks.

—Michael Daconta

Acknowledgements are always the most difficult part of writing a book. So many people are involved and contribute in so many different ways, and I'm always afraid I'll miss someone important. But here goes:

First I'd like to thank my wife Becky and my children Jackie and A.J. and, of course, my parents Al Sr. and Carol, without whose continued support I could never have even entertained the idea of beginning a book, never mind completing one. You put up with more then anyone should ever have too and always had a smile to help me over the rough spots.

I'd also like to thank my friends Mike and Sally and their children Dan and Lauren, who supplied many Saturday night dinners, providing sustenance for both body and soul, not to mention a much-needed distraction from the pressures of everyday life!

No work of this nature could ever have been completed without dedication. I've trained in the martial arts now for years and I owe that dedication to my instructor, Sifu Henrick Hamberg, and my constant training partner Chris Nadeau. Without you two I would never have gotten where I am today.

Many thanks to my co-conspirator Mike Daconta for involving me in yet another great project. You are a wellspring of great ideas and I can only imagine what you will come up with next. And to Steve Anglin and the entire staff at Sams Publishing for patience, understanding, and drive to get it right.

And, of course, the entire crew at the Maynard BEA Education office, especially Tyler, Stephanie, Jay, Jose, and all the other great people of BEA. You guys provide so much insight, ideas, motivation, and inspiration and you are all so much fun to work with!

And finally, special thanks to Jay Cross, who got me involved in the whole Java thing so long ago.

You guys are all the best! Thanks!

—Al Saganich

Tell Us What You Think!

As the reader of this book, *you* are our most important critic and commentator. We value your opinion and want to know what we're doing right, what we could do better, what areas you'd like to see us publish in, and any other words of wisdom you're willing to pass our way.

As Associate Publisher for Sams, I welcome your comments. You can fax, email, or write me directly to let me know what you did or didn't like about this book—as well as what we can do to make our books stronger.

Please note that I cannot help you with technical problems related to the topic of this book, and that due to the high volume of mail I receive, I might not be able to reply to every message.

When you write, please be sure to include this book's title and author as well as your name and phone or fax number. I will carefully review your comments and share them with the author and editors who worked on the book.

Fax: 317.581.4770

Email: xml@mcp.com

Mail: Michael Stephens
         Sams Publishing
         201 West 103rd Street
         Indianapolis, IN 46290 USA

Introduction

XML Development with Java™ *2*

"The first step is putting data on the Web in a form that machines can naturally understand, or converting it to that form. This creates what I call a Semantic Web—a web of data that can be processed directly or indirectly by machines."

—Tim Berners-Lee, *Weaving the Web*

Welcome to *XML Development with Java 2*. This book provides an in-depth guide to developing XML applications with Java. The topics cover implementing XML standards, such as DOM and XSL, in Java, and exploring XML's influence on Java libraries such as Swing and JavaBeans. In addition, nontrivial examples demonstrate all the topics with complete working programs. Last, a building-block approach gets you up and programming quickly and then follows through later with details on the less common features of the standards.

This book assumes that you are familiar with the basics of programming Java. We do not assume you are familiar with XML and walk through all aspects of the key standards. If you are familiar with XML, you can skip over the chapters that teach the basics and focus on the more advanced topics like parsing, XSLT, and EJB integration. Also, this book does not attempt to cover all the XML standards as some are still in flux (or have no implementation) and others are applications of the base standards (such as the Math Markup Language).

Why XML?

Tim Berners-Lee, the inventor of the World Wide Web, hopes to see his creation change in two ways: first, to become more collaborative and, second, to move from presentation to multipurpose processing. While a more collaborative Web requires browsers to morph into full-scale multimedia editors, the second change to the Web requires reengineering of the lingua franca of the Web. In other words, where HTML is a presentation language, the next-generation Web requires a richer communication set that can be automatically processed by computers, traveling software agents and end-user browsers (hopefully of the multimedia-enriched, collaborative kind). So, the key idea is that the next-generation Web will be as easily traversable by computer programs as it is surfed by browsers.

The second-generation Web is approaching and XML is the engine that will take us there. It is not a question of whether XML will become pervasive on the Web but how quickly it will happen. XML's first beachhead will be business-to-business commerce and from there it will spread throughout the entire Web, eventually creating new concepts, opportunities and extrapolated technologies. Now is the time for you to become proficient in XML development to be on the forefront of this technological wave.

Why XML with Java?

Request for Comments (RFC) 2396 describes the syntax of Uniform Resource Identifiers (URIs), which are related to Uniform Resource Locators (URLs). However, the original name of these resource descriptions was *Universal* Resource Identifiers. The goal was and is clear: a *universal* information space. An information space not confined to one type of computer, one type of application, or one geography. The World Wide Web consortium is, in essence, handling the data side of this information space. The applications to take advantage of this universal information space are left up to the software industry. This is where Java becomes the most obvious choice for an implementation vehicle. Java was designed to be a network-savvy universal computing platform. Thus Java aids the adoption of XML by providing implementations that can run anywhere.

Another theoretical example of the affinity of Java and XML is they both represent implementations of user-defined versus technological-defined goals. In other words, both put accomplishing a user-defined task above operating efficiently on computing hardware. Java's interpreted code provides the user benefit of write once, run anywhere. XML's human-readable "text as data" prescription provides the user benefit of application independence. Both have purposely sacrificed computing efficiency for user-defined goals. This is why many people proclaim the convergence of these technologies as nothing short of a technological revolution.

A more practical reason for processing XML with Java is that Java has established itself as the de facto standard for server side computing. So, as XML becomes the de facto standard for storing corporate data, that data will be manipulated, stored and transformed by Java enterprise programs.

Organization of the Book

This book is organized in two ways: The first part of the book follows a loose building-block sequence and the rest covers key topics but in no particular order.

The individual chapters in the book are

- Chapter 1, "An XML Primer"—Walks you through the basics of creating XML documents. Detailed examples demonstrate each component of an XML document. This chapter quickly gives you the basics necessary to understand the key parts of an XML document that you will want to parse for use in a Java application. The key idea is that you need to know just enough XML to get to parsing XML documents.

- Chapter 2, "Parsing XML"—Covers parsing XML documents in detail for both Java applications and applets. The chapter focuses on the two most prevalent standards for parsing: SAX and the `javax.xml` standard extension. Includes a detailed discussion of the Aelfred parser that is specifically designed to be fast and small. Aelfred is perfect for applets.

- Chapter 3, "The Document Object Model (DOM)"—This chapter covers the DOM specification and several implementations. Covers both traversing a DOM and creating a DOM structure from scratch.

- Chapter 4, "Advanced XML"—This chapter fills in all the details of the XML Specification glossed over in Chapter 1. In addition, it covers new and emerging XML areas such as namespaces, XLINK, and XPointer.

- Chapter 5, "Java and the Extensible Stylesheet Language (XSL)"—This chapter covers both the XSL Transformation specification and the XSL Formatting objects specification. Includes demonstrations using several XSLT processors such as XT, LotusXSL, and Microsoft Internet Explorer. Includes numerous style sheet examples covering every major feature of the specification.

- Chapter 6, "Collections and XML"—Introduces the Java collection classes and their similarity to the DOM, then examines how to integrate the DOM with Java's built-in collection classes. Also demonstrates sorting a DOM.

- Chapter 7, "Swing and XML"—Covers the interaction between Swing and XML in the areas of DOM viewing and GUI construction. Demonstrates how to view a DOM using a JTree and a JTable. Demonstrates how simple XML-based markup languages can ease GUI constructions. Demonstrates a simple menu markup language to quickly build menus.

- Chapter 8, "JavaBeans, EJB, and XML"—Covers both JavaBeans and Enterprise JavaBeans. For JavaBeans, demonstrates saving state via XML and XML for Bean composition. For Enterprise JavaBeans (EJB), provides a thorough introduction and exploration of the EJB architecture before examining how XML can be used for Bean-managed persistence.

- Chapter 9, "Servlets and XML"—Introduces the basics of servlets programming before discussing its integration with XML. Uses a real-world example, an aphorisms Web site, to demonstrate the key concepts. The site collects and displays aphorisms. To accomplish this, we cover converting form data inputs to XML, storing XML, and transforming XML to HTML.

- Chapter 10, "XML and Database Access"—This chapter covers the integration of relational databases and XML. The topics range from techniques you can implement today to emerging technologies of tomorrow. First, we cover how to map relational databases to XML. Second, we explain how Oracle integrated XML into Oracle 8i. Last, we cover the current state of the XML Query language specification.

Comments Welcome

This book is written by programmers for programmers. All comments and suggestions from the entire computing community are appreciated. We would like to thank the many readers in the past who have helped improve our books with their thoughtful and constructive comments. We can be reached electronically at the following addresses:

Mike Daconta can be reached at `mdaconta@aol.com`.

Al Saganich can be reached at `al.saganich@bicnet.net`.

Best wishes,

Mike Daconta,
Bealeton, Virginia

An XML Primer

"XML gives Java something to do."

—Jon Bosak, XML, Java, and the Future of the Web

IN THIS CHAPTER

This chapter introduces you to the Extensible Markup Language (XML). I will cover its history, benefits, and components. The components will be discussed and demonstrated in detail that include the prolog, elements, attributes, comments, and the document type definition (DTD). Some advanced topics are deferred to Chapter 4, "Advanced XML." The top priority of this chapter is for you to master enough of the basics to prepare you to begin parsing XML in the next chapter.

History of XML

The first thing to understand about Extensible Markup Language (XML) is that the name is a misnomer. XML is not a markup language. XML is a set of rules for creating new markup languages. So, let's begin with a definition of XML and then deconstruct the definition into its parts:

XML is a subset of the Standard Generalized Markup Language (SGML) that specifies the rules for creating markup languages, such as the Hypertext Markup Language (HTML) that can be shared on the World Wide Web (WWW).

Since XML is a subset of SGML and every valid XML document is also a valid SGML document, let's first examine SGML. SGML was a standardization of the Generalized Markup Language invented by Dr. Charles Goldfarb, Ed Mosher, and Ray Lorie in 1969 while working for IBM. It is interesting to note that GML is the same initials as the three inventor's last names. The idea behind GML was to formalize the markup of text documents that was already occurring in the publishing industry. When a publisher received raw text, a copy editor marked up the document with instructions to the typesetter on layout, fonts, indentation, and spacing. These hand-written instructions are traditionally called markup. Generic markup separates the logical structure of a document from its content. After you have the structure of a document, you can attach a stylesheet to it that specifies formatting instructions for each structural element. In 1974, Dr. Goldfarb produced the first validating parser for GML. Between 1978 and 1986, Dr. Goldfarb acted as technical lead of a team to transition GML into ISO 8879, which they called SGML.

As stated earlier, markup allows you to separate the structure of a document from its content.

The structure denotes the purpose of the document's data. In computer science, this type of data that describes other data is called *meta-data*. For example, if I circle the first sentence in a paragraph and label it as a title, that label is meta-data about the original data (the circled sentence). Both the label title and the sentence are data; however, the label "title" is information intended to clarify or modify the information it is applied to. So, meta-data is data that is outside the original data, for the purpose of enhancing or clarifying the original. So, SGML is a formalized method for capturing the meta-data for a document by using markup on the content. Table 1.1 is an example of data and meta-data.

TABLE 1.1 Data and Meta-data

Data	*Meta-data*
Michael Daconta	Name
4296 Razor Hill Road	Street
Bealeton	City
VA	State
22712	Zip Code

So, SGML defines the rules for creating markup. A markup language is an application of SGML (or the rules thereof). A markup language is composed of a set of markup tags (words that describe purpose) and a specific tree structure to describe one type of document. The legal tags and tree description (also called a *content model*) reside in a file called a *document type definition* (DTD). The best known example of a markup language is HTML. Let's discuss a brief history of HTML to understand how it relates to SGML and its influence on XML.

In 1989, Tim Berners-Lee and Anders Berglund developed a markup language for hyperlinked text documents.[1] It is interesting to note that they started from one of the first published SGML document type definitions from an IBM manual written by Dr. Goldfarb. Their markup language was called the Hypertext Markup Language (HTML). HTML is a language that describes hypertext documents. A hypertext document is a document with a head and body whose body can contain text, lists, links to other documents, images, forms, frames, and other components.

HTML was an application of SGML. The key components of HTML are start tags, end tags, elements, attributes, comments, and entity references. Listing 1.1 is a simple example of an HTML document.

---

1 Berners-Lee, Tim, "Information Management: A proposal" March 1989, May 1990

LISTING 1.1   A Simple HTML Example

```
<HTML>
    <HEAD>
        <TITLE> Java Programming Tutorial </TITLE>
    </HEAD>
    <BODY>
        <!-- Created 2/8/1999 -->
        <UL>
        <LI> <A HREF="chap1.html"> Chapter One </A>
        <LI> <A HREF="chap2.html"> Chapter Two </A>
        </UL>
    </BODY>
</HTML>
```

Table 1.2 highlights the key HTML components from Listing 1.1.

TABLE 1.2   HTML Components

HTML Component	Description
`<BODY>`	Start tag
`</BODY>`	End tag
`<TITLE> Java Programming Tutorial</TITLE>`	Element
`<A HREF="chap1.html">`	Attribute
`<!-- Created 2/8/1999 -->`	Comment

Tim Berners-Lee and his team at the Centre Européen pour la Recherche Nucléaire (CERN, or the European Center for Nuclear Research) also created the Hypertext Transfer Protocol (HTTP), the Web browser, and the Web server. In February of 1993, while a student at the University of Illinois and working at the National Center for Supercomputing Applications (NCSA), Marc Andreessen (and a small team of peers) created a graphical Web browser called Mosaic. Although Mosaic was not the first graphical Web browser, the NCSA team ported it to the three most popular platforms (Windows, Mac, and Unix) and gave it away free. In 1994, Jim Clark (founder of Silicon Graphics, Inc.) and Marc Andreessen co-founded Netscape Communications (originally called Mosaic Communications Corp). Soon after, they released the Netscape Navigator Web browser. As the Web grew in popularity, HTML was extended for new purposes; however, soon it became apparent that proprietary extensions to HTML were counter-productive and ill-suited to general use. So, to solve the problems of interoperability and scalability on the Web without extending HTML, the W3C began work on a simplified version of SGML which it called the Extensible Markup Language (XML).

Some people attempt to qualitatively compare HTML to XML because XML is seen as a replacement to HTML. XML is not intended as a replacement for HTML and both are complementary technologies. XML is a more general and better solution to the problem of sharing data on the Web than extending HTML. It should be obvious that extending a single language to every possible case is impossible. Unique cases require unique languages, which is why each vertical industry quickly develops its own specialized jargon. Those vertical domains of data can be structured and captured by an XML-compliant markup language and presented via HTML or the Extensible Stylesheet Language (XSL), covered in Chapter 5.

The Extensible Markup Language (XML) 1.0 was made a World Wide Web Consortium (W3C) recommendation on February 10, 1998. A recommendation is the final step in the W3C process for creating Web standards. As stated earlier, XML is a subset of SGML, which specifies specific syntactic and semantic rules and constraints for creating new markup languages. Although it is currently common practice to describe documents that follow the XML standard as "XML documents," that description is too generic. You actually create HTML, MathML (Math Markup Language), or CML (Chemical Markup Language) documents, which you design using the rules laid out in the XML specification. So, this makes the term *XML document* an abstract concept that has no concrete implementation. Listing 1.2 is an example of an Address Book Markup Language (ABML) document. ABML is an XML-compliant language.

LISTING 1.2   ABML Document

```
<?xml version="1.0"?>

<!DOCTYPE ADDRESS_BOOK SYSTEM "abml.dtd">
<ADDRESS_BOOK>
    <ADDRESS>
<NAME>Michael Daconta </NAME>
<STREET>4296 Razor Hill Road </STREET>
        <CITY>Bealeton </CITY>
        <STATE>VA </STATE>
        <ZIP>22712 </ZIP>
    </ADDRESS>
    <ADDRESS>
        <NAME>Sterling Software </NAME>
        <STREET> 7900 Sudley Road</STREET>
        <STREET> Suite 500</STREET>
        <CITY>Manassas</CITY>
        <STATE>VA </STATE>
        <ZIP>20109 </ZIP>
    </ADDRESS>
</ADDRESS_BOOK>
```

Since HTML predated XML, it is not currently XML compliant; however, the next version of HTML from the W3C will be XML compliant. So, let's examine some of the differences between HTML and XML. By comparing Listing 1.1 and Listing 1.2, you can see the major constructs of both languages, such as start and end tags. Also, comments and attributes are identical. The differences result in XML being a stricter specification. Here is a list of the differences:

NOTE

The W3C has released a Recommendation of HTML reformulated as an XML 1.0–compliant language and called XHTML 1.0. See http://www.w3.org/TR/xhtml1.

- XML elements (composed of a start and end tag) must be strictly nested. For example, `<B><I> Improper Nesting </B></I>` is legal in HTML but illegal in XML. The proper nesting would be for the `<I>` element to be fully enclosed within the `<B>` element like this: `<B><I> Proper Nesting </I></B>`.

- In XML, every start tag must have an end tag. For example, in HTML the List Item and paragraph tags are not required to have an end tag. In HTML, this is legal: `<LI> Platoon Leader, US Army`. That statement would be illegal in XML. In XML, you would write `<LI> Platoon Leader, US Army </LI>`.

- Both HTML and XML allow empty tags. An empty tag does not have any content associated with it. For example, the HTML image tag is `<IMG SRC="portrait.jpg">`. However, in XML an empty tag must have a forward slash before the closing greater than character like this: `<IMG SRC="portrait.jpg" />` You can think of this as combining a start and end tag.

- XML documents allow only one *root element*. A root element is the top-level element that contains all other elements. For example, in Listing 1.1, `<HTML>` is the root element. While one root element is the norm, this requirement is formalized in the XML specification.

- All attribute values in XML must be surrounded by single or double quotes. In HTML a single value does not require quotes. So, where in HTML you can have `<PARAM value=10>`, in XML it must be `<PARAM="10">`.

- XML tags are case sensitive, whereas HTML tags are not. In HTML, `<BODY>` and `<body>` are the same tag. In XML, they are two different tags.

- Whitespace between tags is ignored in HTML but is preserved in XML and considered relevant and is passed on by the XML parser to the processing application.

Benefits of XML

Much of the fervor over XML is due to the fact that XML provides numerous benefits over our current system of proprietary data formats. Of course, this XML revolution would not have been possible if hardware advances had not given us enough performance to process and translate data into an application-independent format. This is a similar case to the success of an interpreted language such as Java. Hardware advances have given us the luxury of a universal interpreted language that performs on par with compiled languages of the past. Without such hardware advances, these technologies would have languished in the tar pits of inefficiency and immaturity. Both XML and Java require ubiquity to be successful and to progress beyond a good idea and into production systems. The benefits of XML are

- *Data Independence*—Using XML, data is no longer dependent on a specific application for creation, viewing, or editing. In this sense, XML is to data what Java is to applications. Java allows programs to run anywhere. XML allows data to be used by any application. Thus you also see the natural synergy between the two as expressed in the subtitle of this book (*Portable Code Meets Portable Data*). This data independence fosters application interoperability, more choice for users and improved information sharing in and between organizations.

- *Improved domain knowledge, terminology, and communication*—By undergoing the arduous task of creating a meta-language to describe a particular domain, all organizations in that domain will benefit tremendously from the process of articulating such a language. In one sense, this activity represents humans assisting computers so that they can in turn better serve us. In another sense, computers are forcing us to be more explicit and exact in both the content and meaning of our communication.

- *One data source, multiple views*—By formatting our data in a markup language, we allow computer applications to process and present this data to us in different ways. This separation of model and view has been used successfully in both Smalltalk and the Java Foundation Classes. Also, more insight into a large array of data can be obtained by viewing the data in multiple formats. Last, the processing of data into multiple views is the perfect role for a Java-powered client that receives the XML-formatted data from the server. This is the key idea behind Jon Bosak's prophetic statement, "XML gives Java something to do."

- *Enables e-commerce transactions*—An e-commerce transaction requires instant cooperation between a host of agents involved in a single purchase. Commerce requires the connecting of a consumer with a demand to a supplier with a product. This transaction can involve numerous players: the customer, retail Web site, one or more banks, a distributor, and a supplier. For e-commerce to work efficiently and affordably, all these players need to exchange data among their disparate computer systems in real time. XML is the enabler for this new economic model.

- *Improved data searches*—Since XML addresses the purpose of data and not just the content, we can drastically improve our ability to find relevant information by storing our data on the Web in a rich XML-compliant language or set of languages. Current searches of documents (including HTML) are simply full or partial keyword matches against the content. An intelligent search engine against a body of XML-compliant markup languages would search both the content and the meta-data, which would drastically improve the accuracy of searches.

- *Increase in relevant and accessible data*—The world's databases will able to be encoded in an XML-compliant language and published on the Web. This will open up huge amounts of data to any and all applications interested in processing that data. This increases the opportunities for data mining on a global scale. Consider the vast amounts of information recorded over the holiday season on consumer buying habits via credit-card transactions.

- *Data access where you want it*—Similar to presenting different views of data, a single XML-compliant document can be automatically reformatted for different display devices. Data created and viewed one way on a personal computer can also be accessed, though in a more appropriate condensed format, on a palmtop computer or personal digital assistant. This same technique could also benefit handicapped people by reformatting the data for the specialized devices (current and future) that assist them.

- *Simpler application development*—Applications will no longer need to import or export hundreds of proprietary binary data formats. This makes application development simpler, which will lead to more competition, better focus on the main functionality of a particular application, and potentially lower costs for consumers due to the increased competition.

I hope you agree that the benefits of XML are not only interesting but have the potential to cause a revolution in the storage and processing of the world's data.

Components of XML

As stated in the section on the history of XML, XML is a formalization of rules for "marking up" documents with meta-data to convey extra information (the data's purpose) to the user. So, an XML-compliant document can be separated into markup and content. All markup starts with either an ampersand (&) or left angle bracket (<). There are six types of markup defined in XML. They are as follows: elements, attributes, comments, processing instructions, entity references, and CDATA sections.

- *Elements*—Elements are the most common aspect of markup languages. An element is a logical construct of a document. A normal element is composed of start and end tags that surround content, other elements, or both. The tags of an element are delimited by angle brackets. For example:

  ```
  <STREET> 4296 Razor Hill Road </STREET>
  ```

- *Attributes*—An element may have attributes that are specified in name/value pairs and are placed after the start-tag name. In this example, the width and height are the attributes:

  ```
  <APPLET width="100" height="200">
  ```

- *Comments*—A comment allows free text description that is ignored by an XML processor. For example:

  ```
  <!-- Keep this part it is really important. -->
  ```

- *Processing Instructions*—Processing instructions are used to pass information to a processing application. Here is the syntax of a processing instruction:

  ```
  <?application data ?>
  ```

- *Entity References*—Entity references are used to put reserved characters or abbreviations in markup. For example, the left angle bracket (<) is a reserved character. To put that character in your markup, use the reference <. The lt stands for *less than* and the ampersand (&) and semicolon (;) delimit the reference in the content. A list of all the predefined character references is provided in Chapter 4.

- *CDATA Sections*—A CDATA section is a section of text that should not be processed but instead passed directly to the application. This is useful for passing source code to an application. CDATA sections will be covered in detail in Chapter 4.

In addition to marking up your document, you can specify the rules that govern your new markup language. These rules will determine whether a document of your type is valid (follows your rules). You specify the rules for your language in a document type definition (DTD). In your document (called an *instance* of the DTD), you then indicate which DTD specifies the rules for your language in a document type declaration. Inside a DTD, you can declare elements, element attributes, and entity references. Figure 1.1 shows the one-to-many relationship between DTDs and instance documents, as well as the distinction between the document type declaration and the definition.

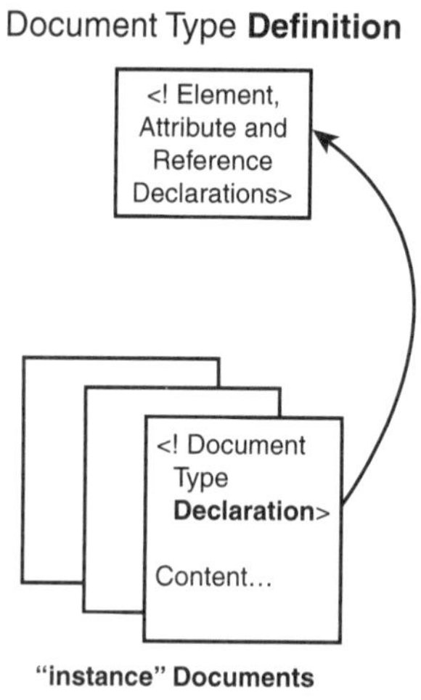

Document Type **Definition**

FIGURE **1.1**

Relationship between DTD and instances.

BNF Grammar

When describing each specific component of XML, at times we will refer to the exact words in the specification. To make sense of the specification, you must understand how it strictly defines the grammar of this language. To express XML in a manner in which computer-generated parsers can be built, the designers defined the language using *Backus-Naur form* (BNF). BNF describes a context-free grammar which is a system of definitions in the following form:

```
part_of_speech ::= definition
```

The ::= means "is defined as". A definition that is composed of a left-hand side (LHS) and a right-hand side (RHS) is called a production. For example, a production for an English sentence would be:

```
sentence ::= subject predicate PERIOD
```

A sentence is a subject followed by a predicate followed by a PERIOD. There are two types of symbols on the right-hand side: *nonterminal* symbols and *terminal* symbols. A nonterminal symbol must be defined further in the grammar (like the subject in a sentence). A terminal symbol is a literal word or symbol (like a "." for PERIOD) that needs no further expansion.

There are other ways to describe the right-hand side of a production. You can have the LHS equate to one among a choice of symbols. To do this, use the pipe symbol (|), which is commonly used as the OR operator in programming languages such as C and Java. Consider the following production:

```
Space ::= (#x20 | #x9 | #xD | #xA)+
```

This production would read as follows:

Space is defined as one or more spaces (character #20 in hex), carriage returns (#9) in hex, line feeds (#13 in hex), or tabs (#10 in hex). Note that in hexadecimal (which is a base-16 numbering system), the values 10 through 15 are represented with the letters A through F. In the production, it is important to notice the plus sign outside of the parentheses. The plus sign is an occurrence indicator that stands for "one or more". You will see this occurrence indicator again, as it is the same one used in the XML document type declaration. Other occurrence indicators are an asterisk (*), which means "zero or more" and a question mark, which means "zero or one".

Now that you have a general idea how a BNF Grammar works, we will examine how the document prolog is precisely defined in the XML Specification using BNF. We will examine BNF in more detail in Chapter 4. It is introduced here to highlight the fact that there is no ambiguity in the language specification. Every component of XML syntax is fully specified in BNF.

Prolog

A prolog is an introduction to a document. Here is a sample prolog of an XML document:

```
<?xml version="1.0"?>
<!DOCTYPE JDATA SYSTEM "javadata.dtd">
```

The prolog consists of two parts that are both optional. The first part is called the XML declaration and the second part the document type declaration. The specification states that both parts of the prolog are optional. Here is the formal definition (in BNF) of the prolog as listed in the XML specification:

```
[22] prolog ::= XMLDecl? Misc* (doctypedecl Misc*)?
[23] XMLDecl ::= '<?xml' VersionInfo EncodingDecl? SDDecl? S?
                 '?>'
[24] VersionInfo ::= S 'version' Eq (' VersionNum ' |
             "VersionNum")
[25] Eq ::= S? '=' S?
[26] VersionNum ::= ([a-zA-Z0-9_.:] | '-')+
[27] Misc ::= Comment | PI | S
```

Let's translate each production rule into a corresponding English sentence. We will cover all the symbols of the BNF syntax in more detail in Chapter 4; this section will just be an introduction.

Production 22 states that "a prolog is defined as an optional XML Declaration followed by one or more miscellaneous symbols (defined in production 27 as a comment or processing instruction or space) followed by an optional document type declaration."

Production 23 states that "an XML declaration is defined as the literal string `<?xml` followed by Version information followed by an optional Encoding declaration followed by an optional standalone document declaration followed by optional space then followed by the literal string `?>`."

Production 24 states that a version number is defined as "space followed by the literal string 'version' followed by an equal sign followed by a version number, which is surrounded by either single quotes or double quotes."

Production 25 states that the equal sign may be preceded or trailed by optional space (remember the production for space or whitespace was given earlier).

Production 26 states that a version number is defined as one or more of the following characters to include lowercase a through z, uppercase A through Z, the digits 0 through 9 or one of the following punctuation marks to include underscore, period, colon or hyphen. Notice that the hyphen must be declared as a literal separately because without the surrounding quotes it refers to a range of characters.

So, as stated more formally earlier, a prolog consists of an optional XML declaration and an optional document type declaration (discussed later). Almost all XML-compliant documents will use an XML declaration. An XML declaration consists of the literal string `<?xml`, followed by version information, followed by an optional encoding declaration, followed by an optional standalone document declaration, and ending with the literal text `?>`. Here is the minimum requirement for an XML declaration:

```
<?xml  version="1.0" ?>
```

If used, this must be the first item in every XML-compliant document you create. It specifies to a processing application which version of the specification your document adheres to. The optional encoding declaration is used to specify what character encoding your document will use. The default is Unicode (same as Java character set) encoded in UTF-8 format. The optional standalone document declaration is rarely used but specifies whether a processing application can skip downloading the document type definition to process the document. It takes the literal values of "yes" or "no." Here is another example of an XML declaration:

```
<?xml  version="1.0" encoding="UTF-8" standalone="no" ?>
```

Elements

An element is a logical component of a document. An element normally contains content, either character data or other elements, and is denoted by a start and end tag. For example:

```
<TITLE> This is an HTML title. </TITLE>
```

or

```
<HTML>
    <HEAD> ... </HEAD>
    <BODY> ... </BODY>
</HTML>
```

In XML, you can only have a single root element. That root element has subelements which may also have subelements. The structure of an XML document is a tree of elements. So, as stated earlier, if you think of an element as a container, an XML document becomes a container of containers. Containers have a name associated with them (the element name) and possible additional characteristics (called attributes). The containers hold the content (or data) of the document. The start and end tags define the boundaries of the container.

A start tag consists of a left angle bracket (<), an identifier or tag name, and a right angle bracket (>). Elements may also have attributes (discussed next). An end tag is identical to a start tag except that the identifier is preceded with a forward slash (/). In the XML specification, the precise definition of tag is < followed by an element-type name, followed by a >.

Some elements contain no content. These are called empty elements. You denote this by preceding the greater-than angle bracket with a forward slash—for example, `<EmptyTag/>`. Usually empty tags have attributes—for example:

```
<IMG SRC="house.jpg" />
```

NOTE

In XML, an element with content must have a start tag and an end tag.

Attributes

In addition to content, elements may have attributes. Attributes allow you to attach characteristics to an element. Attributes have a name and a value and are placed within the start tag—for example:

```
<APPLET code="myapplet.class">
```

In the document type definition (DTD), you define the legal attributes for an element and what values are legal for that attribute. We discuss creating a DTD in a following section.

An element can have multiple attributes—for example:

```
<APPLET code="myapplet.class" height="100" width="100">
```

In XML, the value must be surrounded by single or double quotes. When you use one type of quotes, the other type is legal within the quotes—for example:

```
<PERSON quote=" 'To Be or Not to Be' ">
```

Comments

A comment is extra information for humans who read the document, and is not meant for a program to use. When parsed by a computer program, comments are not passed on to the application. The format of a comment is as follows:

```
<!-- Note: remember to write more stuff here. -->
```

You are not allowed to put the characters "--" inside your comment content. Comments cannot go inside of tags or within other comments. Comments are useful to describe elements, especially cryptic ones such as <P>.

Document Type Definition

We have learned about the elements and attributes that represent the key indicators of the structure or purpose of our content but we have not yet covered how to determine which tags we can use in a document. A document type definition (DTD) declares all the legal elements in a document; the legal attributes those elements can have; and the hierarchy, nesting, and occurrence indicators for all elements. In order for a document to be valid it must specify what DTD it adheres to. A document specifies its DTD in a document type declaration.

If you remember back to the Prolog section, a document type declaration is optional but if present, occurs after the XML declaration and before the root element of the document. There are two forms of document type declarations: internal and external. An internal document type declaration is when you include the declaration in the same document with the markup and content. This is practical only for short DTDs. Listing 1.3 is an example of an internal DTD.

LISTING 1.3   Internal DTD

```
<?xml version="1.0"?>
<!DOCTYPE JDATA
[
<!ELEMENT JDATA (OBJECT)+>
<!ELEMENT OBJECT (PRIMITIVE|OBJECT|ARRAY)+>
<!ELEMENT PRIMITIVE (#PCDATA)>
<!ELEMENT ARRAY (PRIMITIVE+|OBJECT+|ARRAY)>
<!ATTLIST PRIMITIVE
    name    CDATA    #IMPLIED
    type    (string|byte|char|short|int|long|float|double|boolean) #REQUIRED>
<!ATTLIST OBJECT
```

LISTING 1.3   Continued

```
name    CDATA     #IMPLIED
    type CDATA     #IMPLIED>
<!ATTLIST ARRAY
    name    CDATA    #IMPLIED
    type    (array|object|string|byte|char|short|int|long|float|
 double|boolean) #REQUIRED>
]>

<JDATA>
<OBJECT name="test">
<PRIMITIVE name="anInt"
        type="int"> 200 </PRIMITIVE>
</OBJECT>
</JDATA>
```

All document type declarations start with the string literal <!DOCTYPE. The next word is the document name, which must correspond to the root element of the document. For an internal DTD, you include all the element declarations and attribute declarations between the open bracket ([) and the close bracket (]).

An external DTD is stored externally and referenced via a Uniform Resource Identifier (URI) which is similar to the more familiar Uniform Resource Locator (URL). A URL is one form of a URI and is the most common method for accessing external DTDs. Listing 1.4 is an example of an external DTD declaration.

LISTING 1.4   External DTD Declaration

```
<?xml version="1.0"?>
<!DOCTYPE JDATA SYSTEM "javadata.dtd">

<JDATA>
<OBJECT name="test">
<PRIMITIVE name="anInt"
        type="int"> 200 </PRIMITIVE>
</OBJECT>
</JDATA>
```

For external DTDs, the third part of the DTD declaration must be either SYSTEM or PUBLIC. If it is SYSTEM, the final part must be a Uniform Resource Identifier (URI). A URL is a valid URI. The format of a URL is as follows:

```
protocol://host[:port]/path/resource
```

The most common protocol in a URL is HTTP, the Hypertext Transfer Protocol. That is the protocol that Web browsers use to communicate with Web servers. A URI allows URLs to be extended with an optional query and an optional fragment identifier. We will discuss URIs in more detail in a future section on XPointers. In the example above, the URL is a relative URL, which means that the DTD is in the same directory as the current document. If you declare a DTD as PUBLIC it is followed by a unique name so that the software knows where to locate the DTD. In essence, the software vendors would provide these built-in DTDs.

The key benefit of an external DTD is for numerous documents to share a single DTD. By sharing the DTD, any changes to the DTD automatically affect all instance documents that refer to that DTD. Thus you have central management of the specification of your markup language. Secondly, space and time can be saved by not replicating a DTD among all instances of the document.

Element Declaration

Every element in a valid XML Document must correspond to an element type declared in a DTD. Element type declarations start with the string literal <!ELEMENT, followed by the element name, and then by a content specification. Here is the general form for an element declaration:

```
<!ELEMENT  elemName  content-spec>
```

Element type names are XML names. An XML name must begin with a letter or an underscore, followed by any number of letters, digits, hyphens, underscores, or periods.

In general, the content specification states whether this element will contain child elements or character data. If the element will contain child elements, you further specify ordering, repeatability and presence requirements. The content specification is one of four types. Table 1.3 lists the element content types.

TABLE 1.3   Element Content Types

Content Specification Type	Content
EMPTY content	No content
ANY content	May have any content (character data, subelements, or both)
Mixed content	May have character data or a mix of character data and subelements specified in the mixed content specification
Element content	Only has subelements as specified in the element content specification

Now let's describe each content model specification:

- *EMPTY content*—EMPTY content is the model for empty elements.
- *ANY content*—ANY content is rarely used. Normally your elements have a structure. For example, an HTML document has subelements head and body. A head element can have subelements, and so on.
- *Mixed content*—A mixed content allows both character data and subelements. The definition of the subelements is exactly as described in the element content specification below.
- *Element content*—The element content specification is the most common. You specify an element (or child) content specification by creating a content model. A content model is a pattern that specifies what subelements are allowed, and what order they should occur in.

Let's examine the element content specification in more detail by working through a series of examples.

```
<!ELEMENT shipping EMPTY>
```

This declares an element called shipping with an EMPTY content specification. Notice that parentheses are not used because they are in the mixed and element content specifications. The ANY content model would be specified by just replacing the word EMPTY in the above example with ANY.

```
<!ELEMENT memo (name)>
```

This example states that the memo element may only have a single subelement called name. The parentheses are used and form what is called a content particle. Content particles may be nested inside other content particles. This is demonstrated below.

```
<!ELEMENT memo (name, date)>
```

This example states that the memo element will have one name element, followed by one date element. The comma specifies a sequence, meaning that date must follow name. This is a called a sequence content particle.

```
<!ELEMENT FIGURE (GRAPHIC | TABLE | SCREEN-SHOT)>
```

This example states that a figure will have a GRAPHIC or a TABLE or a SCREEN-SHOT subelement. This is called a choice content particle.

To make elements repeatable or optional you use an occurrence indicator. Table 1.4 lists the three occurrence indicators.

TABLE 1.4   The Content Particle Occurrence Indicators

Indicator	Element or Content Particle Can Occur...
?	zero or one time (optional)
*	zero or more times (optional and repeatable)
+	one or more times (required and repeatable)

Now let's examine some examples using occurrence indicators.

```
<!ELEMENT JDATA (OBJECT)+>
```

This example states that a JDATA element must have at least one and maybe more OBJECT elements.

As stated above, if you surround an element or sequence or choice of elements in parentheses you create a content particle. This is important because you can put an occurrence indicator on both an element and a content particle.

```
<!ELEMENT OBJECT (PRIMITIVE|OBJECT|ARRAY)+>
```

This example states that an OBJECT can be one or more of the following choices: PRIMITIVE, an OBJECT, or an ARRAY. The choice forms a content particle which is then repeated one or more times using the '+' occurrence indicator.

```
<!ELEMENT PRIMITIVE (#PCDATA)>
```

This example states that a PRIMITIVE element can contain just character data and no subelements. The literal string #PCDATA stands for parsed character data. Parsed character data is the technical term for the text content of your document.

```
<!ELEMENT ARRAY (PRIMITIVE+|OBJECT+|ARRAY)>
```

This example states that an ARRAY element can contain one of the following: one or more PRIMITIVE elements, one or more OBJECT elements, or a single ARRAY element.

```
<!ELEMENT FOO ( (PRIMITIVE, ARRAY) | (ARRAY, PRIMITVE) )>
```

This example demonstrates nested content particles. It declares an element named FOO that may only have two child elements (PRIMITIVE and ARRAY) but in any order.

Attribute-List Declaration

As stated previously, attributes of an element take the form of name/value pairs. For example:

```
<A HREF="http://www.gosynergy.com">
```

In a DTD, an attribute list declaration begins with the string literal <!ATTLIST and then is followed by the element name these attributes are for. After the name, you add one or more attribute declarations. An attribute declaration consists of three parts: the attribute name, its type, and a default declaration. The general form of an attribute declaration is

```
<!ATTLIST  elemName
               attName  attType  default-decl>
```

Here is an example attribute list declaration:

```
<!ATTLIST A
               HREF CDATA #REQUIRED>
```

This example states that the A element has one attribute called HREF. This element is any character data (that is, no predefined list of legal values) and it is a required attribute. There are three attribute types: a string type (CDATA), a set of tokenized types, or an enumerated type. The two most common are the string or enumerated type. Tokenized types are discussed in Chapter 4.

You can declare many attributes in a single attribute-list declaration. For example,

```
<!ATTLIST EMPLOYEE
           STATUS    (SALARIED|HOURLY)    #REQUIRED
           WORKWEEK  CDATA  #IMPLIED>
```

This example states that the EMPLOYEE element has two attributes, STATUS and WORKWEEK. The STATUS attribute's legal value is one of two choices in an enumerated list. The STATUS attribute is required, whereas the WORKWEEK attribute is optional.

There are four attribute default declaration options: #REQUIRED, #IMPLIED, #FIXED or a default value. A REQUIRED declaration means the attribute must be present with the element. An IMPLIED declaration allows the document writer to optionally include the attribute. With a FIXED declaration you must supply the value at which the attribute is fixed. Last, you can have a default value for an attribute that will be used if the user does not override it. Here is an example that uses a default value:

```
<!ATTLIST REMINDER
               type  (birthday|anniversary|other)  "other">
```

Syntactic Rules

Since XML is a document markup specification, it has syntax rules. Syntax dictates the rules for words to form larger grammatical constructs such as sentences. The following are syntactic rules for XML-compliant documents:

- XML documents are composed of Unicode characters. Unicode is a 16-bit character set that covers all the world's languages.

- XML is case-sensitive. `<HTML>` and `<html>` are two different tags.

- Whitespaces are invisible characters such as space (ASCII 32), tab (ASCII 9), carriage return (ASCII 13), and line feed (ASCII 10). Whitespace is ignored inside of tags; however, whitespace is significant in content. By content, I mean the text between a start tag and an end tag. By significant, I mean that an XML Processor must pass it on to the using application.

- You often name things in XML like elements and attributes. An XML name must begin with a letter or an underscore, followed by any number of letters, digits, hyphens, underscores, or periods. For example:

```
MyUnique123Tag-Identifier
2_an_illegal_tag
```

- An XML name may not begin with `xml` (uppercase or lowercase). That is reserved for the specification creators.

- Literal strings are enclosed in single or double quotes.

- Other syntactic rules (full nesting, empty tags, start and end tag pairs) were listed when explaining differences between HTML and XML. To recap, XML tags must be properly nested. If an element exists inside another element, its end tag must be before the enclosing element's end tag. An empty tag is a start tag that ends with a forward slash before the right angle bracket. Lastly, a start tag must have an end tag.

- An XML document may have only a single root element.

Valid and Well-Formed Documents

There are two tests by which an XML-compliant document's correctness can be assessed: valid and well-formed. An XML document is *valid* if it declares a document type definition and conforms to the element and attribute declarations in the DTD. An XML document is *well-formed* if it follows all the syntax rules specified in the XML specification. A document does not require a document type definition (DTD) to be well-formed.

Several validating XML parsers are available free. A validating parser will ensure that a document is both well-formed and valid and report any violations to the user. Sun Microsystems,

IBM, and Microsoft all provide free validating parsers. In this chapter, we will validate documents using the IBM Java XML parser called xml4j. This parser can be downloaded free from http://www.alphaworks.ibm.com. The download will be in the form of a zip file or a gzipped tar file. Extract the zip file or tar file to a directory. It will create a directory called xml4j with several subdirectories. In the xml4j_x_x_x (The *x*'s will be replaced with version numbers.) directory you will see three jar files: xml4j.jar, xerces.jar and xercesSamples.jar. Add these three jar files to your classpath. For example, in Windows you would type

```
>set classpath=%classpath%;c:\xml4j_x_x_x\xml4j.jar;
➡c:\xml4j_x_x_x\xercesSamples.jar;
➡c:\xml4j_x_x_x\xerces.jar;
```

After installing the xml4j code and a Java virtual machine (1.1 compliant or greater) you can run the class sax.SAXWriter to ensure that your documents are well-formed and valid. You will do this in the next section.

Creating a Markup Language from Scratch

Let's now do a step-by-step walkthrough of creating an XML-based language and a document of that type.

Address books are a very common data item that many applications store in their own proprietary format. Thus they are a good candidate for a standard language so that any application could read and write the data.

The best way to begin creating your language is to first examine several examples of your data so that you can extract the appropriate meta-data that describes the purpose of your data.

Example 1. A home address:
_____

Michael Daconta

4296 Razor Hill Road

Bealeton, VA 22712

Meta-data:
_____

Name

Street

City, State Zip

Example 2. A business address:
_____

Sterling Software

7900 Sudley Road

Suite 500

Manassas, VA 20109

Meta-data:
Name
Street
Street2
City, State Zip

In examining your meta-data it is easy to see the elements that you need for your simple language: NAME, STREET, CITY, STATE, ZIP. The only decision you need to make is how to handle multiple street designations. There are two ways to do this:

- Allow multiple street tags.
- Allow multiple street tags and distinguish the street designations with an attribute.

Let's use the simpler approach, which is the first option. Now you are ready to write a well-formed XML document for your data. Listing 1.5 is an example of an Address Book Markup Language (ABML) document.

LISTING 1.5   An ABML Document with External DTD Declaration

```
<?xml version="1.0"?>

<!DOCTYPE ADDRESS_BOOK SYSTEM "abml.dtd">
<ADDRESS_BOOK>
    <ADDRESS>
<NAME>Michael Daconta </NAME>
<STREET>4296 Razor Hill Road </STREET>
        <CITY>Bealeton </CITY>
        <STATE>VA </STATE>
        <ZIP>22712 </ZIP>
    </ADDRESS>
    <ADDRESS>
        <NAME>Sterling Software </NAME>
        <STREET> 7900 Sudley Road</STREET>
        <STREET> Suite 500</STREET>
        <CITY>Manassas</CITY>
        <STATE>VA </STATE>
        <ZIP>20109 </ZIP>
    </ADDRESS>
</ADDRESS_BOOK>
```

Now that you know generally how you want your language to look, you need to precisely define the rules of a valid document by creating the document type definition. As stated earlier in this chapter, a DTD consists of element type declarations and attribute-list declarations. You start with your elements and describe the allowed sequence, choice, and occurrence of subelements.

- An ADDRESS_BOOK must have one or more ADDRESS elements.
- An ADDRESS must have a NAME, STREET, CITY, STATE, and ZIP element in that sequence.
- An ADDRESS element may have multiple STREET tags.
- NAME, STREET, CITY, STATE, and ZIP elements can only contain parsed character data.

Here are the element declarations for the DTD:

```
<!ELEMENT ADDRESS_BOOK (ADDRESS)+>
<!ELEMENT ADDRESS (NAME, STREET+, CITY, STATE, ZIP)>
<!ELEMENT NAME (#PCDATA)>
<!ELEMENT STREET (#PCDATA)>
<!ELEMENT CITY (#PCDATA)>
<!ELEMENT STATE (#PCDATA)>
<!ELEMENT ZIP (#PCDATA)>
```

Now, these elements were very simple and did not have any attributes; however, you would add an attribute to the STREET element by doing the following:

```
<!ATTLIST STREET TYPE (street|suiteno|aptno|other) #IMPLIED>
```

This would allow people to optionally add a TYPE attribute to the STREET element.

Now run the IBM validating parser on the ABML document to ensure it is both well-formed and valid. First cd to the sams.chp2 directory, where the file myaddresses.xml is located. Then type the following command:

```
> java sax.SAXWriter
➥-p com.ibm.xml.parsers.ValidatingSAXParser myaddresses.xml
```

Running the program produces Figure 1.2. If the document has no errors, the document is printed. If the document is not well-formed or does not match the DTD, errors are printed that detail the exact line where the problem occurs.

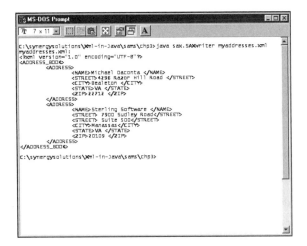

FIGURE 1.2

xml4j *validating parser.*

Summary

This chapter covered the history, benefits, and components of XML. The purpose of the chapter was to prime you for the following chapter on XML parsing. Some details of the XML specification (like some element content specifications and attribute types) have been deferred until Chapter 4. In this chapter we covered the most commonly used components.

"History of XML" was important to understand the maturity of this technology. The history section walked us through the key events leading up to the XML Recommendation to include the creation of the Generalized Markup Language, the standardization of GML, the creation of HTML, and the launch of Netscape Navigator. The section ended with a detailed comparison of HTML to XML.

"Benefits of XML" provided the motivation for working through this chapter and the rest of the book. The section answered the question, "Why should I care about XML?" The key benefits of XML discussed were data independence, improved domain knowledge, multiple views of data, enabling e-commerce, improved data searches, increase in relevant data, data access where you want it, and simpler application development.

"Components of XML" was by far the largest section in the chapter as it covered each item of XML markup and the most common declarations in the document type definition. The coverage included explanations, detailed syntax descriptions, and multiple examples. The markup items covered were the XML declaration, the document type declaration, elements, attributes, and comments. The DTD declarations covered were element type declarations and attribute list declarations. Additionally, this section explained the BNF grammar, XML Syntax rules, and the distinction between well-formed and valid documents. The section ended with a walk-through of how to create a markup language from scratch.

Now you are ready to examine the key technologies and strategies for parsing XML documents.

Suggested for Further Study

1. List the meta-data for the following data for a grocery store transaction:

   Wheaties breakfast cereal

   $3.59

   10 boxes in stock

   2

   Cost: $7.18

   supersaver cust #: 44234

   Michael C. Daconta

2. List three types of proprietary data current stored by multiple parties or organizations (probably in proprietary formats) that would benefit from an XML markup language to foster improved data sharing.

3. Type the Address Book Markup Language DTD into a file called abml.dtd. Then create an ABML document containing your home and work address (and one other address of your choice). Validate your ABML document with the IBM XML parser. To do this, you run two Java programs: sax.SAXWriter and ui.TreeViewer. To run these programs, use the following command lines:

   ```
   > java sax.SAXWriter  -p com.ibm.xml.parsers.ValidatingSAXParser
   ➥myaddress.xml
   > java ui.TreeViewer  myaddress.xml
   ```

4. Create two concrete data examples of event reminders. An event reminder is a note that is scheduled into the computer to remind you of an important occasion. Your event reminder should have at least six parts (such as author, event notice, date of event, time of event, and so on). List your events and then list the meta-data that describes the purpose of each field in your data.

5. Create a well-formed XML document that contains markup and content of your two event reminders.

6. Create a document type definition for your Reminder Markup Language (RML). Validate your DTD and RML document using the IBM parser.

Further Reading

Extensible Markup Language (XML) 1.0. W3C Recommendation 10-February-1998.
`http://www.w3.org/TR/REC-xml.`

The XML Handbook. Charles F. Goldfarb and Paul Prescod. 1998, Prentice Hall PTR.

Parsing XML

"Short for eXtensible Markup Language, XML can convert data into an understandable format for disparate systems, in much the same way that Morse code is used by disparate telegraph operators to transmit their messages in an easily understood format."

—Patrick T. Coleman, "The Morse Code of Data—XML,"
SunExpert Magazine, Feb. 1999

IN THIS CHAPTER

This chapter will deliver a detailed tour of and tutorial on Java XML parsers. We will begin with the theory behind parsers and various parsing strategies implemented in the current crop of parsers. After gaining an understanding of these broad concepts and categories, we will examine the key APIs in XML parsing: SAX and SAX2. Once we know the key APIs, we will examine the current Parser Implementations available from the leading commercial vendors and popular open source alternatives.

Parsing is the process of dissecting a body of text into its individual component pieces. For example, if that body of text is a paragraph, parsing would break the paragraph into sentences. It would then break a sentence into subject and predicate. In turn, the subject and predicate would then be broken down into their components like nouns, verbs, and adjectives. Parsing is a highly developed and formalized discipline in computer science. There are numerous examples in computer science where parsing is necessary. Translating (or compiling) high-level languages (Java, C, C++, Smalltalk, Lisp, and so on) to low-level languages (assembly) requires parsing. Command lines are parsed by programs. Batched commands are parsed in scripting languages. Numerous other languages, such as the Standard Query Language (SQL) and the HyperText Markup Language (HTML), all require parsing.

In computer science, parsing is divided into two distinct activities: lexical analysis and grammatical analysis.

Lexical analysis breaks the body of text into tokens. Tokens are the smallest atomic components of the stream of data. In the paragraph example, tokens would be words. In a computer program, tokens are keywords (such as `while` and `for`), literals (such as `23` or `"mike"`) and identifiers (such as `myInt` and `employeeName`).

Grammatical analysis involves recognizing the syntactical structure of a language—in other words, how words are combined to form larger structures and how those structures form even larger ones. For example, in parsing a computer program, grammatical analysis would determine how tokens form expressions, how expressions and keywords form statements, how statements form blocks, how blocks form modules and, lastly, how modules form programs. Although parsing is often used loosely as an umbrella concept for the activities of lexical analysis and grammatical analysis, it is usually implemented by two separate pieces of software: a scanner and a parser. The scanner extracts tokens from the stream (lexical analysis) and passes them to the parser for grammatical analysis. For XML, an XML processor parses the XML for its using application. An XML processor is just another name for an XML parser.

Parsing Methodologies

Java has some built-in support for lexical analysis. Let's examine those classes and build our own XML scanner to perform lexical analysis.

StringTokenizer and Scanners

StringTokenizer is a class for breaking a single string into a set of tokens by matching all characters between the specified character delimiters as tokens. Though StringTokenizer is adequate for tokenizing simple, uniform strings, it is clearly inadequate for parsing an XML file. Listing 2.1 demonstrates parsing an XML file with StringTokenizer.

LISTING 2.1   A Naive Tokenizer

```
 1: /** SimpleTokenize.java */
 2: package sams.chp2;
 3:
 4: import java.io.*;
 5: import java.util.*;
 6:
 7: public class SimpleTokenize
 8: {
 9:     public static void main(String args[])
10:     {
11:         if (args.length < 1)
12:         {
13:             System.out.println("USAGE: java sams.chp2.SimpleTokenize
                ➥ xmlfile");
14:             System.exit(1);
15:         }
16:
17:         try
18:         {
19:             FileInputStream fis = new FileInputStream(args[0]);
20:             BufferedReader br = new BufferedReader(
21:                                     new InputStreamReader(fis));
22:             String line = null;
23:             while ( (line = br.readLine()) != null)
24:             {
25:                 // spaces as delimiter
26:                 StringTokenizer st = new StringTokenizer(line);
27:                 while (st.hasMoreTokens())
28:                     System.out.println(st.nextToken());
29:             }
30:
31:             fis.close();
32:         } catch (Exception e)
33:             {
34:                 e.printStackTrace();
35:             }
36:     }
37: }
```

Running `SimpleTokenize.java` produces the following output:

```
 1: C:\ >java sams.chp2.SimpleTokenize myaddresses.xml
 2: <?xml
 3: version="1.0"?>
 4: <!DOCTYPE
 5: ADDRESS_BOOK
 6: SYSTEM
 7: "abml.dtd">
 8: <ADDRESS_BOOK>
 9: <ADDRESS>
10: <NAME>Michael
11: Daconta
12: </NAME>
13: <STREET>4296
14: Razor
15: Hill
16: Road
17: </STREET>
18: <CITY>Bealeton
19: </CITY>
20: <STATE>VA
21: </STATE>
22: <ZIP>22712
23: </ZIP>
24: </ADDRESS>
25: ...
26: </ADDRESS_BOOK>
```

The program `SimpleTokenize` split the XML file into a list of strings. It is obvious that just tokenizing based on spaces does not give us proper tokens. As previously defined, a token is a single atom of data. By only delimiting tokens with a space, we had tokens running together, such as the string `<STREET>4296`, which should be two tokens. Of course, we could further post process this list of tokens into a more complete list; however, we can get better results by building our own token scanner specifically tailored to XML.

A scanner is an object that performs lexical analysis on an input stream to create tokens for the language that is being parsed. For example, you could create a scanner for the Pascal language or the C language that would understand the keywords unique to those languages. The key criterion of a good scanner is that it separates the input stream into all the different token types necessary for grammatical analysis. The `StringTokenizer` is inadequate for this task because it basically only has a single type of token, which I will call a *word*. Although the Java I/O package has another class called `StreamTokenizer` that is a more sophisticated, table-driven scanner, it also does not supply enough token types to be useful to adequately parse XML.

Let's code a simple scanner that satisfies the bare minimum requirement to scan XML: to differentiate between markup and content. Listing 2.2 is a simple scanner that fulfills that requirement.

LISTING 2.2   A Simple XML Scanner

```
 1: /* SimpleXmlScanner.java */
 2: package sams.chp2;
 3:
 4: import java.io.*;
 5:
 6: public class SimpleXmlScanner
 7: {
 8:     public static final int TT_PI = 0;
 9:     public static final int TT_TAG = 1;
10:     public static final int TT_CONTENT = 2;
11:     public static final int TT_ENTITY = 3;
12:
13:     public static final String [] constants = { "PI",
14:                                                 "TAG",
15:                                                 "CONTENT",
16:                                                 "ENTITY" };
17:
18:     int ttype;
19:     PushbackReader rdr;
20:     private int c = 0;
21:     private char lastChar = 0;
22:
23:     public final int getType() { return ttype; }
24:
25:     public String nextToken() throws IOException
26:     {
27:         StringBuffer tok = new StringBuffer();
28:         ttype = -1; // initial state
29:
30:         outer:
31:         while ((c = rdr.read()) != -1)
32:         {
33:             switch (c)
34:             {
35:                 case '<':
36:                     if (tok.length() > 0)
37:                     {
38:                         rdr.unread(c);
39:                         break outer;
```

LISTING 2.2   Continued

```
40:                           }
41:                              ttype = TT_TAG;
42:                              break;
43:                          case '>':
44:                              break outer;
45:                          case '?':
46:                              if (lastChar == '<')
47:                                  ttype = TT_PI;
48:                              break;
49:                          case '&':
50:                              ttype = TT_ENTITY;
51:                              break;
52:                          case ';':
53:                              break outer;
54:                          default:
55:                              if (ttype < 0)
56:                                  ttype = TT_CONTENT;
57:                              tok.append((char) c);
58:                      }
59:                  lastChar = (char) c;
60:              }
61:
62:          if (tok.length() < 1)
63:              return null;
64:
65:          return tok.toString();
66:      }
67:
68:      public SimpleXmlScanner(InputStream is)
69:      {
70:          InputStreamReader isr = new InputStreamReader(is);
71:          rdr = new PushbackReader(isr);
72:      }
73:
74:      public static void main(String args[])
75:      {
76:          if (args.length < 1)
77:          {
78:              System.out.println("USAGE: java sams.chp2.SimpleXmlScanner
                 ➥ xmlfile");
79:              System.exit(1);
80:          }
81:
82:          try
```

LISTING 2.2   Continued

```
83:          {
84:              FileInputStream fis = new FileInputStream(args[0]);
85:              SimpleXmlScanner scanner = new SimpleXmlScanner(fis);
86:
87:              String tok = null;
88:
89:              while ( (tok = scanner.nextToken()) != null)
90:              {
91:                  System.out.println(SimpleXmlScanner.constants
92:                  ➥[scanner.getType()] +":{" + tok + "}");
93:              }
94:
95:              fis.close();
96:          } catch (Throwable t)
97:          {
98:              t.printStackTrace();
99:          }
100:     }
101: }
```

Running `SimpleXmlScanner` produces the following output:

```
 1: PI:{xml version="1.0"}
 2: CONTENT:{
 3: }
 4: TAG:{!DOCTYPE ADDRESS_BOOK SYSTEM "abml.dtd"}
 5: CONTENT:{
 6: }
 7: TAG:{ADDRESS_BOOK}
 8: CONTENT:{
 9:      }
10: TAG:{ADDRESS}
11: CONTENT:{
12:          }
13: TAG:{NAME}
14: CONTENT:{Michael Daconta }
15: TAG:{/NAME}
16: CONTENT:{
17:          }
18: TAG:{STREET}
19: CONTENT:{4296 Razor Hill Road }
20: TAG:{/STREET}
21: CONTENT:{
```

```
22:           }
23: TAG:{CITY}
24: CONTENT:{Bealeton }
25: TAG:{/CITY}
26: CONTENT:{
27:             }
28: TAG:{STATE}
29: CONTENT:{VA }
30: TAG:{/STATE}
31: CONTENT:{
32:           }
33: TAG:{ZIP}
34: CONTENT:{22712 }
35: TAG:{/ZIP}
36: CONTENT:{
37:       }
38: TAG:{/ADDRESS}
39: ...
40: TAG:{/ADDRESS_BOOK}
41: CONTENT:{
42: }
```

As you can see, our scanner separated the markup tags and processing instructions from the document content. Unfortunately, this simple scanner is not complete enough yet to support grammatical analysis of XML. A complete scanner would add tokens for XML comments, DOCTYPE declarations, CDATA sections, and possibly parsing of the DTD (to support validating parsers).

The XML Recommendation assisted XML developers by describing the required behavior for XML processors. The standard defines the required behavior as a software module "used to read XML documents and provide access to their content and structure." The Web focus of XML is evident in the care that the standard has taken to ensure that XML processors behave in a consistent manner. Ease of processing is key to making XML ubiquitous.

Requirements for XML Processors

It is beyond the scope of this book to analyze all of the requirements placed on XML processors. You should consult Tim Bray's annotated version of the XML standard at www.xml.com if you are interested in implementing your own XML processors. Instead, I will focus on two types of requirements. I will first focus on the requirements that will affect your decision on which XML processor to use. Second, I will examine the requirements that affect your understanding of the APIs to various processors.

There are three categories of requirements specified by the standard for XML processors. The three categories consist of requirements for validating processors, for non-validating processors, and for both. Both validating and non-validating processors must report XML document violations of well-conformedness. The specification has clearly marked and segregated all validity and well-formedness constraints to which a conforming processor must adhere.

The most basic decision to resolve is whether you need a validating or non-validating XML processor (parser). Validating XML processors must do more work than non-validating processors. Specifically, a validating processor must not only process the XML document but also the entire DTD and all external parsed entities. Another requirement for validating parsers is that they perform text replacement on all entities. Therefore, a non-validating parser will have better performance than a validating parser. In general, if you are not sure whether your performance requirements necessitate a non-validating parser, assume you can afford to validate documents.

In addition to the speed considerations, there are two other ramifications of choosing a non-validating parser. First, some well-formedness errors could go undetected because external entities were not processed. Second, the information passed on to the application may exclude default parameters for attributes and text replacement of external entities. This would result in a validating parser passing different information to an application than a non-validating one. Therefore, the choice of a non-validating parser must also be based on your knowledge of the type and complexity of the XML documents you will need to process. On the other hand, if your XML documents are generated by a computer program and are known to be complete and valid, it is overkill to use a validating parser.

There are several requirements that should be noted in relation to fully understanding the interfaces to XML processors. They are as follows:

- All XML processors must accept documents encoded in both UTF-8 and UTF-16 of International Standard 10646. The full name of these encodings are the Universal Character Set Transformation Format 8-bit form or 16-bit form, respectively. These transformations are used to make characters in standard 10646 quicker to parse. Standard 10646 organizes characters in planes, rows, and cells. Unicode is the first plane and is also known as the Basic Multilingual Plane (BMP). UTF-8 is used as a fast encoding for the BMP. UTF-16 is used for encoding the next 16 planes. Java makes following this rule easy because the classes `DataInputStream` and `DataOutputStream` have `readUTF()` and `writeUTF()` methods, respectively.

- An XML processor must pass on all characters that are not markup to the application. This, of course, includes whitespace. This is important as you will need to determine whether whitespace is significant in your processing of the XML document or not. This also is significant because it is different from how HTML is currently processed.

- An XML processor can resolve a public identifier in an application-specific way. If the processor has no knowledge of the public identifier, it must use the URI of the system identifier. Public identifiers will become more common as XML applications, languages, and users proliferate. You will see the capability to resolve these identifiers available in the parser APIs (like SAX).

- The system and public identifier of both unparsed entities and notations must be passed on to the application by the XML processor. We will go into detail about entities and notations in Chapter 4, "Advanced XML." You will also see this capability provided in the parser APIs, including SAX.

With so many good parsers available, it is unlikely that you will implement your own XML parser. However, understanding the previous rules levied on XML processors will enable you to better choose the type of parser you want to use. There is one more significant selection criterion to evaluate when choosing an XML parser—that is, whether you use an event-based parser or a tree-based parser.

Event-based Versus Tree-based Parsing

While choosing between a validating and non-validating parser revolves around your application's performance constraints, choosing between an event-based or tree-based parser will revolve around your application's memory constraints. A tree-based parser produces a tree data structure, such as the W3C's Document Object Model (DOM), as the result of the parse. This is an in-memory representation of the XML text document. The DOM will be discussed in detail in the next chapter. While this makes the document easy to traverse and manipulate, it can consume a large amount of memory for large XML documents. Because there is no limit to the size of an XML document, you must either be familiar with the average size of an XML document you will process or use an event-based parser.

As more and more data becomes encoded in XML-compliant languages, you may find your applications extracting data from portions of many XML documents. This is another common case where an event-based parser is more efficient than a tree-based parser. With an event-based parser, you can ignore parts of a document and only save the elements and sub-elements in which you are interested. This not only saves memory but will provide better performance than building the entire document tree.

The primary event-based interface to XML documents is the Simple API for XML (SAX). SAX is discussed in the next section.

SAX API

SAX is a simple, event-based application programming interface (API) for XML parsers that was developed by a group of developers who subscribe to the xml-dev mailing list. David

Megginson (`http://www.megginson.com`) spearheaded the effort, gained consensus on design, and wrote the code. The API makes extensive use of Java interfaces as registered callbacks to an XML parser supplied by a third party. The SAX interface is event-based in that it transforms the parsing of an XML document into the invocation (or firing) of a specific method (the type of event) with its associated parameters (the specific state of the event). So an event has two components: a name (the method name) and an associated state (the method parameters).

> **NOTE**
>
> To subscribe to the `xml-dev` mailing list, send an email message to `majordomo@ic.ac.uk` with the following message: "subscribe xml-dev."

SAX is broken into four parts:

- *Interfaces implemented by an XML Parser* (`org.xml.sax` *package*)—`Parser`, `AttributeList`, and `Locator`. `Parser` and `AttributeList` are required, while `Locator` is optional. SAX provides a default implementation for the `Locator` and `AttributeList` interfaces called `LocatorImpl` and `AttributeListImpl`, respectively.
- *Interfaces implemented by your application* (`org.xml.sax` *package*)—`DocumentHandler`, `ErrorHandler`, `DTDHandler`, and `EntityResolver`. All these interfaces are optional.
- *Standard SAX classes* (`org.xml.sax` *package*)—`InputSource`, `SAXException`, `SAXParseException`. These are fully implemented in SAX.
- *Helper classes* (`org.xml.sax.helpers` *package*)—`ParserFactory`, `AttributeListImpl`, and `LocatorImpl`. These are fully implemented in SAX.

Before examining each interface, a simple example demonstrating the event-based interface of SAX will be useful. Listing 2.3 is a simple SAX tester that prints out what methods were called and the parameters passed in to those methods by the parser's SAX driver. The code in bold highlights the key actions your program needs to perform to receive SAX events from a SAX Driver. These steps are covered in detail following the listing.

LISTING 2.3　Catching and Printing All SAX Events

```
1: /** SaxTester.java */
2: package sams.chp2;
3:
4: import java.io.*;
5:
6: import java.net.*;
7:
8: import org.xml.sax.*;
```

LISTING 2.3   Continued

```
 9: import org.xml.sax.helpers.*;
10:
11: public class SaxTester
12: {
13:
14:     public static void main(String args[])
15:     {
16:         if (args.length < 1)
17:         {
18:             System.out.println("USAGE:java -Dorg.xml.sax.parser=
19:             <classname> " +"sam.chp2.SaxTester <document>");
20:             System.exit(1);
21:         }
22:
23:         try
24:         {
25:             File f = new File(args[0]);
26:
27:             // create a SAX input source
28:             InputSource is = new InputSource(f.toURL().toString());
29:
30:             // instantiate a SAX driver
31:             Parser sax = ParserFactory.makeParser();
32:
33:             // create our test handler
34:             TestHandler handler = new TestHandler();
35:
36:             // register a document handler
37:             sax.setDocumentHandler(handler);
38:
39:             // register the DTD handler
40:             sax.setDTDHandler(handler);
41:
42:             // register the entity resolver
43:             sax.setEntityResolver(handler);
44:
45:             // register the error handler
46:             sax.setErrorHandler(handler);
47:
48:             // start the parsing!
49:             sax.parse(is);
50:         } catch (Throwable t)
51:           {
52:             t.printStackTrace();
53:           }
54:     }
```

LISTING 2.3   Continued

```
55: }
56:
57: class TestHandler extends HandlerBase
58: {
59:     /** Locator reference. */
60:     Locator loc;
61:
62:     /** method of the DocumentHandler Interface. */
63:     public void characters(char[] ch, int start, int length)
64:     {
65:         // Receive notification of character data inside an element.
66:         System.out.println("Called characters(ch:"+ new String
67:         (ch,start,length) +",start:" + start + ",length: " + length + ")");
68:     }
69:
70:     /** method of the DocumentHandler Interface. */
71:     public void endDocument()
72:     {
73:         // Receive notification of the end of the document.
74:         System.out.println("Called endDocument()");
75:     }
76:
77:     /** method of the DocumentHandler Interface. */
78:     public void endElement(java.lang.String name)
79:     {
80:         // Receive notification of the end of an element.
81:         System.out.println("Called endElement(name: " + name + ")");
82:     }
83:
84:     /** method of the DocumentHandler Interface. */
85:     public void ignorableWhitespace(char[] ch, int start, int length)
86:     {
87:         // Notification of ignorable whitespace in element content.
88:         System.out.println("Called ignorableWhitespace(ch:" + new String
89:         (ch,start,length) +",start: " + start+ ",length: " + length + ")");
90:     }
91:
92:     /** method of the DocumentHandler Interface. */
93:     public void processingInstruction(java.lang.String target,
94:                               java.lang.String data)
```

2

PARSING XML

LISTING 2.3   Continued

```
 95:    {
 96:        // Receive notification of a processing instruction.
 97:        System.out.println("Called processingInstruction(target:" + target +
 98:                          ",data:" + data + ")");
 99:    }
100:
101:    /** method of the DocumentHandler Interface. */
102:    public void setDocumentLocator(Locator locator)
103:    {
104:        // Receive a Locator object for document events.
105:        System.out.println("Called setDocumentLocator()");
106:        loc = locator;
107:    }
108:
109:    /** method of the DocumentHandler Interface. */
110:    public void startDocument()
111:    {
112:        // Receive notification of the beginning of the document.
113:        System.out.println("Called startDocument()");
114:    }
115:
116:    /** method of the DocumentHandler Interface. */
117:    public void startElement(java.lang.String name, AttributeList
     ➥ attributes)
118:    {
119:        // Receive notification of the start of an element.
120:        System.out.println("Called startElement(name:" + name + ")");
121:        for (int i = 0; i < attributes.getLength(); i++)
122:        {
123:            String attName = attributes.getName(i);
124:            String type = attributes.getType(i);
125:            String value = attributes.getValue(i);
126:            System.out.println("att-name:" + attName + ",att-type:"
             ➥ + type + ", att-value:" + value);
127:        }
128:        if (loc != null)
129:            System.out.println("In " + loc.getSystemId() + ",at line " +
130:                              loc.getLineNumber() + " and col " +
131:                              loc.getColumnNumber());
132:    }
133:
134:    /** method of the DTDHandler Interface. */
```

LISTING 2.3 Continued

```
135:        public void unparsedEntityDecl(java.lang.String name,
136:        java.lang.String publicId, java.lang.StringsystemId,
137:        java.lang.String notationName)
138:        {
139:            // Receive notification of an unparsed entity declaration.
140:            System.out.println("Called unparsedEntityDecl");
141:            System.out.println(name);
142:            System.out.println(publicId);
143:            System.out.println(systemId);
144:            System.out.println(notationName);
145:        }
146:
147:        /** method of the DTDHandler Interface. */
148:        public void notationDecl(java.lang.String name,
149:        java.lang.String publicId, java.lang.String systemId)
150:        {
151:            // Receive notification of a notation declaration.
152:            System.out.println("Called notationDecl(name: " + name +
153:                                ",publicId: " + publicId +
154:                                ",systemId: " + systemId + ")");
155:        }
156:
157:        /** method of the EntityResolver Interface. */
158:        public InputSource resolveEntity(java.lang.String publicId,
159:                                    java.lang.String systemId)
160:        {
161:            // Resolve an external entity.
162:            System.out.println("Called resolveEntity(publicId:" + publicId +
163:                                ",systemId:" + systemId + ")");
164:            InputSource is = null;
165:            if (systemId != null)
166:            {
167:                // create a SAX input source
168:                File f = new File(systemId);
169:                try
170:                {
171:                    is = new InputSource(f.toURL().toString());
172:                } catch (MalformedURLException mfue)
173:                    { }
174:            }
```

LISTING 2.3   Continued

```
175:            else
176:                is = new InputSource(new StringReader("Unknown Entity"));
177:
178:            return is;179: }
180:
181:     /** method of the ErrorHandler Interface. */
182:     public void error(SAXParseException e)
183:     {
184:         // Receive notification of a recoverable parser error.
185:         System.out.println("Called error(e:" + e + ")");
186:         if (loc != null)
187:             System.out.println("In " + loc.getSystemId() + ",at line " +
188:                                 loc.getLineNumber() + " and col " +
189:                                 loc.getColumnNumber());
190:         e.printStackTrace();
191:     }
192:
193:     /** method of the ErrorHandler Interface. */
194:     public void fatalError(SAXParseException e)
195:     {
196:         // Report a fatal XML parsing error.
197:         System.out.println("Called fatalError(e:" + e + ")");
198:         if (loc != null)
200:             System.out.println("In " + loc.getSystemId() + ",at line " +
201:                                 loc.getLineNumber() + " and col " +
202:                                 loc.getColumnNumber());
203:         e.printStackTrace();
204:     }
205:
206:     /** method of the ErrorHandler Interface. */
207:     public void warning(SAXParseException e)
208:     {
209:         // Receive notification of a parser warning.
210:         System.out.println("Called warning()");
211:         if (loc != null)
212:             System.out.println("In " + loc.getSystemId() + ",at line " +
213:                                 loc.getLineNumber() + " and col " +
214:                                 loc.getColumnNumber());
215:         e.printStackTrace();
216:     }
217: }
```

When running `SaxTester`, you pass in the class name of the SAX-compliant parser by adding the Java system property `org.sax.xml.parser`. The following is an example of the command line:

```
C:\>java -Dorg.sax.xml.parser=com.ibm.xml.parser.SAXDriver sams.chp2.SaxTester
➥  myaddresses.xml
```

Running the program produces the following output (abridged for brevity):

```
 1: Called setDocumentLocator()
 2: Called startDocument()
 3: Called resolveEntity(publicId:null,
    ➥ systemId:file:/C:/synergysolutions/Xml-in-Java/sams/chp2/abml.dtd)
 4: Called startElement(name:ADDRESS_BOOK)
 5: In file:/C:/synergysolutions/Xml-in-Java/sams/chp2/myaddresses.xml,at line
    ➥ 3 and col 15
 6: Called ignorableWhitespace(ch:,start: 80,length: 0)
 7: Called ignorableWhitespace(ch:
 8: ,start: 0,length: 1)
 9: Called ignorableWhitespace(ch:     ,start: 82,length: 1)
10: Called startElement(name:ADDRESS)
11: In file:/C:/synergysolutions/Xml-in-Java/sams/chp2/myaddresses.xml,at line
    ➥ 4 and col 11
12: Called ignorableWhitespace(ch:,start: 92,length: 0)
13: Called ignorableWhitespace(ch:
14: ,start: 0,length: 1)
15: Called ignorableWhitespace(ch:        ,start: 94,length: 2)
16: Called startElement(name:NAME)
17: In file:/C:/synergysolutions/Xml-in-Java/sams/chp2/myaddresses.xml,at line
    ➥ 5 and col 9 ??? Author: Above code line too long.
    ➥ -Gus/DE18: Called characters(ch:Michael Daconta ,start:102,length: 16)
19: Called endElement(name: NAME)
20: ...
21: Called endElement(name: ADDRESS_BOOK)
22: Called endDocument()
```

This output should give you a good understanding of how the SAX API works. The SAX-compliant parser calls methods such as `startDocument()`, `startElement()`, `endElement()`, and `endDocument()` on your handler class. In the simple program in Listing 2.3, we created a handler class called `TestHandler` that extended `org.xml.sax.HandlerBase`. The `HandlerBase` class implements all the handler interfaces: `DocumentHandler`, `ErrorHandler`, `DTDHandler`, and `EntityResolver`. We then registered our interface handler with the parser using the set*XXX*Handler methods.

Before moving on to the specific SAX interfaces, let's examine the general steps used in the SAXTester program to receive the events from the SAX-compliant parser (also called a SAX driver). There are four steps:

1. *Create an* InputSource *class*—An XML parser requires an XML input source. The org.xml.sax.InputSource class is a single abstraction that represents multiple methods for identifying an input source to an XML parser. You can create an InputSource class by providing a character stream, a byte stream, or a URI as a string. In SaxTester.java, I created the input source using a file URI. Another possible way would be to use a FileReader, as shown in the following:

   ```
   FileReader rdr = new FileReader(filename);
   InputSource insrc = new InputSource(rdr);
   ```

2. *Instantiate a SAX-compliant parser*—There are two methods to do this. The most direct way is to instantiate a specific SAX-compliant parser with the new operator. However, this will lock your application into only using that implementation. A more flexible method is to use the helper class called ParserFactory. The org.xml.sax.helpers. ParserFactory class has a makeParser() method that will use reflection to instantiate the class referred to in the org.xml.sax.parser System property. Remember that we set this on the command line with the -D option to the Java virtual machine (JVM). In SaxTester.java, I created a parser using the ParserFactory class.

3. *Register the handler classes*—A SAX-compliant parser is required to implement mutator methods (also called setters) for the following interfaces: DocumentHandler, ErrorHandler, DTDHandler, and EntityResolver. As a result, every SAX-compliant parser has a setDocumentHandler(), setErrorHandler(), setDTDHandler(), and setEntityResolver() method that accepts a reference to an object that implements that interface. In SaxTester.java, we have one class that implements all the interfaces, so we pass a reference to it into each method.

4. *Start parsing*—The final step is to call the parse() method on the reference to the Parser class and pass in a reference to the InputSource to parse.

Now that we have covered the general process, I will discuss and demonstrate each handler interface.

The DocumentHandler Interface

This is the primary interface your application will implement to receive events from the SAX-compliant parser. If you do not want to implement all methods in this interface, you can have your class extend HandlerBase and override just the events in which you are interested. The order of events you receive will correspond to the order of markup in the XML document you are parsing. Listing 2.4 is the complete DocumentHandler interface.

LISTING 2.4 DocumentHandler Interface

```
1: package org.xml.sax;
2:
3: public interface DocumentHandler
4: {
5:    public abstract void setDocumentLocator (Locator locator);
6:
7:    public abstract void startDocument ()
8:      throws SAXException;
9:
10:   public abstract void endDocument ()
11:      throws SAXException;
12:
13:   public abstract void startElement (String name, AttributeList atts)
14:      throws SAXException;
15:
16:   public abstract void endElement (String name)
17:      throws SAXException;
18:
19:   public abstract void characters (char ch[], int start, int length)
20:      throws SAXException;
21:
22:   public abstract void ignorableWhitespace (char ch[], int start,
   ➥ int length)
23:      throws SAXException;
24:
25:   public abstract void processingInstruction (String target, String data)
26:      throws SAXException;
27: }
```

I will first examine the purpose of each method (event) in the interface (see Table 2.1) and then demonstrate an example that uses the interface.

TABLE 2.1 DocumentHandler Interface Methods

Method Name	Purpose
setDocumentLocator (Locator l)	This method will be called by the parser if it can provide location information on where the events it is reporting occur in the XML document it is parsing. See the Locator interface described next. You will need to store this reference to this Locator in an instance variable for use in other methods (especially the ones in the ErrorHandler interface, which is described in the next section).

TABLE 2.1 Continued

Method Name	Purpose
startDocument()	Indicates the start of the XML document.
endDocument()	Indicates the end of the XML document.
startElement(String name, AttributeList atts)	Indicates the start of the element specified in the name string. If the element has attributes, the attributes are passed in via a reference to an object that implements the AttributeList interface. SAXTester.java demonstrates iterating through the AttributeList.
endElement(String name)	Indicates the end of the element specified in the name string.
characters(char [] ch, int start, int length)	This method passes character data (all data that is not markup) into your application. It is important that your application does not try to read character data from the array (called ch) outside of the specified range (between start and start + length).
ignorableWhitespace (char [] ch, int start, int length)	This method is required by Section 2.10 of the XML 1.0 Recommendation for validating parsers to report whitespace appearing in element content. An element has element content if it only has child elements (no character data). So, think of this as the whitespace used to separate tags that an application can safely ignore because they are not part of the character data.
processingInstruction (String target, String data)	Passes a processing instruction consisting of a target and data for the target into the application. Remember that processing instructions are application specific (there are no constraints on values for the target or data).

Now that we understand what methods a SAX Parser calls and the parameters it passes into those methods, we need an example of how to translate those events in an application. Let's again parse our addresses.xml file, but this time convert address elements into address objects. Listing 2.5, AbmlParser.java, does just that.

LISTING 2.5 Turning Elements into Objects

```
1: /* AbmlParser.java */
2: package sams.chp2;
3:
4: import java.util.*;
5: import java.io.*;
```

LISTING 2.5   Continued

```
 6:
 7: import org.xml.sax.*;
 8: import org.xml.sax.helpers.*;
 9:
10: public class AbmlParser
11: {
12:     public final static boolean debug;
13:
14:     static
15:     {
16:         String strDebug = System.getProperty("DEBUG");
17:         if (strDebug == null)
18:             strDebug = System.getProperty("debug");
19:
20:         if (strDebug != null && strDebug.equalsIgnoreCase("true"))
21:             debug = true;
22:         else
23:             debug = false;
24:     }
25:
26:     private Parser saxParser;
27:
28:     private AbmlHandler docHandler;
29:
30:     class AbmlHandler implements org.xml.sax.DocumentHandler
31:     {
32:         /** locator object from parser. */
33:         private Locator loc;
34:
35:         /** Vector of addresses. */
36:         private Vector addresses;
37:
38:         /** Current element parsed. */
39:         private int currentElement;
40:
41:         /** current Address */
42:         private Address currentAddress;
43:
44:         /** accessor method. */
45:         public final Vector getAddresses() { return addresses; }
46:
47:         /** method of the DocumentHandler Interface. */
48:         public void characters(char[] ch, int start, int length)
49:         {
```

LISTING 2.5   Continued

```
50:             // Receive notification of character data inside an element.
51:             if (debug) System.out.println("Called characters(ch:" +
52:                         new String(ch,start,length) +
53:                         ",start:" + start + ",length: "+ length + ")");
54:
55:             if (currentAddress == null)
56:                 return; // parser will catch this well-formedness error.
57:
58:             String s = new String(ch, start, length);
59:             switch (currentElement)
60:             {
61:                 case Address.NAME:
62:                     currentAddress.setName(s);
63:                 break;
64:                 case Address.STREET:
65:                     Vector v = currentAddress.getStreets();
66:                     if (v == null)
67:                         v = new Vector();
68:                     v.addElement(s);
69:                     currentAddress.setStreets(v);
70:                 break;
71:                 case Address.CITY:
72:                     currentAddress.setCity(s);
73:                 break;
74:                 case Address.STATE:
75:                     currentAddress.setState(s);
76:                 break;
77:                 case Address.ZIP:
78:                     currentAddress.setZip(s);
79:                 break;
80:             }
81:         }
82:
83:         /** method of the DocumentHandler Interface. */
84:         public void startDocument()
85:         {
86:             // Receive notification of the beginning of the document.
87:             if (debug) System.out.println("Called startDocument()");
88:
89:             // initialize the vector
90:             addresses = new Vector();
91:         }
92:
```

LISTING 2.5 Continued

```
93:            /** method of the DocumentHandler Interface. */
94:            public void endDocument()
95:            {
96:                // Receive notification of the end of the document.
97:                if (debug) System.out.println("Called endDocument()");
98:            }
99:
100:           /** method of the DocumentHandler Interface. */
101:           public void startElement(java.lang.String name,
               ➥ AttributeList attributes)
102:           {
103:               // Receive notification of the start of an element.
104:               if (debug) System.out.println("Called startElement(name:" + name
                   ➥ + ")");
105:               if (name.equals("ADDRESS"))
106:               {
107:                   // create an Address object
108:                   currentElement = Address.ADDRESS;
109:                   currentAddress = new Address();
110:               }
111:               else if (name.equals("NAME"))
112:                   currentElement = Address.NAME;
113:               else if (name.equals("STREET"))
114:                   currentElement = Address.STREET;
115:               else if (name.equals("CITY"))
116:                   currentElement = Address.CITY;
117:               else if (name.equals("STATE"))
118:                   currentElement = Address.STATE;
119:               else if (name.equals("ZIP"))
120:                   currentElement = Address.ZIP;
121:               else
122:                   currentElement = -1;
123:           }
124:
125:           /** method of the DocumentHandler Interface. */
126:           public void endElement(java.lang.String name)
127:           {
128:               // Receive notification of the end of an element.
129:               if (debug) System.out.println("Called endElement(name: "
                   ➥ + name + ")");
130:
131:               if (name.equals("ADDRESS"))
132:                   addresses.addElement(currentAddress);
```

LISTING 2.5   Continued

```
133:          }
134:
135:          /** method of the DocumentHandler Interface. */
136:          public void ignorableWhitespace(char[] ch, int start, int length)
137:          {
138:              // Receive notification of ignorable whitespace in
                ➥ element content.
139:              if (debug) System.out.println("Called ignorableWhitespace(ch:"
140:                          + new String(ch,start,length) +
141:                          ",start: " + start + ",length: " + length + ")");
142:          }
143:
144:          /** method of the DocumentHandler Interface. */
145:          public void processingInstruction(java.lang.String target,
146:                                    java.lang.String data)
147:          {
148:              // Receive notification of a processing instruction.
149:              if (debug) System.out.println("Called processingInstruction
                ➥ (target:" + target + ",data:" + data + ")");
151:          }
152:
153:          /** method of the DocumentHandler Interface. */
154:          public void setDocumentLocator(Locator locator)
155:          {
156:              // Receive a Locator object for document events.
157:              if (debug) System.out.println("Called setDocumentLocator()");
158:              loc = locator;
159:          }
160:      }
161:
162:      public AbmlParser() throws InstantiationException
163:      {
164:          try
165:          {
166:              saxParser = ParserFactory.makeParser();
167:          } catch (Exception e)
168:            {
169:              if (e instanceof InstantiationException)
170:                  throw (InstantiationException) e;
171:              else
172: throw new InstantiationException("Reason:" + e.toString());
```

LISTING 2.5   Continued

```
173:              }
174:
175:          docHandler = new AbmlHandler();
176:          saxParser.setDocumentHandler(docHandler);
177:      }
178:
179:      /**
180:       * method to parse an abml file and return a Vector of Address
             ➥ objects.
181:       * @param is  org.xml.sax.InputSource.
182:       * @returns A Vector of sams.chp2.Address objects.
183:       */
184:      public Vector parse(InputSource is) throws SAXException
185:      {
186:          try
187:          {
188:              saxParser.parse(is);
189:          } catch (IOException ioe) { throw new SAXException(
             ➥ ioe.getMessage()); }
190:
191:          return docHandler.getAddresses();
192:      }
193:
194:      /** main() method for unit testing. */
195:      public static void main(String args[])
196:      {
197:          if (args.length < 1)
198:          {
199:              System.out.println("USAGE: java -Dorg.xml.sax.parser=<classname>
200:              + "sams.chp2.AbmlParser <document>");
201:              System.exit(1);
202:          }
203:
204:          try
205:          {
206:              AbmlParser addressParser = new AbmlParser();
207:              File f = new File(args[0]);
208:              InputSource is = new InputSource(f.toURL().toString());
209:              Vector docAddresses = addressParser.parse(is);
210:
211:              // how many addresses?
212:              int count = docAddresses.size();
```

2

PARSING XML

LISTING 2.5   Continued

```
213:                System.out.println("# of addresses: " + count);
214:
215:                // print out the address names
216:                for (int i=0; i < count; i++)
217:                {
218:                    System.out.println("Address of: " +
219:                    ((Address)docAddresses.elementAt(i)).getName());
220:                }
221:            } catch (Throwable t)
222:              {
223:                t.printStackTrace();
224:              }
225:        }
226: }
```

Listing 2.6 is the Address object that is instantiated by the AbmlParser.java program.

LISTING 2.6   Address Object that Corresponds to an Address Element

```
1: package sams.chp2;
2:
3: import java.util.Vector;
4:
5: public class Address
6: {
7:     public static final int ADDRESS = 1;
8:     public static final int NAME = 2;
9:     public static final int STREET = 3;
10:    public static final int CITY = 4;
11:    public static final int STATE = 5;
12:    public static final int ZIP = 6;
13:
14:    private String name;
15:    private Vector streets = new Vector();
16:    private String city;
17:    private String state;
18:    private String zip;
19:
20:    public String getName() { return name; }
21:    public void setName(String s) { name = s; }
22:    public Vector getStreets() { return streets; }
23:    public void setStreets(Vector v) { streets = v; }
24:    public String getCity() { return city; }
25:    public void setCity(String s) { city = s; }
```

LISTING 2.6   Continued

```
26:    public String getState() { return state; }
27:    public void setState(String s) { state = s; }
28:    public String getZip() { return zip; }
29:    public void setZip(String s) { zip = s; }
30: }
```

Executing Listing 2.5 produces the following output:

```
1: C:\synergysolutions\Xml-in-Java\sams\chp2>java
2: -Dorg.xml.sax.parser=com.ibm.xml.parsers.ValidatingSAXParser
3: sams.chp2.AbmlParser myaddresses.xml
4: # of addresses: 2
5: Address of: Michael Daconta
6: Address of: Sterling Software
```

There are several key points to note about Listing 2.5:

- The purpose of this program is to instantiate a Vector of Address objects given an XML file of Address elements.

- The AbmlParser uses an inner class (called AbmlHandler) to implement org.xml.sax. DocumentHandler. The purpose of this is to make the handler object a part of the larger class.

- The AbmlHandler class declares a reference to a Locator object to allow the SAX-compliant parser to set this variable. Though not used in this program, the Locator is used in error reporting, which is discussed in the next section.

- The key idea behind the program is the creation of a simple finite state machine whereby SAX events trigger the appropriate state changes. The end state we want to reach is a fully populated Vector of Address objects. The key state changes are when to create an Address object, when to populate the fields, and when to store the Address object in the Vector. An Address object is created when the Address element is parsed (see the startElement() method). The fields of an Address object are populated in the characters() method by switching on the appropriate subelement (state which is set in the startElement() method when the appropriate subelement is reached). Lastly, the Address object is stored in the vector at the end of the Address element (see the endElement() method). For uniform XML document types, such as the Address Book Markup Language, the Java Data Binding standard extension will automatically generate Java class files that map to an XML element.

- The main() method of Listing 2.5 demonstrates the use of the AbmlParser. It is important to notice that the use of this parser mirrors the two steps for using a SAX parser—instantiate the parser and then call the parse() method. One important difference is that the AbmlParser.parse() method returns the resultant Vector of Address objects.

Although Listing 2.5 performed the core operations for parsing an XML document and translating it into a useable Java object, it assumed that the XML instance documents contained no errors. Because this is not a wise assumption, I will now examine how SAX reports errors and how to handle them.

The ErrorHandler Interface

This is the interface you implement to customize error handling for your SAX application. A SAX-compliant parser may not throw an exception. Instead it must use this interface to report errors, and your application can determine whether it wants to throw an exception. Listing 2.7 is the ErrorHandler interface.

LISTING 2.7   The ErrorHandler Interface

```
 1: package org.xml.sax;
 2:
 3: public interface ErrorHandler
 4: {
 5:   public abstract void warning (SAXParseException exception)
 6:     throws SAXException;
 7:
 8:   public abstract void error (SAXParseException exception)
 9:     throws SAXException;
10:
11:   public abstract void fatalError (SAXParseException exception)
12:     throws SAXException;
13: }
```

Table 2.2 shows a breakdown and explanation of each method.

TABLE 2.2   ErrorHandler Interface Methods

Method Name	Purpose
warning (SAXParseException e) throws SAXException	The purpose of this method is to report errors that are continuable and minor. The parser will continue to send events.
error (SAXParseException e) throws SAXException	This method reports errors that are considered continuable but major. The parser will continue to send events.
fatalError (SAXParseException e) throws SAXException	This method reports an error that is not recoverable from— Usually a document that is not well-formed. The parser will *not* continue normal processing.

The lowest level of error reporting is a warning. Examples of when the parser reports a warning are when the document encoding is incorrect (but still recognized) and when redefining an internal entity. Listing 2.8 demonstrates redefining an internal entity.

LISTING 2.8 Warning: Redefining an Internal Entity

```
1: <?xml version="1.0"?>
2: <!DOCTYPE ADDRESS_BOOK
3: [
4: <!ENTITY md "Michael Daconta">
5: <!ENTITY md "Medical Doctor">
6: ]>
7: <ADDRESS_BOOK>
8:     <ADDRESS>
9:                 <NAME> &md; </NAME>
10:        <STREET>4296 Razor Hill Road </STREET>
11:        <CITY>Bealeton </CITY>
12:        <STATE>VA </STATE>
13:        <ZIP>22712 </ZIP>
14:    </ADDRESS>
15: </ADDRESS_BOOK>
```

To demonstrate the reporting of this warning, I will use the SaxTester program displayed in Listing 2.3. We run the program using a non-validating parser from Sun Microsystems, Inc., which produces the following output:

```
 1: C:/synergysolutions/Xml-in-Java/sams/chp2>java
➥ -Dorg.xml.sax.parser=com.ibm.xml.
 2: parsers.ValidatingSAXParser sams.chp2.SaxTester addrerr1.xml
 3: Called setDocumentLocator()
 4: Called startDocument()
 5: Called warning()
 6: In file:/C:/synergysolutions/Xml-in-Java/sams/chp2/addrerr1.xml,
 7: at line 5 and col -1
 8: org.xml.sax.SAXParseException: Using original entity definition for "&md;".
 9:         at com.sun.xml.parser.Parser.warning(Parser.java:2721)
10:         at com.sun.xml.parser.Parser.maybeEntityDecl(Parser.java:2276)
11:         at com.sun.xml.parser.Parser.maybeMarkupDecl(Parser.java:1165)
12:         at com.sun.xml.parser.Parser.maybeDoctypeDecl(Compiled Code)
13:         at com.sun.xml.parser.Parser.parseInternal(Compiled Code)
14:         at com.sun.xml.parser.Parser.parse(Parser.java:286)
15:         at sams.chp2.SaxTester.main(SaxTester.java:49)
16: Called startElement(name:ADDRESS_BOOK)
17: In file:/C:/synergysolutions/Xml-in-Java/sams/chp2/addrerr1.xml,
```

```
18: at line 7 and col -1
19: Called characters(ch:,start:132,length: 0)
20: Called characters(ch:
21: ,start:0,length: 1)
22: Called characters(ch:    ,start:134,length: 1)
23: Called startElement(name:ADDRESS)
24: In file:/C:/synergysolutions/Xml-in-Java/sams/chp2/addrerr1.xml,
25: at line 8 and col -1
26: Called characters(ch:,start:144,length: 0)
27: Called characters(ch:
28: ,start:0,length: 1)
29: Called characters(^C
30: Called characters(ch:                    ,start:146,length: 16)
31: Called startElement(name:NAME)
32: ...
```

The key thing to notice in the beginning of the output is that warning() is called. Inside, the warning() method would put out the information provided from the Locator interface and the SAXParseException that was passed into the method. The following is a repeat of the warning() inside the SaxTester class.

```
 1: /** method of the ErrorHandler Interface. */
 2:     public void warning(SAXParseException e)
 3:     {
 4:         // Receive notification of a parser warning.
 5:         System.out.println("Called warning()");
 6:         if (loc != null)
 7:            System.out.println("In " + loc.getSystemId() + ",at line " +
 8:                               loc.getLineNumber() + " and col " +
 9:                               loc.getColumnNumber());
10:         e.printStackTrace();
11:     }
12: }
```

The Locator object (referred to by the reference loc in the previous source) is set in the setDocumentLocator() method of the DocumentHandler interface. All of the error reporting methods should use this interface to inform the user of where in the input XML file the parser encountered the error. From the Locator interface, we report what URL the error occurred in, the line, and column number. However, because it is not required that a SAX-compliant parser provide a Locator object, you must check if the reference is null before trying to use it. Three of the four methods available in the Locator interface are used in the warning() method. The only method not used is getPublicId(), which returns a public identifier if one is available. If your application receives a warning() from the parser, you should merely report this occurrence to the user (or log it if in a server application) and continue processing. It is important to note that the Locator object gives you information about all SAX events. While it can be used with errors, all the methods that exist in Locator also exist in the SAXParseException, which is passed to all of the ErrorHandler methods. So, instead of loc.getLineNumber(), I could have used e.getLineNumber(). The final thing to note about the handling of the warning() error is that the SAX events do not stop but continue even after the warning() method is called.

The second level of SAX error reporting is when the parser calls the error() method. Use of this method conforms to the definition in the XML Specification for error that defines an error as "a violation of the rules of this specification; results are undefined. Conforming software may detect and report an error and may recover from it." While that definition is not very specific and final implementation is up to the individual creators of XML parsers, it is mostly used for validation-type errors. Informally, this group of errors is considered continuable but major. Common validation errors are undeclared elements, undeclared attributes, incorrect root element type, incorrect content model, and incorrect values for a certain attribute type. Listing 2.9 is an example of an XML document that produces a validation error.

LISTING 2.9   Error: Undeclared Element Type

```
 1: <?xml version="1.0"?>
 2: <!DOCTYPE ADDRESS_BOOK
 3: [
 4: <!ELEMENT ADDRESS_BOOK (ADDRESS)+>
 5: <!ELEMENT ADDRESS (NAME, STREET+, CITY, STATE, ZIP)>
 6: <!ELEMENT NAME (#PCDATA)>
 7: <!ELEMENT STREET (#PCDATA)>
 8: <!ELEMENT STATE (#PCDATA)>
 9: <!ELEMENT ZIP (#PCDATA)>
10: <!ATTLIST STREET TYPE (street|suiteno|aptno|other) #IMPLIED>
11: ]>
12: <ADDRESS_BOOK>
13:     <ADDRESS>
14:             <NAME> Michael Daconta </NAME>
15:         <STREET>4296 Razor Hill Road </STREET>
16:         <CITY>Bealeton </CITY>
17:         <STATE>VA </STATE>
18:         <ZIP>22712 </ZIP>
19:     </ADDRESS>
20: </ADDRESS_BOOK>
```

The error in Listing 2.9 is an undeclared element. Although the CITY element is used in the instance of the ADDRESS_BOOK document, it is not declared in the internal document type definition. When we run SaxTester with Sun's validating parser, we get the following output:

```
 1: C:/synergysolutions/Xml-in-Java/sams/chp2>java
 -Dorg.xml.sax.parser=com.ibm.xml.
 2: parser.ValidatingParser sams.chp2.SaxTester addrerr2.xml
```

```
 3: Called setDocumentLocator()
 4: Called startDocument()
 5: Called startElement(name:ADDRESS_BOOK)
 6: In file:/C:/synergysolutions/Xml-in-Java/sams/chp2/addrerr2.xml,
 7: at line 13 and col -1
 8: Called ignorableWhitespace(ch:,start: 332,length: 0)
 9: Called ignorableWhitespace(ch:
10: ,start: 0,length: 1)
11: Called ignorableWhitespace(ch:   ,start: 334,length: 1)
12: Called startElement(name:ADDRESS)
13: In file:/C:/synergysolutions/Xml-in-Java/sams/chp2/addrerr2.xml,
14: at line 14 and col -1
15: ...
16: Called startElement(name:STREET)
17: In file:/C:/synergysolutions/Xml-in-Java/sams/chp2/addrerr2.xml,
18: at line 16 and col -1
19: Called characters(ch:4296 Razor Hill Road ,start:404,length: 21)
20: Called endElement(name: STREET)
21: Called ignorableWhitespace(ch:,start: 434,length: 0)
22: Called ignorableWhitespace(ch:
23: ,start: 0,length: 1)
24: Called ignorableWhitespace(ch:          ,start: 436,length: 2)
25: Called error(e:org.xml.sax.SAXParseException: Element type "CITY" is
26: not declared.)
27: In file:/C:/synergysolutions/Xml-in-Java/sams/chp2/addrerr2.xml,
28: at line 17 and col -1
29: org.xml.sax.SAXParseException: Element type "CITY" is not declared.
30:          at com.sun.xml.parser.Parser.error(Parser.java:2733)
31:          at com.sun.xml.parser.Parser.maybeElement(Compiled Code)
32:          at com.sun.xml.parser.Parser.content(Compiled Code)
33:          at com.sun.xml.parser.Parser.maybeElement(Compiled Code)
34:          at com.sun.xml.parser.Parser.content(Compiled Code)
35:          at com.sun.xml.parser.Parser.maybeElement(Compiled Code)
36:          at com.sun.xml.parser.Parser.parseInternal(Compiled Code)
37:          at com.sun.xml.parser.Parser.parse(Parser.java:286)
38:          at sams.chp2.SaxTester.main(SaxTester.java:49)
39: Called startElement(name:CITY)
40: In file:/C:/synergysolutions/Xml-in-Java/sams/chp2/addrerr2.xml,
41: at line 17 and col -1
42: Called characters(ch:Bealeton ,start:444,length: 9)
43: Called endElement(name: CITY)
44: ...
```

The previous code lines only reveal the middle portion of the output. Sax events are caught before the error and after the error. The error() method is invoked when the CITY element is processed in the XML document. Because we are using a validating parser (notice the setting of the org.xml.sax.parser property), the parser reports that the element called CITY has not been declared in the internal DTD. Although this is a serious error, the parser still passed you the markup and content for the CITY element. One potential remedy for handling validation type errors is to skip the element where the parser encountered the error. Another possibility is to fill in a subelement or attribute with default data. The most serious error the parser can report is a fatal error.

The fatalError() Method

The fatalError() method in the ErrorHandler interface corresponds to the definition of a fatal error in Section 1.2 of the XML Specification. The specification states that a fatal error is "an error which a conforming XML processor must detect and report to the application. After encountering a fatal error, the processor may continue processing the data to search for further errors and may report such errors to the application.... Once a fatal error is detected, however, the processor must not continue normal processing." In relation to SAX, halting normal processing means ceasing all SAX events except the reporting of errors. In informal terms, a fatal error is an uncontinuable error. The most common types of fatal errors are documents that are not well-formed. Listing 2.10 demonstrates an ill-formed document that causes a fatal error.

LISTING 2.10   Fatal Error: A Not Well-Formed Document

```
 1: <!-- not well formed -->
 2: <?xml version="1.0
 3: <<ADDRESS_BOOK>
 4:     <ADDRESS>
 5:                 <NAME> Michael Daconta </NAME>
 6:          <STREET>4296 Razor Hill Road </STREET>
 7:                 <CITY>Bealeton
 8:          <STATE>VA </STATE>
 9:          <ZIP>22712 </ZIP>
10:          </ADDRESS>>
11: </ADDRESS_BOOK>
```

It should be immediately obvious that Listing 2.10 is not well-formed. The version attribute of the XML declaration does not have a closing quote. Also, the processing instruction does not end with a greater-than symbol. Lastly, the ADDRESS_BOOK element has two beginning less-than symbols. When the SaxTester application is run it produces the following output:

```
 1: C:\synergysolutions\Xml-in-Java\sams\chp2>java
➥ -Dorg.xml.sax.parser=com.ibm.xml.
```

```
 2: parsers.ValidatingSAXParser sams.chp2.SaxTester addrerr3.xml
 3: Called setDocumentLocator()
 4: Called startDocument()
 5: Called fatalError(e:org.xml.sax.SAXParseException: XML declaration may
 6: only begin entities.)
 7: In file:/C:/synergysolutions/Xml-in-Java/sams/chp2/addrerr3.xml,
 8: at line 2 and col -1
 9: org.xml.sax.SAXParseException: XML declaration may only begin entities.
10:         at com.sun.xml.parser.Parser.fatal(Parser.java:2755)
11:         at com.sun.xml.parser.Parser.fatal(Parser.java:2743)
12:         at com.sun.xml.parser.Parser.maybePI(Compiled Code)
13:         at com.sun.xml.parser.Parser.maybeMisc(Compiled Code)
14:         at com.sun.xml.parser.Parser.parseInternal(Compiled Code)
15:         at com.sun.xml.parser.Parser.parse(Parser.java:286)
16:         at sams.chp2.SaxTester.main(SaxTester.java:49)
```

When the parser encounters the ill-formed document, it reports the error. Your only recourse for this is to abort the process and report the error to the user. If your document is one member of a set, move on to the next document.

The next two interfaces are less common and are only useful under specific circumstances.

The DTDHandler Interface

This interface provides the minimal amount of DTD processing required by the XML Specification for non-validating parsers. The purpose for this is that SAX 1.0 was meant to be simple for validating and non-validating parsers to implement. Many developers considered the lack of DTD processing a serious deficiency and it has been rectified in SAX 2.0. Listing 2.11 is the DTDHandler interface that reports two DTD declarations—notations and unparsed external entities.

NOTE

The SAX2 API is now complete. Information is available on this API at http://www.megginson.com/SAX/index.html. Unfortunately, at the time of writing, parser support for SAX2 is still spotty at best.

LISTING 2.11   DTDHandler Interface

```
1: package org.xml.sax;
2: public interface DTDHandler
3: {
```

LISTING 2.11   Continued

```
 4:    public abstract void notationDecl (String name,
 5:                        String publicId,
 6:                        String systemId)
 7:      throws SAXException;
 8:
 9:    public abstract void unparsedEntityDecl (String name,
10:                        String publicId,
11:                        String systemId,
12:                        String notationName)
13:      throws SAXException;
14: }
```

Table 2.3 shows a breakdown and explanation of each method.

TABLE 2.3   DTDHandler Interface Methods

Method Name	*Purpose*
notationDecl(String name, String publicId, String systemId)	This method reports the name and translation of a declared notation. A notation represents some method to format binary data (like GIF).
unparsedEntityDecl (String name, String publicId, String systemId, String notationName)	This method reports an unparsed (binary) entity declaration. This is a reference to some external binary data.

To demonstrate the use of the DTDHandler, I will create a simple XML document that contains both a notation and unparsed external entity. We discuss these concepts in more detail in Chapter 4. The source in Listing 2.12 represents a portion of a BOOKMARKS markup language that uses an unparsed (binary) entity to refer to a folder icon. The icon is in GIF format (or in XML-speak, the GIF notation).

LISTING 2.12   A Notation and Unparsed Entity

```
1: <?xml version="1.0" ?>
2: <!DOCTYPE BOOKMARKS [
3: <!NOTATION gif SYSTEM "apps/gifviewer.exe ">
4: <!ENTITY folder SYSTEM "images/folder1.gif" NDATA gif>
5: <!ELEMENT BOOKMARKS (BOOKMARK|FOLDER)* >
6: <!ELEMENT FOLDER (BOOKMARK|FOLDER)* >
```

LISTING 2.12   Continued

```
 7: <!ELEMENT BOOKMARK (#PCDATA)>
 8: <!ATTLIST FOLDER
 9:         icon  ENTITY #REQUIRED>
10: ]>
11: <BOOKMARKS>
12:         <FOLDER icon="folder"> </FOLDER>
13: </BOOKMARKS>
```

With Listing 2.12 as input, the SaxTester program produces the following output:

```
 1: C:\synergysolutions\Xml-in-Java\sams\chp2>java
    ➥ -Dorg.sax.xml.parser=com.ibm.xml.
 2: parsers.ValidatingSAXParser sams.chp2.SaxTester notat1.xml
 3: Called setDocumentLocator()
 4: Called startDocument()
 5: Called notationDecl(name: gif,publicId: null,systemId:
    ➥ file:/C:/synergysolutions
 6: /Xml-in-Java/sams/chp2/apps/gifviewer.exe)
 7: Called unparsedEntityDecl
 8: folder
 9: null
10: file:/C:/synergysolutions/Xml-in-Java/sams/chp2/images/folder1.gif
11: gif
12: Called startElement(name:BOOKMARKS)
13: In file:/C:/synergysolutions/Xml-in-Java/sams/chp2/notat1.xml,
14:  at line 11 and col -1
15: Called ignorableWhitespace(ch:,start: 328,length: 0)
16: Called ignorableWhitespace(ch:
17: ,start: 0,length: 1)
18: Called ignorableWhitespace(ch:          ,start: 330,length: 8)
19: Called startElement(name:FOLDER)
20: att-name:icon,att-type:ENTITY,att-value:folder
21: ...
```

As you can see, the parser informs us of the notation and the binary data. This provides enough information for us to process this binary data. The last interface of interest to SAX application writers also handles a special case.

The EntityResolver Interface

The EntityResolver interface is used to customize the resolution of external parsed entities. Listing 2.13 is the EntityResolver interface.

LISTING 2.13 The `EntityResolver` Interface

```
 1: package org.xml.sax;
 2:
 3: import java.io.IOException;
 4:
 5: public interface EntityResolver
 6: {
 7:   public abstract InputSource resolveEntity (String publicId,
 8:                           String systemId)
 9:     throws SAXException, IOException;
10:
11: }
```

There is only one method in the interface. The `resolveEntity()` method gives you the public identifier and system identifier of the entity to resolve. Your application should only implement this interface if the XML-compliant language you are processing requires custom resolution of external entities. Although entities will be discussed in more detail in Chapter 4, for now you need to know that they are used for text replacement. An internal parsed entity provides the replacement text in the same file. An external parsed entity has the replacement text in some external file. You can specify an external parsed entity with the following syntax:

```
<!ENTITY entityName PUBLIC "publicId" "optionalURI">
```

or

```
<!ENTITY entityName SYSTEM "URI of resource">
```

Listing 2.14 demonstrates the use of both types of external parsed entities. Note that a parsed entity is another way to say a text entity (in contrast to an unparsed entity, which is some binary data).

LISTING 2.14 Parsed External Entities to Resolve

```
 1: <?xml version="1.0" ?>
 2: <!DOCTYPE JOURNAL [
 3: <!ENTITY mcd "Michael Corey Daconta">
 4: <!ENTITY templatexml PUBLIC "boilerplate" "stuff.xml">
 5: <!ENTITY logo SYSTEM "http://www.gosynergy.com/logo">
 6: ]>
 7: <JOURNAL>
 8: <ENTRY> &logo; It was a bright sunny day. - &mcd; </ENTRY>
 9: <ENTRY> Standard legalese here: &templatexml; </ENTRY>
10: </JOURNAL>
```

In Listing 2.14 we see an external entity using the PUBLIC identifier and the SYSTEM identifier. The PUBLIC identifier is for widely used content that crosses many XML applications. A SYSTEM identifier provides a URI and means that the replacement text is located at that URI. When these entities are used in the content of the XML document, SAX calls resolveEntity() on the registered handler to resolve the entity and return the replacement text. When I use Listing 2.14 as the input to SaxTester, it produces the following output:

```
 1: C:\synergysolutions\Xml-in-Java\sams\chp2>java
    ➥ -Dorg.xml.sax.parser=com.ibm.xml.
 2: parsers.ValidatingSAXParser sams.chp2.SaxTester entity1.xml
 3: Called setDocumentLocator()
 4: Called startDocument()
 5: Called startElement(name:JOURNAL)
 6: In file:/C:/synergysolutions/Xml-in-Java/sams/chp2/entity1.xml,
 7: at line 7 and col -1
 8: Called characters(ch:,start:208,length: 0)
 9: Called characters(ch:
10: ,start:0,length: 1)
11: Called startElement(name:ENTRY)
12: In file:/C:/synergysolutions/Xml-in-Java/sams/chp2/entity1.xml,
13:  at line 8 and col -1
14: Called characters(ch: ,start:217,length: 1)
15: Called resolveEntity(publicId:null,systemId:http://www.gosynergy.com/logo)
16: Called characters(ch:Resolved Entity,start:0,length: 15)
17: Called characters(ch: It was a bright sunny day. - ,start:224,length: 30)
18: ...
19: Called startElement(name:ENTRY)
20: In file:/C:/synergysolutions/Xml-in-Java/sams/chp2/entity1.xml,
21: at line 9 and col -1
22: Called characters(ch: Standard legalese here: ,start:277,length: 25)
23: Called resolveEntity(publicId:boilerplate,systemId:
24: file:/C:/synergysolutions/Xml -in-Java/sams/chp2/stuff.xml)
25: Called characters(ch:Resolved Entity,start:0,length: 15)
26: ...
27: Called endDocument()
```

You should notice in the output that resolveEntity is called and then the resolution of the entity is returned in the very next call to the characters() method. Entities and entity resolution are an advanced topic that is discussed in more detail in the next chapter. For now, it is sufficient to know that SAX has the ability to do custom entity resolution if your application will benefit from it. This concludes our examination of interfaces that you as an application writer can implement. Again, the most common interfaces you will implement are `DocumentHandler` and `ErrorHandler`. `DTDHandler` and `EntityResolver` are for special cases. SAX has several other interfaces and classes for the parser writers to deliver the events your application processes.

Interfaces Implemented by Parser Writers

Even though I do not recommend you write yet another XML parser (there are already too many freely distributable ones available), it is worthwhile to briefly examine the interfaces a SAX-compliant parser must implement.

- `Parser` This is the main interface a SAX-compliant parser must implement. It has all the set*XXX*Handler methods like `setDocumentHandler()`. It also has two `parse()` methods that take an `InputSource` to parse.

- `AttributeList` This interface is implemented by the parser and passed into the `startElement()` method of the `DocumentHandler` interface. This interface represents a collection of attributes for the current element. It allows you to either iterate through the entire collection of attributes (using a `getName()`, `getType()`, and `getValue()` method) or access a value on a specific attribute. Listing 2.15 is the `AttributeList` interface.

LISTING 2.15   `AttributeList` Interface

```
package org.xml.sax;

public interface AttributeList
{
public abstract int getLength ();

public abstract String getName (int i);

public abstract String getType (int i);

public abstract String getValue (int i);

public abstract String getType (String name);

public abstract String getValue (String name);
}
```

- `Locator` The `Locator` interface is implemented by the parser and passed to the application via the `setDocumentLocator()` method in the `DocumentHandler` interface. The `Locator` interface provides information on the line number in the XML document in which a SAX event occurs. The `SaxTester` program used the `Locator` in its implementation of the `startElement()` method.

That completes our discussion of SAX interfaces. Now we will finish our discussion of SAX by examining all of the classes provided with SAX.

SAX Standard Classes and Helper Classes

There are two categories of classes provided with the SAX distribution: standard classes and helper classes. The standard classes are part of the org.xml.sax package, and the helper classes are part of the org.xml.sax.helpers package. The following are the standard classes:

- HandlerBase   This is an adapter class that implements all the SAX handler interfaces as a convenience for developers. You can make your handler class extend HandlerBase and then just override the methods you are interested in.

- InputSource   This class is an encapsulation of all the information about an XML input source (to be handed to the parse() method of the Parser interface). The information encapsulated is the public identifier, the system identifier, a byte stream with a specified encoding, or a character stream.

The helper classes are for the convenience of both parser writers and application writers:

- AttributeListImpl   An implementation of the AttributeList interface for use by parser writers.

- LocatorImpl   An implementation of the Locator interface for use by parser writers.

- ParserFactory   A convenience class for SAX application writers to allow a SAX-compliant parser to be instantiated by a static method called makeParser(). There are two forms of makeParser(). The no-arg form instantiates the parser object by using the System property org.xml.sax.parser. A form that takes a string parameter accepts the classname to instantiate using reflection.

The Java API for XML Parsing (JAXP)

As stated earlier, there are two common ways for a computer program to ingest and use an XML document: either as a stream of SAX events or as a Document Object Model (DOM). There are many implementations of these two de facto standards available from numerous vendors; however, there was no way to write code that would work with all vendors' implementations in a plug-and-play manner until now. That is the problem that the Java Community process set out to solve with the Java API for XML Parsing. The package javax.xml defines two Factory and Wrapper class combinations—one for SAX Parsers and one for Document (Object Model) Builders. The following are the four classes in the javax.xml.parser:

- SAXParserFactory   An abstract class whose subclasses represent specific implementations capable of instantiating a compliant SAX Parser. An example of using this class is presented later in this section.

- `SAXParser` A convenience wrapper class that represents a SAX Parser. This class adds some overloaded `parse()` methods that parse common Java IO objects like `java.io.File` and `java.io.InputStream`.

- `DocumentBuilderFactory` An abstract class whose subclasses represent specific implementations capable of instantiating a compliant Document Builder (another name for a parser capable of producing an `org.w3c.dom.Document` object). An example of using this class is presented later in this section.

- `DocumentBuilder` A convenience wrapper class that represents a Document Builder parser. There are several overloaded `parse()` methods that all produce an `org.w3c.dom.Document` object. Additionally, there is a method to obtain a new `Document` object for creating in-memory representations from scratch.

Next we will examine an example using a `SAXParserFactory` object.

> **NOTE**
>
> The JAXP specification and code can be downloaded at `http://java.sun.com/xml`.

The SAX Parser Factory

The SAX Parser Factory is an abstract class designed to allow you to access a SAX Parser implementation and check or set certain facilities of the implementation. The `SAXParseFactory` comes with a default implementation (`com.sun.xml.parser.*`) that can be overridden by setting the System property `javax.xml.parsers.SAXParserFactory` with the name of a class that is a concrete subclass of `SAXParserFactory`.

The Java API for XML parsing is extremely simple and consistent. Listing 2.16 is a rewrite of Listing 2.3 (`SaxTester.java`) that uses a `SAXParserFactory` instead. The class `TestHandler` has been separated out and repackaged as the public class `EchoHandler` (the code is identical to the class `TestHandler` in Listing 2.3, so it is not repeated here).

LISTING 2.16   Example of the SAX Parser Factory

```
/* SaxFactoryExample.java */
package sams.chp2;

import javax.xml.parsers.*;
import java.io.*;
```

LISTING 2.16   Continued

```
public class SAXFactoryExample
{
    public static void main(String args[])
    {
        if (args.length < 1)
        {
            System.out.println("USAGE: java sams.chp2.SAXFactoryExample
➡ xmlfile");
System.exit(1);
        }

        try
        {
            SAXParserFactory factory = SAXParserFactory.newInstance();
            SAXParser sp = factory.newSAXParser();
            sp.parse(new File(args[0]), new EchoHandler());
        } catch (Throwable t)
          {
            t.printStackTrace();
          }
    }
}
```

A run of Listing 2.16 produces the same output as Listing 2.3.

The Document Builder Factory

The Document Builder Factory is an abstract class designed to allow you to access a Document Builder implementation and check or set certain facilities of the implementation. The Document Builder Factory comes with a default implementation (com.sun.xml.tree.*) that can be overridden by setting the System property javax.xml.parsers. DocumentBuilderFactory with the name of a class that is a concrete subclass of DocumentBuilderFactory.

Listing 2.17 demonstrates the use of a DocumentBuilderFactory. We will not elaborate on the Document Object Model in this chapter because it is covered in detail in the next chapter. Listing 2.17 is provided here to provide complete coverage of the Java API for XML Parsing. The usage of the Document Builder Factory follows the same pattern as the SAX Parser Factory. We first obtain an instance of the factory. We then obtain an instance of the builder (or parser). We then build (or parse) some document. To complete the example, Listing 2.17 includes a method to recursively print out the nodes of the document, which is a tree data structure.

LISTING 2.17   Example of the Document Builder Factory

```java
/* DocumentBuilderFactoryExample.java */
package sams.chp2;

import javax.xml.parsers.*;
import java.io.*;

import org.w3c.dom.*;

public class DocumentBuilderFactoryExample
{
    public static void main(String args[])
    {
        if (args.length < 1)
        {
            System.out.println("USAGE: java
sams.chp2.DocumentBuilderFactoryExample xmlfile");
System.exit(1);
        }

        try
        {
            DocumentBuilderFactory factory =
➥ DocumentBuilderFactory.newInstance();
DocumentBuilder builder = factory.newDocumentBuilder();
            Document doc = builder.parse(new File(args[0]));
            Element root = doc.getDocumentElement();
            root.normalize();
            printNodes(root, System.out);
        } catch (Throwable t)
          {
            t.printStackTrace();
          }
    }

    private static void printNodes(Node n, OutputStream out) throws IOException
    {
        if (n == null)
            return;

        out.write(("Node name: " + n.getNodeName() + ", value: "
➥ + n.getNodeValue() + "\n").getBytes());
NodeList list = n.getChildNodes();
        if (list == null)
```

LISTING 2.17   Continued

```
            return;
        else
        {
            int len = list.getLength();
            for (int i=0; i < len; i++)
            {
                printNodes(list.item(i), out);
            }
        }
    }
}
```

When run, Listing 2.17 produces the following output (abridged for brevity):

```
E:\synergysolutions\Xml-in-Java\sams\chp2>java
➥ sams.chp2.DocumentBuilderFactoryExample myaddresses.xml

Node name: ADDRESS_BOOK, value: null
Node name: #text, value:
Node name: ADDRESS, value: null
Node name: #text, value:
Node name: NAME, value: null
Node name: #text, value: Michael Daconta
Node name: #text, value:
Node name: STREET, value: null
Node name: #text, value: 4296 Razor Hill Road
Node name: #text, value:
Node name: CITY, value: null
Node name: #text, value: Bealeton
Node name: #text, value:
Node name: STATE, value: null
Node name: #text, value: VA
Node name: #text, value:
Node name: ZIP, value: null
Node name: #text, value: 22712
```

So, as demonstrated in this section, the Java API for XML parsing provides the key standardized bootstrapping mechanisms for a plug-and-play parsing architecture. Java developers now have simple, standard access to both a DOM or SAX event stream.

Alternative Parsers

There are numerous XML parsers written in Java available for you to use. There are commercial parsers that are freely distributable for both commercial and non-commercial use. There are several open-source parsers. However, it does us no good to study another parser unless it has a value proposition different from the Java Standard extension. Otherwise, there is no use in learning another API. One alternative parser that has a clear value proposition is AElfred.

AElfred

AElfred is a Java-based XML parser from Microstar Software. It is free for both commercial and non-commercial use. It was originally written by David Megginson and is distributed with full source. The key value proposition of AElfred is that it is highly optimized for use with applets. The following are the design goals for AElfred:

- AElfred must be as small as possible. AElfred is currently approximately 26KB in total. The compressed JAR file, including the optional classes, is 15KB.

- AElfred must use as few class files as possible. AElfred consists of only two core class files—the main parser class (`XmlParser.class`) and a small interface for your own program to implement (`XmlHandler.class`). All other classes in the distribution are either optional or for demonstration only.

- AElfred must be compatible with most Java implementations and platforms.

- AElfred must use as little memory as possible, so that it does not take away resources from the rest of your program. To accomplish this, AElfred uses an event-based paradigm nearly identical to SAX.

- AElfred must run as fast as possible, so that it does not slow down the rest of your program.

- AElfred must produce correct output for well-formed and valid documents, but it need not reject every document that is not valid or not well-formed. AElfred is DTD-aware and handles all current XML features, including CDATA and INCLUDE/IGNORE marked sections, internal and external entities, proper whitespace treatment in element content, and default attribute values.

- AElfred must provide full internationalization from the first release. AElfred correctly handles XML documents encoded using UTF-8, UTF-16, ISO-10646-UCS-2, ISO-10646-UCS-4 (as far as surrogates allow), and ISO-8859-1 (ISO Latin 1/Windows). With these character sets, AElfred can handle all of the world's major (and most of its minor) languages. To support other character encodings, you can supply your own reader.

NOTE

You can download AElfred from the Web at `http://www.opentext.com/microstar`.

As you can see from this list, AElfred is designed for production use and not for validation. For validation, the Java Standard Extension validating parser can be used.

AElfred also has a SAX 1.0 driver built in to the main distribution. The class name of the driver is `com.microstar.xml.SAXDriver`. However, the SAX interface is a front-end layer on top of Aelfred, so its use will slow performance. In our example, we use the AElfred API, which is nearly identical to SAX and therefore does not represent a new learning curve.

To learn how to use Aelfred, we will develop an applet that will process an XML document. Our applet will be a `BookmarkViewer` that allows us to view annotations on bookmarks to explain their value and optionally to jump to a bookmark URL that interests us. Our data source for the applet will be a single XML document that conforms to a simple DTD called the Bookmark List Markup Language (BLML). Listing 2.18 is our XML data source in a file called `bookmarks.xml`.

LISTING 2.18   Bookmark List Markup Language Source Document

```
 1: <?xml version="1.0" ?>
 2: <!DOCTYPE BOOKMARK_LIST [
 3: <!ELEMENT BOOKMARK_LIST (FOLDER|BOOKMARK)+>
 4: <!ELEMENT FOLDER (FOLDER|BOOKMARK)+>
 5: <!ELEMENT BOOKMARK (COMMENT) >
 6: <!ELEMENT COMMENT (#PCDATA)>
 7: <!ATTLIST BOOKMARK
 8:         name CDATA #REQUIRED
 9:         href CDATA #REQUIRED>
10: <!ATTLIST FOLDER
11:         name CDATA #REQUIRED>
12: ]>
13:
14: <BOOKMARK_LIST>
15:         <FOLDER name = "Java" >
16:             <BOOKMARK name="Java Technology Home"
17:                     href="http://java.sun.com" >
18:                 <COMMENT> Great site!
19:                         The authoritative source of
20:                         all things Java.  Both
21:                         News and Technical Documentation
22:                         and tutorials for Developers.
23:                         Download all the latest Java
24:                         Software.
25:                     </COMMENT>
26:             </BOOKMARK>
27:         </FOLDER>
28:         <FOLDER name = "XML" >
```

LISTING 2.18　Continued

```
29:                    <BOOKMARK name="IBM's XML site"
30:                          href="http://www.ibm.com/xml" >
31:                       <COMMENT> Cutting edge!
32:                                IBM really showing its depth.
33:                                Just like their very popular
34:                                Java site in its completeness.
35:                       </COMMENT>
36:                    </BOOKMARK>
37:          </FOLDER>
38: ...
39: </BOOKMARK_LIST>
```

Although Listing 2.18 has some sections omitted for brevity, all the basic concepts of a bookmark file are there. We have the ability to have folders, subfolders, and bookmarks in our list. A bookmark has all the relevant information, such as name and href, and a subelement called COMMENT. Now we can write an applet to parse the file using the AElfred parser and display it with a GUI. Figure 2.1 shows the result of running our applet on Netscape Navigator.

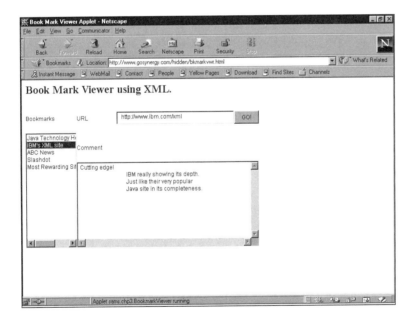

FIGURE 2.1

BookmarkViewer *applet running in Navigator.*

Although this is only useful as an applet, the code will actually run as either an applet or an application. This is handy for testing the functionality before deploying it as an applet. Listing 2.19 is the source code for the BookmarkViewer applet.

LISTING 2.19   Bookmark List Applet

```
 1: /* BookmarkViewer.java */
 2: package sams.chp2;
 3:
 4: import com.microstar.xml.*;
 5:
 6: import java.applet.*;
 7: import java.awt.*;
 8: import java.awt.event.*;
 9: import java.io.*;
10: import java.net.*;
11: import java.util.*;
12:
13: public class BookmarkViewer extends Applet implements XmlHandler,
14:                                                        ActionListener,
15:                                                        ItemListener
16: {
17:     private final boolean debug = false;
18:     private boolean isApplet = true;
19:     public final String datasource = "bookmarks.xml";
20:     XmlParser parser = new XmlParser();
21:     Vector bookmarks = new Vector();
22:     Hashtable lookup = new Hashtable();
23:
24:     final int BOOKMARKLIST = 0;
25:     final int FOLDER = 1;
26:     final int BOOKMARK = 2;
27:     final int COMMENT = 3;
28:
29:     public class Bookmark
30:     {
31:         String name;
32:         String href;
33:         String comment;
34:     }
35:
36:     Bookmark currentBookmark = null;
37:     int currentElement = -1;
38:     String lastName, lastHref;
39:
```

LISTING 2.19 Continued

```
40:      // gui components
41:      Label listLabel = new Label("Bookmarks");
42:      Label commentLabel = new Label("Comment");
43:      Label hrefLabel = new Label("URL");
44:      java.awt.List bookmarkList = new java.awt.List(10);
45:      TextField hrefTF = new TextField(30);
46:      Button goButton = new Button("GO!");
47:      TextArea commentTA = new TextArea(8, 60);
48:
49:      public void init()
50:      {
51:          String surl = null;
52:
53:          if (isApplet)
54:          {
55:              URL codebase = getCodeBase();
56:              surl = codebase.toString() + "/" + datasource;
57:          }
58:          else
59:          {
60:              // use current directory
61:              String currentDirectory = System.getProperty("user.dir");
62:              String fileSep = System.getProperty("file.separator");
63:              String file = currentDirectory.replace(fileSep.charAt(0), '/')
              ➡ + '/';
64:              if (file.charAt(0) != '/')
65:                file = "/" + file;
66:              try
67:              {
68:                  URL baseURL = new URL("file", null, file);
69:                  surl = new URL(baseURL,datasource).toString();
70:              } catch (MalformedURLException mfue) { surl = null; }
71:          }
72:
73:          parser.setHandler(this);
74:          try
75:          {
76:              if (surl != null)
77:                  parser.parse(surl, (String) null, (String) null);
78:          } catch (Exception e)
79:            {
80:                e.printStackTrace();
81:            }
82:
83:
```

2

LISTING 2.19   Continued

```
 84:        // here we should have a full Vector
 85:        // set up our GUI
 86:        GridBagConstraints gbc = new GridBagConstraints();
 87:        gbc.fill = GridBagConstraints.HORIZONTAL;
 88:        gbc.weightx = 1.0; gbc.weighty = 1.0;
 89:        gbc.ipadx = 4; gbc.ipady = 4;
 90:        GridBagLayout gbl = new GridBagLayout();
 91:        setLayout(gbl);
 92:        gbc.gridx = 1; gbc.gridy = 1;
 93:        gbc.gridwidth = 5; gbc.gridheight = 1;
 94:        gbc.anchor = GridBagConstraints.WEST;
 95:        gbl.setConstraints(listLabel, gbc);
 96:        add(listLabel);
 97:        gbc.gridx = 1; gbc.gridy = 3;
 98:        gbc.gridwidth = 5; gbc.gridheight = 7;
 99:        gbc.fill = GridBagConstraints.BOTH;
100:        gbc.anchor = GridBagConstraints.CENTER;
101:        gbl.setConstraints(bookmarkList, gbc);
102:        add(bookmarkList);
103:        gbc.gridx = 7; gbc.gridy = 1;
104:        gbc.gridwidth = 1; gbc.gridheight = 1;
105:        gbc.fill = GridBagConstraints.NONE;
106:        gbc.anchor = GridBagConstraints.WEST;
107:        gbl.setConstraints(hrefLabel, gbc);
108:        add(hrefLabel);
109:        gbc.gridx = 8; gbc.gridy = 1;
110:        gbc.gridwidth = 4; gbc.gridheight = 1;
111:        gbc.fill = GridBagConstraints.HORIZONTAL;
112:        gbl.setConstraints(hrefTF, gbc);
113:        add(hrefTF);
114:        gbc.gridx = 13; gbc.gridy = 1;
115:        gbc.gridwidth = 1; gbc.gridheight = 1;
116:        gbl.setConstraints(goButton, gbc);
117:        add(goButton);
118:        goButton.addActionListener(this);
119:        gbc.gridx = 7; gbc.gridy = 3;
120:        gbc.gridwidth = 4; gbc.gridheight = 1;
121:        gbc.anchor = GridBagConstraints.CENTER;
122:        gbl.setConstraints(commentLabel, gbc);
123:        add(commentLabel);
124:        gbc.gridx = 7; gbc.gridy = 4;
125:        gbc.gridwidth = 8; gbc.gridheight = 6;
126:        gbc.fill = GridBagConstraints.BOTH;
127:        gbl.setConstraints(commentTA, gbc);
```

LISTING 2.19   Continued

```
128:            add(commentTA);
129:
130:            // fill the bookmark list
131:            bookmarkList.addItemListener(this);
132:            int count = bookmarks.size();
133:            if (count > 0)
134:            {
135:                for (int i=0; i < count; i++)
136:                {
137:                    Bookmark b = (Bookmark) bookmarks.elementAt(i);
138:                    /* addItem() replaced by add() in JDK1.2.
139:                       However, most browsers are still on 1.1. */
140:                    if (b != null && b.name != null)
141:                    {
142:                        bookmarkList.addItem(b.name);
143:                        // use the name as the key
144:                        lookup.put(b.name, b);
145:                    }
146:                }
147:            }
148:        }
149:
150:        public void actionPerformed(ActionEvent evt)
151:        {
152:            String cmd = evt.getActionCommand();
153:
154:            if (isApplet)
155:            {
156:                if (cmd.equals("GO!"))
157:                {
158:                    try
159:                    {
160:                        AppletContext context = getAppletContext();
161:                        String surl = hrefTF.getText();
162:                        URL u = new URL(surl);
163:                        context.showDocument(u);
164:                    } catch (MalformedURLException mue)
165:                        { showStatus("Incorrect URL."); }
166:                }
167:            }
168:            else
169:                System.out.println("Operation only supported in an Applet.");
170:        }
171:
```

2

PARSING XML

LISTING 2.19   Continued

```
172:    public void itemStateChanged(ItemEvent evt)
173:    {
174:        if (evt.getStateChange() == ItemEvent.SELECTED)
175:        {
176:            // We can cheat here, we know the List is the source
177:            String key = bookmarkList.getSelectedItem();
178:            // Now get the object
179:            Bookmark b = (Bookmark) lookup.get(key);
180:            if (b != null)
181:            {
182:                hrefTF.setText(b.href);
183:                commentTA.setText(b.comment);
184:            }
185:        }
186:    }
187:
188:    public static void main(String args[])
189:    {
190:        BookmarkViewer viewer = new BookmarkViewer();
191:        viewer.isApplet = false;
192:
193:        // add panel to Frame
194:        Frame f = new Frame("Test Bookmark Viewer Frame");
195:
196:        viewer.init();
197:        f.add("Center", viewer);
198:
199:        f.addWindowListener(new WindowAdapter()
200:                        {
201:                            public void windowClosing(WindowEvent we)
202:                            { System.exit(0); }
203:                        });
204:
205:        // show Frame
206:        f.setLocation(100,100);
207:        //f.setSize(500,400);
208:        f.pack();
209:        f.setVisible(true);
210:    }
211:
212:    private void setElementType(String ename)
213:    {
214:        if (ename.equals("BOOKMARKLIST"))
215:            currentElement = BOOKMARKLIST;
216:        else if (ename.equals("FOLDER"))
```

LISTING 2.19   Continued

```
217:                currentElement = FOLDER;
218:            else if (ename.equals("BOOKMARK"))
219:                currentElement = BOOKMARK;
220:            else if (ename.equals("COMMENT"))
221:                currentElement = COMMENT;
222:        }
223:
224:        /** XmlHandler: Start the document */
225:        public void startDocument () throws java.lang.Exception
226:        {
227:            if (debug) System.out.println("startDocument()");
228:        }
229:
230:
231:        /**
232:         * XmlHandler: End the document.
233:         */
234:        public void endDocument () throws java.lang.Exception
235:        {
236:            if (debug) System.out.println("endDocument()");
237:
238:        }
239:
240:
241:        /**
242:         * XmlHandler: Resolve an External Entity.
243:         */
244:        public Object resolveEntity (String publicId, String systemId)
245:        throws java.lang.Exception
246:        {
247:            if (debug) System.out.println("resolveEntity(publicId: "
248:            + publicId + ",systemId: " + systemId + ")");
249:            return null;
250:        }
251:
252:        /**
253:         * XmlHandler: Begin an external entity.
254:         */
255:        public void startExternalEntity (String systemId)
256:        throws java.lang.Exception
257:        {
258:            if (debug) System.out.println("startExternalEntity(systeId: "
                ➡ + systemId + ")");
```

LISTING 2.19   Continued

```
259:
260:    }
261:
262:    /**
263:     * XmlHandler: End an external entity.
264:     */
265:    public void endExternalEntity (String systemId)
266:    throws java.lang.Exception
267:    {
268:        if (debug) System.out.println("endExternalEntity(systemId: "
            ➥ + systemId + ")");
269:
270:    }
271:
272:
273:    /**
274:     * XmlHandler: Document type declaration.
275:     */
276:    public void doctypeDecl (String name, String publicId,
           ➥ String systemId)
277:    throws java.lang.Exception
278:    {
279:        if (debug) System.out.println("doctypeDecl(name: " + name +
280:                                    ",publicId: " + publicId +
281:                                    ",systemId: " + systemId + ")");
282:
283:    }
284:
285:    /**
286:     * XmlHandler: Attribute.
287:     */
288:    public void attribute (String aname, String value, boolean
           ➥ isSpecified)
289:    throws java.lang.Exception
290:    {
291:        if (debug) System.out.println("attribute(aname: " + aname +
292:                    ",value: " + value +
293:                    ",isSpecified: " + isSpecified + ")");
294:
295:        // Aelfred attribute events are BEFORE the startElement call
296:        if (aname.equals("name"))
297:            lastName = value;
298:        else if (aname.equals("href"))
299:            lastHref = value;
```

LISTING 2.19   Continued

```
300:        }
301:
302:        /**
303:         * XmlHandler: Start an element.
304:         */
305:        public void startElement (String elname)
306:        throws java.lang.Exception
307:        {
308:            if (debug) System.out.println("startElement(elname: " + elname
                ➡ + ")");
309:            setElementType(elname);
310:            if (elname.equals("BOOKMARK"))
311:            {
312:                currentBookmark = new Bookmark();
313:                // NOTE: attribute events are before the startElement event.
314:                //        NON-INTUITIVE!   SAX uses a better way.
315:                if (lastName != null)
316:                {
317:                    currentBookmark.name = lastName;
318:                    lastName = null;
319:                }
320:
321:                if (lastHref != null)
322:                {
323:                    currentBookmark.href = lastHref;
324:                    lastHref = null;
325:                }
326:            }
327:        }
328:
329:        /**
330:         * XmlHandler: End an element.
331:         */
332:        public void endElement (String elname)
333:        throws java.lang.Exception
334:        {
335:            if (debug) System.out.println("endElement(elname: " + elname
                ➡ +")");
336:            if (elname.equals("BOOKMARK") && currentBookmark != null)
337:                bookmarks.addElement(currentBookmark);
338:        }
339:
340:
341:        /**
```

LISTING 2.19   Continued

```
342:       * XmlHandler: Character data. */
343:      public void charData (char ch[], int start, int length)
344:      throws java.lang.Exception
345:      {
346:          if (debug) System.out.println("charData(ch:" +
347:                  new String(ch, start, length) + ")");
348:          switch (currentElement)
349:          {
350:              case BOOKMARKLIST:
351:                  break;
352:              case FOLDER:
353:                  break;
354:              case BOOKMARK:
355:                  break;
356:              case COMMENT:
357:                  if (currentBookmark != null)
358:                      currentBookmark.comment = new String(ch, start,
                    ➡ length);
359:                  break;
360:          }
361:      }
362:
363:
364:      /** XmlHandler: Ignorable whitespace. */
365:      public void ignorableWhitespace (char ch[], int start, int length)
366:      throws java.lang.Exception
367:      {
368:          if (debug) System.out.println("ignorableWhitespace(...)");
369:
370:      }
371:
372:      /** XmlHandler: Processing instruction.*/
373:      public void processingInstruction (String target, String data)
374:      throws java.lang.Exception
375:      {
376:          if (debug) System.out.println("processingInstruction(target: "
377:          + target + ",data: " + data + ")");
378:
379:      }
380:
381:
```

LISTING 2.19   Continued

```
382:        /** XmlHandler: Fatal XML parsing error. */
383:        public void error (String message, String systemId, int line,
            ➥ int column)
384:        throws java.lang.Exception
385:        {
386:            if (debug) System.out.println("error(message:" + message + ")");
387:            if (!isApplet)
388:                System.exit(1);
389:        }
390: }
```

Note the following points about BookmarkViewer.java:

- The best way to understand the program is to separate the parsing aspects from the GUI code. These two are really separate actions. In fact, the GUI is not even instantiated until after the parsing has occurred. When the user interface pops up, the parsing has already been completed.

- The class BookmarkViewer implements three interfaces: two for GUI event handling (ActionListener and ItemListener) and one for AElfred event handling (XmlHandler). The XmlHandler interface has quite a few methods that closely resemble methods in SAX. In the code, all the methods belonging to the XmlHandler interface are clearly identified in a preceding comment.

- The parsing completes and produces a vector of Bookmark objects. Bookmark is a simple inner class.

- The init() method of the applet first parses the XML data source and then instantiates and lays out the user interface in the applet. The XmlParser class in AElfred is the parser. There are three steps to using this parser. First, instantiate an object of type XmlParser. Second, call the setHandler() method on the parser to set the current object as the parser event handler. Lastly, call the parse() method on the parser and pass in a URI. The rest of the init() method is concerned with properly placing the UI elements (an awt List, labels, text field, and text area) using a GridBagLayout.

- The Go button in the GUI fires an ActionEvent. The actionPerformed() method uses the showDocument() method of the Applet class to jump to the specified URL.

- The selection of a list item fires an ItemEvent. The itemStateChanged() method triggers the viewing of a specific bookmark when its name is selected in the list.

- The main() method is used to run the class as an application. It brings up a frame and places the applet (which extends Panel) inside the center of the frame. This allows us to test the GUI before deploying it as an applet.

- The rest of the code is the implementation of the XmlHandler methods. Most are unused. Only four methods are used: startElement(), endElement(), attribute(), and charData(). Note: attribute processing is different in AElfred than in SAX. In AElfred, the attribute events are fired *before* the startElement event (of the element that has the attributes). While this is non-intuitive, it is the way it is currently implemented in AElfred.

After we compile BookmarkViewer.java, we need to collect it and the AElfred classes into a jar file for distribution as an applet. We use the jar tool to add the three classes for BookmarkViewer and the AElfred classes into a single file called bookmark.jar. The bookmark.jar file is only 28,596 bytes (about 28KB). The last step to distribute this code as an applet is to create an HTML page that has an applet tag. Listing 2.20 is the HTML page for this applet.

LISTING 2.20   HTML Page to Display the BoomarkViewer Applet

```
 1: <HTML>
 2: <HEAD>
 3: <TITLE> Book Mark Viewer Applet </TITLE>
 4: </HEAD>
 5: <BODY>
 6: <H2> Book Mark Viewer using XML. </H2>
 7: <APPLET code = "sams.chp2.BookmarkViewer.class"
 8:         archive = bookmark.jar
 9:         width = 400 height = 300>
10: </APPLET>
11: </BODY>
12: </HTML>
```

When loaded in a Web browser, Figure 2.1 is displayed.

Summary

This chapter covered the concepts behind parsing, SAX, JAXP, and AElfred. You can now use the available XML parsers to ingest and break down XML documents to extract the pertinent information for your application.

The two activities involved in parsing are lexical analysis and grammatical analysis. Lexical analysis was examined in detail with two sample programs: an initial obvious but incorrect tokenizer and then a refined approach. Additionally, this section included the requirements the XML specification levies on all XML processors.

The Simple API for XML (SAX) is a simple, event-based API for parsing XML documents. This was the largest section in the chapter because it explained and demonstrated every interface and class in the API. The four steps to parsing a document with SAX are

- Create an input source to the XML document
- Instantiate a SAX Parser (also known as a SAX Driver)
- Register the classes that will handle SAX events (known as handlers)
- Tell the SAX Parser to start parsing

The Java API for XML Parsing (JAXP) provides Factory objects for both styles of XML parsing: event-based (like SAX) and DOM-based. These Factory objects allow you to plug and play any compliant Java implementation into your applications. Sun Microsystems provides a default implementation.

The chapter concluded with a section on alternative parsers, featuring AElfred. AElfred is an XML Parser optimized for use in Java applets. The section walked through a non-trivial applet that downloads, parses (via AElfred), and displays bookmarks from a Bookmark List Markup Language.

Suggested for Further Study

1. Expand `SimpleXmlScanner` to add tokens for XML comments, DOCTYPE declarations, CDATA sections, and both element and attribute declarations in the DTD (to support validating parsers).

2. Make the `AbmlParser` implement the `ErrorHandler` interface and appropriately handle the three levels of errors reported by a SAX-compliant parser.

3. Improve the `BookmarkViewer` application by adding two buttons (and their associated behaviors): Sort and Add. Sort will sort the bookmark names in the list. Add will allow you to add an additional bookmark to the list (note: this will require an additional text field for the URL name).

4. Using AElfred and the `javax.swing` classes, develop an applet that will display an XML document using a JTree.

Further Reading

Building XML Applications. Simon St. Laurent and Ethan Cerami. 1999, McGraw-Hill. This reference has good coverage of XML parsers and several real-world, non-trivial applications that use XML.

Sams Teach Yourself XML in 21 Days. Simon North and Paul Hermans. 1999, Sams. An overview of many XML topics. Geared toward non-programmers.

The Document Object Model (DOM)

"The Document Object Model is an Applications Programming Interface for HTML and XML documents."

—W3C, Document Object Model Level 1 Specification

IN THIS CHAPTER

Defining the Document Object Model

The term "model" is one of those all-purpose terms that everyone uses. For our purposes, a model is a representation of an object. Models can be complete, incomplete, or somewhere in between. In the case of DOM, the model represents an XML document. An incomplete model only partially replicates the object it models, whereas a complete model mimics everything down to the smallest detail. In the DOM specification, each element of an XML document is represented, making the DOM a complete model. The DOM also defines a set of interfaces that developers, and perhaps others, can implement allowing concrete programmatic representations of XML documents. In essence, the DOM is three things:

- *Model*—The DOM models an XML document. The DOM serves as a complete model representing each and every aspect of an XML object, allowing that object to be completely re-created from the model's data. The DOM Core Level I is a complete model providing for all the required manipulations. The DOM Core Specification says explicitly that "With the Document Object Model, programmers can build documents, navigate their structure, and add, modify, or delete elements and content."

- *Set of Requirements*—The DOM is a set of requirements, defined by the W3C, that each implementation of the DOM must follow. The next section introduces and discusses the DOM implementation requirements.

- *Set of Object Definitions*—The DOM is an object-oriented specification that specifies a set of interfaces, properties, and behaviors for each object. We will examine the interfaces in detail shortly. Examples of properties are `getNodeName`, `getParentNode`, and `getChildNodes`. DOM Object definitions also require that every DOM object follow certain behavioral patterns. An example of these patterns is that each object can have only one parent and can have zero or more children. The exception to this pattern is the root document, which does not have any parents.

At first glance, the DOM appears to be one more thing, an implementation. While individual companies may implement the DOM, the W3C specification provides no implementation. The specification leaves implementation to Sun, IBM, Oracle, or to any user. Anyone could, in fact, implement a DOM. Last time I checked, there were implementations for C++, Python, Perl, Smalltalk, Gecko, and a slew of other languages. For Java alone, companies such as Sun, Microsoft, Netscape, Oracle, IBM, Docuverse and others had all committed to supporting the DOM in one fashion or another and providing Java implementations. Let's now get back to what the W3C actually defined and how we might use it.

DOM Requirements

Because the W3C defines specifications rather than implementations, it needs to define the general requirement of any implementation. The following list, taken directly from the W3C's requirements document for DOM, defines each of these requirements. Let's now look at each to understand what they mean.

- *The Document Object Model (DOM) is an Applications Programming Interface (API) for HTML and XML*—Simple enough, the DOM defines the APIs through which we access XML documents.

- *The Object Model is language neutral and platform independent*—This is perhaps one of the most important aspects of the DOM, DOM specification is not dependent on any specific platform or language. As a result of the independence of the specification, developers are free to provide an implementation in any available language. All the DOM does is specify what interfaces, methods, attributes, and properties the DOM objects provide.

- *There will be a core DOM that is applicable to HTML, CSS and XML documents*—Basically, the DOM Core supports only HTML, CSS, and XML. Don't expect to process some other language with the DOM.

- *The Object Model can be used to construct and deconstruct the document*—Models typically vary in how complete they are. The DOM is defined to be complete. Anything that you can validly create can also be read later.

- *The Object Model will not preclude use by either agents external to the document content, or scripts embedded within the document*—The DOM will not stop you from processing your XML document with some other method (perhaps SAX or your own parser).

- *Consistent naming conventions must be used through all levels of the Object Model*—Properties are properties are properties! A good model is consistent and doesn't change its nomenclature for different objects or at different levels.

- *A visual UI component will not be required for a conforming implementation of the Object Model*—The DOM is a programming API and is not designed around how a document is displayed. No requirements are imposed on how the developer presents DOM modeled documents.

- *The specific HTML, CSS or XML document object models will be driven by the underlying constructs of those languages*—Simply put, DOM objects follow the ebb and flow of the thing they represent rather than force all documents to be represented in a generic format.

- *It must be possible to read in a document and write out a structurally isomorphic document*—If you read in and write out a document, the end result will be the same as the starting result (assuming that you didn't change anything).

- *The Object Model will not expose the user to problems with security, validity, or privacy*—DOM Implementors must not reply on platform, security, or language-specific mechanisms to process XML and HTML documents.

- *The Object Model will not preclude other mechanisms for manipulating documents*—If you have another way for processing your documents, great! The DOM is not the only game in town. You aren't forced to use it if you don't want to!

In addition to the things the DOM is, there are a number of things that are beyond the scope of the DOM. The following list describes some of what the DOM specifically is not or does not provide for.

- *The DOM does not implement all of "Dynamic HTML," in particular, events*—The DOM Core Level I does not specify everything under the sun but rather sets a sound foundation for processing XML. Events and other important but secondary concepts are left to Level II.

- *The DOM is not a binary specification*—While the DOM specifies a number of interfaces, it does not require anything beyond source level compatibility between documents.

- *The DOM is not a way of persisting objects to XML*—The DOM specifies how XML objects are represented via an API but leaves the external representation to XML. The primary focus of DOM is to define how objects can be used in programs, not how they are stored externally.

- *The DOM is not a set of data structures*—While the DOM represents parent/child relationships, these relationships are logical and may be implemented as required.

- *The DOM does not define "the true inner semantics" of XML*—While XML documents are represented as objects within DOM, their underlying semantics are defined by the XML language specification and not by the DOM itself. The DOM is simply a vehicle through which these semantics of an XML document can be manipulated.

- *The DOM, despite its name, does not compete with COM (The Component Object Model)*—COM is a mechanism to specify binary interfaces and objects for runtime interoperability in much the same way the *Common Object Request Broker Architecture (CORBA)* does. The DOM specifies a number of logical objects and interfaces but does not specify any binary level compatibility.

DOM Core Level I

The DOM is broken into two parts. The first is the DOM Core Level I. As the name implies, the DOM Core Level I is a *core* or basic set of interfaces and objects that are required to provide a complete platform upon which other features can be added or layered. Only those features needed to manipulate XML documents at their most basic level are required. Support for additional functionality, such as Cascading Style Sheets (CSS) and events, is not part of the DOM Core.

Documents, Elements, and Nodes

The DOM Core Level I covers three main areas—Documents, Elements, and Nodes. Each of these three interfaces represents objects at a different level in the XML hierarchy. Figure 3.1 shows graphically the parent/child relationship between these DOM objects.

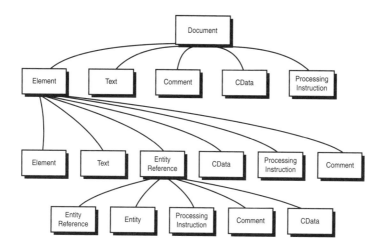

FIGURE 3.1
Parent/child relationships in the DOM.

> **NOTE**
>
> In addition to XML, the DOM also supports modeling HTML 4.0 and greater documents. While our primary focus is handling XML, much of the DOM Core functionality applies equally well to HTML with the exception of those areas that specifically target XML such as entities, notations, and the like.

> **NOTE**
>
> Java developers will find an interesting twist in DOM API, specifically that everything is a node. In reality, what this means is that the DOM API is really two separate APIs— one hierarchical and one flat. A developer could use nothing but the methods provided on the Node object and never, well, almost never, use any other interface. This flat model is designed to eliminate the need for cast operations that are typically costly in languages such as Java. For those more inclined to use traditional inheritance-based hierarchies, the DOM provides one of those as well. Developers can use either API or intermix the two as needs dictate.

Table 3.1 shows the complete node types and their underlying values as defined by
`org.w3c.dom.Node`.

TABLE 3.1   Node Types

Constant	Value
ELEMENT_NODE	1
ATTRIBUTE_NODE	2
TEXT_NODE	3
CDATA_SECTION_NODE	4
ENTITY_REFERENCE_NODE	5
ENTITY_NODE	6
PROCESSING_INSTRUCTION_NODE	7
COMMENT_NODE	8
DOCUMENT_NODE	9
DOCUMENT_TYPE_NODE	10
DOCUMENT_FRAGMENT_NODE	11
NOTATION_NODE	12

If we examine a tree, we see that a typical tree has a root, a number of branches, and sub-
branches, with each ending in a leaf (except the root is normally drawn at the top!). A XML
Document or its DOM representation is no different with the `Document` interface representing
the root, elements representing the branches and sub-branches, and the Nodes representing the
leaves.

Listing 3.1 shows the DTD of a simple catalog representing books that might be used by a
publisher. The catalog has a header (0 or 1), a trailer (0 or 1), and any number of entries (0 or
more). The catalog element is the root, with `catheader`, `cattrailer`, and some number of elements representing entries in the catalog. Figure 3.2 shows the logical tree that represents a
catalog with only a header entry. In reality, things are slightly more complicated than Figure
3.2 suggests. Conceptually, there is a `Document` object, which represents the root, and its one
child node, representing the `catheader` element, which is represented by a leaf node. In actual-
ity, the header node also has a child—a text node—and that text node has a number of children, one for each character. From a programming standpoint, the text node is a node, and the
header node is an `Element`.

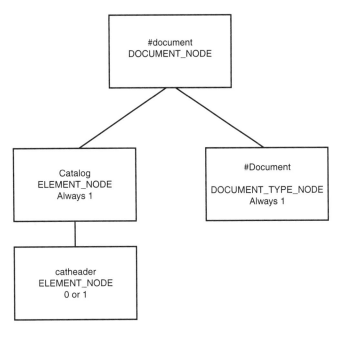

FIGURE 3.2

Catalog with only a header entry.

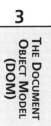

LISTING 3.1   DTD of Book Catalog Markup Language

```
 1: <!-- Book Catalog Markup Language Document Type Definition -->
 2: <!ELEMENT catalog (catheader,entry*,cattrailer)>
 3: <!ELEMENT catheader (#PCDATA)>
 4: <!ELEMENT cattrailer (#PCDATA)>
 5: <!ELEMENT entry (title, author+, publisher,price+, isbn)>
 6: <!ELEMENT title (#PCDATA)>
 7: <!ELEMENT author (#PCDATA)>
 8: <!ELEMENT publisher (#PCDATA)>
 9: <!ELEMENT price (#PCDATA)>
10: <!ATTLIST price
11: cur CDATA #REQUIRED
12: discount (retail|wholesale|other) "retail">
13: <!ELEMENT isbn (#PCDATA)>
14: <!ENTITY AuthorName "Albert J. Saganich Jr">
15: <!ENTITY PublisherInfo "MCP">
```

As we add information to our XML document, the DOM representation changes accordingly. Adding a cattrailer item results in a tree similar to Figure 3.3.

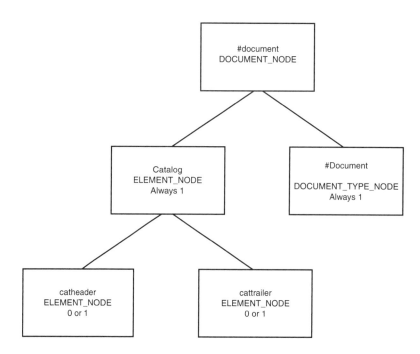

FIGURE 3.3

Catalog with header and trailer.

If we continue to add elements to our catalog, it eventually results in a tree that looks similar to Figure 3.4. Note that we have also shown all the *unexpected* children of our leaf nodes for completeness. As we previously mentioned, one would expect that each leaf, for example the cattrailer element, would be represented as the type text. The leaf would then have an appropriate name and contain the value specified in the XML document. However, this is not the case. Each element results in an accompanying element in the DOM tree with the underlying data represented as a child item. If we examine this for a moment, it makes perfect sense. The element itself is not the data but rather the description of the data. Elements often have other information as well, such as attributes, all of which helps us to understand why the DOM tree is as it is.

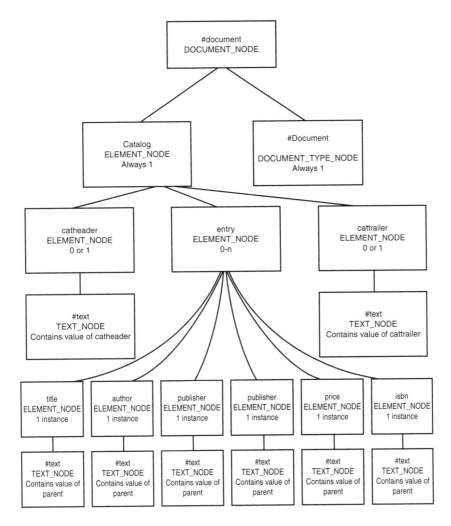

FIGURE 3.4

Catalog with header, trailer, and entry elements.

Creating Document Objects

At this point, we have looked at the theory behind an XML document, how the various objects are laid out, and how we might access them. But how do we create the root document object in the first place? Creating a document is the one area that the W3C did not specify in the DOM Core Level I and, as such, each vendor is free to provide its own mechanism. That is to say that no specific method is defined for creating a DOM document from an XML document. For the remainder of this chapter, we'll examine three different DOM implementations—Sun, IBM, and Oracle. For the majority of the examples, we will be using the Sun implementation. One might speculate that at some point the Sun DOM implementation could become a javax. All java extensions are maintained under the javax tree in the appropriate jar file extension. For that reason, and because all the tested implementations were almost identical, we prefer the Sun implementation.

> **TIP**
>
> The Web page at `http://www.stud.ifi.uio.no/~larsga/linker/XMLtools.html` lists a number of tools by vendor and type and would make a good jumping off point in a search for other DOM implementations.

Listings 3.2 through 3.4 show how each of the implementations create the root Document object.

LISTING 3.2   Creating Document Object Sun Style

```
 1: /*
 2:  * @(#)OpenSun.java          1.0 99/05/28
 3:  *
 4:  * Copyright (c) 1999 Sams Publishing. All Rights Reserved.
 5:  *
 6:  */
 7:
 8: package sams.chp3;
 9:
10: import java.io.*;
11: import com.sun.xml.tree.*;
12: import org.w3c.dom.*;
13:
14: public class OpenSun
15: {
16:     public static void main (String argv [])
```

LISTING 3.2   Continued

```
17:     {
18:         if (argv.length != 1)
19:         {
20:
21:             System.err.println("Usage: java sams.chp3.OpenSun filename");
22:             System.exit(1);
23:         }
24:
25:         FileInputStream inStream;
26:         Document document;
27:         String xmlDocumentPath = argv[0];
28:         try
29:         {
30:             inStream = new FileInputStream(xmlDocumentPath);
31:             document = XmlDocument.createXmlDocument(inStream,true);
32:
33:         }
34:         catch (Exception e)
35:         {
36:             System.out.println(
                   ➥"Unexpected exception reading document!" +e);
37:             System.exit (0);
38:         }
39:
40:         System.out.println("Document successfully created!");
41:         System.exit (0);
42:
43:     }
44: }
```

3

THE DOCUMENT
OBJECT MODEL
(DOM)

LISTING 3.3   Creating Document Object IBM Style

```
 1: /*
 2:  * @(#)OpenIBM.java        1.0 99/05/28
 3:  *
 4:  * Copyright (c) 1999 Sams Publishing. All Rights Reserved.
 5:  *
 6:  */
 7:
 8: package sams.chp3;
 9:
10: import java.io.*;
11: import com.ibm.xml.parser.*;
```

LISTING 3.3   Continued

```
12: import org.w3c.dom.*;
13:
14: public class OpenIBM
15: {
16:     public static void main (String argv [])
17:     {
18:
19: . . .
20:
21:         FileInputStream inStream;
22:         Document document;
23:         String xmlDocumentPath = argv[0];
24:         try
25:         {
26:             inStream =      new FileInputStream(xmlDocumentPath);
27:             Parser parser = new Parser("Using the IBM Parser");
28:             document =      parser.readStream(inStream);
29:         }
30: . . .

31:         System.out.println("Document successfully created!");
32:         System.exit (0);
33:     }
34: }
```

LISTING 3.4   Creating Document Object Oracle Style

```
 1: /*
 2:  * @(#)OpenOracle.java        1.0 99/05/28
 3:  *
 4:  * Copyright (c) 1999 Sams Publishing. All Rights Reserved.
 5:  *
 6:  */
 7: package sams.chp3;
 8:
 9: import java.io.*;
10: import java.net.*;
11: import oracle.xml.parser.XMLParser;
12: import org.w3c.dom.*;
13: public class OpenOracle
14: {
15:
16:     public static void main (String argv [])
17:     {
18: . . .
```

LISTING 3.4 Continued

```
19:
20:         FileInputStream inStream;
21:         Document document;
22:         String xmlDocumentPath = argv[0];
23:         try
24:         {
25:             inStream =      new FileInputStream(xmlDocumentPath);
26:             XMLParser parser = new XMLParser();
27:             parser.setErrorStream(System.err);
28:             parser.setValidationMode(true);
29:             parser.showWarnings(true);
30:             parser.parse(inStream);
31:             document = parser.getDocument();
32:
33:         }
34: . . .

35:         System.out.println("Document successfully created!");
36:         System.exit (0);
37:
38:     }
39: }
```

As previously stated, because the DOM Core does not require any specific mechanism for processing DOM documents, each vendor is free to provide whatever method(s) seem appropriate. There is, however, some commonality. Each implementation supports creating XML documents from URLs and strings. Each uses its own SAX parser to actually do the work of assembling the document, and each provides a method to return the assembled Document object. In fact, the Oracle and IBM implementations are remarkably similar. Each extends the parser interface and provides an additional method to get the completed document. Oracle provides an implementation of the parser interface via oracle.xml.Parser.XMLParser adding a method getDocument() that returns the parse representation as an XML Document object. The IBM implementation provides almost an identical scheme by providing com.ibm.xml.parser, which adds a readStream(inStream) method that returns the resulting document. Only the Sun implementation differs from this approach in that Sun provided a class-factory method to generate the XML Document object. Sun's implementation provides a new class, com.sun.xml.XmlDocument, which provides several static methods for creating a DOM document from a stream or string with or without validation. For clarity, let's review the important lines in the listing. Each implementation requires importing the DOM Core classes as well as the vendor-specific extensions. In the IBM case, the two lines of interest are

```
import org.w3c.dom.*;
import com.ibm.xml.parser.*;
```

Each vendor then supports some mechanism for obtaining a reference to the underlying DOM document. In the Oracle case, we see that extending the parser interface allows a fine level of control with respect to parser errors and validation. We then obtain a handle to the document with a getDocument call.

```
inStream = new FileInputStream(xmlDocumentPath);
XMLParser parser = new XMLParser();
parser.setErrorStream(System.err);
parser.setValidationMode(true);
parser.showWarnings(true);
parser.parse(inStream);
document = parser.getDocument();
```

While each implementation differs slightly, the amount of vendor-specific code is rather small. As we shall see, with the exception of beta code-level anomalies, each implementation performs almost identically.

Now that we can successfully open XML documents, we will move on and look at the three primary Java interfaces representing Node, Element and Document.

> **TIP**
>
> A number of Java DOM methods can raise exceptions. DOM has defined a specific exception, DOMException, to handle such cases as out-of-bounds errors and so on. While we will most often ignore the fact that exceptions can and do occur, the smart developer will wrap sensitive code in try, catch, and finally blocks. The smart developer will anticipate where problems may occur and handle them gracefully.

Node Interface

The root of the inheritance structure for DOM objects is the Node. All other interfaces are descended from Node and inherit a number of its methods. The Node interface provides three basic areas of functionality that allow the developer to do the following:

- Find information about the Node, such as its value, name, and type.
- Read, update, and delete information.
- Find children, parent, and sibling Node information.

What we consider the tips of an XML document tree are typically of the following node types: TEXT_NODE, CDATA_SECTION_NODE, and COMMENT_NODE. Most of the other nodes are normally found as special purpose children of a document, element, or tip node.

As we saw in Figure 3.4, nodes represent the branches, sub-branches, and leaf nodes of an XML tree. At first glance, these nodes appear to be alike. The key to unraveling this mystery is the getNodeType() method. The getNodeType() method returns the underlying node's numeric type. With getNodeType, we can now walk the DOM tree casting nodes, where appropriate, to other interfaces.

If we look closely at any given DOM tree, we see that branches and sub-branches are all of type ELEMENT_NODE, with the various leaf nodes being of type TEXT_NODE, CDATA_NODE, COMMENT_NODE, or one of the other terminal node types. Under normal circumstances, every node on the DOM hierarchy returns one of the node types listed in Table 3.1. Perhaps the most important of the methods in the Node interface are the accessor methods for returning a node's children. The original DOM specification named a number of methods for accessing an object's children, with the final recommendation supporting four important methods (note that the DOM Level II specification provides several more). We will now examine the Node interface in general.

NOTE

The DOM is specified using CORBA IDL. Unfortunately, both CORBA and XML use the term *attribute*. In the CORBA case, an attribute is really a member variable within an IDL definition of an interface. In the XML case, an attribute is a property of a data item. For example, the currency of a monetary value is a property of a data item. The section "The DOM Core Defined" will discuss IDL in more detail. In cases where it is not clear from the context, we will state specifically which we are discussing.

In addition, when a CORBA Interface Definition Language (IDL) file is processed via an IDL compiler, many of the attributes result in mutator (get/set) methods being generated. While these methods are generated, they are methods nonetheless, and we will discuss them interchangeably with developer-written methods.

The Node interface is the primary interface in the DOM Core. It contains 12 member variables (CORBA attributes) and 6 methods (although most of the CORBA attributes result in one or two methods being generated). I've broken down the methods into groups based on properties of the object.

Methods that Return Information About a Node

Each of the following descriptions reference the following XML snippet:

```
<entry>
<title>Better Living Thru Chemistry</title>
<author>I. W. Books</author>
<publisher>Books R Us</publisher>
```

```
<price discount="retail" cur="us">9.95</price>
<price discount="wholesale" cur="us">7.95</price>
<isbn>0101010123</isbn>
</entry>
```

- `short getNodeType()`   Returns the underlying type of the node as defined in `org.w3c.dom.Node.java`. See Table 3.1 for a complete listing. `getNodeType()` on `<isbn>...</isbn>` would return `ELEMENT_NODE` with one child of type `TEXT_NODE`.

- `String getNodeName()`   Returns the name of the node. For example, `cattrailer`.

- `String getNodeValue(), void setNodeValue(String)`   Returns the value of the node or sets the value of the node. Returns `null` if not applicable. Again, on `<author>`, returns `null` but on child of author it would return `I.W. Books`.

- `NamedNodeList getAttributes()`   Returns a `NamedNodeList` of the attributes associated with this node or `null` if no attributes exist. We will examine the `NamedNodeList` class shortly. `getAttributes` on `<price discount="wholesale" cur="us">7.95</price>` would return a list of two attributes.

- `boolean hasChildNodes()`   Returns `true` or `false` depending on whether this node has children.

Methods that Return Information About the Children of a Node

There are a number of methods that can be used to return information about the children of a `Node` object. The most commonly used methods are

- `Node getFirstChild()`   Returns `null` or the first child of the node. This method is useful when we are looking for the actual data of a node. On `<entry>...</entry>`, would return an `ELEMENT_NODE` representing `<title>...</title>`.

- `Node getLastChild()`   Returns null or the last child of the node. On `<entry>...</entry>`, would return an `ELEMENT_NODE` representing `<isbn>...</isbn>`.

- `NodeList getChildNodes()`   Returns a `NodeList` of the children of the current node. Depending on the node type, this list may be empty, but the specification requires it to be returned. Readers should also note that this is a "live" list. That is, it can change and mutate as the underlying object changes and is required to do so. If the XML document changes, for example to add a new child to a given node, any `NodeList` that represents that child must be updated to reflect the change. `getChildNodes` on entry returns a `NodeList` of `ELEMENT_NODE`s representing the 5 children.

Methods Related to the Parent or Siblings

Each of the following descriptions reference the following XML snippet. Note that given our DTD, this snippet is well-formed but not technically valid as no DTD is given.

```
<catalog>
<entry>
<title>Better Living Thru Chemistry</title>
</entry>
<entry>
<title>Conversational French</title>
</entry>
<entry>
<title>Special Edition:Using Java 2 and XML</title>
</entry>
</catalog>
```

- Node getParentNode()   Returns the parent of this node or null in the case of Document, DocumentFragment, or Attribute objects. In addition, nodes that have been created on-the-fly but not inserted into a document may return null. The parent of any <entry...> node is <catalog>.

- Node getPreviousSibling()   Returns the immediate sibling to the current node or null if the first or no prior sibling exists. The previous sibling of Conversational French is Better Living.

- Node getNextSibling()   Same as previous only for next sibling.

Methods that Return Information About the Document a Node Is Contained Within

While there is only a single method for returning the DOM document a node is contained within, it is important to be able to access the parent Document from any given Node.

- Document getOwnerDocument()   Returns null for documents or the Document this Node is contained within.

Methods for Manipulating the Children of a Node

There are a number of methods for manipulating the contents of a node.

- Node insertBefore(Node new, Node reference)   Inserts a node before reference node returns the inserted node.

- Node replaceNode(Node replacement, Node tobereplaced)   Replaces the specified node with the replacement node. Returns the replaced node.

- Node removeNode(Node toberemoved)   Removes the input node. Returns the removed node.

- Node appendChild(Node tobeappended)   Adds a child node to the list of child nodes of the current node. Returns the node appended.

- `Node cloneNode(boolean deep)`   Produces a duplicate of the node. If `deep=true`, all the children of this node are also duplicated recursively. Note that all attributes of the node are copied. If `deep=false`, the node's children are not copied.

NodeList and NamedNodeMap

We have encountered two other interesting interfaces, but we have not yet examined them in detail—`NodeList` and `NamedNodeMap`. These two interfaces exist to process lists of nodes and are surprisingly similar. `NodeList` is the simpler of the two, and we will start with it.

NodeList

`NodeList` has two methods of interest:

- `int getLength()`   Returns the count of nodes within the list
- `Node item(int index)`   Returns the `Node` at index

Otherwise, a `NodeList` is straightforward. One other important aspect of a `NodeList` is that the `Nodes` are returned in the order in which they are specified in the XML or in the order they were specified when added to the parent node.

NamedNodeMap

`NamedNodeMap` is similar to `NodeList` and, in fact, contains `getLength()` and `item` methods exactly like `NodeList`. However, a `NamedNodeMap` has a different purpose, namely to handle and manipulate lists of nodes. `Attributes` of a `Node`, for example, would be handled by a `NamedNodeMap`. While `NamedNodeList` and `NodeList` have similar methods, they are not otherwise related. `NamedNodeLists` are not maintained in any particular order or via any particular representation.

`NamedNodeLists` contain three other methods:

- `Node getNamedItem(String name)`   Returns a node representing *name*.
- `Node removeNamedItem(String name)`   Removes the node represented by *name*. The removed node is returned.
- `Node setNamedItem(Node name)`   Inserts or replaces the given node into the `NamedNodeList`. If the node had name `foo` and value `bar`, it would later be accessible via `getNamedItem(`foo').

Document Interface

The `Document` interface is the topmost interface in the XML document tree. It contains nine defined methods, five additional methods derived from the various document attributes, and those methods and variables inherited from the Node interface. The Document interface performs four major functions, allowing developers to do the following:

- Query for information about the document, such as its name, entities, and notations.
- Query for information about the implementation, such as what version of the DOM core is supported.
- Create documents, DocumentFragments, Elements, Nodes, Attributes, Comments, and so on.
- Traverse the document tree.

The Document object always has Node type DOCUMENT_NODE. The following sections describe the methods on the Document object.

Methods that Return Information About the Document or Implementation

There are a number of methods for returning information about the DTD associated with a document. The most common methods are listed below.

- DocumentType getDocType()   Returns a DocumentType object that has three methods. NamedNodeMap getEntities() returns all the defined entities within the document. NamedNodeMap getNotations() returns all the notations, and String getName() returns the name immediately following the DOCTYPE keyword within the DTD.
- DOMImplementation getImplementation()   Returns a DOMImplementation object that has a single method boolean hasFeature();. A typical use might be getImplementation.hasFeature("XML,"1.0");.

Methods that Return Information About Descendant Nodes

In addition to those inherited from the node interface, two methods exist for accessing the children of a Node.

- Element getDocumentElement(...)   Returns the root Element of the Document. In the case of HTML it is the element containing the <html> tag. In XML, this method returns the Element representing the root of the XML tree.
- NodeList getElementsByTagName(String tag)   Returns a NodeList of all the nodes that match the given tag. This method is interesting in that it returns all the nodes represented by the tag regardless of their level within the XML tree.

Methods that Create Descendant Nodes

There are a number of methods that can be used to create child nodes, which can then be inserted into an XML document. The various Create methods can be used to create empty elements that can then be inserted into a DOM tree.

- Attr createAttribute(*String name*)   Creates an attribute of the given name.
- CDATASection createCDATASection(*String name*)   Creates a CDATA node.
- Comment createComment(*String comment*)   Create a comment.
- DocumentFragment createDocumentFragment()   Creates an empty document that can then be used to add additional elements.
- Element createElement(*String tag*)   Creates an empty element of name tag. This element may later have child nodes added to it.
- EntityReference createEntityReference(*String name*)   Creates an EntityReference of the given name.
- ProcessingInstruction createProcessingInstruction(*String target, String data*)   Creates a ProcessingInstruction node.
- TextNode createTextNode(*String data*)   Creates a TextNode with the given data as its value.

Before we move on and examine the Element interface, a short example of the use of getElementsByTag(...) would be beneficial (see Listing 3.5).

LISTING 3.5   ElementsByTag.java—Using getElementsByTag

```
 1: /*
 2:  * @(#)ElementsByTag.java          1.0 99/05/28
 3:  *
 4:  * Copyright (c) 1999 Sams Publishing. All Rights Reserved.
 5:  *
 6:  */
 7:
 8: import java.io.*;
 9: import com.sun.xml.tree.*;
10: import org.w3c.dom.*;
11:
12: public class ElementsByTag
13: {
14:     public static void main (String argv [])
15:     {
16:         FileInputStream inStream;
17:         Document document;
18:         String xmlDocumentPath = "catalog.xml";
19:         try
20:         {
21:             inStream = new FileInputStream(xmlDocumentPath);
22:             document = XmlDocument.createXmlDocument(inStream,true);
23:
```

LISTING 3.5   Continued

```
24:              NodeList entries = document.getElementsByTagName( "entry" );
25:              if ( entries.getLength()== 0)
26:              {
27:                  System.out.println("No entries in this catalog, exiting");
28:                  System.exit(0);
29:              }
30:
31:              for (int i = 0; i < entries.getLength(); i++)
32:              {
33:                  System.out.print(i + " ");
34:                  Element entryNode = (Element) entries.item(i);
35:                  NodeList titles = entryNode.getElementsByTagName ("title");
36:                  if ( titles.getLength() == 0)
37:                      System.out.println("Unknown");
38:                  else
39:                  {
40:                      Node titleElement = titles.item(0);
41:                      NodeList titleValues = titleElement.getChildNodes();
42:                      Node titleValue = titleValues.item(0);
43:                      System.out.print (" "+titleValue.getNodeValue());
44:                  }
45:
46:                  //
47:                  // Now show author entries
48:                  //
49:                  NodeList authors = entryNode.
                     ➥getElementsByTagName ("author");
50:                  if ( authors.getLength() == 0)
51:                      System.out.println("Unknown");
52:                  else
53:                  {
54: . . .
55:                  }
56:                  //
57:                  // Now show prices
58:                  //
59:                  NodeList prices = entryNode.getElementsByTagName ("price");
60:                  if ( prices.getLength() == 0)
61:                      System.out.println("Unknown");
62:                  else
63:                  {
64: . . .
65:                  System.out.println("");
66:              }
```

3

THE DOCUMENT
OBJECT MODEL
(DOM)

LISTING 3.5 Continued

```
67:          }
68:          catch (Exception e)
69:          {
70:              System.out.println(
                 ➥"Unexpected exception reading document!" +e);
71:              System.exit (0);
72:          }
73:
74:
75:      }
76: }
```

Listing 3.5 produces output similar to Listing 3.6.

LISTING 3.6 Output of GetElementsByTag.java

```
1: C:\java sams.chp3.GetElementsByTab
2: 0   Better Living Thru Chemistry I. W. Books 9.95 discount:retail cur:us 7.95
   ➥discount:wholesale cur:us
3: 1   Special Edition:Using XML and Java 2.0  Al Saganich Mike Daconta 9.95
   ➥discount:retail cur:us 7.95 discount:wholesale cur:us
4: 2   Java 2.0 and JavaScript for C/C++ Programmers Al Saganich Mike Daconta
   ➥59.95 discount:retail cur:us 74.95 discount:wholesale cur:us
5: 3   Converational French R. Weiman 7.00 discount:retail cur:can 4.25
   ➥discount:wholesale cur:us
```

In GetElementsByTag.java, we use the getElementsByTag method multiple times on both the Document object and its underlying Element object. As we'll see in the next section, the Element interface has an identical method to the Document.getElementsByTag() method.

Again we use the method several times, once to return a list of the entry elements and within entries to directly get entry information such as title, author, and price. Both are simple enough, but what is important to understand is that we could have completely ignored the fact that titles exist within entries. If we remember that our catalog contains entries and entry titles, we could have just as easily listed all the titles with the catalog directly with the following code snippet:

```
NodeList document = entryNode.getElementsByTagName ("title");
```

This command takes the parent Document object, rather then acting on a child node somewhere down the DOM document. The code snippet also returns all title objects. For example, if we are only interested in collecting all the currencies associated with a catalog, we could write the following:

```
NodeList document = entryNode.getElementsByTagName ("price");
```

which, again, takes the parent Document object and returns all the child price Elements, regardless of where they fall in the DOM tree. getElementsByTagName is certainly one of the more powerful methods in the entire DOM API.

Element Interface

Up to this point, we have examined the top of an XML tree, the Document interface, and the bottom of the tree—the Node interface. We will now examine the intermediate levels of the tree, which are represented by the Element interface.

Element objects form the intermediary branches of the XML tree. Elements make up the bulk of what a DOM document is. The primary purpose of the Element interface is to support the manipulation of attributes, and many of its methods are designed with this in mind. And, as always, the Element interface is derived from the Node interface and inherits all of its public methods.

The Element interface performs three major functions, allowing you to do the following:

- Access and manipulate the attributes of the Element
- Access the children of the Element
- Access the tag of the Element

And, of course, the Element object always has node type ELEMENT_NODE.

Methods that Return Information About an Element

There is only one informational method on the Element interface.

String getTagName(); returns the tag associated with this element.

Methods for Manipulating Element Attributes

There are a number of methods for manipulating element attributes, the most common of which are listed below.

- String getAttribute(String name);   Returns the value of the given attribute.
- Attr getAttributeNode(String name)   Returns an Attr object that represents the given attribute.
- void removeAttribute(String name)   Removes the given attribute from the Element. For example: If an XML element contained two attributes, <price discount="retail" cur="us">9.95</price> and <price discount="wholesale" cur="us">7.95</price>, removeAttribute("retail"); could remove the first.
- Attr removeAttributeNode(*Attr someAttribute*)   Remove the given Attribute object from the Element.
- void setAttribute(*String name, String value*)   Sets or replaces the attribute *name* with the given *value*.

- `Attr setAttributeNode(Attr newAttribute);` Adds a new `Attribute` object as a child of the current `Element`.

NOTE

`setAttribute` expects its value to be literal text that will need to be *escaped*, if required, when written. If you want to add an attribute that contains an `EntityReference` you need to create an `Attr` object and populate it and its children by setting the name, value, and so on. Then insert that attribute into the element.

Accessing Child Nodes

Element nodes contain one special method for accessing their child nodes.

The `NodeList getElementsByTagName(String tag)` method returns a `NodeList` of all the nodes that match the given tag. This method is identical in function to the method of the same name in the `Document` interface.

One additional method exists in `Element`—`normalize()`. The `normalize()` method handles a special case that occurs when two or more text nodes are added as children of the same element. Say we have a `<title>` element, "Better," and we want to add two or more text nodes as children of the title, "Living" and "Through Chemistry." `normalize` would concatenate all three of these together resulting in a single text node representing the value of the element in question, which in our case would be "Better Living Through Chemistry."

Attr Interface

We introduced the `Attribute` interface in the previous section, and we saw the use of the `Attribute` interface in Listing 3.5. We should now examine the `Attribute` interface in detail. Attributes, represented by the `java` interface `Attr`, allow for creating, examining, and otherwise manipulating the XML representation of attributes via the DOM. Attributes are not part of the DOM tree per se. They are never children of any given node but must be acted on specifically by calling one of the `get`/`set` attribute methods on an element. As a result, `getPreviousSibling`, `getParent`, and `getNextSibling` methods return null. In short, attributes are properties of nodes, are owned by a node, but are not children of nodes. One further note—while `Attributes` are never children of a node, an `Attribute`, which contains `EntityReferences`, can have children.

The `Attr` interface contains only four methods. Note that one additional method exists in the `Attr` interface—`getSpecified()`.

- `String getName()`　Returns the name of the attribute. For example, `discount` or `cur`.
- `String getValue()`　Returns the value of the attribute. Entity references and character data are replaced with their appropriate expanded values.
- `String setValue(String newValue)`　Replaces the value of the `Attr` with the value specified by `newValue`.
- `boolean getSpecified()`　Returns `true` or `false` defined as follows:
    - `true`　The attribute was given a value in the original document.
    - `true`　The user set the value of the attribute programmatically.
    - `false`　The attribute was specified in the DTD but not given a value; this is the default value.
    - `false`　The attribute has no assigned value but is `#IMPLIED` in the DTD.

Additional Interfaces

There are nine additional interfaces that we will not examine in low-level detail but will be required for many applications. The first four have to do with actual content:

- `CharacterData`　The `CharacterData` interface extends `Node`. No DOM objects of type `CharacterData` exist but rather this object represents common methods inherited by other DOM interfaces. The `CharacterData` interface contains eight methods for setting, getting, inserting, appending, and otherwise manipulating normal character data information.
- `Comment`　The `Comment` interface extends `CharacterData` and represents a comment in an XML document. No additional methods are defined on this interface.
- `Text`　The `Text` interface extends `CharacterData`. The `Text` interface contains a single method `splitText(int offset)` that allows the given text node to be split at an offset into two text nodes which may later be recombined with `normalize();`.
- `CDATASection`　The `CDATASection` interface extends `Text` and allows for blocks of text to be contained within a DOM node that would otherwise be considered markup without the need to escape markup characters. No additional methods are defined in this interface.

The next five interfaces represent other elements in XML.

- `Entity`　Extends `Node`. Represents the `Entities` within an XML document. Depending on validation, these entities may or may not be expanded and the object may (not expanded, non-validating parsers) or may not (expanded) have children. Defines three methods for accessing entity information.

- Notation   Extends Node. Represents the Notation elements of an XML document. Defines two methods for accessing information about a Notation.

- DocumentType   Extends Node. The DocumentType interface is used to gather information about the Document itself and has three methods for accessing Entities, Notations, and the name of the DTD itself.

- ProcessingInstruction   Extends Node. The ProcessingInstruction interface represents processing instruction information. This interface specifies three methods for accessing and manipulating processing instruction information.

- DocumentFragment   Extends Node. Contains no additional methods beyond the Node interface. The DocumentFragment interface is designed to allow users and developers to develop XML documents that are not well formed. A document fragment can be built that represents data at any level in an XML tree. After being inserted back into a Document object, the underlying children are inserted and not the DocumentFragment object itself. For these reasons, DocumentFragments can be thought of as *lightweight* Documents.

Listing 3.7, DumpXMLOracle.java, uses the Oracle DOM and wraps up all of the DOM Core Level I interfaces into one neat package that displays, in semi human-readable format, any given XML document. The output is shown in Listing 3.8.

LISTING 3.7   DumpXMLOracle.java

```
 1: /*
 2:  * @(#)DumpXMLOracle.java        1.0 99/05/28
 3:  *
 4:  * Copyright (c) 1999 Sams Publishing. All Rights Reserved.
 5:  *
 6:  */
 7: package sams.chp3;
 8:
 9: import java.io.*;
10: import java.net.*;
11:
12: import oracle.xml.parser.XMLParser;
13:
14: import org.w3c.dom.*;
15:
16: public class DumpXMLOracle
17: {
18:     // map the type to a string
19:     static String mapNodeTypeToString(short nodeType)
20:     {
```

LISTING 3.7 Continued

```
21:          switch(nodeType)
22:          {
23:              case org.w3c.dom.Node.ATTRIBUTE_NODE: return "ATTRIBUTE_NODE";
24:              case org.w3c.dom.Node.CDATA_SECTION_NODE:
                 ➥return "CDATA_SECTION_NODE";
25:              case org.w3c.dom.Node.COMMENT_NODE: return "COMMENT_NODE";
26:              case org.w3c.dom.Node.DOCUMENT_FRAGMENT_NODE:
                 ➥return "DOCUMENT_FRAGMENT_NODE";
27:              case org.w3c.dom.Node.DOCUMENT_NODE: return "DOCUMENT_NODE";
28:              case org.w3c.dom.Node.DOCUMENT_TYPE_NODE:
                 ➥return "DOCUMENT_TYPE_NODE";
29:              case org.w3c.dom.Node.ELEMENT_NODE: return "ELEMENT_NODE";
30:              case org.w3c.dom.Node.ENTITY_NODE: return "ENTITY_NODE";
31:              case org.w3c.dom.Node.ENTITY_REFERENCE_NODE:
                 ➥return "ENTITY_REFERENCE_NODE";
32:              case org.w3c.dom.Node.NOTATION_NODE: return "NOTATION_NODE";
33:              case org.w3c.dom.Node.PROCESSING_INSTRUCTION_NODE:
                 ➥return "PROCESSING_INSTRUCTION_NODE";
34:              case org.w3c.dom.Node.TEXT_NODE: return "TEXT_NODE";
35:
36:          }
37:          return "Unknown";
38:      }
39:
40:      // Display attribute information
41:      static void displayAttributeInfo(String prefix, Node node)
42:      {
43:          // only elements have attributes
44:          if (node.getNodeType() != org.w3c.dom.Node.ELEMENT_NODE) return;
45:
46:          NamedNodeMap attributes = node.getAttributes();
47:          if ( null == attributes || attributes.getLength() == 0)
48:          {
49:              return;
50:          }
51:
52:          System.out.println(prefix +"has " + attributes.getLength() +
                 ➥" attributes");
53:          System.out.println(prefix + attributes.toString());
54:          for (int i = 0; i < attributes.getLength(); i++)
55:          {
56:              Node attribute = attributes.item(i);
57:              System.out.print(prefix+"["+i+"] " + attribute.getNodeName());
58:              System.out.println(" = " + attribute.getNodeValue());
```

3

THE DOCUMENT
OBJECT MODEL
(DOM)

LISTING 3.7   Continued

```
59:         }
60:
61:     }
62:
63:     // Display generalized node properties
64:     static void displayNodeInfo(String prefix,Node node)
65:     {
66:         System.out.println(prefix+ "----------------");
67:         System.out.println(prefix + "name:"+node.getNodeName());
68:         System.out.println(prefix + "type:("+node.getNodeType()+ ")"
            ➥+mapNodeTypeToString(node.getNodeType()));
69:         System.out.println(prefix + "value:"+ node.getNodeValue());
70:         displayAttributeInfo(prefix,node);
71:         if (node.getNodeType() != org.w3c.dom.Node.TEXT_NODE)
72:         {
73:             NodeList children = node.getChildNodes();
74:             System.out.println(prefix + "Children("+
                ➥children.getLength()+"):");
75:             if ( children.getLength() > 0)
76:             {
77:                 System.out.print(prefix+ "      ");
78:                 for (int i = 0; i < children.getLength(); i++)
79:                 {
80:                     Node child = children.item(i);
81:                     System.out.print(" ["+i+"] " + child.getNodeName());
82:                 }
83:                 System.out.println();
84:             }
85:
86:         }
87:     }
88:     // Display Entity Information
89:     static void displayEntityInfo(String prefix, Entity entity)
90:     {
91:         System.out.println(prefix + "Entity information");
92:         System.out.println(prefix + "    public id:"+
            ➥entity.getPublicId());
93:         System.out.println(prefix + "    system id:"+
            ➥entity.getSystemId());
94:         System.out.println(prefix + "    notation name:"+
            ➥entity.getNotationName());
95:         displayNodeInfo(prefix,entity);
96:
97:         NodeList children = entity.getChildNodes();
```

LISTING 3.7 Continued

```
98:          if ( children.getLength() == 0)
99:              System.out.println(prefix + "     Has 0 children");
100:         else
101:             System.out.println(prefix + "     Children(" +
                 ➥children.getLength()+ ")");
102:
103:         for (int i = 0; i < children.getLength(); i++)
104:         {
105:             Node child = (Entity)children.item(i);
106:             System.out.println("    child(" + i + ")");
107:             displayNodeInfo("         ",child);
108:         }
109:
110:     }
111:     // Display Document information
112:     static void displayDocumentInfo(Document document)
113:     {
114:         DocumentType docTypeInfo = document.getDoctype();
115:         System.out.println(" ");
116:         System.out.println("Document Type Information");
117:         System.out.println("---------------");
118:         System.out.println("name:"+document.getNodeName());
119:         System.out.println("type:("+document.getNodeType()+ ")"
                 ➥+mapNodeTypeToString(document.getNodeType()));
120:         System.out.println("value:"+ document.getNodeValue());
121:         System.out.println("    Properties");
122:         System.out.println("    Name Property:"+docTypeInfo.getName());
123:         NamedNodeMap entities = docTypeInfo.getEntities();
124:         System.out.println("    contains " + entities.getLength() +
                 ➥" entities");
125:         NamedNodeMap notations = docTypeInfo.getNotations();
126:         if ( notations != null)
127:             System.out.println("    contains " + notations.getLength() +
                 ➥" notations");
128:         else
129:             System.out.println("    contains (null) notations");
130:
131:         if ( entities != null && entities.getLength() > 0)
132:         {
133:             System.out.println("    Entities");
134:             for (int i = 0; i < entities.getLength(); i++)
135:             {
136:                 //
137:             // Note that in the SUN implementation this works as expected
```

LISTING 3.7   Continued

```
138:                    // The IBM implementation causes a class cast exception.
139:                    try
140:                    {
141:                        Entity entity = (Entity)entities.item(i);
142:                        System.out.println("    Entity(" + i + ")");
143:                        displayEntityInfo("        ",entity);
144:                    }
145:                    catch (Exception e) { System.out.println("exception! "
                    ➥+ e); } ;
146:                }
147:            }
148:
149:        if ( notations != null && notations.getLength() > 0)
150:        {
151:            System.out.println("    Notations");
152:            for (int i = 0; i < notations.getLength(); i++)
153:            {
154:                Node node = notations.item(i);
155:                System.out.println("    Notation(" + i + ")");
156:                displayNodeInfo("        ",node);
157:            }
158:        }
159:
160:
161:    }
162:
163:    // Process all the children of a node.
164:    public static void displayChildren(String prefix,Node parent)
165:    {
166:        NodeList children = parent.getChildNodes();
167:        if ( children == null || children.getLength() == 0) return;
168:        for (int i = 0; i < children.getLength(); i++)
169:        {
170:            try
171:            {
172:                Node node = children.item(i);
173:                displayNodeInfo(prefix,node);
174:                displayChildren(prefix + "    ",node);
175:            }
176:            catch (Exception e)
177:            {
178:            }

179:        }
```

LISTING 3.7 Continued

```
180:
181:
182:     }
183:
184:
185:     public static void main (String argv [])
186:     {
187:         if (argv.length != 1)
188:         {
189:
190:             System.err.println(
                 ➡"Usage: java sams.chp3.DumpXMLOracle filename");
191:             System.exit(1);
192:         }
193:
194:         try
195:         {
196:             XMLParser parser = new XMLParser();
197:             FileInputStream inStream =  new FileInputStream(argv[0]);
198:             parser.setErrorStream(System.err);
199:             parser.setValidationMode(true);
200:             parser.showWarnings(true);
201:
202:             parser.parse(inStream);
203:
204:             Document document = parser.getDocument();
205:             System.out.println("Sucessfully created document on " +
                 ➡argv[0]);
206:
207:             //
208:             // Print relevent info about the document type
209:             //
210:             displayDocumentInfo(document);
211:             displayNodeInfo("",document);
212:
213:             //
214:             // Now walk the document itself displaying data
215:             //
216:             displayChildren("    ",document);
217:         }
218:         catch (Exception e)
219:         {
220:             System.out.println("Unexpected exception reading document!"
                 ➡+e);
```

LISTING 3.7   Continued

```
221:              System.out.println(e);
222:              System.exit (0);
223:          }
224:
225:
226:      }
```

LISTING 3.8   Abbreviated Output of `DumpXMLOracle.java`

```
 1: C:\java sams.chp3.DumpXMLOracle
 2: Sucessfully created document on catalog.xml
 3:
 4: Document Type Information
 5: ----------------
 6: name:#document
 7: type:(9)DOCUMENT_NODE
 8: value:null
 9:     Properties
10:     Name Property:catalog
11:     contains 2 entities
12:     contains (null) notations
13:     Entities
14:     Entity(0)
15:        Entity information
16:             public id:null
17:             system id:null
18:             notation name:null
19:        ----------------
20:        name:PublisherInfo
21:        type:(6)ENTITY_NODE
22:        value:MCP
23:        Children(0):
24:             Has 0 children
25:     Entity(1)
26:        Entity information
27:             public id:null
28:             system id:null
29:             notation name:null
30:        ----------------
31:        name:AuthorName
32:        type:(6)ENTITY_NODE
33:        value:Albert J. Saganich Jr
34:        Children(0):
```

LISTING 3.8   Continued

```
35:               Has 0 children
36: ----------------
37: name:#document
38: type:(9)DOCUMENT_NODE
39: value:null
40: Children(4):
41:     [0] xml [1] #comment [2] catalog [3] catalog
42:     ----------------
43:     name:xml
44:     type:(7)PROCESSING_INSTRUCTION_NODE
45:     value: version = '1.0' encoding = 'UTF-8'
46:     Children(0):
47:     ----------------
48:     name:#comment
49:     type:(8)COMMENT_NODE
50:     value:
51:
52:     A Simple catalog of books a bookstore might carry
53:
54:     Al Saganich for Macmillan Computer Publishing
55:
56:     Children(0):
57:     ----------------
58:     name:catalog
59:     type:(10)DOCUMENT_TYPE_NODE
60:     value:null
61:     Children(0):
62:     ----------------
63:     name:catalog
64:     type:(1)ELEMENT_NODE
65:     value:null
66:     Children(7):
67:         [0] #comment [1] catheader [2] entry [3] entry [4] entry [5]
            ➥ entry [6] cattrailer
68:         ----------------
69:         name:#comment
70:         type:(8)COMMENT_NODE
71:         value:
72:
73: This is a comment.
74:
75: It follows after <catalog> entry
76:
77:         Children(0):
```

LISTING 3.8   Continued

```
78:         ---------------
79:         name:catheader
80:         type:(1)ELEMENT_NODE
81:         value:null
82:         Children(1):
83:             [0] #text
84:             ---------------
85:             name:#text
86:             type:(3)TEXT_NODE
87:             value:This is the catalog header only one instance of this guy
88:         ---------------
89: . . .
90:         name:entry
91:         type:(1)ELEMENT_NODE
92:         value:null
93:         Children(7):
94:             [0] title [1] author [2] author [3] publisher [4] price [5]
                ➥ price [6] isbn
95:             ---------------
96:             name:title
97:             type:(1)ELEMENT_NODE
98:             value:null
99:             Children(1):
100:                [0] #text
101:                ---------------
102:                name:#text
103:                type:(3)TEXT_NODE
104:                value:Special Edition:Using XML and Java 2.0
105:             ---------------
106:             name:author
107:             type:(1)ELEMENT_NODE
108:             value:null
109:             Children(1):
110:                [0] #text
111:                ---------------
112:                name:#text
113:                type:(3)TEXT_NODE
114:                value:Al Saganich
115:             ---------------
116:             name:author
117:             type:(1)ELEMENT_NODE
118:             value:null
119:             Children(1):
120:                [0] #text
```

LISTING 3.8   Continued

```
121:                    - - - - - - - - - - - - - - -
122:                    name:#text
123:                    type:(3)TEXT_NODE
124:                    value:Mike Daconta
125:               - - - - - - - - - - - - - - -
126:               name:publisher
127:               type:(1)ELEMENT_NODE
128:               value:null
129:               Children(1):
130:                    [0] #text
131:                    - - - - - - - - - - - - - - -
132:                    name:#text
133:                    type:(3)TEXT_NODE
134:                    value:Sams Publishing
135:               - - - - - - - - - - - - - - -
136:               name:price
137:               type:(1)ELEMENT_NODE
138:               value:null
139:               has 2 attributes
140:               [oracle.xml.parser.XMLAttr@29be915b, oracle.xml.parser.
                   ➡XMLAttr@2b06915b]
141:               [0] discount = retail
142:               [1] cur = us
143:               Children(1):
144:                    [0] #text
145:                    - - - - - - - - - - - - - - -
146:                    name:#text
147:                    type:(3)TEXT_NODE
148:                    value:9.95
149:               - - - - - - - - - - - - - - -
150:               name:price
151:               type:(1)ELEMENT_NODE
152:               value:null
153:               has 2 attributes
154:               [oracle.xml.parser.XMLAttr@28ae915b, oracle.xml.parser.
                   ➡XMLAttr@2872915b]
155:               [0] discount = wholesale
156:               [1] cur = us
157:               Children(1):
158:                    [0] #text
159:                    - - - - - - - - - - - - - - -
160:                    name:#text
161:                    type:(3)TEXT_NODE
162:                    value:7.95
```

LISTING 3.8   Continued

```
163:               - - - - - - - - - - - - - -
164:               name:isbn
165:               type:(1)ELEMENT_NODE
166:               value:null
167:               Children(1):
168:                   [0] #text
169:                   - - - - - - - - - - - - - -
170:                   name:#text
171:                   type:(3)TEXT_NODE
172:                   value:0101010124
173:               - - - - - - - - - - - - - -
174: . . .
175:          name:entry
176:          type:(1)ELEMENT_NODE
177:          value:null
178:          Children(6):
179:              [0] title [1] author [2] publisher [3] price [4]
                 ➥price [5] isbn
180: . . .
181:          - - - - - - - - - - - - - -
182:          name:cattrailer
183:          type:(1)ELEMENT_NODE
184:          value:null
185:          Children(1):
186:              [0] #text
187:              - - - - - - - - - - - - - -
188:              name:#text
189:              type:(3)TEXT_NODE
190:              value:This is the catalog trailer only one instance of
                 ➥this guy as well
```

Creating DOM Elements

One area we have not examined closely is how to create and insert objects into a DOM tree. There are two methods for doing this. The first is to build an item from scratch and then insert it. The second it to use the `Clone` method to clone a given element and then the `setNodeValue` method to manipulate its contents before inserting it into the tree. The second approach is left as an exercise for the reader. Let's examine how we build an element from scratch.

Adding information to a DOM tree is simple enough if we remember that DOM documents are hierarchical. Looking back to our original catalog example, we remember that a catalog contained "entry" items, each containing a number of subelements. So we can create a new entry as follows:

1. First, we create the new element that represents our new "entry".

   ```
   Element newEntry = document.createElement("entry");
   ```

2. Next, we create each of the child items and populate them. For example, the title item

   ```
   Element newTitle = document.createElement("title");
   newTitle.appendChild(document.createTextNode("A new book"));
   ```

3. Finally, we insert the new child item into its parent.

   ```
   newEntry.appendChild(newTitle);
   ```

In addition to being a child of the entry element, we see that the title item itself has one child item—a TextNode that represents its value.

We would continue for any other children of "entry" elements, such as author, publisher, and price. Price has one other interesting twist to it; it contains attributes. We can create and populate the attributes of the price element one of two ways. We can either create an Attribute object and insert it into the price element, or we can create it directly into the price element. Both methods are shown next.

```
// We can build attributes either of two ways.
// by building it up from scratch and inserting it.
Attr currAttr= document.createAttribute("cur");
currAttr.setValue("frc"); // this book prices in french francs
newPrice.setAttributeNode(currAttr);

// insert it whole
newPrice.setAttribute("discount","other");
// or by inserting it whole
newEntry.appendChild(newPrice);
```

The final step is to insert the information back into the DOM tree.

```
// Now insert it into the document
Element root = document.getDocumentElement();
root.appendChild(newEntry);
```

Listing 3.9 shows the complete source for adding elements into a DOM tree.

3

THE DOCUMENT
OBJECT MODEL
(DOM)

> **NOTE**
>
> The DOM Core Level I contains no provisions for storing a changed representation of an XML document in memory. If you wish to save the results of an update or change, it is up to you to use either proprietary extensions or your own code!

LISTING 3.9   CreateElement.java—Adding Elements into a DOM Tree

```
 1: /*
 2:  * @(#)CreateEntry.java  1.0 99/05/28
 3:  *
 4:  * Copyright (c) 1999 Sams Publishing. All Rights Reserved.
 5:  *
 6:  */
 7: package sams.chp3;
 8:
 9: import java.io.*;
10: import com.sun.xml.tree.*;
11: import org.w3c.dom.*;
12:
13: public class CreateEntry
14: {
15:  public static void main (String argv [])
16:  {
17:   FileInputStream inStream;
18:   Document document;
19:   String xmlDocumentPath = "catalog.xml";
20:   try
21:   {
22:    inStream = new FileInputStream(xmlDocumentPath);
23:    document = XmlDocument.createXmlDocument(inStream,true);
24:
25:    NodeList entries = document.getElementsByTagName( "entry" );
26:     System.out.println("Original catalog contains " + entries.getLength()
         ➥+ " entries");
27:
28:    // Create a new entry element.
29:    Element newEntry = document.createElement("entry");
30:    // Since entry's contain titles we need a title entry
31:    Element newTitle = document.createElement("title");
32:    newTitle.appendChild(document.createTextNode("A new book"));
33:    newEntry.appendChild(newTitle);
34:
35:    // Likewise add the author and publisher items
36:    Element newAuthor = document.createElement("author");
37:    newAuthor.appendChild(document.createTextNode("I.Also Write"));
38:    newEntry.appendChild(newAuthor);
39:    Element newPublisher = document.createElement("publisher");
40:    newPublisher.appendChild(document.createTextNode("We Publishem, Inc."));
41:    newEntry.appendChild(newPublisher);
42:
43://We also need a price which contains two attributes, currency and discount
```

LISTING 3.9 Continued

```
44:    Element newPrice = document.createElement("price");
45:    newPrice.appendChild(document.createTextNode("5.95"));
46:
47:    // We can build attributes either of two ways.
48:    // by building it up from scratch and inserting it.
49:    Attr currAttr= document.createAttribute("cur");
50:    currAttr.setValue("frc"); // this book prices in french francs
51:    newPrice.setAttributeNode(currAttr);
52:
53:    // insert it whole
54:    newPrice.setAttribute("discount","other");
55:    // or by inserting it whole
56:    newEntry.appendChild(newPrice);
57:
58:    /note that the toString method has no defined behavior for DOM objects
59:    System.out.println("newEntry = " + newEntry.toString());
60:
61:    // Now insert it into the document
62:    Element root = document.getDocumentElement();
63:    root.appendChild(newEntry);
64:
65:    //
66:    //  Now list the entries
67:    //
68:    entries = document.getElementsByTagName( "entry" );
69:    if ( entries.getLength()== 0)
70:    {
71:     System.out.println("No entries in this catalog, exiting");
72:     System.exit(0);
73:    }
74:
75:    for (int i = 0; i < entries.getLength(); i++)
76:    {
77: . . .
78:    }
79:    }
80:    catch (Exception e)
81:    {
82:     System.out.println("Unexpected exception reading document!" +e);
83:     System.exit (0);
84:    }
85:
86:
87:  }
88: }
```

DOM Level II

The Document Object Model Level II (the DOMII) defines a set of interfaces to create, manipulate, track, and view an XML document. DOM Level II goes beyond Level I and, for the most part, fills in areas where it is clear that additional functionality is required.

NOTE
As of this writing, the DOM Level II specification is in the final stages of being accepted by the W3C. However, no implementations currently exist and, as a result, we can examine each of the areas covered by the specification but give no concrete examples. It's more than likely that by the time you have this book in hand implementations will exist. Because the specification itself is in its final stages and not likely to change the information significantly, this section can be thought of as a quick reference to the DOM Level II interfaces.

Specifically, the DOMII provides interfaces for the following:

- *HTML*—A set of HTML-specific interfaces, such as `HTMLDocument` and `HTMLElement`, which allow for processing HTML documents by the DOM. We will not look closely at the HTML interfaces because they are outside the scope of this text.

- *Views*—A set of interfaces for working with views. A view is like a window into a document. DOMII views are very much like the traditional concepts of a view with two different applications, or different objects in the same application, looking onto different parts of a document. A view could be thought of in terms of an HTML frame or a computed view after a stylesheet has been applied.

- *Stylesheets*—The DOMII introduces a number of interfaces that represent the generic concept of a stylesheet. The DOMII specification provides for examining stylesheets in a generic fashion and treating them very much like XML `Document` objects.

- *CSS Stylesheets*—Because CSS use is so prevalent, the DOMII contains a set of interfaces for accessing CSS stylesheets. We will only give light coverage of this area of the specification because it's superceded by XSL stylesheets.

- *Events*—One of the long-awaited features of DOMII is support for events. The event interfaces cover such areas as basic event flow and event registration and define User Interface (UI), Mouse, Key, Mutation, and HTML events. We will concentrate on Mutation events because they are the most applicable to Java programming/XML.

- *Traversal*—The DOMII defines a set of interfaces that are collectively lumped into the group Traversal. These interfaces, much like the JDK1.2 collections interfaces, define mechanisms for walking a tree in either tree or list order.

- *Range*—The final area covered by the DOMII is Range. Ranges cover what we traditionally think of as selections and define the concepts of boundary elements and what is meant by a range of elements between two boundary elements.

> **NOTE**
>
> DOM implementations can be queried to determine if they support one or more of the previously mentioned features by using the `hasFeature(DOMString)` method on a `DOMImplementation` object. The `DOMString` returns `true` if the specified feature is supported.

View Interfaces

Perhaps the simplest set of interfaces in DOMII is the view interfaces. View defines a window or view onto a XML `Document` object. Views are optional and may not be provided by an implementation. There are two view interfaces:

- `AbstractView`   An abstract view contains a single, read-only attribute `DocumentView` `document`.

- `DocumentView`   The `DocumentView` interface is implemented by `Document` objects and contains a single, read-only attribute, `AbstractView defaultView`, which refers to the default document.

The view interfaces can be used collectively to get the original document from a view and views from documents.

Stylesheet Interfaces

There are a five stylesheet interfaces:

- `StyleSheet`   An interface representing a generic stylesheet. In XML documents, `StyleSheet` objects are created in reference to stylesheet processing instructions. The `StyleSheet` interface contains attributes:
  - `DOMString type`   The type of the stylesheet (`'test/css'` for example).
  - `Boolean disabled`   Is this stylesheet associated with a document?
  - `Node ownerNode`   The document the stylesheet is associated with.

- StyleSheetList   An ordered list of all the StyleSheet objects. Contains a length attribute representing the number of stylesheets in the list and a StyleSheet item() method for returning a given stylesheet.

- MediaList   An unordered list of all the media type associated with a StyleSheet. The MediaList interface provides methods for accessing each of the media types associated with a stylesheet, as well as methods to add and delete media types.

- LinkStyle   The LinkStyle interface is provided so that the stylesheet object associated with a document can be retrieved, for example via a processing instruction. It contains a single attribute StyleSheet sheet.

- DocumentStyle   The DocumentStyle interface provides a mechanism for accessing stylesheets from a Document object and contains a single attribute StyleSheetList styleSheets. The DocumentStyle interface is normally implemented by Document objects.

Events

From a Java developer's perspective, events are one of the more interesting areas of the DOMII specification. Events are interesting because they define a mechanism whereby an application can determine easily at runtime how a Document is changing. Events fall into three broad categories:

- *UI Events*—UI Events are those events generated by the user interface. UI events are typically the result of external devices, such as a mouse click or a key press.

- *UI Logical Events*—UI Logical Events are a step above normal UI Events in that they detail higher level happenings, such as changes to fonts, pointer focus changes, and so on.

- *Mutation Events*—From a Java/DOM perspective, Mutation Events are the most interesting type of event. Mutation events alert applications to changes in the underlying structure of a DOM Document. Every time a node is changed, added, or deleted, the potential exists for a UI event to occur.

There are three principal participants in DOM event parsing. Event producers, any class that implements the Node interface, generate events that can be consumed by event consumers. Event consumers are informed whenever something happens to an object to which they are listening. And Events themselves are passed from an event generator to an event consumer to inform a consumer what has happened. In fact, there is no reason that an event consumer could not produce events as well, perhaps to propagate information from one area of an application to another.

Because DOM Documents are tree structured, a single event type does not suit all event happenings. The DOMII specification defines three kinds of event processing:

- *Capturing*—Capturing allows an event consumer to capture an event; that is, stop it from propagating from one event consumer to another.

- *Bubbling*—Bubbling is the process whereby a single event at a leaf node is propagated or *bubbled* all the way up a tree from one node to its parent. When a node is bubbled, each event consumer is given the chance to act on it. Using bubbling, an application can register to receive an event on the root of a `Document` and see all events on that document's children.

- *Cancelable*—Cancelable events can be stopped from being processed by a given event listener. Cancelable events are normally used to override the additional processing that might be incurred as an event bubbles up through a `Document` tree.

There are three main interfaces used with DOMII events.

- `EventTarget`   `Node` objects implement the `EventTarget` interface. The `EventTarget` interface contains three methods:

  - `addEventListener(String type, EventListener listener, boolean useCapture)`   Registers classes to handle events

  - `removeEventListener(String type, EventListener listener, boolean useCapture)`   Removes previously registered listeners

  - `dispatchEvent(Event)`   Generates an event

- `EventListener`   Classes that want to consume events on a given `Node` or `Document` do so by implementing the `EventListener` interface. This interface has a single method, `handleEvent(Event)`, which is called when an event happens.

- `Event`   The `Event` class itself is the currency that `EventListeners` and `EventTargets` trade in. Event objects contain a number of fields that the consumer can act on, such as the `Node` associated with the event—whether the event is cancelable or not, whether the event bubbles or not. The `Event` class also contains a number of methods that allow an `EventListener` to change how the event is processed. For example, the `stopPropagation()` method allows a listener to stop a bubbling event from being delivered to listeners registered higher up in the DOM tree.

There are a number of additional classes that derive from the `Event` class:

- `UIEvent`   Events that encapsulate additional information about the View in which they happened.

- `MouseEvent`   Events that contain pointer-related information, such as screen x/y position, and keyboard state, such as whether the Ctrl key was pressed or not, and so on.

- `MutationEvent`   Events that contain related `Node` information, previous and current value, and other applicable `Node` information. `MutationEvents` have a number of derived events, such as `DOMSubtreeModified`, `DOMNodeInserted`, `DOMNodeRemoved`, `DOMAttrModified`, and so on.

Traversal Interfaces

Anyone who has used the JDK1.2 collection classes will be comfortable with the DOMII Traversal interfaces. There are two main interfaces for Document traversal—NodeIterator and TreeWalker. A third interface, NodeFilter, allows developers to write filters to limit the number of elements returned by the two traversal interfaces.

Iterators

The Iterator interface provides a mechanism whereby a developer can walk a flattened version of a Document. Iterators are created by calling the createNodeIterator() on a Document object as shown in the following:

```
NodeIterator iterator = document.createNodeIterator(rootNode,whatToShow,filter);
```

where *rootNode* is the starting Node object, *whatToShow* is a bitwise ored combination from Table 3.2, and *filter* is any class that implements the NodeFilter interface or null.

There are three methods of note on the Iterator interface:

- Node nextNode()   Returns the next node in the list.
- Node previousNode()   Returns the previous node in the list.
- void detach()   Releases any resources associated with the Iterator. Subsequent calls to the iterator will raise an exception.

One of the interesting aspects of iterators is how they react in the face of change. Iterators are defined to represent the current structure of a Document tree and must correctly handle situations where the previous or next node has been deleted or new nodes added.

Conceptually an Iterator has a concept of a *current* node. Consider, for a moment, the following list of nodes:

```
* A B C D E F G *

^(current node)
```

When the iterator is first created, the current node is null. Calls to getNext() would return A, and calls to getPrevious() would return null. Likewise, if the current node was after G, as shown next, getNext() would return null and getPrevious() would return G.

```
* A B C D E F G *

                ^(current node)
```

If a node was added or removed, the Iterator would still behave as you would expect with the list effectively "shifting" left or right as required. For example, assume we have the following situation:

```
* A B C D E F G *

      ^(current node)
```

where the current node *D*, and next returning *E* and previous returning *C*. If node *E* was removed, the Iterator would correctly return node *F*. If an additional node was inserted after *D* called *D'*, the iterator would return *D'* for next.

In addition to the logical behavior of Iterators we've already seen, Node objects also have a behavior known as *visibility*. The second and third parameters to the createNodeIterator() method are a bit mask and a filter, respectively. These two parameters define whether a node is visible and will be returned by getNext() or getPrevious(). The functioning of the bit mask is fairly common. For example, if you only want TEXT and COMMENT nodes, provide a mask of NodeFilter.SHOW_TEXT | NodeFilter.SHOW_COMMENT. Or in additional constants to return other Elements of the Document. We will examine filters shortly.

TABLE 3.2   NodeFilter Constants

Constant	Description
NodeFilter.SHOW_ALL	Return all elements
NodeFilter.SHOW_ELEMENT	Return Element objects
NodeFilter.SHOW_ATTRIBUTE	Return Attribute objects
NodeFilter.SHOW_TEXT	Return Text objects
NodeFilter.SHOW_CDATA_SECTION	Return CDATA objects
NodeFilter.SHOW_ENTITY_REFERENCE	Return EntityReference objects
NodeFilter.SHOW_ENTITY	Return Entity objects
NodeFilter.SHOW_PROCESSING_INSTRUCTION	Return ProcessingInstruction objects
NodeFilter.SHOW_COMMENT	Return Comment objects
NodeFilter.SHOW_DOCUMENT_TYPE	Return DocumentType objects
NodeFilter.SHOW_DOCUMENT_FRAGMENT	Return DocumentFragment objects
NodeFilter.SHOW_NOTATION	Return Notation objects

3

THE DOCUMENT OBJECT MODEL (DOM)

TreeWalkers

TreeWalkers provide a mechanism whereby developers can walk the actual tree structure of a Document.

TreeWalkers are created by calling the createTreeWalker() method on a Document object, as shown in the following:

```
TreeWalker walker = document.createTreeWalker(rootNode,whatToShow,filter);
```

where *rootNode* is the starting Node object, *whatToShow* is a bitwise ored combination from Table 3.2, and *filter* is any class that implements the NodeFilter interface or null.

There are seven methods of note on the TreeWalker interface:

- Node parentNode()   Returns the parent of the current node
- Node firstChild()   Returns the first child of the current node
- Node lastChild()   Returns the last child of the current node.
- Node previousSibling()   Returns the sibling logically to the left of the current node.
- Node nextSibling()   Returns the sibling logically to the right of the current node.
- Node previousNode()   Returns the previous node in the document. Note that previousNode() and nextNode() can move up and down the tree, whereas the sibling methods will not.
- Node nextNode()   Returns the next node in the tree, moving down the tree as required.

If we consider the following tree:

```
            A

       B    C

        D E   F G

      H I
```

and B is the current node:

- getParent() returns A
- previousSibling() returns null
- nextSibling() returns C
- firstChild() returns D
- lastChild() returns E
- previousNode() returns A
- nextNode() returns C

Filters
The final interface in the Iterator set of interfaces is the NodeFilter interface. Node filters provide developers with a finer level of control over when Elements are returned by Iterators and TreeWalkers by allowing a developer to examine a node and return NodeFilter.FILTER_ACCEPT, NodeFilter.FILTER_REJECT, or NodeFilter.FILTER_SKIP to have the Iterator or TreeWalker return, ignore, or skip a given node. The NodeFilter interface has a single method, short acceptNode(Node node), and must return one of the three previously listed constants.

For example, the following snippet of code defines a node filter that returns comment nodes but ignores all other nodes:

```
Class commentsOnlyFilter implements NodeFilter
{
    short acceptNode(Node n)
    {
        if (n instanceof Comment)
            return NodeFilter.FILTER_ACCEPT;
        else
            return NodeFilter.FILTER_SKIP;
    }
}
```

It's important to understand the difference between `FILTER_SKIP` and `FILTER_REJECT`. When walking a tree, if a filter returns `FILTER_REJECT`, the node will be rejected as well as all of its children. With `FILTER_SKIP`, the node will be rejected but its children will still be processed. For iterators `FILTER_SKIP` and `FILTER_REJECT` have the same behavior.

DOM Ranges

DOMII ranges behave in a fashion similar to what you would expect from a word processor or text editor. Ranges have what is termed a mark or start of range and an offset or end of range. DOMII ranges allow a number of logical operations to be performed on a `Document` object, such as adding a new element (`insertNode()`), deleting elements (`deleteContents()`), and copying elements (`cloneRange()`).

We create a range as follows:

```
Document d;
Range range = (DocumentRange)d.createRange();
```

After we have a range object, we then can set its start and end points using the following methods, all of which are from the `Range` interface:

- `Range.setStartBefore(Node startNode)`   Sets the start of the range to be before the current node, including the current node.
- `void setStartAfter(Node startNode)`   Sets the start of the range to be after the current node and not include the current node.
- `void setEndAfter(Node endNode)`   Sets the end of the range to be after the current node, including the given node.
- `void setEndBefore(Node endNode)`   Sets the end of the range to be before the endNode and not include the end node.

3

THE DOCUMENT
OBJECT MODEL
(DOM)

After we have a range of nodes, we can manipulate its content using the following:

- void deleteContents()   Deletes all Nodes between the starting and ending points from the Document object.

- DocumentFragment extractContents()   Creates a new DocumentFragment that represents the contents of the range. The extracted contents are deleted from the Document object.

- DocumentFragment cloneContents()   Creates a new DocumentFragment that is a copy of the contents of the range. The original Document is unchanged.

- void InsertNode(Node new)   Inserts the node into the range. The newly inserted node becomes the new start of the range.

Using range objects, we can manipulate the contents of a DOM tree easily using a graphical metaphor.

The DOM Core Defined

At this point, we've examined in detail the DOM Core Level I and Level II interfaces to understand how they are used. However, we have glossed over how the DOM Level I and Level II are actually specified. In this section, we examine this issue in detail and see that DOM interfaces are specified using something known as the *Interface Description Language* or IDL. After all, seeing the Java descriptions is good, but sometimes we want to go right to the source.

The concept of IDL gained popularity a long time ago, in computer terms anyway, with Sun-RPC. More recently, CORBA has built on past work to create a concise IDL standard. DOM interfaces are defined using the common CORBA IDL syntax. For the most part, IDL is fairly easy to read and we won't get into CORBA specifics. The interested reader can refer to Chapter 13 of *Java 2 and JavaScript for C/C++ Programmers,* (Daconta, Saganich, Monk; John Wiley and Sons, 1999) for a better understanding. However, because the DOM Specification is written in IDL, there are a few conventions you should be aware of. Three of the more useful ones are noted here.

- interface *name: parentclass* { .... };   Defines a new interface *name* that extends *parentclass.*

- *[readonly] attribute type name;*   Defines a variable *name* of type *type.* Defines an attribute (member variable), that may be read-only and results in get/set methods being defined.

  For example, *readonly attribute DocumentType doctype;* also defines the java method DocumentType getDoctype();. Note that attributes marked read-only do not define a set method.

> **NOTE**
>
> Unfortunately, both CORBA and XML use the term *attribute*. In the CORBA case, an attribute is really a member variable within in IDL definition of an interface. In the XML case, an attribute is a property of a data item.

The third IDL syntax convention supports defining methods. For example

```
type methodname([in/out/inout]arguments...) raise(someexception)
```

specifies a method *methodname*, returning type *type* with the specified arguments (which can input/output or both), which may cause an exception. For example, the Document interface defines a method for creating attributes:

```
Attr createAttribute(in DOMString name) raises(DOMException);
```

These are only three of the many important syntax definitions in IDL. Many more exist for defining objects within packages and specifying scope and a variety of other language constructs. We needn't go any further with CORBA at this point except to understand one additional aspect. Normally, an IDL definition is processed via an IDL compiler and results in a language-specific binding for a given definition. Earlier, we stated that a definition results in methods getting defined. What actually happens is that when the IDL compiler is executed, the interface definition generates language-specific code (Java-specific code, for example). All the definitions are processed and so-called mutator (get/set) methods are generated for attributes and the like. As we can see, IDL does not really "define" methods per se but is close enough for our purposes.

Listing 3.10 shows the complete IDL definition of the DOM Document interface (with line numbers added for clarity).

LISTING 3.10   IDL Definition of the DOM Document Interface

```
1    interface Document : Node {
2        readonly attribute DocumentType doctype;
3        readonly attribute DOMImplementation implementation;
4        readonly attribute Element documentElement;
5        Element createElement(in DOMString tagName)
6            raises(DOMException);
7        DocumentFragment createDocumentFragment();
8        Text createTextNode(in DOMString data);
9        Comment createComment(in DOMString data);
10       CDATASection createCDATASection(in DOMString data)
11           raises(DOMException);
12       ProcessingInstruction createProcessingInstruction
```

LISTING 3.10   Continued

```
13                              (in DOMString target, in DOMString data)
14              raises(DOMException);
15         Attr createAttribute(in DOMString name)
16              raises(DOMException);
17         EntityReference createEntityReference(in DOMString name)
18              raises(DOMException);
19         NodeList getElementsByTagName(in DOMString tagname);
20   };
```

If we examine it closely it can be analyzed as follows:

Line 1 defines the interface Document that is derived from the interface Node.

Lines 2, 3, and 4 define four member variables, all of which are read-only and result in the getDoctype, getImplementation, and getDocumentElement methods being generated when the IDL is processed.

Lines 5–18 define methods for creating child objects.

Line 19 defines an additional method that returns an ordered list of nodes of type *tagname*.

And that's all there is to it! IDL is fairly clear to Java developers. CORBA is well suited to Java and maps well to Java syntax. For a larger taste of IDL, refer to any of the W3C Java language binding specifications.

Implementation Anomalies

The following section details findings discovered while using each of the aforementioned DOM implementations. Each implementation has its own warts and idiosyncrasies. It should be kept in mind that the implementations are in various forms of compliance with the specifications. Any and all of these issues may be addressed with newer releases.

Processing Instructions

```
<?xml version="1.0" encoding="UTF-8" ?>
```

Only the Oracle implementation returned anything for this line. It was returned as a ProcessingInstruction node with appropriate contents.

Unexpected Child Nodes

The IBM implementation returned a number of child nodes off of the DOCUMENT_TYPE_NODE object. Both the Sun and Oracle implementations return 0 children for this node. The IBM implementation listed the entities of the XML as children of this node as well as a number of other nodes that appear to represent the structure of the DTD.

Results Using `toString`

Many Java developers, myself included, use the `toString` method to examine object contents. Various results were obtained by using this method on different objects in the DOM hierarchy. It is strongly recommended that you *not* depend on the results of this method because the DOM Core does not specify what it should return. With that said, the following results were observed.

`node.getAttributes().toString` returned differing results.

- Sun returned `'discount="wholesale" cur="us"'`.
- IBM returned `'[retail, us]'`.
- Oracle returned what appears to be the underlying result of `toString`ing the actual attribute objects.

CR/LF in XML Document Text

One of the requirements of the DOM is that it reports structurally isomorphic results. That is to say that two documents are identical from a processing perspective if formatting that makes no structural difference, such as whitespace outside real content, is not considered. In English, that means what goes in should come out. However, different implementations handle Carriage Return/Line Feed pairs differently. Specifically, the CR/LF pair between lines in the XML document is discarded by the Sun parser but returned as a text node by the IBM parser. The Oracle implementation returned CR/LF pairs where expected.

Comments

Comments are another area where implementations differed significantly.

- Sun—Lost comments
- IBM—Shown in appropriate places as comment nodes
- Oracle—Shown in appropriate places as comment nodes

Entities

Because the DOM Core allows for validating and non-validating parsers, entities can be expected to be handled slightly differently between implementations. The following results were observed.

- Sun—Entities returned but values shown always as null
- IBM—Entity class cast exception when casting to entity
- Oracle—Returned as expected

As we can see, there are differences between the implementations. However, we can assume that, as of this writing, all the implementations are beta and many of these issues will be addressed.

Summary

In this chapter we examined the Document Object Model (DOM). Particularly, we focused on the DOM and DOMII APIs in detail. We began the chapter by explaining what the DOM is as well as what it is not in order to ground the remainder of the chapter. We introduced the DOM `Document` object and saw how `Documents` are logically represented. We walked through each of the interfaces defined in the DOM and DOMII APIs giving numerous examples where applicable. We ended by examining a number of DOM implementations and the differences between those implementations.

Suggested for Further Study

The following questions use the Docuverse DOM implementation, which can be found at `www.docuverse.com`.

1. How does one create a DOM document using the Docuverse SDK?

2. Compare the result of question 1 with any of the previously mentioned Java SDK for DOM. Describe how the `Document` methods differ from one of the other implementations.

3. Several known anomalies were found in the IBM, Sun, and Oracle DOM implementations. Expand the anomalies list to include the Docuverse DOM SDK and explain if it exhibits any of the previous anomalies or adds new ones of its own.

4. We have not touched on the issues of valid and well-formedness within the DOM. Please give an example of how these issue impact a DOM implementation. Hint: Is this a DOM issue or a SAX issue?

5. Modify the `CreateElement.java` example to use the `Clone` method on an entry. Which method, `Clone` or build from scratch, is better and why?

Further Reading

The Document Object Model (DOM) Level 1 Specification, Version 1.0. W3C Members. 1-October-1998, W3C. The definitive reference to the DOM Core Level 1. Not for the faint of heart!

The Document Object Model (DOM) Level 2 Specification, Version 1.0 Working Draft. W3C Members. 1-March-1999, W3C. The definitive reference to the DOM Core Level 2. Subject to change.

CORBA-Fundamentals and Programming. Jon Seigel. 1996, John Wiley and Sons. An older but still excellent CORBA reference.

COM and DCOM:Microsoft's Vision for Distributed Objects. Roger Sessions. 1998, John Wiley and Sons. An excellent book on COM and distributed objects from the Microsoft perspective. For entry-level to advanced engineers.

Java 2 and JavaScript for C and C++ Programmers. Michael C. Daconta, Al Saganich, Eric Monk. 1999, John Wiley and Sons. A must have for those C++ programmers looking to get into Java. For entry-level to advanced C++ engineers moving to Java.

Advanced XML

"Readers and users be forewarned, however; if you thought Java was a rush of wave on wave of new standards, APIs, and tools—surf's up! XML is incoming."

—Jacques Surveyer, "XML Meets Java," Java Pro, April 1999

IN THIS CHAPTER

In Chapter 1, "An XML Primer," you learned just enough XML to begin experimenting with programming it using SAX and DOM. In this chapter, I will cover areas that we previously glossed over and advanced topics not yet discussed. Due to this "fill-in-the-blanks" approach, this chapter will sometimes skip from topic to topic with little cohesion between the topics. However, in the end, what you learn in this chapter combined with your knowledge acquired in the previous chapters will give you a thorough understanding of XML.

Advanced Markup

In this section, we will cover advanced topics of XML markup like entities, mixed and content specifications, and the remaining attribute types. We begin with how and why to add character references to your XML document.

Character References

XML uses the *Unicode* character set. Unicode is a standard that allows characters from all existing, and even ancient, languages. If your keyboard does not have a key for a particular international character you can insert that character into an XML document using a *character reference*.

Character Representation

It is important to distinguish between the varying facets of representing characters in documents. Each definition represents one facet of such representation:

- *Character*—A letter in a language.
- *Glyph*—The picture or rendered illustration of the character.
- *Coded character set*—An agreed-on mapping of characters to positions in a code space. XML uses the Unicode character set. Unicode supports a base of 1,114,112 positions and each character can be encoded in one or two 16-bit words.
- *Font*—A collection of glyphs for a character set.
- *Character set encoding*—The final step in using characters in an electronic document is deciding how to represent the numeric positions in the chosen character set in binary form in the file on disk. Simple character sets like ASCII or Latin1 encode using a byte of storage per character, with the value of the byte being the integer value of the position in the character set. This only worked because these character sets only supported 128 and 256 characters, respectively. Because Unicode is a much larger character set, some other encoding is needed. There are four possible encodings of Unicode characters: UCS-2, UTF-7, UTF-8,

and UTF-16. The last two are the most common. UCS-2 only encodes the first 65,536 positions. UTF-7 uses only the first seven bits in a byte and was suitable for older email handling agents. UTF stands for Universal Character Set Transformation Format. UTF-8 uses one or more eight-bit bytes to encode Unicode characters with the first 256 characters encoding using a single byte just like Latin1. UTF-16 is similar to UCS-2 but has an escape mechanism to encode all the Unicode characters.

There are two formats for a character reference: decimal and hex. The decimal representation is

```
CharRef :== '&#' [0-9]+ ';'
```

For example:

```
<P> Here is a special character: &#169; </P>
```

In Unicode, as in Latin1, position 169 is the copyright symbol (©).

The hex representation is

```
CharRef :== '&#x' [0-9a-fA-F]+ ';'
```

Here is an example of a character reference in hex:

```
<P> Here is another special character: &#xB6; </P>
```

In decimal, this character is position 182, which is a paragraph symbol.

4

ADVANCED XML

NOTE

The Unicode standard lists its characters in hex notation.

Just as character references are abbreviations for Unicode characters, the XML specification also allows you to define your own abbreviations called entities and refer to them with entity references.

Entities and Entity References

Entities and entity references are techniques for enabling reuse of both content and markup in your XML documents. Entities can be confusing because there are many different categories of entities; however, after you clearly understand the various categories and to what category a particular entity belongs, they make sense. Figure 4.1 depicts the hierarchy of entity categories.

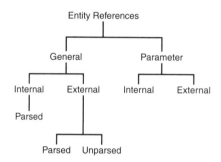

FIGURE 4.1

Hierarchy of entity categories.

Before demonstrating each category, let's look at Table 4.1, which provides definitions of each category.

TABLE 4.1   Entity Categories

Category	Definition
General entity	Entities used only in document content.
Parameter entity	Entities used only in document type definitions (DTDs).
Parsed entity	An entity whose replacement content is text.
Unparsed entity	Normally used for binary (non-text entities). If it is text, it may not be XML. Has an associated notation.
Internal parsed entity	An entity that is declared in an instance of the XML document.
External entity	An entity fetched from an external source. The external source is specified via a URI.

> **NOTE**
>
> An internal entity must be a parsed entity.

General Entities

In its simplest form (an internal, general parsed entity) an entity is just an abbreviation for larger text. For example, an entity `dtd` could be used to abbreviate the phrase *document type definition.*

You declare entities in your document type definition like this:

```
<!ENTITY dtd  "document type definition">
```

Another way to think about an entity is as a box with a label. The label is the entity's name. The contents of the box can be text or data. If the content of the entity is text, the standard calls this a parsed entity. Because the content is text it may also contain markup. For example:

```
<!ENTITY line "<P>This is a parsed entity. </P>">
```

An entity can be fetched from an external source specified by a URI. This is called an external entity. Here's another example:

```
<!ENTITY intro SYSTEM "http://www.gosynergy.com/intro.xml">
```

In an XML document, an entity is referred to via an *entity reference*. Here is the formal definition of an entity reference.

```
EntityRef :== '&'  Name  ';'
```

Table 4.2 shows the predefined entities for the characters used to delineate markup

TABLE 4.2 Predefined Entities

Entity Reference	*Character*
&amp;	&
&lt;	<
&gt;	>
&apos;	'
&quot;	"

4

ADVANCED XML

> **NOTE**
>
> Unlike HTML, which has many predefined entities, the entities listed in Table 4.2 are the only ones predefined in XML.

Here is a more complete example that uses a parsed general entity:

```
<!DOCTYPE BOOK [
<!ENTITY publisher "SAMS Professional publishing">
]>
<BOOK>
<PUBLISHER> &publisher; </PUBLISHER>
<P> Welcome to this book published by &publisher;.  This
```

```
&publisher; produces numerous professional titles every year.
</BOOK>
```

There are also unparsed entities for data such as images:

```
<!ENTITY image SYSTEM "http://www.wyweb.com/myhouse.gif" NDATA GIF>
```

Notice that unparsed entities are differentiated with the keyword NDATA followed by a notation name for that data. The notation name must be a declared notation. You declare notations in the DTD similar to the way you declare elements. The declaration of the GIF notation would be

```
<!NOTATION GIF SYSTEM "apps/imgviewer.exe ">
```

So far we have seen parsed and unparsed entities and external and internal entities. There is one more distinction that can be applied to entities: *general* or *parameter*. So far, we have seen only general entities. Remember, a general entity is an entity used for text replacement in a document instance.

Parameter Entities

A *parameter* entity is an entity that is only used in a DTD. It is differentiated in both its declaration and reference by a % symbol.

Here is an example of an internal parameter entity declaration:

```
<!DOCTYPE EXAMPLE [
<!ENTITY % obj "<!ELEMENT OBJECT (#PCDATA)>">
%obj;
]>
```

Parameter entities have different rules for an internal DTD (called an internal subset) versus an external DTD (called an external subset). In an internal DTD you can only have whole declarations (as shown above). In an external DTD you can have a parameter entity for partial declarations. This is to make parsing for non-validating parsers (which must parse the internal subset) easier—for example:

```
<!ENTITY % nameAtt  "name CDATA #REQUIRED">
<!ATTLIST folder
        %nameAtt;>
<!ATTLIST bookmark
        %nameAtt;
        type CDATA #IMPLIED>
```

External parameter entities allow you to reuse common declarations. For example, an employee element may be used in several different markup languages across the business. Here is an example of an external parameter entity:

```
<!ENTITY % employee SYSTEM "http://www.super.com/xml/employee.dtd">
...
%employee;
```

Markup may not span entity boundaries. The following is illegal:

```
<!DOCTYPE SAMPLE [
<!ENTITY start-tag  "<title>This is very">
<!ENTITY end-tag  "illegal. </title>">
]>
&start;&finish;
```

I'd like to make the following points about entities:

- In an attribute value you can use an internal, general entity. For example:

```
<!ENTITY favrest "Tippy's Taco house">
<!ATTLIST menu
          date CDATA #REQUIRED
          restaurant CDATA #FIXED "&favrest;">
```

- Entities must be declared before they are used.

Entities are a concept that will take experience to master. A good way to speed up your learning curve on entities is to examine DTDs and documents written by others. See XML.org for a repository and catalog of XML documents and DTDs.

Understanding Attribute Types

In Chapter 2, "Parsing XML," you learned how to declare attributes in a document type declaration using an attribute-list declaration. For example:

```
<!ELEMENT CONTACT (#PCDATA)>
<!ATTLIST  CONTACT  EMAIL CDATA #REQUIRED>
```

Attributes have types that enforce both lexical and semantic constraints. Table 4.3 provides a summary of the attribute types.

TABLE 4.3   Attribute Types

Type	Definition
CDATA	Any character data
Enumeration	A list of Nmtokens ("name tokens") where only one may be used (similar to a choice content model)
NOTATION	A list of names and a declared notation name
ID	A name that uniquely identifies an element

4

TABLE 4.3   Continued

Type	Definition
IDREF	A reference to an element (by its ID)
IDREFS	May refer to one or more IDs (space delimited)
ENTITY	A name of a declared entity
ENTITIES	One or more declared entities (space delimited)
NMTOKEN	An Nmtoken (see definition later in the chapter)
NMTOKENS	One or more Nmtokens

Many of the definitions in Table 4.3 specify using either a name or a name token. A *name* is any valid XML name. An XML name must begin with a letter or an underscore, followed by any number of letters, digits, hyphens, underscores, periods, or colons. Colons are now used to denote namespaces (discussed next). XML names are used for all element and attribute names. For example:

```
<!ELEMENT BODY (#PCDATA)>
```

An NmToken or *name token* is any combination of legal name characters for XML names. In other words, all XML names are name tokens, but not all name tokens have XML names. Here are some sample name tokens:

```
.1.a.name.token.but.not.a.name
234_also_a_name_token_but_not_a_name
A_name_token_and_a_name
```

In Chapter 2, I covered the most common attribute data types (CDATA and enumeration); now I will both define and demonstrate all the available attribute types.

- CDATA is the simplest type of attribute. It allows any character data except <, & (unless it starts a reference), or the quotation character used to surround the string. For example:
  ```
  <!ATTLIST QUOTE  DATE  CDATA #REQUIRED>
  ]>
  <QUOTE  DATE="February 9, 1999"> ... </QUOTE>
  ```
- An Enumeration type allows an attribute to take one name token among a choice of any number of name tokens. For example:
  ```
  <!ATTLIST CHOICE (option1|option2|option3) #REQUIRED>
  ```
- Name token (NMTOKEN) attributes are similar to CDATA except that they are restricted to valid name tokens (only name characters). An empty string is not a valid name token. Also, a name token cannot have whitespace. For example:
  ```
  <!ATTLIST QUOTE DATE NMTOKEN #REQUIRED>
  ```

```
... ]>
<QUOTE  DATE="1999-02-09"> ... </QUOTE>
```

The NMTOKENS declaration allows an attribute value to be one or more NMTOKENS separated by a space.

• An ID attribute allows you to name a particular element so that it may be referred to later using an IDREF attribute. These ID attributes will also be used with XLINKS, which are discussed later. IDs are XML names. Every element can have at most one ID. All IDs specified in an XML document must be unique. IDREF attributes must refer to an ID in the document. Also, if you use the IDREFs designation, you may have an attribute that has one or more IDREFs as its value. For example:

```
<!DOCTYPE PAPER [
<!ELEMENT SECTION (TITLE, PARAGRAPH*)>
<!ATTLIST  SECTION SEC-ID  ID  #IMPLIED>
<!ELEMENT  CROSS-REFERENCE  EMPTY>
<!ATTLIST  CROSS-REFERENCE  TARGET  IDREF  #REQUIRED>
... ]>
<PAPER>
<SECTION  SEC-ID="java.features"> <TITLE> Java's Best
features </TITLE>  ...  </SECTION>
...
To refresh your memory, see the section titled <CROSS-REFERENCE
TARGET="java.features" /> </PAPER>
```

• An ENTITY attribute is used to refer to an unparsed external entity.

```
<!DOCTYPE BOOKREVIEW [
...
<!ATTLIST BOOK COVER ENTITY #REQUIRED>
<!NOTATION GIF SYSTEM "apps/gifview.exe ">
<!ENTITY  java-book1  SYSTEM
    "http://www.sellbooks.com/java/book1.gif" NDATA GIF>
]>
<BOOKREVIEW>
<BOOK  cover = "java-book1"> ... </BOOK>
</BOOKREVIEW>
```

You may also declare an attribute to refer to one or more entities using the ENTITIES designation.

• A NOTATION attribute type is used to specify that an attribute value is one of several declared NOTATIONS. For example:

```
<!ATTLIST COVER_IMG
          type NOTATION (GIF|JPEG|BMP) "GIF">
```

After you declare your attributes and assign them to an appropriate type, you can use attributes in your document. The values assigned to those attributes are modified by a process called "normalization," which is discussed next.

4

ADVANCED XML

Attribute Value Normalization and Whitespace Handling

Normalization and whitespace handling are detailed processes for handling specific text processing situations. This type of fine granularity is the basis of a good standard.

Attribute Value Normalization

Element attributes are `name="value"` pairs; however, the value between the quotes is first passed through a process called normalization. Here are the steps in the normalization process:

- Surrounding quotes are stripped out.
- Character references are replaced with their corresponding characters. For example, `&#169;` would be replaced with a copyright symbol.
- General entity references are replaced with their corresponding text. This is a recursive process, which means that if the replacement text also contains references, they are replaced, and so on.
- Whitespace characters (carriage return, line feed, tab and space) in attribute values are replaced by spaces. Also, the sequence CR-LF is replaced by a single space.
- If an attribute type is anything other than CDATA, leading and trailing spaces are removed. Also, if using tokenized types, spaces between tokens are collapsed to a single space.

It is important to remember the distinction between unnormalized attribute value text and attribute value data (after normalization). For example:

```
<GRAPHIC  ALTERNATE-TEXT="This is a picture of
                         a penguin dancing.">
The attribute value is normalized to
This is a picture of a penguin dancing.
```

Whitespace Handling

You may remember that in Chapter 2 we contrasted XML to HTML in its treatment of whitespace. Whereas HTML disregarded whitespace, XML preserved whitespace in your document content. To be technically accurate, the specification requires that an XML processor (usually a parser) pass whitespace on to the application (the consumer program of the data). The application then can determine whether whitespace is significant. The specification provides a special attribute called `xml:space` that can be attached to any element in order to specify the proper treatment of whitespace to the application. Here is the form of the `xml:space` attribute:

```
<!ATTLIST elemName
        xml:space (default | preserve) 'preserve'>
```

The `elemName` in the general form is any element you want to attach the element to. By convention, the attribute applies to that element and its children elements. The value `'preserve'` specifies that the application should preserve all whitespace. The value `'default'` indicates that the application's default processing for whitespace is acceptable (whatever that may be).

Another aspect of handling whitespace across heterogeneous platforms is the processing of end-of-line characters. The problem is that there are three widespread methods for handling end-of-line: Mac OS uses a carriage return (CR), UNIX uses a line feed (LF) and Windows uses a carriage return line feed (CR-LF) sequence. The XML specification requires that the XML processor convert any of the stated conventions to a single LF to signify end-of-line.

Any and Mixed Element Content Models

As previously stated, element type declarations start with the literal string `<!ELEMENT` followed by an element name and then a content specification:

```
<!ELEMENT html (head, body) >
```

The content specification can be one of four types: EMPTY, ANY, mixed content, or element content. The element content model is the most common. The EMPTY content model is for empty elements.

The ANY content model allows an element to contain any character data or child elements. This is a completely unstructured content specification and therefore is rarely used.

A mixed content element may contain character data, optionally interspersed with child elements. Here is the grammar for the mixed content specification:

```
Mixed ::= '(' S? '#PCDATA' (S? '|' S? Name) * S? ')*'
        | '(' S? '#PCDATA' S? ')'
```

This grammar states that you can either have the literal #PCDATA followed by zero or more child element names or just have the literal #PCDATA by itself. PCDATA stands for parsed character data.

```
Example 1:  <!ELEMENT  NAME  (#PCDATA) >
```

```
Example 2:  <!ELEMENT  paragraph  (#PCDATA|quote|reference)* >
```

CDATA Sections

A CDATA section is used in a document when you do not want the content to be treated as markup. The most obvious example of using a CDATA section would be to pass XML markup into an application (instead of having it parsed as markup). A CDATA section starts with the string `<![CDATA[` and ends with the string `]]>`. For example:

```
<![CDATA[<TITLE> an XML example </TITLE>]]>
```

Another possible use of a CDATA section would be to pass source code to an application without having to use character references for reserved characters like the < or > symbol.

> **NOTE**
>
> A CDATA section is only allowed where #PCDATA is allowed in your XML document.

Conditional Sections

Conditional sections can only occur in the external subset of the document type declaration and in external entity references from the internal subset. A conditional section allows you to turn on and off a series of markup declarations. There are two keywords used with conditional sections: INCLUDE and IGNORE.

A conditional section may include one or more complete declarations, comments, processing instructions, or nested conditional sections. If the keyword used is INCLUDE, the section is processed. If the keyword is IGNORE, the section is not processed.

Here is an example of using conditional sections:

```
<! [INCLUDE [
<!ELEMENT  article (title, section+, references*)>
] ]>
<![IGNORE [
<!ELEMENT  article  (title, section+)>
]]>
```

This is very useful for turning on and off parts of a DTD during development. You can use an entity for the keyword of a conditional section. The processor will replace the reference before determining whether it should include or ignore the section. For example, the document could be rewritten like this:

```
<!ENTITY % editor "INCLUDE">
<!ENTITY % author "IGNORE">
<! [%editor [
<!ELEMENT  article (title, section+, references*)>
] ]>
<![%author [
<!ELEMENT  article  (title, section+)>
]]>
```

Processing Instructions

A processing instruction is used to pass additional information to one specific processing application without changing the way the document is processed by other applications. In general, processing instructions should be used infrequently. The format of a processing instruction is the literal <? followed by a name (the name of the target application), followed by any text and ending with the literal string ?>.

> **NOTE**
>
> The name of the application in a processing instruction may not be any variation of the letters *XML*.

Here is an example to change the font of the first word of a paragraph. You may have to do this if you are using someone else's DTD that does not have markup for something you want to do. For example:

```
<SECTION> The man stood on the beach.
<p> <?EZFormat Font="24Pt"?> Hey! <?EZFormat endFont ?>
</SECTION>
```

Another reason for processing instructions could be for sending special commands to a CGI program processing the XML prior to passing it to a client.

XML uses a special processing instruction for attaching XSL stylesheets to a document instance.

```
<?xml:stylesheet
         href="http://www.mystuff.com/memo.xsl"
         type="text/xsl" ?>
```

Last, remember that the XML declaration is a form of processing instruction.

Encoding and the Standalone Document Declarations

In the primer on XML, I discussed the XML declaration and stated that it contained some literal text <?xml, followed by version information, an optional encoding declaration, an optional standalone document declaration, and the literal text ?>. I will now examine the two optional parts of the XML declaration: the encoding declaration and the standalone document declaration.

The encoding declaration specifies the character set encoding for the following document. The earlier section "Character References" contains a note that defines character set encoding and how it relates to both characters and character sets. The specification requires all XML processors to support both UTF-8 and UTF-16 encoding. Support of all other encodings is optional. In the absence of an encoding declaration or a byte order mark (this allows auto-detection of a UTF-16 encoded file), the encoding must be UTF-8. Because ASCII is a subset of UTF-8, ordinary ASCII files do not need an encoding declaration. Here are some examples of encoding declarations:

```
<?xml version='1.0' encoding='UTF-16' ?>
<?xml version='1.0' encoding='ISO-10646-UCS-2' ?>
```

A list of Internet-supported character set names can be retrieved from

```
ftp://ftp.isi.edu/in-notes/iana/assignments/character-sets
```

> **NOTE**
>
> Any external parsed entity may begin with a text declaration. A text declaration is identical to an XML declaration with the exception that the version declaration is optional and minus the standalone document declaration. For example:
>
> ```
> <?xml encoding='UTF-16' ?>
> ```

The standalone document declaration is only used rarely and is not recommend for general use. As we stated previously, a DTD can be composed of both an external subset and an internal subset. An external subset is stored elsewhere and referenced via a URI. A standalone document declaration declares whether an application needs to fetch the external subset of the DTD to process the document correctly. For example:

```
<?xml version="1.0"  standalone="yes" ?>
<!DOCTYPE  HTML  SYSTEM  http://www.xmlstuff.com/html.dtd>
<HTML> ... </HTML>
```

This example would state to a processor that the client does not need to fetch the DTD to properly process the document. It is important to note that a document is not valid unless both the external subset and internal subset of a DTD has been processed.

Another scenario for using the standalone document declaration is if multiple programs process a document but only the first one validates the document. All ensuing programs could safely skip that step.

The XML Grammar

The XML grammar is specified using an Extended Backus-Naur form (EBNF) notation. Using an EBNF defines a context-free grammar—a grammar that is independent of the context in which it is used. The notation for definitions in the grammar is

```
symbol ::=  expression
```

where expression defines the rule for creating the symbol on the left-hand side. This formal grammar ensures that there is no ambiguity in the XML syntax. All the legal expressions are precisely defined via EBNF.

NOTE

It is important to keep in mind that this section refers to EBNF syntax and not XML syntax. The purpose for reviewing EBNF is to give you the ability to consult the XML specification when necessary.

EBNF statements are also called production rules, because they express the way in which valid symbols are constructed or produced using other symbols or specific fixed strings.

Table 4.4 shows EBNF notations in the grammar and their meaning.

TABLE 4.4   EBNF Notations

Notation	Description
(expression)	A group expression treated as a single unit.
#xN	Where *N* is a hexadecimal integer. This notation matches a specific UCS character.
"string"	Matches a literal string.
'string'	Matches a literal string.
A?	Matches A or nothing; Means A is optional.
A+	Matches one or more occurrences of A.
A*	Matches zero or more occurrences of A.
A B	Matches A followed by B.
A | B	Matches A or B, but not both.
A - B	Matches any string that matches A but does not match B.
[a-zA-Z] [#xN-#xN]	Matches any character with a value in the ranges (inclusive).
[^a-z], [^#xN-#xN]	Matches any character with a value outside the range.
[^abc]	Matches any character not among the given characters.

4

ADVANCED XML

Here is a snippet of the XML grammar in the XML specification:

```
elementdecl ::= '<!ELEMENT' S  Name  S  contentspec S? '>'
S ::= (#x20 | #x9 | #xD | #xA)+
Name ::= (Letter | '_' | ':') (NameChar)
```

```
contentspec ::=  'EMPTY'  |  'ANY'  |  Mixed  |  children
children  ::=  (choice  |  seq) ('?'  |  '*'  |  '+') ?
cp  ::=  (Name  |  choice  |  seq) ('?'  |  '*'  |  '+') ?
choice  ::=  '('  S?  cp  ( S?  '|'  S?  cp  )*  S?  ')'
seq  ::=  '('  S?  cp  ( S?  ','  S?  cp  )*  S?  ')'
Mixed  ::=  '('  S?  '#PCDATA'  (S?  '|'  S?  Name)*  ?  ')*'
             |  '('  S?  '#PCDATA'  S?  ')'
```

> **NOTE**
>
> See Letter and NameChar rules in the XML Recommendation. They occupy several pages and were left out for brevity.

Here is a partial translation of the production rules:

An element declaration is the literal `<!ELEMENT`, followed by a space, a legal XML name, a symbol called `contentspec`, (optionally) a space, and finally the literal `>`.

A `contentspec` is either the literal `EMPTY` or `ANY`, or the translation of the symbol `Mixed` or the symbol `children`.

A `children` symbol is translated as either a choice or a sequence followed optionally by an occurrence indicator, which is the literal `?`, `*`, or `+`.

A choice symbol is translated as the literal `(`, an optional space, a symbol called `cp` (a content particle), zero or more literals `|` with more content particles (and optional space), and a literal `)`.

Namespaces in XML

As markup languages proliferate, markup language designers will want to reuse portions of languages instead of reinventing the wheel. This poses the problem of naming collisions. For example, what if we mixed HTML tags with our own Book Review Markup Language that also had a `<TITLE>` tag?

For example:

```
<HTML>
<HEAD>
     <TITLE> Book Review Page </TITLE>
</HEAD>
<BODY>
     <BOOK>
          <TITLE>  Developing XML in Java </TITLE>
```

```
            <AUTHOR>  Michael C. Daconta   </AUTHOR>
      </BOOK>
</BODY>
</HTML>
```

If a program were to parse this document, how would the programmer know which TITLE was the book title? In order to accomplish this, element and attribute names must be universal. To create a universal name, an XML name is separated into two parts: a namespace prefix and a local part. The World Wide Web Consortium (W3C) formalized the rules for creating these universal names in the Namespaces Specification, which became a W3C Recommendation on January 14, 1999. So, rewriting the previous example using namespaces produces

```
<ht:HTML xmlns:ht="http://www.w3.org/1999/xhtml"
                  xmlns:bk="http://www.gosynergy.com/brml">
<ht:HEAD>
     <ht:TITLE> Book Review Page </ht:TITLE>
</ht:HEAD>
<ht:BODY>
     <bk:BOOK>
           <bk:TITLE>  Developing XML in Java </bk:TITLE>
           <bk:AUTHOR>  Michael C. Daconta   </bk:AUTHOR>
     </bk:BOOK>
</ht:BODY>
</ht:HTML>
```

Declaring Namespaces

A namespace is declared using an attribute whose prefix is xmlns as follows:

```
<TEST  xmlns:syn="http://www.gosynergy.com/example">
```

The value of the xmlns attribute is any Uniform Resource Identifier, which functions as the namespace name. The URI does not have to actually exist. Attributes, not just elements, can also have namespaces. As an example, we could use an HTML alignment attribute to align our book title like this:

```
<ht:HTML xmlns:ht="http://www.w3c.org/HTML/1999/html4"
                  xmlns:bk="http://www.gosynergy.com/brml">
<ht:HEAD>
     <ht:TITLE> Book Review Page </ht:TITLE>
</ht:HEAD>
<ht:BODY>
     <bk:BOOK>
           <bk:TITLE ht:ALIGN="left">  Developing XML in Java </bk:TITLE>
           <bk:AUTHOR>  Michael C. Daconta   </bk:AUTHOR>
     </bk:BOOK>
</ht:BODY>
</ht:HTML>
```

4

ADVANCED XML

Before a prefix can be used in a document, it must be declared in the current tag or in an ancestor tag that contains the current tag. Lastly, a namespace has scope. This means that the namespace applies to the element in which it is declared and all elements within the content of that element.

How Namespaces Affect the DTD

Attribute and element names are also given as qualified names (what we called universal names) in the DTD declarations. Here is an example of the DTD for our BOOK example:

```
<!ELEMENT bk:BOOK (bk:TITLE, bk:AUTHOR?)>
<!ATTLIST bk:BOOK
          xmlns:bk CDATA #FIXED
                    "http://www.gosynergy.com/brml">
<!ATTLIST bk:BOOK
          bk:pages CDATA #IMPLIED>
```

You should understand that to keep backward compatibility with SGML (which allows a colon as part of an SGML name), this is really just a syntactic trick to separate one name into two parts. Therefore, to validate the document, all names in the DTD must be modified to include the prefix part in each element and attribute declaration. Here is another example of a simple markup language that uses namespaces:

```
<?xml version="1.0" ?>
<!DOCTYPE slf:entries [
<!ELEMENT slf:entries (entry)* >
<!ELEMENT slf:entry (field)* >
<!ELEMENT slf:field (#PCDATA) >
<!ATTLIST slf:entries
          xmlns:slf CDATA #FIXED "http://www.gosynergy.com/slf">
<!ATTLIST slf:entry
          slf:type (general|security|fatalerror|
          error|warning|info|trace)    #REQUIRED
          slf:source CDATA #IMPLIED>
<!ATTLIST slf:field
          slf:name CDATA #REQUIRED >
]>

<slf:entries>

<slf:entry slf:type = 'trace'>
<slf:field slf:name='timestamp'>January 24, 2000 12:21:13 PM EST</slf:field>
<slf:field slf:name='class'> java.lang.Exception</slf:field>
<slf:field slf:name='method'>&lt;init&gt;</slf:field>
<slf:field slf:name='message'>View</slf:field>
</slf:entry>
```

```
<slf:entry slf:type = 'trace'>
<slf:field slf:name='timestamp'>January 24, 2000 3:51:48 PM EST</slf:field>
<slf:field slf:name='class'>GOV.dia.mditds.audit.AuditManagerApplet</slf:field>
<slf:field slf:name='method'>actionPerformed</slf:field>
<slf:field slf:name='message'>View</slf:field>
</slf:entry>

</slf:entries>
```

Applying Namespaces

In order to remove the burden of redundant typing, the specification allows a default name-space. A default namespace will apply to the current element where the namespace is declared if it does not have a prefix and to all subelements that do not have a prefix. So the example could be rewritten:

```
<HTML xmlns="http://www.w3.org/1999/xhtml"
       xmlns:bk="http://www.gosynergy.com/brml">
<HEAD>
      <TITLE> Book Review Page </TITLE>
</HEAD>
<BODY>
      <bk:BOOK>
              <bk:TITLE ALIGN="left">  Developing XML in Java </bk:TITLE>
              <bk:AUTHOR>  Michael C. Daconta    </bk:AUTHOR>
      </bk:BOOK>
</BODY>
</HTML>
```

In this example, the HTML namespace is the default namespace for all tags that do not have a prefix. A namespace can be overridden by another namespace declaration with the same name-space attribute name (either xmlns or xmlns:name). Lastly, the default namespace can be set to the empty string. This has the same effect, within the scope of the declaration, of there being no default namespace.

Parser Support for Namespaces

At the time of this writing, SAX is being extended to incorporate namespace support with a new set of interfaces referred to as *SAX2*. SAX2 will support namespace processing by default. This means that every element and attribute will be reported with a two-part name. The new API for an element is as follows:

```
public void startElement (String uri, String localName,
                                 String rawName, Attributes atts)
        throws SAXException;
```

4

ADVANCED XML

```
public void endElement (String uri, String localName, String rawName)
        throws SAXException;
```

NOTE

At the time of this writing, SAX2 is not widely supported. Go to the URL
`http://www.megginson.com/SAX/` for more information.

The XLink Specification

The popularity of the World Wide Web is directly related to the mass appeal of hypertext links. In fact, a new phrase was coined to describe the process of moving between hyperlinked documents—*Web surfing*. Despite their popularity, current Web links are considered primitive in comparison to other linking specifications like those in the Hypermedia/Time-based Structuring language (HyTime) and the Text Encoding Initiative (TEI) guidelines. The XLink specification takes into account the advances of these predecessors to provide the capability to link XML documents.

NOTE

At the time of this writing, the XLink specification is still a candidate recommendation. The latest specification can be found at `http://www.w3c.org/TR`.

Comparison to HTML Hyperlinks

Hyperlinking has two basic components: linking and addressing. Linking is declaring a relationship between two objects. Addressing is a method for finding an object you want to associate with another object. In HTML, the A tag stands for *anchor*, the term in HTML for a resource. The A element describes a link and its HREF attribute points to the destination resource. The source of the link is the text in the content of the A element. For example:

```
<A HREF="http://java.sun.com"> Java Technology Home </A>
```

An HTML link is analogous to a simple link in XLink. Here is an implementation of a simple link using XLink:

```
<MYLINK  xlink:type="simple"
        xlink:href="http://java.sun.com"> Java Home </MYLINK>
```

All XLink attributes and elements can only be used after you have declared the `xlink` namespace. For example:

```
<MYDOC xmlns:xlink="http://www.w3.org/1999/xlink/namespace/ ">
```

Link Types

A link type can be one of seven values: `"simple"`, `"extended"`, `"locator"`, `"arc"`, `"resource"`, `"title"`, or `"none"`. Before we explain each type, it is important to note that the value of the type attribute may be inferred by the application. In other words, the `xlink:type` attribute may be a `#IMPLIED` attribute whereby the processing application can infer its meaning from the other attributes available. This provides the flexibility for an application to treat an element as a link only under certain circumstances based on the value of other non–link-related attributes.

The definitions for each link type are

- `simple`—A constrained link between two resources that is functionally identical to an HTML A element.
- `extended`—A more powerful type of link that allows one-to-many connections and bidirectional traversal.
- `locator`—Identifies an element that refers to a remote resource that is participating in a link.
- `arc`—For use with an extended link in order to supply traversal, behavior, and semantic attributes for one traversal of the link (for one to-from combination).
- `resource`—For use with an extended link to specify local resources that are participating in the link.
- `title`—Both extended and locator type elements can have multiple human-readable titles by using any number of title type elements. One potential use of this is for internationalization.
- `none`—Denotes the element as a non-XLink element. This allows an element to be conditionally treated as an XLink.

Link Attributes

There are four categories of XLink attributes: locators, arc ends, behavior, and semantics. Locator attributes define where a remote resource is located. Arc ends define the context of a link traversal (like direction). Behavior attributes define how the link is activated and what action should be taken with the resource it refers to. Semantic attributes give additional information about the link. Each category will have one or more attributes. All the attributes discussed later must be prepended with the `xlink` prefix.

There is only a single `Locator` attribute, which is `href`. The value of the `href` attribute must be a valid URI.

There are two arc end attributes: `from` and `to`. The values for both attributes must be an ID in an XML document. The intent of the `from` and `to` attributes are to provide contextual information to the processing application.

There are two attributes for specifying behavior: `show` and `actuate`. In contrast, HTML link (anchor) behavior is hardwired. The HTML link behavior is to activate the link based on a user click and replace the current document with the remote resource. The `show` attribute describes what action occurs when a link is traversed. The `actuate` attribute describes when a link traversal should occur. The `show` attribute may take one of four values: `embed`, `replace`, `new`, or `undefined`. Here are definitions for those four values:

- `embed`—The designated resource should be integrated in the body of the resource at the start of the link.
- `replace`—The designated resource should replace (for the purposes of display or processing) the resource at the start of the link.
- `new`—The designated resource should be displayed in a new window.
- `undefined`—The behavior of the application traversing the link is unconstrained by the XLink specification.

The `actuate` attribute may take one of three values: `onLoad`, `onRequest`, or `undefined`.

- `onLoad`—The link should be traversed automatically as soon as the starting resource is loaded.
- `onRequest`—The link should be traversed only on request (like a click) from the user.
- `undefined`—When the link is traversed is unconstrained by the XLink specification. The application is free to use other cues.

Replace and user are the behaviors we are familiar with in HTML links. For example:

```
<A xlink:type="simple" xlink:show="replace" xlink:actuate="onRequest"

   xlink:href="http://www.mysite.com"> This is my Site! </A>
```

Here is another example that would place the target resource into a separate window:

```
<NEWLINK xlink:type="simple" xlink:show="new" xlink:actuate="onRequest"
xlink:href="http://www.mysite.com"> This is my Site! </NEWLINK>
```

There are attributes associated with semantics: `role` and `title`. The role is a link attribute that allows a free-form description of the purpose of the link. The `title` attribute provides human-readable text describing the link. The title is useful for presentation of the link.

The inline attribute can only have the value "true" or "false." If a link is inline, its contents count as the local resource of the link. An out-of-line link is one that is completely outside the resource it is linking.

There are constraints on where attributes can occur. Table 4.5 shows where attributes can occur by type. The columns are `xlink:types` and the rows represent attributes. An X indicates that the attribute is allowed within an element of that `xlink:type`.

TABLE 4.5   Attribute Placement Constraints

	simple	extended	locator	arc	resource	title
type	X	X	X	X	X	X
href	X		X			
role	X	X	X	X	X	
title	X	X	X	X	X	
show	X	X		X		
actuate	X	X		X		
from				X		
to				X		

Extended Links

An extended link is more powerful than a simple link and has these features:

- Can connect any number of resources
- Can create links to and from documents from outside the documents they are linking (create them out-of-line)

In order to create multi-ended links, an extended link separates the source from the targets of the link by using two subelement types: locator and arc. Here is an example of an extended link:

```
<TOPPICK  xlink:type="extended">
  <book xlink:type = "locator" xlink:href="book1.html" xlink:role="original" />
```

```
<book xlink:type = "locator" xlink:href="book2.html" xlink:role="sequel" />
<magazine xlink:type = "locator"  xlink:href="article.html"
          xlink:role="review" />
</TOPPICK>
```

Locator type elements can also have title, show, and actuate attributes. Locators are very similar to simple links. You can add attribute value defaults to the DTD to reduce the number of xlink attributes needed for a particular element.

When referring to resources, XML links can use XPointers, which are URIs that can refer inside an XML document. XPointers are discussed in the next section.

The XPointer Specification

XPointer is a complex specification for addressing into the internal structures of XML documents. In XLink, the resource can be referred to by a Uniform Resource Identifier (URI). A URI is a URL followed by an optional query and then an optional fragment identifier. XPointers are fragment identifiers that can be used in conjunction with a URL.

> **NOTE**
>
> At the time of this writing, the XPointer specification is a candidate recommendation. The latest specification can be found at http://www.w3c.org/TR.

XPointers operate on the tree structure defined by the elements and markup of an XML document. From the discussion of the Document Object Model in Chapter 3, you should know that an XML document contains seven types of nodes: root nodes, element nodes, text nodes, attribute nodes, namespace nodes, processing instruction nodes, and comment nodes. The purpose of an XPointer is to refer to a particular portion of this tree, sometimes in relation to another part. In general, XPointers select a portion of the tree with axes and predicates. An axis selects a node or group of nodes in an XML document. A predicate tests either the selected nodes or nodes relative to the selected nodes. The XPointer specification builds on another specification, called XPath, that is a common syntax used by both XPointer and the extensible stylesheet language transformation (XSLT) specification, which is discussed in Chapter 5, "Java and the Extensible Stylesheet Language (XSL)."

XPath

XPath defines a language for creating expressions that operate on an XML document tree. The most important type of expressions are location paths. There are two types of location paths:

absolute and relative. A location path consists of a set of location steps separated by a /. A location step has three parts: an axis, a node-test, and zero or more predicates. Here is an example of an absolute location path that selects the chapter child (or children) with a title attribute that has the value `Introduction`:

```
xpointer(/child::chapter[attribute::title='Introduction'])
```

In the example, the / is the absolute location for the root of the document. The term `child` is the axis. The double colon (`::`) separates the axis from the node-test. The node-test is the term `chapter`. The predicate is enclosed in quotes. For absolute location path, XPath provides / for the root and `id("name")` to locate a specific element with a unique ID.

Here is another example:

```
/descendant::para
```

This location path selects all the `para` elements in the document. In this example, `descendant` is the axis and `para` is the node-test.

An axis works in respect to a context node. A context node is defined either by an absolute location or a previous relative location step. The following keywords are the available axes:

- `child`—Identifies a child node of the context node.
- `descendant`—Nodes appearing anywhere in the content of the context node.
- `parent`—Identifies a parent node of the context node.
- `ancestor`—Element nodes containing the context node.
- `preceding`—Nodes before the location source.
- `following`—Nodes after the location source.
- `preceding-sibling`—Identifies sibling nodes sharing their parent with the location source that appears before the location source.
- `following-sibling`—Identifies sibling nodes sharing their parent with the location source that appears after the location source.
- `attribute`—Attributes of the context node.
- `namespace`—Namespaces of the context node.
- `self`—The context node.
- `namespace`—Contains the namespace nodes of the context node; the axis will be empty unless the context node is an element.
- `descendant-or-self`—Contains the context node and the descendants of the context node.
- `ancestor-or-self`—Contains the context node and the ancestors of the context node; thus, the ancestor axis will always include the root node.

4

ADVANCED XML

An axis is either a forward axis or a backward axis. If the axis produces the context node and nodes after it then it is a forward axis. If the axis produces the context nodes and nodes before it (higher in the tree) then it is a backward axis.

A node-test filters nodes from an axis if those nodes do not meet certain criteria. Here are the possible node-tests:

- A qualified name—This will filter nodes if they exactly match the name. For example, `child::para` will return all the `para` elements that are children of the current node. The qualified name may include a namespace.
- One of three type tests: `comment()`, `text()`, and `processing-instruction()`—These tests return the node if it matches the type.
- An asterisk `(*)`—This is a wildcard that returns all nodes in the axis.
- An asterisk as the `localpart` of a fully qualified name—For example `child::bk:*` will return all the child elements that are part of the `bk` namespace.

A predicate filters a node-set with respect to an axis to refine the selection. Predicates evaluate to a Boolean value (true or false). There is a core function library that can be used in predicates. Table 4.6 presents the available functions in the core function library.

TABLE 4.6 XPath Core Function Library

Function Prototype	*Description*
number *last*()	Returns a number equal to the context size.
number *position*()	Returns a number equal to the context position.
number *count*(node-set)	Returns the number of nodes in the node-set argument.
node-set *id*(object)	Selects elements by their unique ID.
string *local-name* (node-set?)	Returns the local part of an expanded name.
string *namespace-uri* (node-set?)	Returns the namespace part of an expanded name.
string *name*(node-set?)	Returns the qualified name of the first node in the node-set.
string *string*(object?)	Converts an object to a string.
string *concat* (string, string, string*)	Returns the concatenation of its arguments.
boolean *starts-with* (string, string)	Returns true if the first argument string starts with the second argument string.

TABLE 4.6   Continued

Function Prototype	Description
boolean *contains* (string, string)	Returns true if the first argument string contains the second argument string.
string *substring-before* (string, string)	Returns the substring of the first argument string that precedes the first occurrence of the second argument string.
string *substring-after* (string, string)	Returns the substring of the first argument string that follows the first occurrence of the second argument string.
string *substring* (string, number, number?)	Returns the substring of the first argument starting at the position of the second argument for the length of the third argument.
number *string-length* (string?)	Returns the number of characters in the string.
string *normalize-space* (string?)	Returns the argument with leading and trailing whitespace removed and sequences of whitespace replaced by a single space.
string *translate* (string, string, string)	Returns the first argument string with occurrences of the second argument string replaced with the third argument string.
boolean *boolean*(object)	Converts its argument to a Boolean.
boolean not(boolean)	Returns the negation of its argument.
boolean *true*()	Returns true.
boolean *false*()	Returns false.
boolean *lang*(string)	Returns true if the argument matches the current value of xml:lang.
number *number*(object?)	Converts its argument to a number.
number *sum*(node-set)	The sum of the node-set calculated by converting the string values of the node to a number.
number *floor*(number)	Returns the largest integer not greater than the number.
number *ceiling*(number)	Returns the integer not less than the argument.
number *round*(number)	Returns the number that is closest to the argument and that is an integer.

4

ADVANCED XML

Let's examine a complete example:

```
<!DOCTYPE  SCREENPLAY [
<!ELEMENT  LINES  (#PCDATA | SPEAKER  |  DIRECTOR)* >
<!ATTLIST  SCREENPLAY
           ID            ID  #IMPLIED>
<!ELEMENT  SPEAKER  (#PCDATA) >
<!ELEMENT  DIRECTOR (#PCDATA)> ]>
<SCREENPLAY  ID="Miller1">
  <SPEAKER> Linda </SPEAKER>
  You didn't crash the car, did you?
  <DIRECTOR> Willy looks irritated. </DIRECTOR>
  <SPEAKER> Willy </SPEAKER>
  I said nothing happened. Didn't you hear me?
</SCREENPLAY>
```

Now, let's create some XPointers in this document.

```
xpointer(id('Miller1')/child::SPEAKER[position() = 2])
    selects the 2nd "SPEAKER" element whose content is "Willy"

xpointer(id('Miller1')/child::text()[position() = 2])
    selects the second child  text element which
          is "I said nothing happened".
```

XML Schemas

There are two parts to the XML Schema specification: Structures and Data Types. The Structures specification describes a replacement syntax for describing XML documents to a finer granularity than is possible with a document type definition (DTD—the current method standardized with the XML 1.0 recommendation). The Data Types specification defines primitive data types that can be used in XML schema and other XML specifications like XSL and RDF.

NOTE

At the time of this writing, the XML Schema specification is still a working draft. The latest specification can be found at http://www.w3c.org/TR.

The purpose of an XML Schema is to define and describe a class of XML documents by using XML-compliant markup to constrain and document the meaning, usage, and relationships of the document's datatypes; elements and their content; attributes and their values; entities and their contents; and notations.

The XML Schema:Structures formalism will allow a useful level of constraint checking to be described and validated for a wide spectrum of XML applications.

XML Schema:Structures has a dependency on the data typing mechanisms defined in its companion document, XML Schemas:Datatypes, published simultaneously.

These are key definitions in the specification:

- *Instance*—An XML document whose structure conforms to some schema. Documents are associated with the schema to which they conform.

- *Schema*—A set of rules for constraining the structure and articulating the information set of XML documents.

Schema Structures

The key idea behind XML Schema is to define the vocabulary and content model of a markup language using the rules of XML. The basic features of XML Schema are listed in Table 4.7.

TABLE 4.7   XML Schema Features

Feature	Definition
Schema	All definitions and declarations are contained within a Schema element. Uses `<schema ...> </schema>`.
Simple Type Definition	The mechanisms for typing character data for either attribute values or element contents. Rules for this are specified in XML Schemas:Datatypes specification.
Complex Type Definition	A complete set of constraints for elements in a document. Uses `<type> </type>`.
Element Type Declaration	Associates an element name with a type. Uses `<element ...> </element>`.
Attribute Declaration	Associates an attribute name and a data type. Uses `<attribute ...> </attribute>`.
Content Type	Either a simple type or a content model.
Element Content Model	A type that constrains the contents of an element. Has specifications for sequences and grouping.
Attribute Group Definition	Ability to group a set of attributes under a name for reusability.
Deriving Type Definitions	A type may be based on another type and acquire content type and attributes from the other type.

4

TABLE 4.7   Continued

Feature	Definition
References to Schema Components Across Namespaces	Integrates definitions and declarations defined elsewhere into the schema as if they were defined/declared locally.
Unique Key and Key Reference Constraints	Provides powerful uniqueness and intradocument reference mechanisms.

Schema Datatypes

XML 1.0 does not provide any facility for rigorous type checking of data elements in an XML-compliant document. This specification defines standard data types for constraining values in element content and attributes' values.

The current specification concerns itself with scalar datatypes. A scalar is a single constrained value (formally, a value described in its entirety by magnitude).

Future versions of this specification will also cover aggregate data types like sets and bags (collections).

In this specification, a datatype has a set of distinct values, called its value space, and is characterized by facets or properties of those values and by operations on or resulting in those values. Further, each datatype is characterized by a space consisting of valid lexical representations for each value in the value space. A value space is an abstract collection of permitted values for the datatype. The lexical space for a datatype consists of a set of valid literals. Each value in the datatype's value space maps to one or more valid literals in its lexical space.

Datatypes can be broken down into several dichotomies. The first of these is atomic versus aggregate:

- *Atomic* datatypes are those having values that are intrinsically indivisible.
- *Aggregate* datatypes are those having values that can be decomposed into two or more component values.

Next is primitive versus generated:

- *Primitive* datatypes are those that are not defined in terms of other datatypes.
- *Generated* datatypes are those that are defined in terms of other datatypes.

Finally, built-in versus user-generated:

- *Built-in* datatypes are those that are entirely defined in the XML Schemas:Datatypes specification and can be either primitive or generated.
- *User-generated* datatypes are those generated datatypes whose base types are built-in datatypes or user-generated datatypes and are defined by individual schema designers by giving values to constraining facets.

Table 4.8 shows a description of primitive and generated datatypes.

TABLE 4.8   Primitive and Generated Datatypes

Datatype	Description
string	UCS characters of some specified length.
boolean	A binary-state value.
binary	Sequence of bytes.
uriReference	A uniform resource locator.
language	Represents natural language identifiers as defined by RFC 1766
ID	From XML 1.0 spec.
IDREF	From XML 1.0 spec.
IDREFS	From XML 1.0 spec.
ENTITY	From XML 1.0 spec.
ENTITIES	From XML 1.0 spec.
NMTOKEN	From XML 1.0 spec.
NMTOKENS	From XML 1.0 spec.
NOTATION	From XML 1.0 spec.
name	An XML name as defined by the XML 1.0 spec.
QName	A qualified XML name as defined by the XML Namespace recommendation.
NCName	NCName represents XML "non-colonized" names as defined by the XML Namespace recommendation.
integer	Whole numbers.
PositiveInteger	Derived from nonNegativeInteger by fixing the value of minInclusive to be 1.
nonPositiveInteger	Negative integers where the value of maxInclusive is fixed at 0.
negativeInteger	Negative integers where the value of maxInclusive is −1.
nonNegativeInteger	Derived from integer by fixing the value of minInclusive to be 0.

4

ADVANCED XML

TABLE 4.8   Continued

Datatype	Description
long	`long` is derived from `integer` by fixing the values of `maxInclusive` to be 9223372036854775807 and `minInclusive` to be –9223372036854775808.
int	`int` is derived from `long` by fixing the values of `maxInclusive` to be 2147483647 and `minInclusive` to be –2147483648.
short	`short` is derived from `int` by fixing the values of `maxInclusive` to be 32767 and `minInclusive` to be –32768.
byte	`byte` is derived from `short` by fixing the values of `maxInclusive` to be 127 and `minInclusive` to be –128.
unsignedLong	Derived from `nonNegativeInteger` by fixing the values of `maxInclusive` to be 18446744073709551615.
unsignedInt	Derived from `unsignedLong` by fixing the values of `maxInclusive` to be 4294967295.
unsignedShort	Derived from `unsignedInt` by fixing the value `maxInclusive` to be 65535.
unsignedByte	Derived from `unsignedShort` by fixing the value `maxInclusive` to be 255.
decimal	Numbers with an exact fractional part.
real	Floating-point numbers expressed with a mantissa and an exponent.
float	IEEE single-precision 32-bit floating point type.
double	IEEE double-precision 64-bit floating point type.
date	Date as a string as defined in ISO 8601.
month	A `timePeriod` that starts at midnight on the first day of the month and lasts until the midnight that ends the last day of the month.
year	A `timePeriod` that starts at the midnight that starts the first day of the year and ends at the midnight that ends the last day of the year.
century	A `timePeriod` that starts at the midnight that starts the first day of the century and ends at the midnight that ends that last day of the century.
time	Time as a string as defined in ISO 8601.
timeInstant	Represents a specific instant of time.
timePeriod	A period of time as a string as defined in ISO 8601.

TABLE 4.8   Continued

Datatype	Description
timeDuration	Represents a duration of time as defined in ISO 8601.
recurringDay	A specific day that recurs within a specific timeDuration.
recurringDate	A specific date that recurs.

Strings can be constrained using either picture elements (from COBOL) or regular expressions.

A Sample Schema

To demonstrate and compare schemas in relation to DTDs, I present a schema for our Address Book Markup Language (ABML) that we created a DTD for in Chapter 1:

```
<schema targetNameSpace="http://www.gosynergy.com/abml"
        xmlns = "http://www.w3.org/TR/1999/WD-xmlschema-1-19991217"
    xmlns:abml = "http://www.gosynergy.com/abml" >

<element name="ADDRESS_BOOK" type = "ADDRESS_BOOK_TYPE" />

<type name="ADDRESS_BOOK_TYPE">
    <element name="ADDRESS" type="ADDRESS_BOOK_TYPE" minOccurs="1"
            maxOccurs="*" />
</type>

<type name="ADDRESS_TYPE" >
    <element name="NAME" type="string" />
    <element name="STREET" type="string" />
    <element name="CITY" type="string" />
    <element name="STATE" type="string" />
    <element name="ZIP" type="string" />
</type>
</schema>
```

Summary

This chapter covered a lot of ground. Some of the specifications discussed are completed and others are still works in progress. The five primary categories discussed were advanced markup, namespaces, XLink, XPointer, and XML Schemas.

The advanced markup section covered all the areas of the XML 1.0 specification left out in Chapter 1. Here is a brief description of the topics covered in this section:

- Character references enable you to represent any Unicode character in your XML document.

4

ADVANCED XML

- Entities allow you to abbreviate some replacement data and refer to that data via an entity reference. There are several categories of references to include general, parameter, internal, external, parsed, and unparsed.

- All attributes are typed in order to constrain the values that may be assigned to them. The legal attribute types (in a DTD) are CDATA, Enumeration, NOTATION, ID, IDREF, IDREFS, ENTITY, ENTITIES, NMTOKEN, and NMTOKENS.

- Attribute values are normalized before being passed on to the processing application.

- The xml:space attribute can be attached to any element to determine how whitespace should be handled.

- Element content specifications describe how subelements may be nested. We discussed the ANY and mixed content models.

- CDATA sections allow you to pass raw text (even XML) on to your processing application without it being treated as XML.

- A processing instruction may be used to pass additional information on to one specific application.

- The standalone document declaration is used to signify whether the XML processor is required to fetch the DTD.

Namespaces are a W3C recommendation to create element and attribute names that are globally unique. A unique name is created by separating an XML name into two parts: a prefix and a local part. The prefix is further mapped to a URI.

The XLink specification defines how to create links in XML documents. Links are created via attributes in the XLink namespace. XLink defines two types of links: simple and extended.

The XPointer and XPath specifications define a syntax to refer to a specific element or set of elements inside of an XML document. XPointers use location path expressions. A location path is a series of location steps separated by a /.

XML Schemas define a new syntax for describing the structure and datatypes of a class of XML documents. Unlike DTDs, XML Schemas are a markup language that conforms to XML syntax. XML Schemas also have a larger set of built-in datatypes than DTDs to include float, int, date, and uriReference.

Suggested for Further Study

1. Create a DTD for a Bookmark List Markup Language (BLML). A bookmark list can contain folder elements and bookmarks. A folder element should have a name attribute. A bookmark element must have the following information associated with it: name, URI, and comment. The DTD must use the following entities:

    a. A general entity (that is, an abbreviation for your full name as the author of the comments).

    b. A parameter entity (that is, the name attribute is common between the folder and the bookmark elements).

2. Here's a suggestion for an advanced DTD study. Define an element called STUFF with the following constraints:

- The element can have A, B, and C subelements.

- The element must have at least one of those subelements.

- The element cannot have any duplicates. For example, if you have an A, you cannot have a second A.

(HINT: a good solution will use only three particles.)

3. Add a namespace to your BLML DTD and in an instance of a BLML document.

4. Create a schema for the Bookmark List Markup Language.

Further Reading

XML Specification Guide. Ian S. Graham and Liam Quin. 1999, John Wiley & Sons, Inc. This book is an authoritative reference that explains every line of the XML specification in detail.

XML Unleashed. Michael Morrison. 1999, Sams Publishing. This book covers XML technology broadly, including DTDs, XSL, and XPointers, and manipulating XML with Java and JavaScript. The book includes XML applications involving e-commerce, database access, Web management, real estate, and healthcare as well as reference material on SMIL, the XML-based language for Web multimedia.

4

ADVANCED XML

Java and the Extensible Stylesheet Language (XSL)

"XSL is a language for expressing stylesheets."

> —W3C, Extensible Stylesheet Language (XSL)

"XSLT is a language for transforming XML documents into other XML documents."

> —W3C, XSLT Transformations (XSLT) Version 1.0 Specification

IN THIS CHAPTER

The XSL Language

Extensible Stylesheet Language (XSL) is actually two languages in one (three if we include XPath!). First, XSL is a *transformation* language. XSL Transforms, more commonly called XSLT and using the `xsl:` namespace, defines how an XML Stylesheet is applied to an XML document to transform one XML document into another. The second thing that XSL provides is *formatting*. Formatting Objects, using the `fo:` namespace, define how a document is rendered or *formatted* for display and is normally the second step when applying a stylesheet. Finally, XSL is XPath. XPath is a rather recent addition to XML and is used in both XPointer and XSLT. As we shall see, XSLT extends XPath in certain useful ways. XPath is actually a rather simple expression language, but don't confuse simplicity with lack of power. While XPath is simple, it is also quite powerful!

The XSLT Specification and the W3C Recommendation Process

As of this writing, the XSLT specification was about to be accepted as a recommendation (the final stage in the W3C standards process). Several implementations of XSLT are currently available, with James Clark's XT being exceptionally close to the final specification. Most examples, with differences noted, were developed with XT. However, because the XSLT specification was not yet accepted, some minor changes may be required. XSL Formatting objects, on the other hand, were still changing rapidly and no implementations of formatting object currently exist.

The XSL language is actually composed of two parts, translation and formatting. Each of these processes happens sequentially—first transformation and then formatting. The XSLT Translation specification details the underlying template rules for translating one XML Document to another, and the XSL specification itself contains the definition of XSL Formatting Objects for transmogrifying the result tree into output formatted for display or some other rendering. Figure 5.1 shows how an XML document is processed using XSL. If we remember back to Chapter 4, "Advanced XML," we saw that XML documents are actually represented as trees. What XSLT provides is a mechanism to translate from one XML tree to another. Early versions of the specification required that both the input tree and the output tree be well-formed XML (readers will also remember that HTML can be completely well formed although not always strictly enforced). However, the current version of the specification, and the form most likely to become a recommendation, allows for arbitrary output via `xsl:text`, removing the requirement that both input and output be XML.

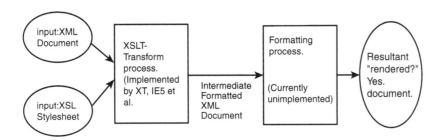

FIGURE 5.1
The XSL process applied.

Why XSL at All?

Many detractors of XSL basically ask the question, "Why XSL at all?" The question is actually a good one; we have CSS Level 2 after all. Why not apply CSS stylesheets to XML documents and be done with it?

The biggest reason is XSL itself. CSS was designed with HTML in mind and supports HTML well. XML is more powerful, in general, than HTML, and XSL is more powerful than CSS, allowing operation on not just whole elements but portions of elements alone (attributes, for example). XSL excels beyond CSS in other ways as well. While CSS targets HTML, XSL supports other output formats such as print. For these and other reasons, XSL is an important part of XML!

The Format of a Stylesheet

Listing 5.1 shows a simple XSL stylesheet. Let's examine it and break it down line by line before moving on to examine each of the features of XSL.

LISTING 5.1 `catalog-simple.xsl`—A Simple Stylesheet

```
1: <?xml version="1.0"?>
2: <!--
3: A simple style sheet for placing a header and footer on any document.
4:    Al Saganich for Macmillan USA
5: -->
6:
7: <!-- Use the transform version 1.0 namespace -->
8:<xsl:stylesheet
```

LISTING 5.1   Continued

```
 9:xmlns:xsl="http://www.w3.org/XSL/Transform/1.0"
10: indent-result="no" default-space="strip">
11:<!-- <xsl:output method="text"> -->
12: <!--
13: Format for transforms are match rule followed by action.
14: This transform matches the root element
15: Prints [header] followed by a cr-lf pair
16:
17: Then the contents of the document
18:
19: followed by [trailer]
20: -->
21: <xsl:template match="/">
22: <xsl:text>[heading]&#xD;&#xA;</xsl:text>
23: <xsl:apply-templates />
24: <xsl:text>[trailer]</xsl:text>
25: </xsl:template>
26: </xsl:stylesheet>
27:
```

Examining Listing 5.1, we see the standard XML prolog as well as a number of comments. The first lines of note are actually lines 8 and 9, which state that this is, in fact, an XSL stylesheet and is specified using the XSL namespace (refer to the section, "The FO Namespace," in this chapter). Remember that the XSL namespace is never accessed as a real URI and may in fact not point to anything useful at all. Namespaces are simply a method of specifying the input and/or output of the XSL transformations. An XSL transform will never attempt to access the URI's namepaces. Line 11, even though it's commented out, specifies the output method for this stylesheet, in this case `text`. Lines 12–20 describe the expected result of applying the stylesheet to an appropriate document. Lines 21 through 26 are the real meat of the stylesheet and bear more serious review.

`xsl:output` and `xsl:strip-space`

The most recent version of the XSLT specification replaces the `result-ns`, `result-version`, `result-encoding`, and `indent-result` attributes of the `xsl:stylsheet` with `xsl:output` and `xsl:strip-space`. However, the version of XT shipped with the CD-ROM only supports these attributes, so all examples use the older mechanism. Many of the examples in Chapter 7, "Swing and XML," contain the newer code, albeit commented out.

XSL is actually specified via XML. Appendix A, "XML Tools," contains the complete non-normative description of XSL. As such, XSL is normally thought of in general terms as XML in that it has elements, nodes, attributes, and so on. The `xsl:stylesheet` element, which is the root of the XSL Stylesheet XML tree, can have eleven child elements. We will examine each in turn. Table 5.1 briefly describes each and its purpose.

TABLE 5.1   XSL Top-Level Elements

Element	Description
`xsl:import`	Import another stylesheet into the current one. Rules from the stylesheet to be imported are always of lower precedence than the rules specified in the parent stylesheet.
`xsl:include`	Include another stylesheet into the current one. Performs exactly as if the import statement was replaced character for character with the included stylesheet.
`xsl:strip-space`	Defines whether whitespace is stripped and for what elements based on the `elements=` attribute. Top level may be specified 0 to *n* times.
`xsl:preserve-space`	Defines whether whitespace is preserved and for what elements based on the `elements=` attribute. Top level may be specified 0 to *n* times.
`xsl:output`	Defines the output method. Supported values for the `method=` attribute are `html`, `text`, `xml` (default). Top level may be specified.
`xsl:key`	Defines a way to work with documents that contain an implicit reference structure. Keys can be used to generate tables of hyperlinks and so on.
`xsl:locale`	Defines a locale that controls how certain number formatting is applied (decimal, comma usage, percent, trailing zeros, and so on).
`xsl:attribute-set`	Allows for the definition of attribute sets, which are named groups of attributes that can later be used as a whole.
`xsl:variable`	Allows the developer to specify variables that can be used within a stylesheet either directly or within expressions.
`xsl:param`	Similar to `xsl:variable`. Can be used to pass variables to named templates.
`xsl:template`	Defines the template construction rules for translating one XML document to another.

5

JAVA AND XSL

CAUTION

Note that with the exception of xsl:import, the order in which top-level attributes are specified is arbitrary. xsl:import must precede all other top-level XSL elements or an error will occur.

Working with the `xsl:template`

xsl:template is perhaps the most important top-level element in an xsl stylesheet. While all the other elements add to a stylesheet, xsl:template is its heart and soul.

NOTE

The remaining sections in this chapter all use the XML Document defined in Listing 5.2 unless otherwise noted.

Figure 5.2 shows a graphical representation of Listing 5.2. Examining Figure 5.2, we see that its root contains two elements—the REListing element and the xsl-stylesheet processing instruction. Don't forget that the root of the document is not the same as the root element. The document root contains the stylesheet element and the root element. The root element, in our case the REListing element, contains all the document's children. Specifically, the REListing element contains a Header, a Trailer (both optional), a State, and some number of County elements. Each County element contains some number of Town elements. And Towns contain some number of, among other things, Listing elements. At the bottom of the hierarchy, Listings contain a number of data items representing each listing such as Price, Address, and other information important to real estate.

To use XSL, one must understand how XSL Transformations function. XSL Transformations work by applying one or more template rules to an XML document. Template rules then work by looking for matches on XML elements and then exercising the remainder of the rule on the matching element or elements in the order encountered. If many elements match the rule, the rule is applied to each in the order it appears. In addition, a template rule might contain instructions to continue to match on children of the current element. In this way, XSL Transforms work sequentially throughout a document (although as we will see later they can be applied other ways) and recursively through the children of an element.

All `xsl:template` rules follow the pattern

```
<xsl:template match="some match criteria">
    Some replacement text and/or additional rules
</xsl:template>
```

The simplest `xsl:template` rule, one that causes all data in an XML document to be ignored, can be written as follows:

```
<xsl:template match="/|*"/>
```

Simply stated, match any document or any text, and do nothing.

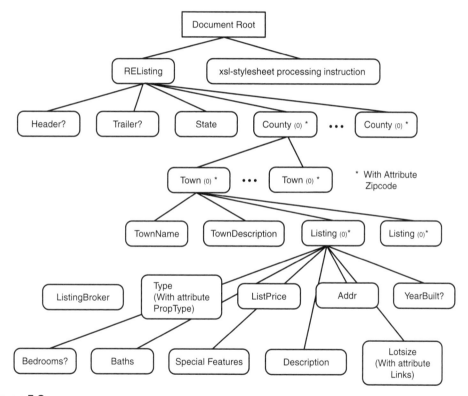

FIGURE 5.2

A graphical representation of the XML document in Listing 5.2.

Specifically, each xsl:template rule contains match criteria as well as replacement text and/or more rules. For example, we can easily imagine an XSL stylesheet that translates book text into HTML. We might want to replace each instance of the tag <chapter> with <H1>Chapter</H1>. We could do this easily with the following xsl:template rule:

```
<xsl:template match="chapter">
<H1>Chapter</H1>
</xsl:template>
```

Of course, this is not a very useful rule. What we are more likely to want to do is insert the chapter tag's *value* along with some text. The following rule does just that for our real estate listings. Each time a Listing element is encountered, we prefix it with the <H1> and then the word *Listing* and finally the contents of the listing itself using xsl:value-of (more on this element of XSL shortly) followed by </H1>.

```
<xsl:template match="Listing">
<H1>Listing: <xsl:value-of select="."/></H1>
</xsl:template>
```

LISTING 5.2   REListing.xml—An XML Document Representing Real Estate Listings

```
<?xml version="1.0" encoding="UTF-8" ?>
<!--
A XML Document representing real estate listing
Al Saganich for Macmillan USA
-->

<!DOCTYPE REListing [
<!ELEMENT REListing (Header,State,County*,Trailer?)>
<!ELEMENT Header (#PCDATA)>
<!ELEMENT State (#PCDATA)>
<!ELEMENT Trailer (#PCDATA)>
<!ELEMENT County (Town*)>
<!ATTLIST County
Name CDATA #REQUIRED
Description CDATA #REQUIRED>
<!ELEMENT Town (TownName, TownDescription, Listing*)>
<!ATTLIST Town Zipcode CDATA "Unknown">
<!ELEMENT TaxRate (#PCDATA)>
<!ELEMENT TownName (#PCDATA)>
<!ELEMENT TownDescription (#PCDATA)>
<!ELEMENT Listing (ListingBroker, Type, ListPrice,Addr,
      YearBuilt?,Bedrooms?, Baths?, SpecialFeatures?, Lotsize,Description)>
<!ELEMENT ListingBroker (#PCDATA)>
<!ELEMENT Type (#PCDATA)>
<!ATTLIST Type
```

LISTING 5.2   Continued

```
PropType CDATA #REQUIRED
PropType (residential|commercial|land|farm|other) "residential">
<!ELEMENT Addr (#PCDATA) >
<!ELEMENT YearBuilt (#PCDATA)>
<!ELEMENT Bedrooms (#PCDATA)>
<!ELEMENT Baths (#PCDATA)>
<!ELEMENT SpecialFeatures (#PCDATA)>
<!ELEMENT Lotsize (#PCDATA)>
<!ATTLIST Lotsize Units (acres|sq.feet) "sq.feet">
]>


<REListing>
<Header>Real Estate Listings for Middlesex and Worchester Counties</Header>
<State>Massachusetts</State>
<County Name="Worchester" Desc="A wondeful county in Central Massachusetts">
<Town>
<Name Zipcode="01464">Shirley</Name>
<TaxRate>14.86</TaxRate>
<TownDescription>A small rural town of approximately 7000
. . .   <!--
Note that the complete contents of listing 5.2 can be found
In the chp7 subdirectory of the CDRom as REListing.xml
        -->
. . .
<Listing>
<ListingBroker>Successful Home Sellers</ListingBroker>
<Type PropType="land">Land</Type>
<ListingPrice>1,249,999</ListingPrice>
<Addr>Groton Country Wood Road</Addr>
<SpecialFeatures>Open farm land</SpecialFeatures>
<Lotsize Units="acres">25</Lotsize>
<Description>A wonderful site ready for the right developer!</Description>
</Listing>
</Town>
</County>
</REListing>
```

Templates Are Recursive

One of the more important concepts to understand about XML is that it is recursive in nature. `xsl:template` rules are for the most part also recursive via the `xsl:apply-templates` element. What exactly does `xsl:apply-templates` do? Well, most times XML data is represented as a hierarchy of data within data. We saw in Figure 5.2 that Countys contained Towns, Towns contained Listings, and Listings contained a number of data items. Earlier, we showed a simple example (which can be found on the CD-ROM as `re-listing.xsl`) that manipulated `Listings`. But suppose we wanted to manipulate `Towns` rather than `Listings`? A rule such as the following appears to do the trick:

```
<xsl:template match="Town">
<h1>Town: <xsl:value-of select ="."/></h1>
</xsl:template>
```

However, what this rule really does is bracket `Towns` and all their underlying data elements in `<h1>...</h1>`. Perhaps what we really wanted was to bracket only the town name and then apply other template rules to each `Listing` child.

The following rule does the trick but does a little more as well, thanks to the default rules, which we'll see more of in a moment.

```
<xsl:template match="Town">
    <h1><xsl:value-of select="TownName"/> </h1>
    <xsl:apply-templates match="Listing"/>
 </xsl:template>
```

Default Rules

As I stated a moment ago the previous rule produced "a little more as well." Well, that "little more" came from the default rules. At first glance, default rules seem to be more of an inconvenience than anything else, causing output we didn't expect or want. However, if we look closely, we can see that it would be much more of an inconvenience to specify a rule for every single element within an XML document! There are two default rules within XSL that output something. They are

```
<xsl:template match="*|/">
    <xsl:apply-templates/>
<xsl:template>
```

which applies to any element or the root element and simply applies all other templates to it.

```
<xsl:template match="text()|@*")>
    <xsl:value-of select="."/>
</xsl:template>
```

which matches any text element or any attribute and outputs its contents.

There are other default rules as well. The following default rule matches processing instructions and comments and outputs nothing:

```
<xsl:template match="processing-instruction()|comment()"/>
```

We could easily override this rule to produce comments and processing instructions as follows:

```
<xsl:template match="processing-instruction()|comment()">
    <xsl:value-of select="."/>
</xsl:template>
```

One interesting note about these two rules is their order of application or *precedence*. Rule precedence defines which rule will be applied if two rules match a given input pattern. The default rules are of lowest precedence, treated as if they were the last rules encountered via xsl:import, and are overridden by any other rule with the same matching criteria. We will provide more examples of precedence in detail in the section "Precedence for Rules" later in this chapter.

We've now seen a few examples of XSL and how we can use it. Before we move on, let's see how we would actually attach a stylesheet to an XML document.

Working with `xsl:output`

There are two things we need to consider when generating output from our XML Document. The first is how the output is generated (what tool does the work), and the second is the format of the output. Of course, all XSL transformations produce some sort of output. XSLT would be of dubious worth otherwise. Control over the output format is provided via the xsl:output element. xsl:output is a topmost element within an XSL stylesheet and is responsible for how the output of the stylesheet is actually formatted. xsl:output has a number of attributes, but one of the most important is the method attribute. The method attribute must contain one of three values: xml, html, or text. For example

```
<xsl:output method="html"/>
```

specifies that the XSL transform will produce well-formed HTML. In addition, the method attribute, if it matches a namespace, is expanded into that namespace on output.

The following stylesheet fragment

```
<?xml version="1.0"?>
<xsl:stylesheet
    xmlns:xsl="http://www.w3.org/XSL/Transform/1.0"
    xmlns="http://www.w3.org/TR/REC-html40">
<xsl:output method="html"/>
```

when applied to an XML document, might produce

```
<html xmlns="http://www.w3.org/TR/REC-html40">...
```

Table 5.2 lists the most common attributes of xsl:output.

TABLE 5.2   Attributes of xsl:output

Attribute	Description
version=	The version of the output method. Combines with, for example, version="4.0".
indent=(yes|no)	Defines whether the processor can add additional whitespace to the output.
media-type	Specifies the output media type. Note that output types must be MIME compliant. Only applicable to method="text". One example might be media-type="text/plain".
standalone=(yes|no)	Specifies whether the result will be a standalone document or not.
xml-declaration=(yes|no)	Specifies whether the transform should output an XML declaration.
cdata-section-elements	Specifies elements that should be output as CDATA sections.

It should be noted that multiple xsl:output statements, either via one stylesheet or through multiple stylesheets included or embedded, are logically merged together into a simple xsl:output element.

In general, the xsl:output statement allows the developer to state exactly what he or she expects the output to look like, and the XSL processor would then take this information into account when generating the result. For example, HTML supports the tag <br> that results in a paragraph or hard break in a document. Any rule that resulted in
</br> or </br> could be output simply as <br> because HTML supports it. Likewise, escaping and/or implicit conversion to CDATA sections may also be implied. Again, using HTML as a guide, an output result containing a well-known entity, such as &lt, should normally be output as < rather then [CDATA [<]]. In a similar fashion, method="text" results in nothing being escaped at all.

Multiple xsl:output statements come in handy when processing elements that can be interpreted as, perhaps, JavaScript, or if we knew that every element of a certain type should be output as CDATA. In our earlier example, if we wanted all <County> elements to be encased as CDATA sections, we could write the following:

```
<xsl:output cdata-section-elements="County"/>
```

As a result, elements found with contents such as &lt, for example

```
<County>Middlesex County, a county with &lt 10000 people</County>
```

would generate something to the effect of

```
<!CDATA[Middlesex County, a county with < 10000 people]>
```

> **disable-output-escaping="yes"**
>
> For XML output, output escaping can be disabled for specific text elements written to the result tree. For example, `<xsl:text>` *something to be output* `&lt</xsl:text>` would normally result in *something to be output &lt* being written to preserve the entity less-than. However, the same rule with output escaping disabled would result in *something to be output* < being output; note the replacement of *&lt* with <. In this fashion, a fine grain of control can be established where required, perhaps to correctly generate script or other elements of HTML.

With output formatting in mind, let's move on to output generation!

Using XSL Processors

To use an XSL stylesheet, we need a way to associate the stylesheet with a document. The W3C provides a single method for this—the `xml:stylesheet` processing instruction. As we shall see shortly, `xml:stylesheet` allows you to embed into your XML document the URI of its associated stylesheet. However, especially in the case of Java servlets, ASP, and similar technologies, we also would like other mechanisms for associating a stylesheet with a document. XT, LotusXSL, MSIE 5.0, and other XSL-enabled applications allow for specifically associating, at runtime, a stylesheet with a given XML document. Each has its own benefits and drawbacks. Let's look at the standard first—embedding a reference to a stylesheet within an XML document.

Using `xml:stylesheet`

The W3C defines the `xml:stylesheet` processing instruction to associate a stylesheet with an XML document. Many people are familiar with HTML and under normal circumstances a stylesheet, for example a CSS stylesheet, could be associated with a document as follows:

```
<link href="somestylesheet.css" rel="stylesheet" type="text/css"?>
```

The equivalent `xml:stylesheet` processing instruction would be as follows:

```
<?xml:stylesheet href="somestylesheet.css" type="text/css">
```

Note that under normal circumstances, the `xsl:stylesheet` processing instruction would most likely be more of the flavor

```
<?xml:stylesheet href="ImaXslsheet.xsl" type="text/xsl"?>
```

`xml:stylesheet` supports a syntax identical to HTML's `<LINK.rel="stylesheet"..>`, but uses the following attributes:

- `href="..."`—The URI to the stylesheet, required.
- `type="..."`—The type of the stylesheet, `text/xsl` for an XSL stylesheet, required.
- `title="..."`—The title of the stylesheet, implied. Titles are used to group multiple `xml:stylesheets` together to define a single style.
- `charset="cdata"`—The characterset of the stylesheet, implied.
- `media="..."`—The intended media, for example `print,screen` and so on. Default is `all`. Normally stylesheets are designed for use in printing or displaying a document to the screen. However, there's nothing to stop you from rendering a document in braille or some other way.
- `alternate="yes|no"`—Is this an alternate stylesheet? Default is `no`. This is an additional attribute for `xml:stylesheet`'s `alternate=...`. Alternate is designed so that you can associate multiple stylesheets with a given XML document, each with its own purpose in mind.

```
<?xml:stylesheet alternate="yes" title="mini"
➥ href="styles/mini.xsl" type="text/xsl"?>
<?xml:stylesheet alternate="yes" title="bigger"
➥ href="styles/bigger.xsl" type="text/xsl"?>
<?xml:stylesheet alternate="yes" title="huge"
➥ href="styles/huge.xsl" type="text/xsl"?>
```

To associate an XSL stylesheet, say `dogs.xsl`, with an XML document, say `allDogBreeds.xml`, we might write the following:

```
<!-- allDogBreeds.xml -->
<xml version="1.0"?>
<!DOCTYPE dogbreeds [...]>
<?xml:stylesheet type="text/xml" href="dogs.xsl"?>
<!-- Remainder of XML document...-->
</dogbreeds>
```

You Can Use CSS with XML

While we will not discuss CSS at all (well almost not at all), you can use a CSS stylesheet with an XML document. The regular nature of XML lends itself well to CSS. Simply specify the CSS stylesheet as just shown and you're on your way! As always, *caveat emptor.* The buyer beware, your mileage may vary!

Running XT

XT is an implementation of the XSL transforms portion of the XSL specification. XT was developed by James Clark and, as of this writing, can be obtained from http://www.jclark.com. For simplicity, a version of XT is available on the CD-ROM. Two versions of XT exist. One is specific to Win32 and is used in most of the examples in this chapter. The other can be used via command line with any of the more recent Java SDKs. To use XT, simply follow the installation instructions. For the Win32 version, all you need to do is be sure that XT is in your PATH. Note that for the Win32 version of XT you need to be running Internet Explorer version 4.01 or later. Actually, what you really need is the Microsoft Virtual machine, but it ships with IE and so it's easier to just get the whole kit and install it.

The XT command line is as follows:

```
c:\xt inputdoc.xml stylesheet
```

where inputdoc is some XML document and xml stylesheet is a stylesheet to associate with it. For example

```
C:\Xt catalog.xml catalog-simple.xsl
```

results in

```
[heading]
This is the catalog header only one instance of this guy


. . .
This is the catalog trailer only one instance of this guy as well
[trailer]
```

when executed using the files in the Chapter 5 directory of the CD-ROM.

Running XT using Java is fairly simple as well, although the command line is longer. Assuming xt.jar and sax.jar are in your CLASSPATH, you simply type

```
c:\java -Dcom.jclark.xsl.sax.parser=
➡com.jclark.xml.sax.CommentDriver com.jclark.xsl.sax.Driver catalog.xml
➡catalog-simple.xsl catalog.output.
```

In general the command is

```
c:\java -Dcom.jclark.xsl.sax.parser=
➡com.jclark.xml.sax.CommentDriver com.jclark.xsl.sax.Driver
➡ Input_file.xsl somestylesheet.xsl outputfile
```

Note that other XSL processors do exist and, at least in a perfect world, would work similarly, albeit with different command-line syntax. LotusXSL, available on the CD-ROM, is another such XSL processor.

Running LotusXSL

LotusXSL is another of a large crop of XSL applications that implement the transform portion of the XSL specification (XSLT). As I was developing this chapter, LotusXSL was at version 0.18 and supported the most recent draft of XSLT. It's almost a certainty that by the time you are reading this a newer version will be available from http://www.alphaworks.ibm.com. LotusXSL was written completely in Java and can be used in servlets, from the command line, or as part of other Java applications.

LotusXSL is run in a fashion similar to XT. You simply specify the starting class as well as the input and output parameters.

Typically your command line will look something like the following:

```
c:\java com.lotus.xsl.xml4j.ProcessXSL
➡ -IN xmlfile -XSL xsl-stylesheet -OUT filename
```

In addition, a number of other command-line switches exist for manipulating LotusXSL functions. See the LotusXSL software documentation for a complete list.

Buyer Beware!

LotusXSL, while not trivial, was fairly straightforward to configure and use. Several additions were required to the CLASSPATH, as well as having the Java 1.2 SDK or later correctly installed. The installation documentation describes the process in depth and was invaluable when I began experimenting with the LotusXSL tool. However, rather than giving any detailed installation and functionality descriptions, I direct the savvy developer—after all, you'd have bought one of the other early, mostly outdated, or just wrong XML books and not this one if you were not a savvy developer—to the IBM Web site for the most up-to-date information, source, and documentation for LotusXSL. As with all developing standards, your mileage may vary!

XML/XSL with Microsoft Internet Explorer 5.0

Microsoft was not to be forgotten and worked hard to get an XML/XSL-enabled product to market. Microsoft Internet Explorer 5.0 goes a long way toward implementing support for XML and XSL. However, as with any bleeding-edge product, MSIE 5.0 shipped before the standards had solidified and, unfortunately, much has changed. In addition, MSIE 5.0 added to XML in many non-standard ways. XML Island discussions as well as other MS proprietary extensions have been debated for what seems like ages on the XML newsgroups. Unfortunately, as with any early release, much of what Microsoft did does not match the current W3C recommendations. Microsoft will most certainly move closer to the XML and XSL standards as time progresses. However, MSIE 5.0 was too far afield to be of much use during this specific chapter's development. Some of the most common differences between MSIE 5.0 and the W3C standards were

- *Namespaces*—MSIE 5.0 supports an old, out-of-date namespace and flags an error when the correct, current, XSL namespace is specified. After the error, all processing stops.
- *Default rules*—MSIE 5.0 did not support any of the default XSL rules requiring developers to do much more work to create useful XSL stylesheets.
- *Expression Syntax*—Most of the power of XSL is in its expression syntax, much of which was omitted from MSIE 5.0.

Other less important differences exist as well, many of which may have been addressed by the time this book comes to print.

Pattern Matching with `match=` and `select=`

We've seen some basic XSL as well as several tools for processing and using XSL. What we need now is a more in-depth understanding of how the `match=` and `select=` attributes to `xsl:template` and `xsl:apply-templates` elements function.

Let's start from the top and examine the whole pattern matching process more closely. Each document contains a root element. The root element is selected via the `match="/"` attribute to `xsl:template`. The `select=` attribute of the `xsl:value-of` element works almost identically. Both `match=` and `select=` work on *patterns*. Examples of patterns might be

- `match="/"`—Match the root element.
- `select="Listing"`—Select any `Listing` element child.
- `match="*"`—Match any element.
- `match="Town|County"`—Match any `Town` element or any `County` element.
- `match="@attribute"`—Match any source element with the named attribute.

In addition to the `match=` attribute of `xsl:template` and the `select=` attribute of `xsl:apply-templates`, patterns are also used in numbering and keys. The rules in this section apply equally well to both of these areas.

Of course many other possibilities exist. In fact the XSLT specification contains a complete set of production rules for specifying patterns. However, they are a little dry and are perhaps better explained via example. As we shall see, `match=` and `select=` can contain rather sophisticated expressions for matching and selecting elements.

> ### Source Element
>
> Each time a template rule is applied, a source element is selected. That is to say that as each element that matches the specified match criteria is processed, the selected element is termed the *source element*. If we had matched on a Listing element, which has children ListingBroker, Type, Addr, Price, and so on, the Listing element would be considered the source element. The select= attribute of xsl:value-of would then act on the children of Listing.

The following sections detail the various pattern rules.

Matching the Root

Under most circumstances, unless we specify output as <xsl:output method="text"/>, XSL output is well formed. In practice, it makes good sense to list rules in a stylesheet from most granular to least granular. Prudence then suggests that we start at the root of our document and we do this with the following rule (did you ever wonder whom this person Prudence is and why she is always suggesting things?):

```
<xsl:template match="/">
. . .
</xsl:template>
```

If we were translating an XML document to the HTML namespace, we would most likely write this rule as follows:

```
<xsl:template match="/">
<html>
<xsl:apply-templates/>
</html>
</xsl:template>
```

which would wrap the result document in traditional <html> </html> tags. We could then further define that processing should only continue on Listing elements via the select= attribute to xsl:apply-templates:

```
<xsl:template match="/">
<h2>
<xsl:apply-templates select="Listing"/>
</h2>
</xsl:template>
```

In fact, we could create a simple table of our listings by applying the stylesheet specified in Listing 5.3, which, when displayed, would look something similar to Figure 5.3. This stylesheet works from most granular to least, matching and processing elements down the hierarchy of our XML document.

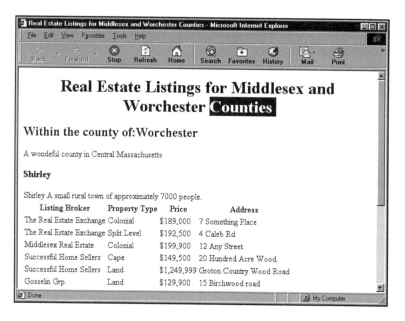

FIGURE 5.3

A table of real estate listings.

LISTING 5.3   RETable.xsl—A Stylesheet for Producing a Table of Listings

```xml
<?xml version="1.0"?>
<xsl:stylesheet
    xmlns:xsl="http://www.w3.org/XSL/Transform/1.0"
    xmlns="http://www.w3.org/TR/REC-html40" result="ns">


<xsl:template match="/">
    <html><body>
    <xsl:apply-templates/>
    </body></html>
</xsl:template>

<xsl:template match="Header">
    <head><title><xsl:value-of select="."/></title></head>
    <center><h1><xsl:value-of select="."/></h1></center>
</xsl:template>
<!--This rule causes the State tag to be ignored-->
<xsl:template match="State"></xsl:template>
```

LISTING 5.3   Continued

```
<xsl:template match="County">
    <h2>Within the county of:<xsl:value-of select="@Name"/></h2>
    <xsl:value-of select="@Description"/>
    <xsl:apply-templates match="Town"/>
</xsl:template>

<xsl:template match="Town">
    <h3><xsl:value-of select="TownName"/> </h3>
    <table>
    <th>Listing Broker</th>
    <th>Property Type</th>
    <th>Price</th>
    <th>Address</th>
    <xsl:apply-templates match="Listing"/>
    </table>
</xsl:template>

<xsl:template match="Listing">
    <tr>
    <td><xsl:value-of select="ListingBroker"/></td>
    <td><xsl:value-of select="Type"/></td>
    <td><xsl:text>$</xsl:text><xsl:value-of select="ListingPrice"/></td>
    <td><xsl:value-of select="Addr"/></td>
    </tr>
</xsl:template>

<!-- If there isn't a template rule ignore it -->
<xsl:template/>
</xsl:stylesheet>
```

Literal Result Elements

There is one special case of the `<xsl:template match="/">` element rule called the literal result element. This special case is designed for use when there is only a single rule within a stylesheet. Such a stylesheet is shown next. Note the differences from the average stylesheet where the root match template rule is implied:

```
<html xmlns:xsl="http://www.w3.org/XSL/Transform/1.0"
      xmlns="http://www.w3.org/TR/REC-html40" >
<head>
    <title>Real Estate Listing</title>
</head>
```

```
<body>
    <p><xsl:value-of select-"."/></p>
</body>
</html>
```

Which produces a result identical to the one produced by

```
<?xml version="1.0"?>
<xsl:stylesheet
    xmlns:xsl="http://www.w3.org/XSL/Transform/1.0"
    xmlns="http://www.w3.org/TR/REC-html40" result="ns">

<xsl:template match="/">
    <head>
        <title>Real Estate Listing</title>
    </head>
    <body>
        <p><xsl:value-of select-"."/></p>
    </body>
</xsl:template>
</xsl:stylesheet>
```

Matching Specific Elements

The second most likely case in matching patterns is matching a particular element within an XML document. Listing 5.3 showed several examples of this. In general, we simply specify the exact name of the element we want to match. Note that, as with XML in general, spelling counts. It's not an error to create a rule to match listings, even though there are none and what we most likely meant was Listing. The general rule is the same as before and is shown next. We simply replace *someelement* with the exact element name we are interested in.

```
<xsl:template match="someelement">
. . .
</xsl:template>
```

For example, we saw we could match Listing elements with

```
<xsl:template match="Listing">
<!-- Listing processing here -->
</xsl:template>
```

Matching Attributes

Attributes are one of the simplest patterns within XSL. We can match any attribute by simply specifying it with the at symbol (@). The template rule outputs the value of the Name attribute within County.

```
<xsl:template match="County">
    <xsl:value-of select="@Name"
</xsl:template>
```

In addition, we can combine attribute matching with the asterisk wildcard (*) and match any attribute. The following rule shows an example of this:

```
<xsl:template match="County">
    <xsl:for-each select="@*">
        <xsl:value-of select="."/><xsl:text>&#xD;&#xA;</xsl:text>
    </xsl:for-each>
</xsl:template>
```

Using `xsl:value-of` Review

While we haven't examined it specifically, we've used `xsl:value-of` repeatedly in past examples. `xsl:value-of` allows you to specify what value to output into the result document based on the value of the source document and on how we specify the `select=` attribute. We've seen the most common usage, `select="."`, which outputs the entire contents of the selected element as well as all its children. We've also seen how to output the value of a specific child node using `select="ChildElement"`. And, more recently, we've seen how we can output the value of an attribute using `select="@SomeAttribute"`. In fact, there are much more sophisticated methods to specify parent-child relationships or, more generally, ancestor-descendant relationships.

Patterns for Ancestor-Descendant Relations

So far, we have shown some of the more common methods for specifying match and select criteria and examined `xsl:value-of` and `xsl:template` as well as `xsl:apply-templates` in some detail. We've seen how to select one of the children of an element. However, sometimes we might want to specify ancestor-descendant relationships skipping intermediate generations, perhaps to handle arbitrary hierarchical relations between elements. We can do this by specifying these relationships separating various generations using the slash ("/").

Remembering back to our real estate listings, REListing contained Countys which contained Towns which, in turn, contained Listings which had a number of leaf elements representing individual listings. If we wanted to output only the listing broker, we could have written a rule something like that shown in Listing 5.4.

LISTING 5.4   ListingBroker.xsl—Output Listing Brokers

```
<?xml version="1.0"?>
<xsl:stylesheet
    xmlns:xsl="http://www.w3.org/XSL/Transform/1.0"
    indent-result="no" default-space="strip">
```

LISTING 5.4 Continued

```
<xsl:template match="/">
    <xsl:apply-templates select="REListing"/>
</xsl:template>

<xsl:template match="REListing">
    <xsl:apply-templates/>
</xsl:template>

<xsl:template match="County/Town/Listing">
    Broker:<xsl:value-of select="ListingBroker"/>
</xsl:template>
</xsl:stylesheet>
```

In fact, we could specify the previous rule more simply by stating

```
<xsl:template match="County//Listing">
    Broker:<xsl:value-of select="ListingBroker"/>
</xsl:template>
```

which says, give me any `ListingBroker` within any `Listing` element that's descended from `County`, regardless of the level at which it appears. The following rules show exactly how we tunnel down into an XML document hierarchy.

The following code matches the root of the XML Document, which, in our `REListing.xml` example, has two child elements—REListing and the `xsl:stylesheet` processing instruction.

```
<xsl:template match="/">
<!--Other rules -->
</xsl:template>
```

The following code matches the root element, which is not the same as the root, of the XML Document.

```
<xsl:template match="/*">
<!--Other rules -->
</xsl:template>
```

The following code matches the named element:

```
<xsl:template match="SomeElement">
<!--Other rules -->
</xsl:template>
```

The following matches the child of parent.

```
<xsl:template match="Parent/Child">
<!--Other rules -->
</xsl:template>
```

For example

```
<xsl:template match="Town/Listing">
    <xsl:value-of select="."/>
</xsl:template>
```

The select="." applies to the Listing element, that is the child element!

The following matches any elements with Parent, any single intermediate level, and then GrandChild elements.

```
<xsl:template match="Parent/*/GrandChild">
<!--Other rules -->
</xsl:template>
```

The following matches any elements that have a descendant somewhere beneath ancestor in the document hierarchy.

```
<xsl:template match="ancestor//descendant">
<!--Other rules -->
</xsl:template>
```

Patterns Using Built-ins

There are a number of built-in functions that can be used to match or process various elements within an XML Document.

Matching with text()

As we've seen before in Chapter 4, every leaf element has a text element child that contains the actual text associated with the element. XSL provides a built-in function for matching on and selecting text—text(). In fact, we've already seen this built-in at work in the default processing rule for nodes, shown here:

```
<xsl:template match="text()|@*">
    <xsl:value-of select="."/>
</xsl:template>
```

Most likely, we might modify this rule to override the default processing of text nodes to discard the contents of an element rather then display it by respecifying the default rule as follows:

```
<xsl:template match="text()"/>
```

This causes text nodes not handled by another processing rule to be ignored.

Matching on `ids`

We can match only on elements that have a specified `id` by using the template rule given next. Note that this rule only matches an element with the given `id`. For example, if we had specified that listings each have a required `id`, perhaps for quick lookup, we could use that `id`. That is, assuming every listing had a required `ID` attribute, `ListingNumber`, we might write the following:

```
<xsl:template match="id('ListingID1')">
    <xsl:value-of select="."/>
</xsl:template>
```

to output the value of the given `id`.

Matching on Processing Instructions

In a similar fashion, we could output the value of a processing instruction associated with the root (again, not the root element) of an XML document as follows. Notice how we combined the "`/`" with `processing-instruction` to match PIs at the root of the document only

```
<xsl:template match="/processing-instruction()">
    <xsl:value-of select="."/>
</xsl:template>
```

Selecting Comments

While most often ignored because they imply knowledge of an XML document outside that which is provided by the DTD, we could output the value of a comment. We saw previously that comments are ignored via one of the default rules, specifically

```
<xsl:template match="processing-instruction()|comment()"/>
```

We might have wanted to output our comments and could have easily done so with the following rule:

```
<xsl:template match="comment()">
    <xsl:value-of select="."/>
</xsl:template>
```

There are a number of other built-in functions in XML stylesheets, and we will examine the remainder more closely when we look at some of the advanced features of XSL. But before we do, we need to examine one more aspect of pattern matching and selection—namely expressions.

Matching with Predicates (`[]`)

Most of what we've done up to this point has been matching against simple location paths. Predicates can be simply thought of as a way to index into an array of nodes. Predicates can be used in other ways as well—for example:

5

JAVA AND XSL

Matches on position:

- `<xsl:template match="Listing[1]">`...

    matches the first `Listing`

- `<xsl:template match="Listing[last()]">`...

    matches the last `Listing`

Matches on attributes:

- `<xsl:template match="County[@Name | @Desc="Some description"]">`...

    matches any `County` element that contains a `Name` attribute or has a description element containing the given text

Matches on children and descendants:

- `<xsl:template match="County[Town | Listing]">`...

    Matches any `County` that has either `Town` or `Listing` children.

See the Xpatch specification for a complete description of the XMPath expression syntax.

In general, predicates can be expressed by the following grammar (snipped from the XPath specification):

```
[8]               Predicate ::=   '[' PredicateExpr ']'
[9]               PredicateExpr::=   Expr
```

Expressions are further defined as:

```
[14]              Expr      ::=  OrExpr
[15]              PrimaryExpr ::=   VariableReference
                            | '(' Expr ')'
                            | Literal
                            | Number
                            | FunctionCall
```

And so on, recursively defining expressions of greater and greater complexity. Basically, what we see is that predicates are just expressions and can be variables, other expressions using parentheses for specify precedence, literals (such as `Listing` and `County`), numbers, calls to the built-in functions, and other expressions. Let's look at expressions in more detail.

Working with Expressions

Most readers are familiar with expressions. $1+1=2$, $a^2 + b^2=c^2$, and if $(a>b)$ then x are all examples of simple expressions. XSL supports expressions of surprising sophistication and power. In fact, XSLT derives much of its power from its expression language. Expressions allow developers to do several things, chief of which are

- Selecting nodes to be further processed
- Specifying conditions for processing nodes
- Generating output text

There are five types of expressions:

- *Node Sets*—Expressions that act on node sets. Node sets are just that, unordered collections of nodes generated by applying `<xsl:template match="...">` and `<xsl:apply-template select="..."">` rules. We've been working with node sets all along but haven't known it! There are a number of built-in functions for node sets, and we'll see them shortly.
- *Booleans*—Boolean expressions are those that result in either a true or false result.
- *Strings*—A string is just that, a string! More precisely, a string is a set of Unicode characters. The `string()` built-in can be used to convert a node, node set, result tree, Boolean, or number to a string.
- *Numbers*—Numbers are 64-bit IEEE floating-point double values. The `number()` built-in function can convert various types to numbers. Numbers can be combined in expressions in the normal way using `+`, `-`, `*`, `div`, and so on (can't use `/`).
- *Result tree fragments*—Result tree fragments are portions of XML documents that are not complete and are often not well formed.

XSLT uses the powerful expression language defined by XPath. Expressions can be used to select specific nodes, specify conditions for processing nodes (perhaps in different ways), and generate output.

In addition, it's important to understand the context within which the expression is evaluated. Two specific points are important:

- The context comes from the currently selected node.
- The position of the current node comes from its position in its current context. A node might be the fifth in the document but the second in a particular context.

Let's now look at each of these expression types in detail.

Boolean Expressions

Boolean expressions are those whose result is determined by applying one of the following operations

- *Equality*—Something = something else.
- *Less than, or less than or equal to*—Something < something else (really < and <=).
- *Greater than, or greater than or equal to*—Something > something else (> or >=).

5

We've already seen an example using equals, but another wouldn't hurt. Listing 5.5 shows how we might select listings that pertain only to land (because we'd rather build than buy).

LISTING 5.5   Land.xsl—Select Land Only Listings

```
 1: <?xml version="1.0"?>
 2: <xsl:stylesheet
 3:     xmlns:xsl="http://www.w3.org/XSL/Transform/1.0"
 4:     indent-result="no" default-space="strip">
 5: <xsl:template match="text()"/>
 6: <xsl:template match="Type[@PropType='land']">
 7:     land:<xsl:value-of select=".."/>
 8: </xsl:template>
 9: </xsl:stylesheet>
10:
```

The two lines or importance here are 6 and 7. Line 6 simply says match any Type elements that have a PropType attribute whose value equals (=) the literal land. Line 7 is interesting only because it selects the parent of the property type, which is a Listing element.

Listings 5.6–5.8 show that we could, in a similar fashion, select the first, last, and anything but the first and last Listing elements:

LISTING 5.6   first.xsl—Select the First Listing

```
 1: <?xml version="1.0"?>
 2: <xsl:stylesheet
 3:     xmlns:xsl="http://www.w3.org/XSL/Transform/1.0"
 4:     indent-result="no" default-space="strip">
 5: <xsl:template match="text()"/>
 6: <xsl:template match="Listing[1]">
 7:     First:<xsl:value-of select="."/>
 8: </xsl:template>
 9: </xsl:stylesheet>
10:
```

Line 6 illustrates the number grammar rule and selects the first Listing element. In fact, the [1] could have been the *n*th element!

LISTING 5.7   last.xsl—Select the Last Listing

```
 1: <?xml version="1.0"?>
 2: <xsl:stylesheet
 3:     xmlns:xsl="http://www.w3.org/XSL/Transform/1.0"
```

LISTING 5.7 Continued

```
4:     indent-result="no" default-space="strip">
5: <xsl:template match="text()"/>
6: <xsl:template match="Listing[position() = last()]">
7:     Last:<xsl:value-of select="."/>
8: </xsl:template>
9:</xsl:stylesheet>
```

Line 6 in Listing 5.7 combines the or and function rules to select the last Listing element. Table 5.3 lists the primary functions that can be used on node sets.

TABLE 5.3 Node Set Functions

Function	Description
count()	Returns a number equal to the total number of elements in the node set.
id(*someid*)	Returns a node set of nodes that match the given id. We could then act directly on the result node set and perform other operations. For example, id(*someid*)[5] returns the 5th element whose id is someid.
last()	Returns a number equal to the last element in the node set.
local-name(*node set*)	Like name, local-name returns the name of the first element in the node set. Unlike name, local-name returns on the local part (deepest in the element hierarchy).
name(*node set*)	Returns a string representing the complete name of the first element in the node set in the order originally given in the input document.
position()	Returns a number equal to the position of the node being acted on in the node set.

LISTING 5.8 middle.xsl—Select the Middle Listings

```
1: <?xml version="1.0"?>
2: <xsl:stylesheet
3:     xmlns:xsl="http://www.w3.org/XSL/Transform/1.0"
4:     indent-result="no" default-space="strip">
5: <xsl:template match="text()"/>
6: <xsl:template match="Listing[not(position()=1 or position() = last())]">
7:     Middle(not first or last):<xsl:value-of select="."/>
8: </xsl:template>
9: </xsl:stylesheet>
10:
```

Line 6 of Listing 5.8 actually shows several things. First, it shows that we can combine expressions using or. Second, line 6 shows that we can establish precedence or order of evaluation using parentheses, and third that we can use the not operator to negate the value of an expression. Finally, we could have written the "middle" expression more simply using > and <, as follows:

```
<xsl:template match="Listing[position() > 1 or  position() &lt; last()]">
```

Table 5.4 lists the functions that return Boolean values or can be used in Boolean expressions.

TABLE 5.4   Boolean Functions

Function	Description
boolean()	Converts its argument to a Boolean value
false()	Always returns false
not(expression)	Inverts the value of the result
true()	Always returns true

In general we see that

- Boolean expressions can be either true or false.
- Boolean expressions on node sets are true if and only if after converting both sets to strings, the result of applying the comparison is true.
- Two strings are true if and only if they contain the exact same sequence of characters.
- A non-zero length string is true. A zero length string is false.
- An empty node set is false; a nonempty set, true.
- If at least one element is a number, the other is converted to a number and the value of the expression is based on the resulting comparison.
- We can convert an expression to a Boolean using the boolean() built-in function.

Combining Expressions with Logical Operators

Before we go on, let's digress just a moment to see how expressions can be combined. We'd first like to examine our expressions. In fact, when we examined the default template rule for processing instructions and comments, we saw that the rule applied to processing-instructions() | comments()—that is, processing instructions *or* comments. The logical "or" operator, represented by the vertical bar (|), can be used to apply this template if either the first expression or the second expression is true. In fact, there is nothing to stop us from combining any of the rules we've seen before using or. For example, and it's quite a stretch, if we wanted to output as bold HTML any processing instructions, comments, ListingBrokers who are descended from County, or Prices, we might write

```
<xsl:template match="Price|County//ListingBroker |
 processing-instruction() | comment()>
    <xsl:value-of select="."/>
</xsl:template>
```

We could also combine expressions using and. For example, if we were interested in nodes that had two specific attributes, say AttrA and AttrB, we might write the following:

```
<xsl:template match="SomeNode[@AttrA and @AttrB]">
    <xsl:value-of select="."/>
</xsl:template>
```

Note that I used whitespace, although inconsistently, within the match expression. Whitespace is ignored, so how it's used is up to you.

Let's move on and examine each of the expression types more closely.

Number Expressions

Expressions involving numbers and numeric operations are perhaps even simpler than Boolean expressions. There are a number of operations that can be used with numbers. First, all the standard operations—such as + (plus), - (minus) and * (multiplication)—can be used. div is used for division because we can't use a slash (/). mod takes the remainder after division. For example, 9 mod 3 is 0, but 10 mod 3 is 1. Most often, we will use number expressions in <xsl:template elements. For example, Listing 5.9 outputs listings that are priced less that $150,000 (specifically via line 6). However, Listing 5.10 shows how we could use them in xsl:value-of elements as well.

LISTING 5.9   cheap.xsl—Select Listings Less Than $150,000

```
1: <?xml version="1.0"?>
2: <xsl:stylesheet
3:     xmlns:xsl="http://www.w3.org/XSL/Transform/1.0"
4:     indent-result="no" default-space="strip">
5: <xsl:template match="text()"/>
6: <xsl:template match="Listing[ListingPrice &lt; 150000]">
7:     Cheap!:<xsl:value-of select="."/>
8: </xsl:template>
9: </xsl:stylesheet>
```

5

AVA AND XSL

We all know that listing price in only one factor in buying a home. Taxes are a fact of life, and property taxes are one more factor determining the perceived value of a property. Listing 5.10 factors in tax rates.

LISTING 5.10 cheap-2.xsl—Select Listings Less Than $150,000 with Factoring for Tax Rates

```
 1: <?xml version="1.0"?>
 2: <xsl:stylesheet
 3:     xmlns:xsl="http://www.w3.org/XSL/Transform/1.0"
 4:     indent-result="no" default-space="strip">
 5: <xsl:template match="text()"/>
 6: <xsl:template match="Listing[ListingPrice &lt; 150000]">
 7:     Cheap:<xsl:value-of select="."/>
 8:             taxrate:<xsl:value-of select="../TaxRate"/>
 9:             applied rate:$<xsl:value-of
    ➥select="round((ListingPrice div 1000) * ../TaxRate)"/> a year
10: </xsl:template>
11: </xsl:stylesheet>
```

Line 9—the meat of this example—selects for output the current listing price in thousands times the tax rate to give the estimated yearly taxes. Breaking line 9 down even further, we can see that we used one of the numeric functions to round the result to the nearest dollar. Table 5.5 lists the various functions that can be applied to numeric results.

TABLE 5.5 Numeric Functions

Function	Description
ceiling()	Returns the smallest (closest to negative infinity) number that is not less than the argument and that is an integer.
floor()	Returns the largest (closest to positive infinity) number that is not greater than the argument and that is an integer.
number()	Convert the given object to a number. true converts to 1, false to 0. Strings are converted to numbers by stripping whitespace and then proceeding as normal. Other objects are converted in a fashion appropriate for the object.
round()	Returns the number that is closest to the argument and that is an integer. If there are two such numbers, the one that is closest to positive infinity is returned.
sum()	Sums the arguments by first calling string to convert to a string and then converting to a number and adding the result.
true()	Always returns true.

In fact, we could put many of the ideas we've come across to work and determine the average property value in all our listings. Listing 5.11 does just that. Listing 5.12 shows the result.

LISTING 5.11   avgprice.xsl—Average Real Estate Listing Prices

```
 1: <?xml version="1.0"?>
 2: <xsl:stylesheet
 3:     xmlns:xsl="http://www.w3.org/XSL/Transform/1.0"
 4:     indent-result="no" default-space="strip">
 5: <xsl:template match="text()"/>
 6: <xsl:template match="/REListing">
 7:     <xsl:for-each select="//Listing">
 8:         <xsl:value-of
➥select="ListingPrice"/><xsl:text>&#xD;&#xA;</xsl:text>
 9:     </xsl:for-each>
10:     Total value: <xsl:value-of select="sum(//ListingPrice)"/>
11:     Count of properties: <xsl:value-of select="count(//ListingPrice)"/>
12:     Average Property Cost:
➥<xsl:value-of select="floor(sum(//ListingPrice) div count(//ListingPrice))"/>
13: </xsl:template>
14: </xsl:stylesheet>
```

LISTING 5.12   Applying avgprice.xsl to relisting.xml

```
189000
. . .
529900

    Total value: 5,105,399
    Count of properties: 11
    Average Property Cost:464127
```

The interesting portions of Listing 5.11 are lines 10–12. Lines 7, 8, and 9 show the `<xsl:for-each. . . >`, which printed all prices (I used this as a debugging aid as the average seemed very high to me when I first ran this example). Line 10 simply sums all the ListingPrice children of the REListing element. Line 11 does the same, counting up the Listing elements. Line 12 combines the two and uses the `floor()` function to truncate the result to whole dollars.

In general we see that

- A number represents an IEEE 64-bit floating point number. This representation includes values for NaN (Not a number) positive, negative infinity, and positive and negative zero.
- Applying +, -, *, div, mod, and the numeric built-in functions produces a result that is a number.
- Boolean true is 1 and false is 0.

5

JAVA AND XSL

- Strings are converted to numbers by trimming all leading and trailing whitespace and then converting to a number. Strings that make no sense after conversion convert as 0.

- We can convert an expression to a number using the number() built-in function.

Listing 5.13 shows a simple stylesheet that executes a number of sample conversions using the number() built-in function.

LISTING 5.13   numbertext.xsl—Sample Conversions

```
<?xml version="1.0"?>
<xsl:stylesheet
    xmlns:xsl="http://www.w3.org/XSL/Transform/1.0"
    indent-result="no" default-space="strip">
<xsl:template match="text()"/>
<xsl:template match="/">
    Number test for ('123') :<xsl:value-of select="number('123')"/>
    Number test for ('1,230') :<xsl:value-of select="number('1,230')"/>
    Number test for ('-123.00') :<xsl:value-of select="number('-123.00')"/>
    Number test for ('123.45') :<xsl:value-of select="number('123.45')"/>
    Number test for ('   +123.45   ') :<xsl:value-of select="number('   +123.45
➡')"/>
    Number test for (true()) :<xsl:value-of select="number(true())"/>
    Number test for (false()) :<xsl:value-of select="number(false())"/>
</xsl:template>
</xsl:stylesheet>
```

LISTING 5.14   Result of Running numbertest.xsl Using *XT*

```
Number test for ('123') :123
Number test for ('1,230') :NaN
Number test for ('-123.00') :-123
Number test for ('123.45') :123.45
Number test for ('   +123.45   ') :123.45
Number test for (true()) :1
Number test for (false()) :0
```

String Expressions

At this point, we've seen Boolean and numeric expressions. We can also write quite sophisticated expressions based on strings. At first glance, strings seem somewhat plain in comparison to number and Boolean expressions, but we can perform a number of operations on strings and string expressions in general. Table 5.6 lists the various functions that can be used on strings. For example, suppose we only wanted to output the first 20 characters of a listing broker? The following rule does the trick:

```
<xsl:template match="//Listing">
   Listing brokers truncated to 20 characters:
➡<xsl:value-of select="substring(ListingBroker,0,20)"/>
</xsl:template>
```

TABLE 5.6   String Functions

Function	Description
concat(str1,str2[...])	Returns a string representing appending str2 to str1. concat() can work on more than two strings.
contains(sourcestr, matchstr)	Returns true if the source string contains the matchstr.
substring(sourcestr, start[,len])	Returns the portion of sourcestr starting at start for len. The length is optional. Start is 1-based.
substring-after(sourcestr, matchstr)	Returns the portion of sourcestr that occurs after matchstr. For example, substring-after('200 Forest Street,Marlboro, Mass',',') returns Marlboro, Mass.
substring-before(sourcestr, matchstr)	Returns the portion of sourcestr that occurs before matchstr. For example, substring-before('200 Forest Street,Marlboro, Mass',',') returns 200 Forest Street.
starts-with(sourcestr, matchstr)	Returns true if the source string starts with the match string.
string()	Converts the given argument to a string.
string-length(string)	Returns the length of the string.
normalize(string)	Returns a string with leading and trailing whitespace stripped and internal whitespace compressed to a single space.
translate(sourcestr, targetstr, replacestr)	Returns sourcestr with all instances of targetstr replaced with replacestr.

In general we see that

- A number is converted to a string as follows: NaN converts to "NaN"; -zero and +zero convert to "0"; positive infinity converts to "+Infinity", likewise "-Infinity".

- Boolean values translate into the English word "true" or "false."
- Node sets are converted to strings concatenating together all the string values of each underlying element in original document order.

Node Set Expressions

Basically a node set is simply an unordered list of nodes. We've seen expressions involving node sets before. In fact, most of the early part of this chapter involved expressions using node sets. The following template rule was one of the first we encountered and, in fact, is an expression for selecting the root node RElisting. Table 5.3 listed a number of built-in functions that operate on node sets.

```
<xsl:template match="/RElisting">
       . . .
</xsl:template>
```

Node set expressions are often thought of in terms of an *axis*. An axis describes the tree relationship between the current selected or context element and its various ancestors and descendants. Table 5.7 lists all the axis names and their descriptions

TABLE 5.7   Abbreviations for the XPath Axes

Axis	Description
child	Contains all the children of the current node.
descendant	Contains all the descendants of the current node—children, grandchildren, great-grandchildren, and so on.
parent	The parent of the current node.
ancestor	The parent, grandparent, great-grandparent, and so on of the current node.
following-sibling	Contains the next sibling of the current node. Attributes and namespace elements do not have siblings, and this axis returns an empty node set if applied to either.
preceding-sibling	Contains the previous sibling of the current node. Attributes and namespace elements do not have siblings, and this axis returns an empty node set if applied to either.
following	Contains all nodes, in document order, after the current node, excluding descendants, attributes, and namespace elements.
preceding	Contains all nodes, in document order, before the current node, excluding descendants, attributes, and namespace elements.
attribute	Contains the attributes of the element.
namespace	Contains all the namespace nodes of the current node.

TABLE 5.7   Continued

Axis	Description
self	The current or selected node.
descendant-or-self	Contains the current node as well as all its descendants.
ancestor-or-self	Contains the current node as well as all its ancestors.

Listings 5.15–5.20 show various axes in action, as well as their abbreviations where applicable. Note that these listings have been abbreviated somewhat. The CD-ROM versions contain the complete listings.

LISTING 5.15   axis-self.xsl

```
<?xml version="1.0"?>
<xsl:stylesheet
    xmlns:xsl="http://www.w3.org/XSL/Transform/1.0"
    indent-result="no" default-space="strip">
. . .
<xsl:template match="/REListing//ListingBroker">
    .:<xsl:value-of select="."/>
    self::node()/TownName:<xsl:value-of select="self::node()"/>
    <xsl:apply-templates/>
</xsl:template>
</xsl:stylesheet>
```

LISTING 5.16   axis-parent.xsl

```
<?xml version="1.0"?>
. . .
<xsl:template match="/REListing//Listing">
    ../TownName:<xsl:value-of select="../TownName"/>
    parent::node()/TownName:<xsl:value-of select="parent::node()/TownName"/>
</xsl:template>
</xsl:stylesheet>
```

LISTING 5.17   axis-child.xsl

```
<?xml version="1.0"?>
. . .
<xsl:template match="/REListing">
    child::Header:<xsl:value-of select="child::Header"/>
        abbrev:<xsl:value-of select="Header"/>
</xsl:template>
</xsl:stylesheet>
```

5

JAVA AND XSL

LISTING 5.18   `axis-attribute.xsl`

```
<?xml version="1.0"?>
. . .
<xsl:template match="/REListing/County">
    attribute::Name:<xsl:value-of select="attribute::Name"/>
        abbrev(@Name):<xsl:value-of select="@Name"/>
</xsl:template>
</xsl:stylesheet>
```

LISTING 5.19   `axis-aos.xsl`

```
<?xml version="1.0"?>
. . .
<xsl:template match="/REListing/County/Town/Listing">
    <xsl:value-of select="ancestor-or-self::node()/child::State"/>
</xsl:template>
</xsl:stylesheet>
```

LISTING 5.20   `axis-dos.xsl`

```
<?xml version="1.0"?>
. . .
<xsl:template match="/">
    /descendant-or-self::node()/child::
➡ListingBroker<xsl:value-of
➡select="/descendant-or-self::node()/child::ListingBroker"/>
    //ListingBroker:<xsl:value-of select="//ListingBroker"/>
</xsl:template>
</xsl:stylesheet>
```

In general, we see that

- `Node SetsExpression` may be empty
- Node sets can be converted to Booleans, strings, or numbers, as previously stated.
- Node sets can be acted on to generate other node sets based on their relationship to other nodes and elements.
- Node sets can be specified using axes or abbreviations for axes.
- There is no abbreviation for some axes, such as `ancestor` or `ancestor-or-self`.

- The most common abbreviations for axes are
  - `.` for `self::node()`
  - `ElementName` for `child::ElementName`
  - `../SomeElement` for `parent::SomeElement`
  - `@AttributeName` for `attribute::AttributeName`
  - `//` for `/descendant=or-self::node()/`
- Axes and axes abbreviations can be combined in the same expression.

Result Tree Fragment Expressions

Result tree fragment expressions are perhaps the least useful of all expressions, and we only mention them for the sake of completeness. A result tree fragment is the tree that results from creating an XML document on-the-fly. Such a tree is not well formed. Because the tree is not well formed, we can't apply most of the previous expressions to it. In fact, the only expressions we can apply are `boolean()` and `string()`, which return `true` or `false`, respectively, depending on whether the fragment is populated or not.

Precedence for Rules

Before we move on and examine some of the more advanced features of XSL, we need to look at one more topic—*precedence*. Precedence is a simple idea, really, that defines the order in which we will apply a rule, given that two rules match an input. For example, the following two rules each match `Listing` elements.

```
<xsl:template match ='Listing'...</xsl:template>
```

and

```
<xsl:template match ='//Listing'...</xsl:template>
```

Which would win if we were processing an XSL stylesheet? What if one of the rules were from an imported stylesheet? Would that matter? In this section we will find out.

`xsl:import` and Import Precedence

As we discussed at the very beginning of this chapter, XSLT supports importing other stylesheets via `xsl:import`. We import another stylesheet as shown in the following:

```
<?xml version="1.0"?>
<xsl:stylesheet
```

```
    xmlns:xsl="http://www.w3.org/XSL/Transform/1.0"
    indent-result="no" default-space="strip">
<xsl:import href="another stylesheet.xsl"/>
<xsl:import href="another stylesheet2.xsl"/>
. . .
<xsl:import href="another stylesheetn.xsl"/>

<!-Other XSLT statements -->
</xsl:stylesheet>
```

We can import any number of stylesheets that result in what is called an *import tree*. If we assume for a moment that we have a stylesheet called main.xsl that imports several other spreads, 1.xsl, 2.xsl, and 3.xsl—with 1.xsl also importing a.xsl and b.xsl, and 3.xsl importing c.xsl—we generate an import tree that looks like Figure 5.4.

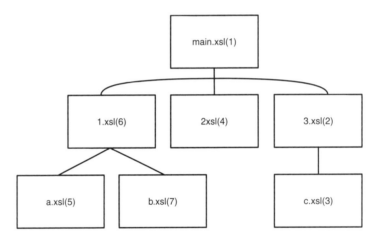

FIGURE 5.4

An import tree.

Precedence is then applied based on post-order traversal of the import tree. Effectively, we can imagine that rules that we have encountered more recently have higher precedence than those encountered in the past. We can see that rules in main.xsl have been encountered most recently because xsl:imports must be the first child element of our stylesheet, so they are of highest precedence. In reverse order, we encounter 3.xsl, which imported c.xsl, resulting in rules in c.xsl being of higher precedence than rules in 3.xsl and likewise backwards through the tree. If you are having trouble with this concept, work through Figure 5.4 a few times and it should help. Remember, most recently encountered equals highest precedence, least recently encountered equals lowest precedence. Figure 5.5 shows the import tree from the bottom up and helps with understanding import order.

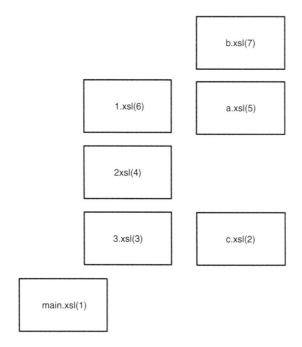

FIGURE 5.5

An import tree from the bottom up.

But what about multiple rules at the same level in the import tree? How are they ordered? In general, the more complex a rule, the lower its priority. Section 5.5 of the XSLT specification gives the following rules for determining priority:

1. Ignore all rules with a lower precedence as reported by the import tree.
2. For all other rules:
   a. Treat rules or'd together as multiple rules all of priority 0.
   b. If the rule is a simple name or @simple name, its priority is 0.
   c. If the rule pattern is an NCName followed by a colon followed by a simple name (i.e., foo:name), its priority is -0.25.
   d. If the rule contains a node test (i.e., comment(), text(), processing-instruction(), and so on), its priority is -0.5.
   e. Otherwise the rule's priority is 0.5.

If we look back at our original example, we see that the match pattern "Listing" is simpler than the match pattern "//Listing", so the first is matched and the second is ignored.

Including Stylesheets with `xsl:include`

In addition to `xsl:import`, we can also include other XSL documents. The primary difference between import and include is that included stylesheets act as if there were part of the stylesheet in which they were included. That is, they do not create a new node in the import tree. The following XSL snippet shows a sample of how we could include a stylesheet:

```
<?xml version="1.0"?>
<xsl:stylesheet
    xmlns:xsl="http://www.w3.org/XSL/Transform/1.0"
    indent-result="no" default-space="strip">
<xsl:include href="another stylesheet.xsl"/>
<!-Other XSLT statements -->
</xsl:stylesheet>
```

Explicit Priority

There is one exception to the previous rule and that is that we can state a priority specifically. We could have made the second rule override the first if we had specified its priority specifically as

```
<xsl:template match ='//Listing' priority='1.0'>...</xsl:template>
```

This specifically tells the XSLT processor to use this rule first and then any others.

Advanced XSL

Up to now, we have examined the basics of XSLT. In fact, we could get along very nicely using just what we have learned so far. However, there are a number of situations that the XSLT basics do not cover. We will look at some of the more advanced features of XSL in this section. These features are not advanced in terms of complexity—in fact, some are quite simple—but advanced in that they move beyond what a simple stylesheet might do.

Sequential and Non-Sequential Processing

Up to now, we have processed all XML documents in a sequential fashion—in original document order. However, it is possible to process documents non-sequentially, multiple times and conditionally. We shall see examples of these kinds of processing in the following sections.

Modes

Modes are a way by which the same elements within an XML document can be processed more than once, each time with a different result. Listing 5.21 shows an XSL stylesheet that processes County elements twice. Lines 7 and 8 cause each of the template rules (lines 10 and 14) to be processed.

LISTING 5.21   mode.xsl—Processing Elements Multiple Times

```
 1: <?xml version="1.0"?>
 2: <xsl:stylesheet
 3:     xmlns:xsl="http://www.w3.org/XSL/Transform/1.0"
 4:     indent-result="no" default-space="strip">
 5: <xsl:template match="text()"/>
 6: <xsl:template match="/">
 7:     <xsl:apply-templates match="County" mode="name"/>
 8:     <xsl:apply-templates match="County" mode="all"/>
 9: </xsl:template>
10: <xsl:template match="County" mode="name">
11:     CountyName:<xsl:value-of select="@Name"/>
12: </xsl:template>
13:
14: <xsl:template match="County" mode="all">
15:     <xsl:for-each select="Town">
16:         TownName:
   ➥<xsl:value-of select="TownName"/><xsl:text>&#xD;&#xA;</xsl:text>
17:     </xsl:for-each>
18: </xsl:template>
19: </xsl:stylesheet>
20:
```

The rules for using the mode= attribute are simple:

- If an xsl:template element does not have a match= attribute, it cannot have a mode= attribute.

- For xsl:apply-template elements, if the rule has a mode= attribute, it is only applied to xsl:template rules with a matching mode= attribute.

Conditional and Repeat Processing

We've seen many ways to process XML documents, most of which are sequential in nature. Basically, we find some element that matches an xsl:template rule and then apply the rule. However, sometimes we know more about the structure of the original document and want to apply other processing to its elements. We've already encountered `xsl:for-each` in several examples but never discussed it specifically. `xsl:for-each` allows us to apply the same processing to each child element of a selected element in their original document order. In Listing 5.11, we wanted to show every listing price, and `xsl:for-each` worked nicely.

But suppose we wanted to see each listing and categorize each as in our price range, slightly above our price range, or completely out of our price range? We can handle the first case simply with `xsl:if`. The following XSL snippet labels real estate listing either within our price range or not and can be found on the CD-ROM as `xsl-if.xsl`.

```
<xsl:template match="Listing">
   <xsl:if test="ListingPrice &lt;= 150000" >
      In our range:<xsl:value-of select="."/>
   </xsl:if>
   <xsl:if test="ListingPrice > 150000" >
      Out of range:<xsl:value-of select="."/>
   </xsl:if>
```

`xsl:if` is simple to use and has a single attribute `test=` where any XSL expression can be evaluated. If the expression evaluates to `true`, the rule is applied; otherwise, it's not. We could output only even-numbered elements by writing

```
<xsl:template match="Listing">
   <xsl:if test="position() mod 2 = 0" >
      Evens<xsl:value-of select="position()"/>):<xsl:value-of select="."/>
   </xsl:if>
   </xsl:if>
```

We can perform much more sophisticated processing via `xsl:choose`. Anyone familiar with a C, C++, or Java switch statement will be comfortable with `xsl:choose`. The format of `xsl:choose` statements is as follows:

```
<xsl:choose>
   <xsl:when test='some test to perform'>
      <!-- Some processing -->
   </xsl:when>
   <xsl:when test='another test to perform'>
      <!-- Other processing -->
   </xsl:when>
   <xsl:otherwise>
      <! Default processing when no xsl:when is applicable>
   </xsl:otherwise>
</xsl:choose>
```

Each `xsl:choose` element has one or more `xsl:when` children and optionally an `xsl:otherwise` child. The test described for each `xsl:when` is performed sequentially in the order listed and, if all tests fail, the `xsl:otherwise` element is processed. In reality, `xsl:choose` is nothing more than a standard switch statement in XSL clothing.

Sorting

Sorting and numbering are two areas we have only briefly discussed. We've seen the `position()` built-in function repeatedly but have not used it in anything more than a trivial way. Let's look at sorting first. We can put position, or any expression really, to use for the purpose of ordering output. For example, suppose rather than determining whether listings are within a price range we'd rather sort all listings in ascending order. Listing 5.22 does something like that, using `xsl:sort`.

LISTING 5.22   `sort.xsl`—Sort Listings by price

```
 1: <?xml version="1.0"?>
 2: <xsl:stylesheet
 3:     xmlns:xsl="http://www.w3.org/XSL/Transform/1.0"
 4:     indent-result="no" default-space="strip">
 5: <xsl:template match="text()"/>
 6:
 7: <xsl:template match="//Town[TownName='Shirley']">
 8:     <xsl:apply-templates select="Listing">
 9:         <xsl:sort select="numberListingPrice"/>
10:     </xsl:apply-templates>
11: </xsl:template>
12:
13: <xsl:template match="Listing">
14:     <xsl:value-of select="."/>
15: </xsl:template>
16: </xsl:stylesheet>
```

The reason I said "something like that" rather than "exactly that" or something similar is because we don't get exactly what is expected; our prices are treated like strings. This brings us to the exact usage of `xsl:sort`. `xsl:sort` has four attributes in addition to the `select=` attribute. Each of these optional attributes adds additional control over sort order. They are

- `order='ascending|descending'`—Defines the order of the sort—default is ascending.
- `data-type='text|number'`—Defines how the data should be interpreted—default is text.
- `lang='somelang'`—Defines the language in which the data should be interpreted. Uses the same set of values as `xml:lang`. For example, `lang='fr'` for French, or `lang='en-US'` for U.S. English—default is determined by the system environment.
- `case-order='upper-first|lower-first'`—Default case order is language specific.

5

JAVA AND XSL

Numbering

Numbering is the natural companion to sorting. Suppose we wanted to number the `Listing` elements from the prior section as well as sorting them. We could have added a single line to Listing 5.21, line 13a, and caused our elements to be numbered neatly on output.

```
13:<xsl:template match="Listing">
13a:    <xsl:number value="position()"/>
14:     <xsl:value-of select="."/>
15: </xsl:template>
```

`xsl:number` also has several additional attributes other than the `value=` attribute that control the format of the resulting output number:

- `level='single|multiple|any'`—Specifies what levels of the tree should be considered. Default is `single`. `single` counts all siblings at the current level +1 (for itself) that match the `count=` pattern. Thus for our two sets of `Listing` elements (one within each `Town`), each list would be counted separately.

  `multiple` counts all ancestors of the current node +1 (for itself) that match the `count=` pattern. any counts nodes that match at any level within the document.

- `from='starting'`—Specifies the starting value to count from. For example, `from='10'` would starting numbering at 10.

- `count='somepattern'`—The `count=` attribute specifies a pattern that the selected node must match to be counted.

- `format='a format'`—The `format=` attribute specifies how the output should look and is a subset of the `type` attribute of the HTML 4.0 element `OL`. Example formats might be

  '1.' For 1., 2., 3., and so on

  'a' for a, b, c, and so on

  'A' for A, B, C, and so on

  'i' for i, ii, iii, iv, v, and so on

Number Formatting

In general, number formatting is defined by section 7.7.1 of the XSLT specification, Number to String Conversion Attributes. See this section for a complete list of all the attributes for formatting numbers.

Listing 5.23 shows a much more complete listing of numbering that makes use of the `count=` attribute to count `County`, `Town`, and `Listing` entries, each of which has its own template rule that uses `<xsl:number...>` with a format to number the individual levels. Listing 5.24 shows an abbreviated result after running `XT` using this stylesheet and our original input `REListing.xml`

LISTING 5.23   `sort-2.xsl`—Sort and Number at Multiple Levels

```
<?xml version="1.0"?>
<xsl:stylesheet
    xmlns:xsl="http://www.w3.org/XSL/Transform/1.0"
    indent-result="no" default-space="strip">
<xsl:template match="text()"/>
<xsl:template match="/REListing">
    <xsl:number level="multiple" count="County|Town|Listing" />
    <xsl:apply-templates/>
</xsl:template>

<xsl:template match="County">
    <xsl:number format="I"/>
    <xsl:text> </xsl:text>
    <xsl:value-of select="@Name"/>
    <xsl:text>&#xD;&#xA;</xsl:text>
    <xsl:apply-templates/>
</xsl:template>
<xsl:template match="Town">
    <xsl:number format="i"/>
    <xsl:text> </xsl:text>
    <xsl:value-of select="TownName"/>
    <xsl:text>&#xD;&#xA;</xsl:text>
    <xsl:apply-templates/>
</xsl:template>

<xsl:template match="Listing">
    <xsl:number format="1."/>
    <xsl:text> </xsl:text>
    <xsl:value-of select="."/>
</xsl:template>
</xsl:stylesheet>
```

LISTING 5.24   Result of Applying `sort-2.xsl` to `REListing.xml`

```
I Worchester
  i Shirley
       1.
          The Real Estate Exchange
          Colonial
          189000
          7 Something Place
          1999
          3
          1.5
          40,000
          A Small Three Bedroom Colonial set on 1 acre
. . .
       6.
          Gosselin Grp.
          Land
          129900
          15 Birchwood road
          Last lot in pristine neighborhood
          1.5
          Will not last!
  ii Lunenburg
       1.
          R.E. LLP
          Mansion
          1200000
          1 Lakeside Ave
          1952
          10
          5
          2
          Absolutely incredible mansion right on the lake!
. . .
       5.
          Gosselin Grp.
          Land
          529900
          4 Lakeshore Drive
          Deep water dock rights!
          2.5
          One of the last lots on the lake!
```

Variables

Before we move on to creating content, there is one other area of XSL that we need to explore: `xsl:variable`. XSL allows us to define variables, which are just content bound to a name, using the `xsl:variable` element. In its simplest form, variables are simply placeholders for other contents. For example, we could define a simple variable as follows:

```
<xsl:variable name='author'>Al Saganich</xsl:variable>
```

We could then reference this variable via `xsl:value-of`. For example:

```
<xsl:value-of select="$author"/>
```

In fact, there are two ways to define variables, although the second is not supported by XT at the time of this writing.

```
<xsl:variable name="SomeName">some value</xsl:variable>
```

and

```
<xsl:variable name="SomeName" select="some value"/>
```

We can use variables in expressions. For example, we could have created a variable that defined the position we wanted to select from a set of listings or perhaps the maximum price we could afford for a home. Let's re-examine selecting inexpensive homes using variables as shown in Listing 5.25.

LISTING 5.25   `Cheap-3.xsl`—Using Variables

```
<?xml version="1.0"?>
<xsl:stylesheet
    xmlns:xsl="http://www.w3.org/XSL/Transform/1.0"
    indent-result="no" default-space="strip">
<xsl:variable name='maximum'>150000</xsl:variable>
<xsl:template match="text()"/>
<xsl:template match="Listing[ListingPrice &lt; $maximum]">
    Cheap!:<xsl:value-of select="."/>
</xsl:template>
</xsl:stylesheet>
```

A few notes on variables:

- `xsl:param` is another way to say `xsl:variable`.
- Variables can reference other variables.

  The current version of XT does not support this and does not expand the underlying variables.

- We insert the value of a variable into an expression by prefixing the variable name with a dollar sign ($).

- Variable values cannot be changed on-the-fly and are similar to variables defined with Java's final keyword.

- Two variables cannot be of the same name and the same scope. For example

```
<xsl:template ...>
    <xsl:variable name='a'>some value</xsl:variable>
    <xsl:param name='a'>some other value</xsl:param>
</xsl:template>
```

is illegal, whereas

```
<xsl:template ...>
    <xsl:variable name='a'>some value</xsl:variable>
</xsl:template>
<xsl:template ...>
    <xsl:param name='a'>some other value</xsl:param>
</xsl:template>
```

is perfectly legal.

Creating Content

There are a number of other ways to insert content directly into an output document. We sometimes want to insert unchanged text (xsl:text), add an attribute (xsl:attribute) or entire elements (xsl:element), or entire lists of elements (xsl:copy). Whatever the case may be, XSL has a construct for it

xsl:text

We've already seen xsl:text several times. It allows us to insert information directly into our output document as well as allowing us to disable output escaping. For example:

```
<xsl:text disable-output-escaping="no">&lt;</xsl:text>
```

results in < being output. Whereas

```
<xsl:text disable-output-escaping="yes">&lt;</xsl:text>
```

results in < being output.

Outputing Scripting Elements

Earlier versions of the XSL Specification had a real problem with outputting JavaScript and the like because most scripting languages use less than as a character and don't recognize the HTML 4.0 entity set. With xsl:text and disabling output escaping, we can output pretty much whatever we want without worrying that the XSL translation engine will muck it up.

xsl:attribute

We can add attributes directly into elements via `xsl:attribute`. For example, suppose we had a separate `.html` file for each town in our original example? We could generate HTML links for each by writing the following:

```
<xsl:template match="//Town">
    <a>
    <xsl:attribute name="href">
        <xsl:value-of select="TownName"/>.html</xsl:attribute>
    The wonderful town of <xsl:value-of select="TownName"/>
    </a>
</xsl:template>
```

Simple and straightforward enough!

A few important notes on adding attributes:

- The attribute must be written within an element. For example, the `<a>`...`</a>`.

- Attributes must be written before any child elements.

- Attributes must not contain non-textual data except for `[cr]` and `[nl]`, which can be inserted exactly as given or via their appropriate entities.

xsl:element

Rather than a single attribute, we sometimes want to create an entire element, and with `xsl:element` we can. If we look back to our original `REListing.xml` file, we can see that `County`s have `Name` and `Description` as attributes rather than as child elements. We could recreate the `County` element with `Name` and `Description` as child elements via listing 5.26

LISTING 5.26   `Element.xsl`—Recreate County Elements with Children

```
<?xml version="1.0"?>
<xsl:stylesheet
    xmlns:xsl="http://www.w3.org/XSL/Transform/1.0"
    indent-result="no" default-space="strip">
<xsl:template match="text()"/>
<xsl:template match="//County">
    <xsl:element name="County2">
        <name><xsl:value-of select="@Name"/></name>
        <desc><xsl:value-of select="@Desc"/></desc>
    </xsl:element>
</xsl:template>
</xsl:stylesheet>
```

In fact, we could have added comments and attributes to the result as well.

5

Attribute Value Templates

We know we can go from attributes to elements, but what about the other way around? Suppose we wanted to create a stylesheet that changed the underlying elements of a Listing into attributes? Given our original definition of a Listing

```
<!ELEMENT TownDescription (#PCDATA)>
<!ELEMENT Listing (ListingBroker, Type,
➥ListPrice,Addr, YearBuilt?,Bedrooms?,
➥Baths?, SpecialFeatures?, Lotsize,Description)>
<!ELEMENT ListingBroker (#PCDATA)>
<!ELEMENT Type (#PCDATA)>
<!ATTLIST Type
PropType CDATA #REQUIRED
PropType (residential|commercial|land|farm|other) "residential">
<!ELEMENT Addr (#PCDATA) >
<!ELEMENT YearBuilt (#PCDATA)>
<!ELEMENT Bedrooms (#PCDATA)>
<!ELEMENT Baths (#PCDATA)>
<!ELEMENT SpecialFeatures (#PCDATA)>
<!ELEMENT Lotsize (#PCDATA)>
<!ATTLIST Lotsize Units (acres|sq.feet) "sq.feet">
```

Our first inclination would be to write the following:

```
<xsl:template match="Listing">
    <NewListing
        ListingBroker="<xsl:value-of select='ListingBroker'"
. . .
    />
</xsl:template>
```

But this code violates the rule that we must output correctly formed XML and this result is malformed. We can, however, get the job done by using an attribute template and replacing the xsl:value-of with {ListingBroker}. For example

```
<xsl:template match="//Listing">
    <NewListing
        ListingBroker="{ListingBroker}"
        Type="{Type}"
    />
</xsl:template>
```

We can see that {ListingBroker} is just a shortcut for saying xsl:value-of select='ListingBroker'.

Copying Nodes with `xsl:copy`

Sometimes, we just want an exact copy of the input generated to the output. `xsl:copy` does just that for us, as shown in Listing 5.27. In fact, the XSLT Specification defines a transform called the identity transform that generates its input as output using `xsl:copy`.

LISTING 5.27   `Identity.xsl`—Generate Input as Output

```
<?xml version="1.0"?>
<xsl:stylesheet
    xmlns:xsl="http://www.w3.org/XSL/Transform/1.0"
    indent-result="no" default-space="strip">

<xsl:template match="@*|node()">
    <xsl:copy>
        <xsl:apply-templates select="@*|node()"/>
    </xsl:copy>
</xsl:template>
</xsl:stylesheet>
```

Formatting Objects

At the beginning of this chapter, it was stated that XSL is really a two-step process. We've examined the transformation step closely. The second step is formatting or page layout and is provide by formatting objects. In this section, we examine how formatting objects work and how we can use them to lay out an XML document.

XSL Formatting Objects Specification

This chapter is based on the April 1999 release of the XSL Formatting Objects specification. Currently, a partial implementation of the specification exists for rendering to PDF from `xml.apache.org/FOP`. It's likely that the syntax will have changed slightly by the time this book reaches print.

Formatting Objects Overview

Formatting objects are based on and extend both CSS2 and DSSSL. Perhaps the largest difference between XSL Formatting Objects, often referred to as FO objects or just FO, and other page layout mechanisms is the way FO objects are used. FO objects don't define layout *per se* but, rather, they specify constraints under which objects are positioned. The exact layout of any object is handled by the formatter itself.

For the most part, each FO object is based on a similar CSS construct. However, as of the most recent XSL specification, CSS constructs and FO objects are similar in name and function, but an exact mapping was not completed.

Using the Formatting Object Specification (FOP)

Currently, or at least when this chapter was completed, there was a single partial implementation of the XSL Formatting Objects specification, FOP. FOP is available from xml.apache.org/fop and was donated by J. Tauber of www.jtauber.com. You will need to download the latest version of FOP (at last report, fop_bin_0_12_1.jar) and add it to your CLASSPATH. For convenience, v0.12.1 is available on the CD-ROM.

You can run FOP in one of several ways. The most common is via the command line using a FOP or FOB file, which is just an XML file containing formatting objects. The format of the FOP command is

```
java [-DDorg.xml.sax.parser=parser.class]
➥org.apache.fop.apps.CommandLine fo.input output.pdf
```

where *fo.input* is any file containing formatting objects and *output.pdf* is the resulting PDF. In addition, you can specify the sax parser to use with FOP by passing the -Dorg.xml.sax.parser switch and setting it to an appropriate parser. For example, to use FOP to process simple.fop to simple.pdf using J. Clarks sax parser, assuming it's in the CLASSPATH, you would execute the following:

```
java   -Dorg.xml.sax.parser=com.jclark.xml.sax.Driver
➥org.apache.fop.apps.CommandLine simple.fob   simple.pdf
```

The previous method assumes that you ran XT or some other XSL Transform engine on an original XML document and produced a formatting objects–based file using a stylesheet. You can skip this intermediate step by executing the following command:

```
java org.apache.fop.apps.XTCommandLine file.xml stylesheet.xsl output.pdf
```

where *file.xml* is an input XML document, *stylesheet.xsl* is a stylesheet that transforms *file.xml* into the formatting objects namespace, and *output.pdf* is the result rendered as a PDF.

The Apache FOP distribution comes with one additional tool that can be used to render to the screen the resultant FO object file using the AWT toolkit. To execute AWTCommandline, type the following command:

```
java org.apache.fop.apps.AWTCommandLine fo.file
```

where *fo-file* contains formatting objects. Figure 5.6 shows a screen shot of running AWTCommandLine on a simple formatting objects file.

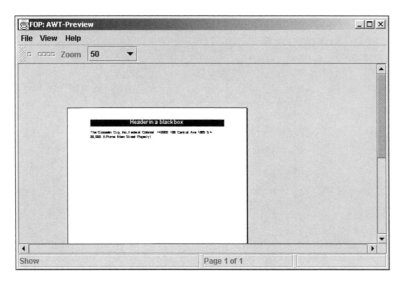

FIGURE 5.6
AWTCommand on `simple.fob`.

With the ability to actually process formatting objects, let's now look at *Areas* and how they affect the page layout process.

> **FOP and the XSL Formatting Objects Specification**
>
> No complete implementation of FO objects existed at the time of this writing. While FOP implements about 28 for the FO elements and 48 FO properties, there are well over 50 elements and more than 100 properties in the XSL specification. See the `xml.apache.org/fop` Web page for a complete list of what is supported in FOP.

Areas

XSL formatting objects are based on a page model in which pages are broken into five regions: `region-before`, `region-after`, `region-start`, `region-end`, and `region-body`. Figure 5.7 shows a typical layout of these five regions from a Western language perspective. Writing modes define the actual layout of each region. Many of the readers of this text might be English speaking and expect text to be displayed in a specific fashion—left to right and top to bottom. Using the *Western* writing mode, `region-before` corresponds to the header, `region-after` the footer, `region-start` the left margin, `region-end` the `right margin`, with `region-body` representing the space left over. Other writing modes correspond to other written languages. Table 5.8 shows many of the common writing modes with common languages that use them and a description of their layouts and reading rules. A number of less common modes also exist that correspond to no specific language and are used in various publishing applications.

Western Page Layout

FIGURE 5.7
Western page layout.

TABLE 5.8   Writing Modes and Screen Layouts

Mode	Common Language	Description
lr-tb	Latin/Western	Read left to right, top to bottom.
rl-tb	Arabic/Hebrew	Read right to left, top to bottom.
tb-rl	Chinese/Japanese	Read top to bottom, right to left.
tb-lr	Mongolian/Western Advertising	Read top to bottom, left to right.
bt-lr	None	Read bottom to top, left to right.

In addition to the five main regions concepts, FO objects are divided into areas. Areas are the basic building blocks of page layout. The XSL Formatting Objects specification defines four rectangular areas: area containers, block areas, line areas, and inline areas. Area containers are constrained by their writing mode and have a number of common properties, such as borders and padding. The four main areas are

- *Area containers*—Area containers are the highest level container in the Formatting Objects specification. Area containers are used to reserve space and hold content and may contain other area containers. Area containers can be precisely positioned and contain many other area types. Area containers have borders and can be padded. Hierarchically, area containers can contain other area containers or block areas and display spaces. In a typical book model, the highest level container is the page. Pages are further broken down into headers/footers and left/right margins with the main body contained in the area in between. Examples of area containers are `region-start`, `region-end`, `region-before`, `region-after`, and `region-body`.

- *Block areas*—Block areas are the next level of area in the FO specification. Block areas typically represent paragraphs or lists and contain other block areas, line areas, and display spaces. The bullet points in this list would have been represented using a list-block, a kind of block area prepended with a number, character, or glyph. Block areas can contain nested block areas, line areas, and display spaces. Within a given area container, block areas are "stacked" one on top of the other and are constrained by the writing mode. Stacking is the process of ordering sequentially one area after another within its bounding area. Block areas grow and shrink as required to contain the text and other areas represented within them. Examples of block areas are: `block`, `display-rule`, `display-graphic`, `display-link`, and `list-block`.

- *Line areas*—Line areas are placed within block areas and contain what we would normally consider lines of text. Line areas contain inline areas and inline spaces. Like block areas, line areas are "stacked" one after another, shrinking or growing as required to contain their content. There are no formatting objects that correspond directly to line areas but they are created by the formatter as required to contain inline areas. Unlike the other areas, line areas do not have borders or padding.

- *Inline areas*—Inline areas are the lowest level area container in the Formatting Objects specification and typically represent characters or "glpyhs." Inline areas are always stacked and may be separated by inline spaces. An example of an inline area is a `glyph-area` representing a single character or glyph within a given language. Note that glyph-areas are atomic elements and cannot contain other areas.

Each of the four areas, with the exception of line areas, have two common properties—border and padding. Borders can have before, after, end, and start color as well as style and width. Padding can be specified to precede, follow, be above, or below a given area.

The FO Namespace

Before we go on and look at the anatomy of a FO Object file, we need to examine the FO namespace.

FOP and Java

Formatting is an important aspect of XML. However, because this is a book on Java and XML, we will not go into elaborate detail on XSL formatting objects but rather give a sufficient introduction such that the reader can progress on his or her own.

5

The FO Name space is defined by xmlns:fo=http://www.w3.org/XSL/Format/1.0.
However, for the remainder of this chapter, we will be using the namespace
xmlns:fo=" http://www.w3.org/1999/XSL/Format" because the most current namespace
is not yet supported by FOP.

There are more then 50 formatting objects defined by the April 1999 specification, and perhaps
more will be added over time. In addition, there are over 100 properties that can be applied to
FO objects. Table 5.9 lists the elements currently supported by FOP, in the FO namespace, in
roughly the order they are defined in XSL specification.

TABLE 5.9   The FO Namespace

Namespace Elements	
fo:root	fo:layout-master-set
fo:simple-page-master	fo:region-body
fo:region-before	fo:region-after
fo:page-sequence	fo:sequence-specification
fo:sequence-specifier-simple	fo:sequence-specifier-repeating
fo:sequence-specifier-alternating	fo:flow
fo:static-content	fo:block
fo:list-block	fo:list-item
fo:list-label	fo:list-body
fo:page-number	fo:display-sequence
fo:inline-sequence	fo:display-rule
fo:display-graphic	fo:table
fo:table-column	fo:table-body
fo:table-row	fo:table-cell

A number of properties apply to the FO namespace elements. Table 5.10 lists the current set of
properties supported by FOP.

TABLE 5.10   FO Namespace Properties

Namespace Properties	
end-indent	page-master-name
page-master-first	page-master-repeating
page-master-odd	page-master-even
margin-top	margin-bottom

TABLE 5.10   Continued

Namespace Properties	
margin-left	margin-right
extent	page-width
page-height	flow-name
font-family	font-style
font-weight	font-size
line-height	text-align
text-align-last	space-before.optimum
space-after.optimum	provisional-distance-between-starts
provisional-label-separation	rule-thickness
color	wrap-option
white-space-treatement	break-before
break-after	text-indent
href	column-width
background-color	padding-top
padding-left	padding-bottom
padding-right	

Anatomy of a FO Document

FO documents are nothing more than normal XML documents, containing a root element and some number of child elements. They need to follow XML syntax and well formed-ness requirements, as well as use the FO namespace. Listing 5.28 shows a simple FO file with a common extension `.fob` or `.fop`, although `.xml` would have been appropriate as well. We can break this file down and see that it is made up of the following parts:

1. Line 1—An `fo:root` root element that encapsulates the entire document   `fo:root` must contain the `xmlns` property. In production environments, this is going to be `http://www.w3.org/XSL/Format/1.0`. However, for FOP we need to use the older `http://www.w3.org/1999/XSL/Format` namespace. The root element contains a `fo:layout-master-set` and a `fo:page-sequence` element.

2. Line 2—`fo:layout-master-set`   Layout master sets contain 1 or more `simple-page-master` elements, each named using the `name=<pagename>` property. Simple-page-masters define the margin, extents and, in general, the layout of a given page. You must have at least one `fo:simple-page-master`, but you can certainly have more. Books often have first, last, odd, and even specifications, each with different margins and layout.

3. Line 11—fo:region-before, fo:region-body, fo:region-after, fo:region-start, and fo:region-end   The fo:region-* elements define what regions are actually contained within our page. In this example, we choose to have three regions (because that's all FOP supports), each of which will be populated later on in the document.

4. Line 16—fo:page-sequence   Every FO document will have a fo:page-sequence element that defines the content of the page. Each fo:page-sequence element starts with a fo:sequence-specification element that defines what page master to use for this layout. There may be fo:sequence-specifier-* children within a sequence specifier, each representing a different portion or the result.

5. Lines 20, 32, and 42—Defines the actual content of the region-before, region-body, and region-after portions of the document   The fo:flow element, starting in line 42, represents the running content of the result and normally spans multiple pages. The two fo:static-content elements, starting on lines 20 and 32, represent content that will be placed on all pages. In Listing 5.28, we specify a header and footer for the pages.

LISTING 5.28   Simple.fob—A Simple FO Object File

```
 1: <?xml version="1.0" encoding="utf-8"?>
 2: <fo:root xmlns:fo="http://www.w3.org/1999/XSL/Format">
 3:     <fo:layout-master-set>
 4:     <fo:simple-page-master page-master-name="cheap"
 5:                   height="8.5in"
 6:                   width="11in"
 7:                   margin-top="0.5in"
 8:                   margin-bottom="0.5in"
 9:                   margin-left="1in"
10:                   margin-right="1in">
11:       <fo:region-before extent="1in"/>
12:       <fo:region-body margin-top="0.5in"/>
13:       <fo:region-after extent=".75in"/>
14:     </fo:simple-page-master>
15:     </fo:layout-master-set>
16:     <fo:page-sequence>
17:       <fo:sequence-specification>
18:         <fo:sequence-specifier-single page-master-name="cheap"/>
19:       </fo:sequence-specification>
20:       <fo:static-content flow-name="xsl-before">
21:       <fo:block font-size="18pt"
22:               font-family="sans-serif"
23:               line-height="24pt"
```

LISTING 5.28   Continued

```
24:                background-color="black"
25:                color="white"
26:                    space-after.optimum="15pt"
27:                    text-align="centered"
28:                    padding-top="3pt">
29:                    Header in a black box
30:                </fo:block>
31:            </fo:static-content>
32:        <fo:static-content flow-name="xsl-after">
33:        <fo:block font-size="18pt"
34:                font-family="sans-serif"
35:                line-height="24pt"
36:                space-after.optimum="15pt"
37:                text-align="centered"
38:                padding-top="3pt">
39:                page:<fo:page-number/>
40:                </fo:block>
41:        </fo:static-content >
42:        <fo:flow flow-name="xsl-body">
43:            <fo:block>
44:            The Gosselin Grp, Inc.
45:            Federal Colonial
46:            149900
47:            106 Central Ave
48:            1865
49:            5
50:            4
51:            80,000
52:            A Prime Main Street Poperty!
53:            </fo:block>
54:        </fo:flow>
55:    </fo:page-sequence>
56: </fo:root>
57:
```

Listing 5.28 was rather simplistic in that all information was hard-coded into the FO document. In real situations, an XSL transform, via a stylesheet, would have been applied to yield the FO document. Listing 5.29 shows a stylesheet that takes as input the REListing.xml document and creates the output shown in Figure 5.8. We will refer back to this listing periodically during the remainder of this section.

LISTING 5.29   fo1.xsl—Stylesheet to Convert FO Objects

```
 1: <?xml version="1.0"?>
 2: <xsl:stylesheet
 3:     xmlns:xsl="http://www.w3.org/XSL/Transform/1.0"
 4:     xmlns:fo="http://www.w3.org/1999/XSL/Format"
 5:     indent-result="no" default-space="strip" > <!-- result-ns="fo"> -->
 6:
 7:
 8:     <xsl:template match="/">
 9:             <fo:root xmlns:fo="http://www.w3.org/1999/XSL/Format">
10:             <fo:layout-master-set>
11:             <fo:simple-page-master page-master-name="cheap"
12:                     height="8.5in"
13:                     width="11in"
14:                     margin-top="0.5in"
15:                     margin-bottom="0.5in"
16:                     margin-left="1in"
17:                     margin-right="1in">
18:               <fo:region-before extent="1in"/>
19:               <fo:region-body margin-top="1.25in"/>
20:               <fo:region-after extent=".75in"/>
21:                 </fo:simple-page-master>
22:             </fo:layout-master-set>
23:
24:     <fo:page-sequence>
25:         <fo:sequence-specification>
26:             <fo:sequence-specifier-single page-master-name="cheap"/>
27:         </fo:sequence-specification>
28:         <fo:static-content flow-name="xsl-before">
29:             <fo:block font-size="18pt"
30:             font-family="sans-serif"
31:             line-height="24pt"
32:             background-color="black"
33:             color="white"
34:             text-align="centered"
35:             padding-top="3pt">
36:                 <xsl:apply-templates select="/REListing/Header"/>
37:             </fo:block>
38:         </fo:static-content>
39:         <fo:static-content flow-name="xsl-after">
40:             <fo:block font-size="18pt"
41:             font-family="sans-serif"
42:             line-height="24pt"
43:             text-align="centered"
44:             padding-top="3pt">
45:                 page:<fo:page-number/>
46:             </fo:block>
47:         </fo:static-content >
```

LISTING 5.29 Continued

```
48:            <fo:flow>
49:                <xsl:apply-templates/>
50:            </fo:flow>
51:        </fo:page-sequence>
52:    </fo:root>
53:    </xsl:template>
54:
55:    <xsl:template match="Header">
56:        <xsl:value-of select="."/>
57:    </xsl:template>
58:
59:    <xsl:template match="Listing[ListingPrice &lt; 150000]">
60:        <fo:block font-size="12pt" font-family="sans-serif">
61:        <xsl:value-of select="."/>
62:        </fo:block>
63:        <fo:block font-size="10pt" font-family="sans-serif">
64:            taxrate:<xsl:value-of select="../TaxRate"/>
65:            applied rate:$<xsl:value-of
➥select="round((ListingPrice div 1000) * ../TaxRate)"/> a year
66:        </fo:block>
67:    </xsl:template>
68: </xsl:stylesheet>
```

FIGURE 5.8

Result of Applying FO1.xsl *to* REListing.xml.

Let's look more closely at each of the parts of a FO document.

Master Pages

We saw in Listing 5.28, and again in Listing 5.29, a `fo:simple-page-master` element. In our examples, we only had a single page. However, in a more complete document, a single page layout is not enough; we typically need several. Listed next are the more common properties of `fo:simple-page-master` elements. For any property not specified, the formatter provides a reasonable default.

- `name=""string""`—The name of the page master. Left, right, first, last are all common. For example `name="first"`.

- `height=""value""`—The height of the page in inches (in), centimeters (cm), or pixel (px). For example, `height=""8in""` for U.S. Letter or `""8.26in""` for European A4.

- `width=""value""`—The width of the page. Same units as height. For example `width=""11.69in""` for A4.

- `margin-top`, `margin-bottom`, `margin-left`, `margin-right`—We can also specify page margins. Values are in inches, centimeters, or pixels.

The following code snippet provides for a common book layout where left and right facing pages have a 1 inch inner margin. Note that the *left* page has `fo:region-start`, `fo:region-body`, and `fo:region-end` areas, whereas the *right* page has only a `fo:region-body` area.

```
<fo:layout-master-set>
    <fo:simple-page-master page-master-name="left"
        height="8.5in"
        width="11in"
        margin-top="0.5in"
        margin-bottom="0.5in"
        margin-left="1in"
        margin-right="0.5in">
        <fo:region-start/>
        <fo:region-body/>
        <fo:region-end/>
    </fo:simple-page-master>
    <fo:simple-page-master page-master-name="right"
        height="8.5in"
        width="11in"
        margin-top="0.5in"
        margin-bottom="0.5in"
        margin-left="0.5in"
        margin-right="1in">
        <fo:region-body/>
    </fo:simple-page-master>
</fo:layout-master-set>
```

Page Sequences

Each FO document must have one or more `fo:page-sequence` elements, each containing `fo:sequence-specification`, `fo:static-content`, and `fo:flow` child elements. `fo:sequence-specification` elements describe how to use the previously defined master pages. As we've stated, it's not uncommon to have many pages defined for a given FO document. Books typically have a start page, a back page, first chapter pages, last chapter pages, body pages, and so on. We can use `fo:sequence-specificier-*` elements of a `fo:sequence-specification` to specify which pages to use and in what order. The `page-master-name` property of the sequence specifier tells the formatter which master page to use. There are several flavors of sequence specifiers:

- `fo:sequence-specifier-single`—Use this page only once. Uses the `page-master-name` property to specify the name of the master page.
- `fo:sequence-specifier-repeating`—Specifies a repeating page. Uses `page-master-first` and `page-master-repeating` to specify the names of the first and repeating pages, respectively.
- `fo:sequence-specifier-alternating`—Specifies different pages that are used in an alternating fashion. Uses `page-master-first` for the first page, `page-master-[odd|even]` for the odd/even pages, and `page-master-last-[odd|even]` for the last odd/even page. A final page, `past-master-blank-even`, is used when a format requires that all starting pages for a given page start on a odd page, as most books do.

> **NOTE**
>
> FOP currently only supports the properties `page-master-name`, `page-master-first`, `page-master-repeating`, `page-master-odd`, and `page-master-even`.

There are a number or properties that can be used with `fo:page-sequence` elements to control how page numbering will be applied. Some of the most common are

- `initial-page-value=`*integer*—Where *integer* is any positive integer.
- `format=""`*format*`""`—Where *format* is one of the formats used in XSLT. Examples include I (generates uppercase roman numerals), i (lowercase), A to generate A B C…AA AB, and so on.
- `digit-group-separator=""`*separator*`""`—Where *separator* is a grouping separator character, such as a comma.
- `n-digits-per-group=`*integer*—Where *integer* is some signed integer between 1 and 10.

5

JAVA AND XSL

After you have defined how pages will look, via `fo:sequence-elements`, you need to describe the contents of a page. The next sections describe both static and flowing content in detail.

Static Content

There are two kinds of content that are placed into a FO area. Static content is unchanging from page to page. Flowing content flows from page to page. The headers and footers of a document are typically static content, whereas the actual text, figures, diagrams, and so on are flowing content. We specify static content using the `fo:static-content` element. Lines 28–38 of Listing 5.28 describe the static content of a page. The following snippet of code shows a `fo:static-content` element that defines a page header based on the `/REListing/Header` element of our `REListing.xml` document.

```
<fo:static-content id="header" flow-name="xsl-before">
    <fo:block font-size="18pt"
    font-family="sans-serif"
    line-height="24pt"
    background-color="black"
    color="white"
    text-align="centered"
    padding-top="3pt">
    <xsl:apply-templates select="/REListing/Header"/>
    </fo:block>
</fo:static-content>
```

Examining the code, we see that content elements, both static and flow, are placed into an area based on the `flow-name=<area_name>` property. Flow names are linked to areas based on the following mapping:

```
xml-body maps to region-body

xml-after maps to region-after

xml-before maps to region-before

xml-start maps to region-start

xml-end maps to region-end
```

It's unclear from the specification why there is a separate set of mappings rather than simply using the `region-*` names. Perhaps, with the final version of the specification, this minor issue will have been resolved.

We can also use the `id=<name>` property to uniquely identify this element.

We will discuss the remainder of the information, basically the `<fo:block>...</fo:block>` portion, when we examine block-level objects. In general, there can be zero or more `fo:static-content` elements within a `fo:page-sequence` element. Furthermore, `fo:static-content` elements must precede any `fo:flow` elements.

Flow Objects

Flow objects represent some sort of content distribution, such as a paragraph, a chapter, a section or similar concept, and immediately follow static content. There are typically one or more `fo:flow` elements within a page sequence element, each of which contains text, links, tables, lists—simply put, flowing content. Anything that is not fixed on a given page belongs in a `fo:flow` element. In Listing 5.29, the `fo:flow` elements represented the listings from `REListing.xml`. Further `fo:flow` elements contain block-level objects.

There are five block-level objects. They are

- `fo:block`—Used to format paragraphs, titles headings, and so on. For example

  `<fo:block font-size="10pt", font-family="sans-serif">This is 10pt text sans serif text<fo:block>`.

- `fo:display-graphic`—Used to insert an image into a flow. For example

  `<fo:display-graphic image="someimage.jgp" height="1.0in" width="2.0in"/>`.

- `fo:display-included-container`—Used to generate block-level areas that have a different writing mode than the current mode.

- `fo:display-rule`—Used to insert a line into a block. For example

  `<fo:display-rule length="1.0in" line-thickness="1pt"/>`.

- `fo:display-sequence`—Used as a container for child block elements and specifies a number of properties that will be inherited by its children.

More Properties

There are a large number of properties that apply to block-level formatting. See the XSL Formatting Objects specification for a complete list of all the properties and which ones apply to a given FO element.

Other Content Elements

There are a number of other content elements that can appear within a `fo:flow` element or children of a `fo:flow` element. Some of the most common are

- `fo:inline-sequence`—Used as a container for properties for its children. For example

  `<fo:inline-sequence font-style="italic">italic text</fo:inline-sequence>` produces *italic text*.

- `fo:table`—Used for inserting tables and has a number of child elements, such as `fo:table-caption`, `fo:table-body`, and `fo:table-row`.

- `fo:list-block`—Used for inserting lists and has a number of child elements, such as `fo:list-item`, `fo:list-item-body`, and `fo:list-item-label`.

There are also a number of other less common `fo:flow` child elements, such as footnotes, links, characters, and so on. All these elements, when combined with their appropriate properties, give an incredible level of control over formatting and page layout.

Summary

In this chapter, we examined the issues related to translating and formatting XML documents using stylesheets and formatting objects. Both are large topics befitting whole books rather than a single chapter. It was our goal to give readers a sufficient understanding of these areas such that an interested reader could read the actual XSLT and XSL specification and understand how to apply that information.

Suggested for Further Study

1. Redraw Figure 5.5 assuming that `3.xsl` includes its child stylesheets rather then imports them.

2. Name the four most important, in your opinion, top-level elements in the XSL namespace and describe what each does and why it's important.

3. What does the template rule `<xsl:template match="/|*"/>` do?

4. List the XSL default rules and describe what each is used for.

5. Pattern matching is the process of producing content from input. Using the `REListing.xml` document, define one or more template rules as required that produces a header element from the header field of the DTD. Describe what each part of the template(s) does for you.

6. Describe 6 of the 13 axes. What does each do? Give examples.

7. Write a template rule or rules that output any listings that have a listing price greater than $149,000 and less than $300,000. Output the original listing plus the tax rate per $1,000 and an estimate of how much in taxes will be paid in 1 year, 5 years, and 10 years. *Challenge: Can you format the output to sort by lowest tax rate?*

Further Reading

Associating Style Sheets with XML documents Version 1.0. W3C Members. 29-June-1999, W3C. Can be found at `http://www.w3.org/TR/xml-stylesheet`.

Extensible Stylesheet Language (XSL) Specification Working Draft. W3C Members. 21-April-1999, W3C. Can be found at `http://www.w3.org/TR/WD-xsl`.

Cascading Stylesheets. Level 1. W3C Members. 11-Jan-1999, W3C. Can be found at `http://www.w3.org/TR/REC-CSS1`.

HTML and Stylesheets. W3C Members. 24-March-97, W3C. Can be found at `http://www.w3.org/TR/WD-style-970324`.

Collections and XML

"One of these days I'd really love to stop talking about what is and isn't XML, though I know it's fun, and start talking about what we can do with it."

—Heard on the XML-Dev mailing list

IN THIS CHAPTER

In Chapter 4, "Advanced XML," we learned about the DOM and how to use it to manipulate XML documents. In addition, there are a number of things developers might want to do beyond the basics provided by the DOM Level I and Level II interfaces. The Java 2.0 JDK specifically provides a number of collection classes, each adding specific functionality. In this chapter we will examine these classes and see how we can extend the DOM interfaces and classes in a natural way via Java collections.

Collection Basics

Interestingly enough, none of the Java books I have go into much detail on how to use the JDK collection classes, not even my own! So before we jump in and examine how we might model an XML document via a collection, it's important to understand exactly what collections are and how they can be used.

The JDK provides for what are commonly called *collections*. Collections, in the simplest sense, are just that: collections of objects. Collections are normally used to store, manipulate, and transmit data from one method to another. Examples of collections might be addresses in a phone book, cards in a playing hand, or any other natural grouping of objects. The JDK goes beyond simple collections and provides a framework for manipulating sets of objects. But what exactly is a *framework*? The *American College Dictionary* defines a framework as follows:

> **framework** *(fraym-wurk), n.* (1) A structure composed of parts fitted and united together. (2) One designed to support or enclose something; frame or skeleton.

In the case of Java, the JDK provides a uniform architecture, or *framework*, for manipulating collections of objects. There are a number of benefits to providing the framework around which collections are developed. The most obvious benefit is that since all the collection classes are defined using uniform underlying principles they can all act and be acted on in similar ways. The JDK states a number of benefits to the collections framework. The most important are

- *Reduces development effort*—The collection framework reduces development effort by providing a number of ready-to-use collections and algorithms that act on them.

- *Provides interoperability between unrelated APIs*—By establishing a number of common interfaces that all collections must implement, classes can pass collections around and know in advance how to manipulate them.

- *Reduces the time required to learn the APIs*—Since each collection is based on a uniform set of functionality, the learning curve for new collections is reduced.

And my two personal favorites:

- *Fosters code reuse*—Since all collections implement a common set of APIs, we can develop algorithms that act on the interfaces and ignore the underlying details. We can reuse these classes again and again as new situations arise.

- *Reduces the effort required to design and implement APIs*—Since the interfaces to the collection classes are well known, we need not agonize over how to implement something but can instead examine the details of only a specific implementation.

The framework sounds all well and good, but without some meat on these bones, it's all just fluff. The JDK provides that meat by way of a number of interfaces and some concrete implementations as well as some abstract classes. Specifically provided for are the following (each addresses in one way or another the important tenets of the collections framework):

- *Interfaces*—The interfaces portion of the collections framework provides the *supporting structure* of our framework. Collections provide a number of interfaces for `Sets`, `Lists`, and `Maps`. The most basic, `Collection`, is a simple list of elements that might be ordered and might contain duplications. `Sets` are collections, still unordered, but cannot contain duplications. `Lists` may contain duplications but are ordered and allow for access by position. `Maps` are not truly collections but rather map from keys to values. `Maps` are ordered, via the keys, and cannot contain duplicates. Additionally, interfaces exist for `SortedMap` and `SortedSets`.

- *General-purpose implementation*—The general-purpose implementations support a number of our framework ideas. The collection classes provide a set of ready-made implementations that a developer can use immediately. Six general-purpose implementations exist: `HashSet`, `TreeSet`, `ArrayList`, `LinkedList`, `HashMap`, and `TreeMap`.

- *Algorithms*—Algorithms are provided by the JDK 1.2 for sorting, searching, shuffling, copying, and otherwise manipulating collections. All are provided via static methods on the `Collection` class.

- *Abstract implementations*—In addition to general implementations, a number of partial implementations exist that developers can build on. Examples of these partial implementations are `AbstractCollection`, `AbstractSet`, and `AbstractList`.

- *Basic infrastructure*—In addition to actual implementations and algorithms, a number of basic infrastructure classes exist for working with collections. We can move through a collection using `Iterators`. `Iterators` are similar to `Enumerations` but go beyond their basic functionality. We can compare collections using the `Comparable` and the `Comparator` interfaces, providing partial and complete orderings on collections.

- *Other aspects of the framework*—The collections framework covers a number of other aspects as well, from special purpose implementations to convenience classes to support for legacy collections such as `Vector` and `Hashtable`.

All in all, the JDK does an excellent job of both defining the collections framework and providing a starting point for using and developing new collections.

Using a Collection

Before we get into developing our own collection-based classes around the DOM, an example of using one of the predefined collections is in order. Listing 6.1 makes use of several of the collection classes and allows for manipulating a list of book titles. In the following sections, we will expand these ideas to develop our own simple collections on top of the DOM.

> **NOTE**
>
> It's really a shame that when the DOM II specification was being drafted its developers didn't spend more time examining the Java 2.0 collections interfaces. Back in Chapter 4 where we discussed the DOM II interfaces, you might remember the nodeIterator interface. The nodeIterator goes much of the way toward providing a traditional JDK 2.0 collection. With only a little more time and effort, nodeIterator and the filter interfaces could have been collections in the Java sense and would have provided interesting definitions for other languages to build on. During the remainder of this chapter we will just build them ourselves!

LISTING 6.1   SortExample.java—Using a Simple Collection

```
 1: /*
 2:  * @(#)SortExample.java        1.0 2000/815
 3:  *
 4:  * Copyright (c) 1999 Macmillan USA.
 5:  * All Rights Reserved.
 6:  *
 7:  */
 8: package sams.chp6;
 9:
10: import java.io.InputStreamReader;
11: import java.io.BufferedReader;
12: import java.io.IOException;
13: import java.util.*;
14:
15: public class SortExample
16: {
17:     ArrayList bookList = new ArrayList();
18:     public SortExample (String sTitle)
19:     {
```

LISTING 6.1 Continued

```
20:         System.out.println("Creating array of books");
21:         bookList.add(new Book("Better Living Thru Chemistry",
22:                               "A. Publisher", 4.27));
23:         bookList.add(new Book("Java 2 for C/C++ Programmers",
24:                               "J.Wiley & Sons", 62.50));
25:         bookList.add(new Book(
26:                       "The Microsoft Visual J++ 1.1 Sourcebook",
27:                       "J.Wiley & Sons", 39.95));
28:         bookList.add(new Book("XML and Java",
29:                       "Macmillian Computer Publishers", 49.95));
30:         bookList.add(new Book("Inside Visual C++ 5.0",
31:                       "Microsoft Press", 99.99));
32:
33:         sortList("(Default)");
34:         boolean done = false;
35:         InputStreamReader isr = new InputStreamReader(System.in);
36:         BufferedReader br = new BufferedReader(isr);
37:         while ( !done)
38:         {
39:             System.out.println("Sort by:");
40:             System.out.println(" 1 for Title");
41:             System.out.println(" 2 for Publisher");
42:             System.out.println(" 3 for Price");
43:             System.out.println(" 4 to add new book");
44:             System.out.println(" 5 to exit");
45:             System.out.println("Enter (1,2,3,4,5): ");
46:             System.out.flush();
47:             String command;
48:             try
49:             {
50:                 command = br.readLine();
51:                 if (command.equals("done"))
52:                 {
53:                     done=true;
54:                     continue;
55:                 }
56:                 if (command != null && command.length() > 0)
57:                 {
58:                     switch (Integer.parseInt(command))
59:                     {
60:                         . . .
61:                     } // end switch
62:                 } // end if command
63:             } catch (IOException e) { done = true;}
```

LISTING 6.1   Continued

```
64:          } // end while not done
65:
66:      }
67:
68:      private void sortList (String sSortCriteria)
69:      {
70:          if (sSortCriteria == null || sSortCriteria.equals(""))
71:              return;
72:
73:          Comparator c = null;
74:          if (sSortCriteria.equals("Title"))
75:              c = new TitleComparator();
76:          else if (sSortCriteria.equals("Publisher"))
77:              c = new PublisherComparator();
78:          else if (sSortCriteria.equals("Price"))
79:              c = new CostComparator();
80:          if ( null == c)
81:              Collections.sort(bookList);
82:          else
83:              Collections.sort(bookList,c);
84:
85:          displayList(bookList);
86:      }
87:
88:      private void displayList(ArrayList list)
89:      {
90:          Iterator it = list.iterator();
91:          while (it.hasNext())
92:          {
93:              Book p = (Book) it.next();
94:              System.out.println(p.sTitle + ", " + p.sPublisher+ ", "
➥+ p.dPrice);
95:          }
96:      }
97:      public static void main (String args[])
98:      {
99:          new SortExample("Sort Example");
100:     }
101:
102:     class Book implements Comparable
103:     {
104:         String sTitle = "";
105:         String sPublisher = "";
106:         double dPrice = 0.0;
```

LISTING 6.1 Continued

```
107:
108:         public Book ()
109:         {
110:             try
111:             {
112:                 InputStreamReader isr =
113:                     new InputStreamReader(System.in);
114:                     . . .
115:             } catch (IOException e) {
116:                 sTitle = sPublisher = "";
117:                 dPrice=0;
118:                 return;
119:             }
120:         }
121:         public String toString()
122:         {
123:             String result= "Title:" + sTitle +"Publisher:"+
➥sPublisher + "Price:" + dPrice;
124:             return result;
125:         }
126:         public Book (String sTitle,
127:                         String sPublisher,
128:                         double dPrice)
129:         {
130:             this.sTitle = sTitle;
131:             this.sPublisher = sPublisher;
132:             this.dPrice = dPrice;
133:         }
134:
135:         private Comparator defaultComparator = new TitleComparator();
136:         public int compareTo (Object o)
137:         {
138:             return (defaultComparator.compare(this, o));
139:         }
140:     }
141:
142:
143:     class TitleComparator implements Comparator
144:     {
145:         public int compare (Object book1, Object book2)
146:         {
147:             String sTitle1 = ((Book)book1).sTitle;
148:             String sTitle2 = ((Book)book2).sTitle;
149:             return (sTitle1.compareTo(sTitle2));
```

LISTING 6.1   Continued

```
150:            }
151:        }
152:
153:    class PublisherComparator implements Comparator
154:    {
155:        public int compare (Object book1, Object book2)
156:        {
157:            String sPublisher1 = ((Book)book1).sPublisher;
158:            String sPublisher2 = ((Book)book2).sPublisher;
159:            return (sPublisher1.compareTo(sPublisher2));
160:        }
161:    }
162:    class CostComparator implements Comparator
163:    {
164:        public int compare (Object book1, Object book2)
165:        {
166:            double price1 = ((Book)book1).dPrice;
167:            double price2 = ((Book)book2).dPrice;
168:            if ( price1 == price2 )
169:                return 0;
170:            else if (price1 < price2)
171:                return -1;
172:            else
173:                return 1;
174:        }
175:    }
176: }
177:
```

Listing 6.1 implements a simple java.util.ArrayList collection. An ArrayList extends from an AbstractList, then List, and ultimately Collection and provides the basics of a growable array object. Methods exist for adding objects, clearing the array, and for the normally expected operations such as size(), isEmpty(), and so forth. SortExample.java shows a number of the most commonly used features of a collection. In fact, most developers will use precisely these operations when they develop code that uses collections.

Examining the listing line by line, we can see the more important aspects of collections in use. First, on line 13 we import the collection classes that are part of java.util. In our simple example we use ArrayList, although List would have worked as well, to manipulate instances of Book objects. Examining line 102 we see the definition of the Book inner class. Book implements the Comparable interface, which requires the method compareTo() to be defined. The important aspect of the Comparable interface is that it is used to define an *ordering* on books.

What exactly is meant by an ordering? We won't go into the mathematical definition of an ordering, but suffice it to say that an ordering defines how we might list our books. If we were defining words in a dictionary, a natural ordering would be lexicographical order. By default, we'll order by title. Lines 135–139 define the `compareTo()` method, which defines how `Book` objects are ordered relative to one another.

Often users need to traverse a collection of objects. Two specific interfaces are supplied just for this purpose, `Iterator` and `ListIterator`. Lines 88–96 define a simple method, `displayList()`, which traverses our list using an `Iterator`. For those familiar with the `Enumeration`, the methods of `Iterator` will come as no surprise. `hasNext()` returns `true` or `false` depending on whether the `Iteration` has more elements. `next()` returns the next object, which we cast to type `Book`, and throws `NoSuchElementException` if no additional elements exist. One additional method that goes beyond what `Enumerations` provide is the `remove()` method. `Remove` removes the last item returned by the `Iteration` and throws `UnsupportedOperationException` or `IllegalStateException` if it fails. In addition to `Iterator`, we could have traversed the list using a `ListIterator`. `ListIterator` extends `Iterator` and so contains all its methods, but adds methods for traversing the list backward as well as forward and other methods for adding and changing the underlying collection. Developers interested in `ListIterator` should see the JDK documentation for a complete list of its methods. In any case, we obtain a reference to an instance of `Iterator` or `ListIterator` interfaces on a given collection via the `iterator()` or `listIterator()` methods on the collection of interest.

We've examined much of the example, but two areas have not yet been covered: adding elements and sorting. Lines 21 and 22 handle the adding of elements nicely. Sorting is another matter altogether. Collections can be manipulated using a set of polymorphic algorithms. *Polymorphic* is one of those 10-cent big words, but for our purposes its simple definition of "many forms" is enough. Our `sortList` method, lines 68–86, uses the `Collections` sort algorithm to sort our list using a given ordering—in this case, title, price, or publisher order. In each case an instance of a class that implements the `Comparator` interface is used. `Comparator` orders objects and requires a single method to be implemented, `compare`, which is much like the `compareTo` method defined on lines 136–139.

Translating a DOM to Other Collections

We've examined a simple `Collections` example, now we move on and examine how we can model the DOM as a `Collection`.

DOM to Array

The simplest way to provide the DOM as an array is to extend the `ArrayList` class. Listing 6.2 shows a very simple class that extends `ArrayList` and takes a document and a tag and creates an array collection, which can then be used anywhere a collection can be used.

The example itself is simple enough: Import `java.util` and then define the class to extend `ArrayList` (line 6). We then populate the array in the constructor as shown in lines 8–20. We can then use the class like any other collection and lines 33–39 simply exercise our new DOM-based collection.

TIP

A little trick you can use to test a class is to define a normal static main method and then use that method to create an instance of your class. Any class that can stand alone can be tested this way. DOMArray.java is written this way and avoids the need for a separate class for testing and debugging.

LISTING 6.2   DOMArray.java—Converting DOM to an Array

```
 1: package sams.chp6;
 2: import java.io.*;
 3: import java.util.*;
 4: import org.w3c.dom.*;
 5:
 6: public class DOMArray extends ArrayList
 7: {
 8:     public DOMArray (Document parent,String tag)
 9:     {
10:         NodeList elements = parent.getElementsByTagName( tag);
11:         if ( elements.getLength()== 0)
12:         {
13:             return;
14:         }
15:         for (int i = 0; i < elements.getLength(); i++)
16:         {
17:             Element anElement = (Element) elements.item(i);
18:             this.add(anElement);
19:         } // end for
20:     }
21:     public static void main (String argv [])
22:     {
```

LISTING 6.2 Continued

```
23:          if (argv.length != 2)
24:          {
25:              System.err.println("Usage:
➥java sams.chp6.DOMArray filename tag");
26:              System.exit(1);
27:          }
28:          Document document;
29:          try
30:          {
31:              document = XMLUtil.openDocument(argv[0]);
32:              System.out.println("Document successfully created!");
33:              DOMArray test = new DOMArray(document, argv[1]);
34:              Iterator it = test.iterator();
35:              while (it.hasNext())
36:              {
37:                  Element e = (Element) it.next();
38:                  XMLUtil.displayNodeInfo("",e);
39:              }
40:
41:          }
42:          catch (Exception e)
43:          {
44:              System.out.println(
➥"Unexpected exception reading document!" +e);
45:              System.exit (0);
46:          }
47:          System.exit (0);
48:      }
49: }
```

DOM as a List

Another type of collection is a *list*, which is simply an ordered group of elements that can contain duplicates. Listing 6.3 goes beyond the simple DOMArray we implemented in listing 6.2 and provides a base implementation of almost every method in the AbstractList interface. For a complete definition of all the methods in an AbstractList, see the JDK documentation. Most of the class is self-explanatory; however, the Iterator interator() method bears some explanation.

As we've already seen, iterators are like enumerations and allow us to move forward through the contents of a collection. However, iterator is only an interface and we are required to provide an implementation. In the case of DOMList, we do not want to expose the underlying mechanisms behind our implementation. That would compromise the framework concepts and principles. But we do need to know how the DOMList does its work in order to provide an appropriate implementation. Lines 108–129 of DOMList define an inner class, DOMIterator, which implements the iterator interface, taking advantage of the underlying workings of DOMList but hiding its implementation.

NOTE

If you're unfamiliar with inner classes you should read Chapter 3, Section 5 of <ShamelessPlug> *Java 2 and JavaScript for C and C++ Programmers* by M. Daconta, A. Saganich and E. Monk, J. Wiley and Sons, publisher.</ShamelessPlug>

LISTING 6.3   DOMList.java—Converting DOM to a List

```
 1: package sams.chp6;
 2:
 3: import java.io.*;
 4: import java.util.*;
 5: import org.w3c.dom.*;
 6:
 7: public class DOMList extends AbstractList
                         implements Cloneable, Serializable
 8: {
 9:
10:     private transient Document parent;
11:     private transient Object elementData[];
12:     private int size;
13:
14:     private void inRangeCheck(int pos)
15:     {
16:     if (pos >= size || pos < 0)
17:         throw new IndexOutOfBoundsException(
18:             "Position: "+pos+", DOMList size: "+size);
19:     }
20:
21:     public DOMList (Document parent,String tag)
22:     {
23:         super();
24:         this.parent = parent;
25:         NodeList elements = parent.getElementsByTagName( tag );
26:         if ( elements.getLength()== 0)
27:         {
28:             size=0;
29:             return;
30:         }
```

LISTING 6.3 Continued

```
31:          elementData= new Object[elements.getLength()];
32:          for (int i = 0; i < elements.getLength(); i++)
33:          {
34:              Element anElement = (Element) elements.item(i);
35:              elementData[i] = anElement;
36:
37:          } // end for
38:      }
39:      public int size()
40:      {
41:          return size;
42:      }
43:      public boolean isEmpty()
44:      {
45:          return size == 0;
46:      }
47:        public void add(int index, Object element)
48:         {
49:           throw new UnsupportedOperationException(
   ➡"DOMList does not support add(int,element) operation" );
50:         }
51:        public boolean add(Object element)
52:         {
53:           throw new UnsupportedOperationException(
   ➡"DOMList does not support add(element) operation" );
54:         }
55:      public Object get(int position)
56:      {
57:          inRangeCheck(position);
58:          return elementData[position];
59:      }
60:      public Object set(int position, Object element)
61:      {
62:          inRangeCheck(position);
63:          throw new UnsupportedOperationException(
   ➡"DOMList does not support set(int,element) operation" );
64:      }
65:      public Object remove(int position)
66:      {
67:          inRangeCheck(position);
68:          throw new UnsupportedOperationException(
   ➡"DOMList does not support remove(int) operation" );
```

LISTING 6.3   Continued

```
69:      }
70:      public int indexOf(Object elem)
71:      {
72:          if (elem == null)
73:              return -1;
74:          else
75:          {
76:              for (int i = 0; i < size; i++)
77:              if (elem.equals(elementData[i]))
78:                  return i;
79:          }
80:          return -1;
81:      }
82:      public int lastIndexOf(Object elem)
83:      {
84:          if (elem == null)
85:              return -1;
86:          else
87:          {
88:              for (int i = size-1; i >= 0; i--)
89:                  if (elem.equals(elementData[i]))
90:                      return i;
91:          }
92:          return -1;
93:      }
94:
95:      public void clear()
96:      {
97:          throw new UnsupportedOperationException(
➥"DOMList does not support clear operation" );
98:      }
99:      public boolean addAll(int index, Collection c)
100:     {
101:         throw new UnsupportedOperationException(
➥"DOMList does not support addAll(int, Collection) operation" );
102:     }
103:
104:     public Iterator iterator()
105:     {
106:         return new DOMIterator();
107:     }
108:     private class DOMIterator implements Iterator
109:     {
110:         Object[] table = DOMList.this.elementData;
```

LISTING 6.3   Continued

```
111:            int length = elementData.length;
112:            int pos = 0;
113:            DOMIterator() {};
114:
115:            public boolean hasNext()
116:            {
117:                if (pos < length)
118:                    return true;
119:                return false;
120:            }
121:
122:            public Object next()
123:            {
124:                if (pos >= length)
125:                    throw new NoSuchElementException();
126:                pos++;
127:                return table[pos-1];
128:
129:            }
130:
131:            public void remove()
132:            {
133:                throw new UnsupportedOperationException(
➥"DOMIterator does not support remove() operation" );
134:            }
135:        }
136:
137:    public static void main (String argv [])
138:    {
139:        if (argv.length != 2)
140:        {
141:
142:            System.err.println(
➥"Usage: java sams.chp6.DOMArray filename tag");
143:            System.exit(1);
144:        }
145:
146:        Document document;
147:        try
148:        {
149:            document = XMLUtil.openDocument(argv[0]);
150:            System.out.println("Document successfully created!");
151:
152:            DOMList test = new DOMList(document, argv[1]);
153:            Iterator it = test.iterator();
154:            while (it.hasNext())
```

LISTING 6.3   Continued

```
155:              {
156:                  Element e = (Element) it.next();
157:                  XMLUtil.displayNodeInfo("",e);
158:              }
159:
160:          }
161:          catch (Exception e)
162:          {
163:              System.out.println(
➥"Unexpected exception reading document!" +e);
164:              System.exit (0);
165:          }
166:          System.exit (0);
167:
168:      }
169:
170: }
```

Sorting a DOM

We briefly examined the elements of sorting in Listing 6.1. Since the `Collections` algorithms are polymorphic we should be able to apply them to our DOM-based collections. However, we still need appropriate `Comparator` methods. Listing 6.4 gives three such methods, each of which can be applied to DOM elements to provide an appropriate ordering. Listing 6.5 then exercises our newly created `Comparator` methods.

LISTING 6.4   `DOMCollectionUtilities.java`—Comparator Methods

```
1: package sams.chp6;
2:
3: import org.w3c.dom.*;
4: import java.util.Comparator;
5:
6: public class DOMCollectionUtilities
7: {
8:     static class StringElementComparator implements Comparator
9:     {
10:         public int compare (Object e1, Object e2)
11:         {
12:             if ( !( e1 instanceof Element)
13:                 || !( e2 instanceof Element)
14:                 )
15:                 return 0;
```

LISTING 6.4 Continued

```
16:            Element element1 = (Element) e1;
17:            Element element2 = (Element) e2;
18:            String content1 = element1.getNodeName();
19:            String content2 = element2.getNodeName();
20:            if (element1.getNodeType() == org.w3c.dom.Node.TEXT_NODE &&
21:                element2.getNodeType() == org.w3c.dom.Node.TEXT_NODE)
22:            {
23:                content1 = element1.getNodeValue();
24:                content2 = element2.getNodeValue();
25:            }
26:            return (content1.compareTo(content2));
27:        }
28:    }
29:
30:    static class IntegerElementComparator implements Comparator
31:    {
32:        public int compare (Object e1, Object e2)
33:        {
34:            if ( !( e1 instanceof Element)
35:                 || !( e2 instanceof Element)
36:                 )
37:                return 0;
38:            Element element1 = (Element) e1;
39:            Element element2 = (Element) e2;
40:
41:            // we can only compare convert text elements to integers
42:            if (element1.getNodeType() != org.w3c.dom.Node.TEXT_NODE ||
43:                element2.getNodeType() != org.w3c.dom.Node.TEXT_NODE)
44:                return 0;
45:
46:            String content1 = element1.getNodeValue();
47:            String content2 = element2.getNodeValue();
48:
49:            return new Integer(content1).compareTo(new Integer(content2));
50:        }
51:    }
52:
53:    static class FloatElementComparator implements Comparator
54:    {
55:        public int compare (Object e1, Object e2)
56:        {
57:            if ( !( e1 instanceof Element)
58:                 || !( e2 instanceof Element)
59:                 )
```

LISTING 6.4   Continued

```
60:                    return 0;
61:              Element element1 = (Element) e1;
62:              Element element2 = (Element) e2;
63:
64:              // we can only compare convert text elements to float
65:              if (element1.getNodeType() != org.w3c.dom.Node.TEXT_NODE ||
66:                  element2.getNodeType() != org.w3c.dom.Node.TEXT_NODE)
67:                  return 0;
68:
69:              String content1 = element1.getNodeValue();
70:              String content2 = element2.getNodeValue();
71:
72:              return new Float(content1).compareTo(new Float(content2));
73:          }
74:      }
75: }
```

LISTING 6.5   TestDOMList.java—DOMList Test Driver

```
 1: package sams.chp6;
 2:
 3: import java.io.*;
 4: import java.util.*;
 5: import org.w3c.dom.*;
 6:
 7: public class TestDOMList
 8: {
 9:     public static void main (String argv [])
10:     {
11:         if (argv.length < 2)
12:         {
13:             System.err.println(
14:     "Usage: java sams.chp8.DOMArray filename tag [comparison method]" );
15:             System.exit(1);
16:         }
17:         Document document;
18:         try
19:         {
20:             document = XMLUtil.openDocument(argv[0]);
21:             System.out.println("Document successfully created!");
22:             DOMList test = new DOMList(document, argv[1]);
23:             if (argv.length == 3)
24:             {
25:                 String which = argv[2];
```

LISTING 6.5   Continued

```
26:             System.out.println("Attempting to sort by "+ which);
27:             Comparator c = null;
28:             if (which.equals("int"))
29:                 c = new
30:             DOMCollectionUtilities.IntegerElementComparator();
31:             else if (which.equals("float"))
32:                 c = new
33:             DOMCollectionUtilities.FloatElementComparator();
34:             else if (which.equals("string"))
35:                 c = new
36:             DOMCollectionUtilities.StringElementComparator();
37:             if ( null != c)
38:                 Collections.sort(test,c);
39:         }
40:         Iterator it = test.iterator();
41:         while (it.hasNext())
42:         {
43:             Element e = (Element) it.next();
44:             XMLUtil.displayNodeInfo("",e);
45:         }
46:     }       catch (Exception e)
47:     {
48:         System.out.println(
➥"Unexpected exception reading document!" +e);
49:         System.exit (0);
50:     }
51:     System.exit (0);
52:     }
53: }
```

TestDOMList.java makes use of the Comparator methods we defined and shows, on lines 27–38, another example of employing custom Comparator methods. The CD version of Listing 6.5 goes slightly farther than the one displayed here in the text and adds a listIterator method, which is required by the generic Collections.sort() method. ListIterators are much like Iterators but allow for both backward and forward list traversal. Interested readers can see a complete implementation of ListIterator.

Custom Collections

Before we close this chapter we need to look at one additional topic: Why develop custom collections in the first place? Up to this point, we've seen two custom collections. DOMArray.java is an exceptionally simple collection that helps us understand better how collections work. DOMList.java goes a step further and gives a much better understanding about the inner workings of a collection.

There are a number of reasons to develop custom collections, the most important of which follow:

- *Application Specific*—Perhaps the most obvious reason for a custom collection might be application-specific collections. The previous DOM-based collections are excellent examples of application-specific collections. Certainly other application domains might warrant specific collections.

- *Concurrency*—One of the drawbacks of the collection classes is that they are not designed to be used concurrently. In fact, they are designed *not* to be used concurrently with specific wrapper collections designed to support concurrent access, but at a high price: reduced performance. Each time a collection is accessed, via a concurrent wrapper, the entire collection is locked. A *very* high price to pay. Financial or trading applications could very well need special-purpose high-performance collections that are highly concurrent. Concurrent collections that lock specific records or in other ways better manage concurrent access can easily be imagined.

- *Persistence*—None of the collections defined in the JDK are persistent. In fact, it might make excellent sense for a DOM-based collection to persist to secondary store. Collections that manage relational or object-oriented databases, Enterprise JavaBeans (EJBs), or other persistent objects might be candidates for persistent collections.

- *Special Purpose*—Each of the standard JDK collections is by definition general purpose and therefore designed to be useful to the broadest range of developers. But suppose you only need a subset of the functionality? Collections could be developed that offer significantly better `insert` or `get` performance but trade off other collection aspects. What about one-way access collections? More and more devices are being developed almost daily. It's not hard to envision a collection that represents all the lights or outlets in a home and provides runtime information on their current use and state.

- *Adapter*—DOM-based collections are examples of *adapter-based* collections. Those collections allow you to access some legacy data structure as if it were a collection class. Although Java has only been in existence for a short time, code that we might consider *legacy* already exists and might be candidates for adapter collections allowing access to legacy data structures but via the newer collection-based interfaces.

- *Other Reasons*—Convenience, enhanced functionality, the list goes on and on. The JDK collections are general purpose and as a result will not fit every desire.

So how do we choose? Use a existing general-purpose collection or develop a new custom collection? The answer is up to you. If existing collections don't fit your needs, develop a new one, or override an existing collection to add functionality or improve performance in some application-specific domain. But before you do, read the collections documentation, understand all the different collection types and how you might use one, and then proceed from there!

Summary

In this chapter we examined the Java Collection APIs. We started by examining exactly what collections are and how they can be used. We then created our own collections on top of the Document Object Model (DOM) and examined how we could sort and access a collection. We concluded our examination of collections by extending DOM-based collections from simple arrays to more complex lists. We invite you to go one step further and use the following section to continue to advance your understanding of Java Collections.

Suggested for Further Study

1. The collections framework defines a number of principles through which the framework itself makes development easier. Take any two of these principles and describe them in your own words. Give examples where applicable.

2. Update `SortExample` to use a `ListIterator` for traversal. Provide methods for displaying the list in backward and forward order.

3. Update `DOMList` to be a real list. That is, implement the unsupported methods. You will need to map the `DOMList` back to its underlying parent document and make sure that any operations on the `DOMList` are applied to the parent.

4. The sort methods in `DOMCollectionUtilities.java` are not quite correct in that they operate almost exclusively on `ELEMENT_NODE` elements. As we saw in Chapter 4, `ELEMENT_NODE`s can be almost terminal, in that they can have a single child node of type `ELEMENT_TEXT` which represents their actual content. Add three new `Comparator` methods that act on the children of `ELEMENT_NODE`s and sort based on the content of those children.

Further Reading

The Collections Framework section of the JDK documentation.

Java 2 and JavaScript for C and C++ Programmers. Michael C. Daconta, Al Saganich, Eric Monk. 1999, John Wiley and Sons.

Swing and XML

"Clearly, with Java emerging as the predominant Internet-system programming language and XML emerging as the dominant model for Internet data, these two technologies are bound to intersect in interesting ways."

—Jeremy Allaire, *"Java, XML and Web Syndication,"* Java
Developers Journal, August 1999

IN THIS CHAPTER

In this chapter, we will examine the basics of displaying XML with a Swing graphical user interface. We begin by discussing how to render the DOM with a JTree widget. For those Java programmers new to Swing user interfaces, we present an overview of the Swing components. We then examine how XML fits into Swing's Model-View-Controller (MVC) architecture. That is followed by a second example that renders an XML document as a table. We end the chapter with a discussion and demonstration of how XML can be used to create flexible, data-driven graphical user interfaces.

Displaying the DOM

As described in Chapter 3, "The Document Object Model (DOM)," the DOM represents an XML document as a hierarchical data structure or tree. The Java Platform Standard Edition (SE) includes support for a graphical tree view in the Swing package (javax.swing) called a JTree. The JTree component renders a tree model. Our job will be to encapsulate the DOM data model inside a Swing tree model so that it can be rendered as a JTree. The result of this is presented in Figure 7.1.

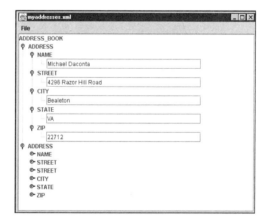

FIGURE 7.1
A DOM rendered with a JTree.

The DOM represents an XML document in two ways—a flat representation in which every member of the tree is a node and a hierarchical (or inheritance-based) representation in which tree members are specific subclasses like element, text node or attribute. I will use the flat representation because a JTree view is not concerned with the type of node, just its position in the tree and rendering.

Swing Component Basics

For those not experienced with building graphical user interfaces in Swing, the following are the prerequisite Swing concepts relevant to this chapter:

- Swing components are pure Java components called lightweight components. The only exceptions to this are Swing's top-level containers: frames, applets, windows, and dialogs. Swing's UI components all begin with the letter J: `JFrame`, `JLabel`, and `JMenu`. The rest of the numerous classes in the Swing packages are supporting classes.

- Swing components are not simple and are composed of multiple cooperating objects. The Swing components extend `java.awt.Container`. They support a cross-platform look-and-feel, pluggable look-and-feels (including native), and multiple views of a single data model.

- For backward compatibility with the AWT, the components in the AWT all have Swing counterparts with nearly identical APIs. The one significant exception is the `JFrame`, in which you add components to the `contentPane` instead of to the `JFrame`.

- The Swing component architecture is based on the Model-View-Controller paradigm. This is the same architecture used by Smalltalk for managing multiple look-and-feels. This architecture separates components into three types of objects: models, views, and controllers.

  Models are responsible for maintaining data and notifying views when the data changes.

  Views provide a visual representation of the models data and update themselves when the model changes.

  Controllers modify the model. For graphical user interface components, the most common way to do this is via handling events from the view (mouse clicks, key strokes, and so on). The Swing MVC implementation combines the view and controller into a UI delegate.

These concepts are demonstrated in the sample applications that follow.

The `DomViewer` Application

There are several options for converting a DOM tree into a tree suitable for rendering in a `JTree`. The requirements for a `JTree` model are defined by the interface `TreeModel` (see Listing 7.1).

LISTING 7.1 `TreeModel` Interface

```
package javax.swing.tree;
import javax.swing.event.*;
```

LISTING 7.1   Continued

```
public interface TreeModel
{        ′
public Object getRoot();
public Object getChild(Object parent, int index);
public int getChildCount(Object parent);
public boolean isLeaf(Object node);
public void valueForPathChanged(TreePath path, Object newValue);
public int getIndexOfChild(Object parent, Object child);
void addTreeModelListener(TreeModelListener l);
void removeTreeModelListener(TreeModelListener l);
}
```

The requirements for a TreeModel are simple for any tree data structure to implement; however, your implementation of this interface must be consistent. For example, the Object returned via the getChild() method must be able to determine if it is a leaf node when passed into the isLeaf() method. There are two options for creating the necessary TreeModel: wrap a DOM in a new class that translates TreeModel method calls into DOM method calls or use the DefaultMutableTreeNode class to create a new tree by extracting the values from the DOM tree.

While creating a DefaultMutableTreeNode tree requires less understanding of the workings of Jtree, wrapping the DOM is the better method because a DOM is already a tree. Therefore it is wasteful to create a second tree that mirrors the DOM tree. The better solution is to make the DOM's tree model conform to the JTree's TreeModel interface. The DomTreeModel inner class in Listing 7.2 implements the TreeModel by wrapping the DOM. The implementation boils down to returning the correct DOM child node, returning the number of children for a node, and other housekeeping operations.

The following are the salient features of the DomViewer application presented in Listing 7.2:

- The user interface sports a frame, a menu bar with one menu (File), and two options (Save and Exit), and the frame is filled with a graphical representation of the DOM tree.

- On startup, you enter the XML file to render and an optional -default argument that chooses between default rendering and custom rendering. If you do not specify the -default, the program uses a custom TreeCellRenderer and a custom TreeCellEditor.

- With the custom renderer and editor, the leaf nodes of the DOM tree will be available to be edited using a JtextField. After nodes are edited and the user hits return, the new value is stored in the DOM. The Save option in the File menu will allow you to write the new XML file to disk.

LISTING 7.2   DomViewer Application

```java
/* DomViewer.java */
package sams.chp7;

import java.io.*;
import java.util.*;
import java.awt.*;
import java.awt.event.*;
import javax.swing.*;
import javax.swing.event.*;
import javax.swing.tree.*;
import com.sun.xml.tree.XmlDocument;
import org.xml.sax.InputSource;
import org.xml.sax.SAXException;
import org.xml.sax.SAXParseException;
import org.w3c.dom.*;

public class DomViewer extends JFrame implements ActionListener
{
    XmlDocument doc;

    public Insets getInsets()
    {
        return new Insets(25,5,5,5);
    }

    class DomTreeModel implements TreeModel
    {
        Document doc;
        ArrayList listeners = new ArrayList();

        public DomTreeModel(Document doc)
        {
            this.doc = doc;
        }

        // Tree model methods
        public Object getRoot()
        {
            return doc.getDocumentElement();
        }

        public Object getChild(Object parent, int i)
        {
```

LISTING 7.2   Continued

```java
        Object o = null;
        NodeList children = ((Node)parent).getChildNodes();
        return children.item(i);
    }

    public int getChildCount(Object parent)
    {
        NodeList children = ((Node)parent).getChildNodes();
        return children.getLength();
    }

    public int getIndexOfChild(Object parent, Object child)
    {
        NodeList children = ((Node)parent).getChildNodes();
        int size = children.getLength();
        int i = -1;
        for(i = 0; i<size; i++)
        {
            Node n = children.item(i);
            if (n == child)
                break;
        }
        return i;
    }

    public boolean isLeaf(Object node)
    {
        boolean hasChildren = ((Node)node).hasChildNodes();
        return !hasChildren;
    }

    public void valueForPathChanged(TreePath path, Object newValue)
    {
        Node n = (Node) path.getLastPathComponent();
        n.setNodeValue((String)newValue);
    }

    public void addTreeModelListener(TreeModelListener l)
    {
        listeners.add(l);
    }

    public void removeTreeModelListener(TreeModelListener l)
    {
        listeners.remove(l);
    }
}
```

LISTING 7.2   Continued

```java
class DomTreeCellRenderer implements TreeCellRenderer
{
    public Component getTreeCellRendererComponent(JTree tree,
                                                  Object value,
                                                  boolean selected,
                                                  boolean expanded,
                                                  boolean leaf,
                                                  int row,
                                                  boolean hasFocus)
    {
        Component c = null;
        Color highlight = new Color(102,255,255);

        //find and see if the node is element node
        if (!leaf)
        {
            JLabel l = new JLabel();
            l.setOpaque(true);
            c = l;
            if ( selected )
            {
                l.setBackground(highlight);
                l.setForeground(Color.black);
                l.setText(((Node)value).getNodeName());
            }
            else
            {
                l.setBackground(Color.white);
                l.setForeground(new Color(0,51,204));
                l.setText(((Node)value).getNodeName());
            }
        }
        else  // a leaf node
        {
            JTextField f = new JTextField(30);
            //f.setEditable(true);
            c = f;
            if ( selected )
            {
                f.setBackground(new Color(195, 195, 250));
                f.setForeground(Color.black);
                f.setText(((Node)value).getNodeValue());
            }
            else
            {
```

LISTING 7.2   Continued

```java
                    f.setBackground(Color.white);
                    f.setForeground(Color.black);
                    f.setText(((Node)value).getNodeValue());
                }
            }

            return c;
        }
    }

    class DomTreeCellEditor  extends DefaultCellEditor
                             implements TreeCellEditor
    {
        private JTree tree;

        public DomTreeCellEditor(JTree tree)
        {
            super(new JTextField(30));
            this.tree = tree;
        }

        public boolean canEditImmediately(EventObject e)
        {
            return true;
        }

        public boolean isCellEditable(EventObject e)
        {
            boolean result = false;

            if (e instanceof MouseEvent)
            {
                MouseEvent me = (MouseEvent) e;
                TreePath path = tree.getPathForLocation(me.getX(), me.getY());
                if (path != null)
                {
                    Node n = (Node) path.getLastPathComponent();
                    if (n != null && !n.hasChildNodes())
                        result = true;
                }
            }

            return result;
        }
```

LISTING 7.2 Continued

```
public Component getTreeCellEditorComponent(JTree tree,
                                            Object value,
                                            boolean selected,
                                            boolean expanded,
                                            boolean leaf,
                                            int row)
{
    JTextField f = (JTextField) getComponent();
    Color highlight = new Color(102,255,255);
    if (leaf)
    {
        if ( selected )
        {
            f.setBackground(highlight);
            f.setForeground(Color.black);
            f.setText(((Node)value).getNodeValue());
        }
        else
        {
            f.setBackground(Color.white);
            f.setForeground(Color.black);
            f.setText(((Node)value).getNodeValue());
        }
    }
    else
        return null;

    return f;
    }
}
public DomViewer(String fileName, boolean defaultRenderer) throws Exception
{
    super(fileName);

    // add a simple menu
    JMenuBar bar = new JMenuBar();
    setJMenuBar(bar);
    JMenu fileMenu = new JMenu("File");
    JMenuItem saveItem = new JMenuItem("Save");
    saveItem.addActionListener(this);
    JMenuItem quitItem = new JMenuItem("Quit");
    quitItem.addActionListener(this);
    fileMenu.add(saveItem);
    fileMenu.add(quitItem);
    bar.add(fileMenu);
```

LISTING 7.2 Continued

```
        // create a SAX InputSource
        InputSource is = new
                    InputSource(new File(fileName).toURL().toString());

        // create a DOM Document
        doc = XmlDocument.createXmlDocument(is, true);
        DomUtil.normalizeDocument(doc.getDocumentElement());

        // Create a Tree Model from the Document
        DomTreeModel model = new DomTreeModel(doc);

        // Create a renderer
        DomTreeCellRenderer renderer = new DomTreeCellRenderer();

        // Create the JTree
        JTree tree = new JTree(model);
        tree.putClientProperty("JTree.lineStyle", "Angled");

        // Create an editor
        DomTreeCellEditor editor = new DomTreeCellEditor(tree);

        if (!defaultRenderer)
        {
            tree.setCellRenderer(renderer);
            tree.setEditable(true);
            tree.setCellEditor(editor);
        }

        // Create a scroll pane
        JScrollPane scroll = new JScrollPane(tree);

        getContentPane().add("Center", scroll);

        addWindowListener(new WindowAdapter()
                        {
                            public void windowClosing(WindowEvent we)
                            { System.exit(1); }
                        });

        setLocation(100,100);
        setSize(600,400);
        setVisible(true);
    }

    public void actionPerformed(ActionEvent evt)
    {
```

LISTING 7.2   Continued

```java
        String command = evt.getActionCommand();
        if (command.equalsIgnoreCase("Quit"))
        {
            System.exit(0);
        }
        else if (command.equalsIgnoreCase("Save"))
        {
            JFileChooser chooser = new
                        JFileChooser(System.getProperty("user.dir"));
            int stat = chooser.showSaveDialog(this);
            if (stat == JFileChooser.APPROVE_OPTION)
            {
                File f = chooser.getSelectedFile();
                try
                {
                    FileWriter fw = new FileWriter(f);
                    doc.write(fw);
                    fw.close();
                } catch (IOException ioe)
                  {
                    System.out.println("Error writing to: " + f);
                  }
            }
        }
    }

    public static void main(String args[])
    {
        if (args.length < 1)
        {
            System.out.println("USAGE: java
    sams.chp7.DomViewer xmlfile [-default]");
            System.exit(1);
        }

        try
        {
            boolean defaultRendering = false;
            if (args.length == 2 && args[1].equals("-default"))
                defaultRendering = true;

            new DomViewer(args[0], defaultRendering);
        } catch (Throwable t)
          {
            t.printStackTrace();
          }
    }
}
```

When Listing 7.2 is run without the `-default` option, it produces Figure 7.1. When run with the `-default` option, it produces Figure 7.2.

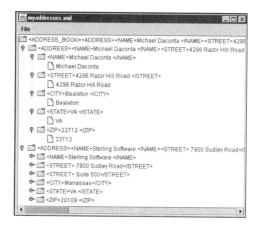

FIGURE 7.2

A DOM with default JTree *rendering.*

Note the following key points about the source code in Listing 7.2:

- The `main()` method merely instantiates a `DomViewer` object and passes in the arguments from the command line (filename and optionally a `-default` argument).

- The `DomViewer` constructor parses the XML document using the Sun Microsystems parser which produces an `XmlDocument` object that implements the DOM `Document` interface. This `XmlDocument` is passed into the constructor for the `DomTreeModel` object. The `DomTreeModel` is the most important object in this program.

- The `DomTreeModel` is an implementation of the `TreeModel` interface as a pass-through to the DOM API. Each requirement for a `JTree TreeModel` is translated into the corresponding DOM API call for the DOM Document object that is passed in to the constructor. All of the methods in this interface are straightforward implementations to satisfy the requirements of the interface method. For example, `getChild(parent, i)` requests the ith child of the parent object that was passed in. Because we know that all children we return will be DOM nodes, we can cast the incoming parent object to a DOM node and then get the `NodeList` of child nodes (using the `getChildNodes()` method) and from that object, the ith child. Note: For the default renderer, returning a node object will render a `JLabel` with whatever the node's `toString()` method returns. Because this is not always what we want, a custom `TreeCellRenderer` object is needed.

- The `DomTreeCellRenderer` object has only one method: `getTreeCellRendererComponent()`. The default `Renderer` returns a `JLabel`. The policy this renderer follows is that it returns a `JLabel` for non-leaf nodes and a `JTextField` for leaf nodes. In addition, this method uses the `nodeName` for non-leaf nodes and the `nodeValue` for leaf nodes. The reason you cannot always use a node value is because there are certain cases (such as an element) in which the node value is null. Using a `JTextField` for the leaf nodes allows us to edit the values in those nodes. To allow editing of these nodes, a `TreeCellEditor` was necessary.

- The key responsibilities of the `DomTreeCellEditor` are to allow editing to take place and return the component to be used as the editor.

- The last method to cover in the `DomViewer` application is the `actionPerformed()` method. This is the only method in the `ActionListener` interface, and is called in response to a menu selection. The Save command makes use of the `JFileChooser` component to display the Save As dialog box. After a valid file is returned, the `write()` method of the `XmlDocument` object is used to write the DOM to a text file.

Since the DOM will have text nodes of just whitespace, we need to normalize the tree to strip out these blank text nodes. To do that we use the `DomUtil` class and the `normalizeDocument()` method in Listing 7.3:

LISTING 7.3   DomUtil.java

```
package sams.chp7;
import java.util.*;
import org.w3c.dom.*;

public class DomUtil
{
    public static void normalizeDocument(Node n)
    {
        if (!n.hasChildNodes())
            return;

        NodeList nl = n.getChildNodes();
        for (int i = 0; i < nl.getLength(); i++)
        {
            Node cn = nl.item(i);
            if (cn.getNodeType() == Node.TEXT_NODE &&
                isBlank(cn.getNodeValue()))
            {
                n.removeChild(cn);
                i--;
            }
```

LISTING 7.3   Continued

```
            else
                normalizeDocument(cn);
        }
    }

    public static boolean isBlank(String buf)
    {
        if (buf == null)
            return false;

        int len = buf.length();
        for (int i=0; i < len; i++)
        {
            char c = buf.charAt(i);
            if (!Character.isWhitespace(c))
                return false;
        }

        return true;
    }
}
```

The Model-View-Controller Architecture and XML

I introduced you to Swing's usage of the Model-View-Controller (MVC) paradigm in the previous section. Though well suited for the design of graphical user interface components, the MVC architecture scales upward to applications and even systems. It is important to understand where XML fits in this picture, from Swing components on up.

Figure 7.3 is a high-level representation of the MVC architecture. The key elements of the diagram are the one-to-many relationships between the model and the controllers and the model and the views. Of course, the model being the abstract representation of some data correlates perfectly with XML as the premiere format for structured data. Another interesting artifact of the MVC architecture is its suitability for distributed applications. The connections between model, views, and controllers can span multiple applications, hosts and networks (including the Internet). So again, the distributed nature of MVC correlates well with the Web-centric domain of XML.

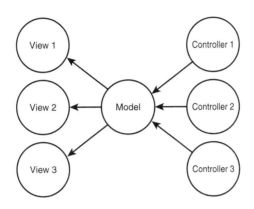

FIGURE 7.3

The MVC architecture.

The Swing components use models to allow multiple components to view and react to a single data structure. Many, but not all, Swing components use a model. Table 7.1 lists all the Swing components, describes them, and lists any models they use.

TABLE 7.1   Swing Component Models

Component	Model	Description
JApplet	None	An extension of an applet to allow Swing MenuBars and multiple panes.
JButton	ButtonModel	A pushbutton.
JCheckBox	ButtonModel	A check box (item that maintains state).
JCheckBoxMenuItem	ButtonModel	A menu item that can be selected or deselected.
JColorChooser	ColorSelection	A set of controls in a pane to allow the selection of a color.
JComboBox	CombBoxModel	A combo box (combination of a text field and a drop-down list).
JComponent	None	Base class for all Swing components.

TABLE 7.1   Continued

Component	Model	Description
JDesktopPane	None	Container used to create a multiple document object (MDI) desktop.
JDialog	None	A dialog window for both custom and standard dialog boxes.
JEditorPane	Document	A text component to edit a pluggable content type (using an EditorKit implementation).
JFileChooser	None	A dialog box to select a file to open or save.
JInternalFrame	None	A MDI window inside a JDesktopPane.
JLabel	None	A static text string or image that does not react to events.
JLayeredPane	None	A component to add depth to a container via multiple layers.
JList	ListSelection ListModel	A list of objects (text or images).
JMenu	ButtonModel	A menu in either a menu bar or popup menu.
JMenuBar	SingleSelectionModel	A menu bar.
JMenuItem	ButtonModel	A menu item.
JOptionPane	None	A standard set of dialog boxes to prompt the user.
JPanel	None	An invisible container for other components.
JPasswordField	Document	A text field that does not echo characters.
JPopupMenu	SingleSelectionModel	A popup menu (menu that pops up with a right click).

TABLE 7.1 Continued

Component	Model	Description
JProgressBar	BoundedRange	A graphical bar that displays the progress of some action.
JRadioButton	ButtonModel	A radio button (item that displays its state and can belong to a group).
JRadioButtonMenuItem	ButtonModel	A group of menu items of which only one can be selected.
JRootPane	None	The root of all JFC windows/panes.
JScrollBar	BoundedRange	A scrollbar (a knob to set a viewable display area).
JScrollPane	None	A container that automatically manages scrollbars for its contents.
JSeparator	None	A menu separator.
JSlider	BoundedRange	A slider (a slidable knob within a bounded interval).
JTabbedPane	SingleSelectionModel	A component that allows switching between panes (tabbed folder metaphor).
JTable	TableModel TableColumn ListSelection	A two-dimensional spreadsheet view.
JTextArea	Document	A multi-line editing area.
JTextField	Document	A single-line editing area.
JTextPane	Document	An extension of editor pane that models paragraphs and styles.

7

SWING AND XML

TABLE 7.1   Continued

Component	Model	Description
JToggleButton	ButtonModel	A two-state button.
JToolBar	None	A button bar with image buttons for common actions.
JToolTip	None	A "tip" display for all components when the mouse "hovers" over it.
JTree	TreeModel TreeSelection	A display for hierarchical data.
JViewPort	None	A viewable area (porthole) in a window that can be changed via scrolling.
JWindow	None	A window with no title bar.

The model this section focuses on is TableModel in Listing 7.4. TableModel abstracts a two-dimensional table of data with columns, rows, and a header line of column names. Any object that implements this interface can be rendered with a JTable.

LISTING 7.4   TableModel.java

```java
package javax.swing.table;
import javax.swing.*;
import javax.swing.event.*;

public interface TableModel
{
    public int getRowCount();
    public int getColumnCount();
    public String getColumnName(int columnIndex);
    public Class getColumnClass(int columnIndex);
    public boolean isCellEditable(int rowIndex, int columnIndex);
    public Object getValueAt(int rowIndex, int columnIndex);
    public void setValueAt(Object aValue, int rowIndex, int columnIndex);
    public void addTableModelListener(TableModelListener l);
    public void removeTableModelListener(TableModelListener l);
}
```

The `DomTable` Application

The `DomTable` application wraps a DOM in a table model and produces Figure 7.4 for `myaddresses.xml`. To execute the `DomTable` application you type:

```
> java sams.chp7.DomTable myaddresses.xml ADDRESS
```

When run, the code generates the output shown in Figure 7.4.

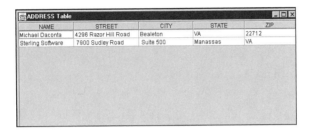

FIGURE 7.4
A DOM presented in table form.

The features of the `DomTable` application are as follows:

- Accepts any XML document to render in a table. The only constraint is that the user specifies one element (referred to as a `recordTag` in the program) to equate to a record (or row of the table). The chosen record element can be arbitrarily nested in the XML document because the list of rows (or candidate elements) is created by traversing the entire tree.
- The elements subelements become the columns of the table.

LISTING 7.5   DomTable.java

```java
/* DomTable.java */
package sams.chp7;

import java.io.*;
import java.util.*;
import java.awt.*;
import java.awt.event.*;
import javax.swing.*;
import javax.swing.event.*;
import javax.swing.table.*;
import com.sun.xml.tree.XmlDocument;
```

LISTING 7.5   Continued

```java
import org.xml.sax.InputSource;
import org.xml.sax.SAXException;
import org.xml.sax.SAXParseException;
import org.w3c.dom.*;

public class DomTable extends JFrame
{
    XmlDocument doc;

    public Insets getInsets()
    {
        return new Insets(25,5,5,5);
    }

    class DomTableModel extends AbstractTableModel
    {
        Document doc;
        ArrayList listeners = new ArrayList();
        NodeList records, columns;

        public DomTableModel(Document doc, String recordTagName)
        {
            this.doc = doc;
            records =
              doc.getDocumentElement().getElementsByTagName(recordTagName);
            columns = records.item(0).getChildNodes();
        }

        // Table model methods
        public int getRowCount()
        {
            return records.getLength();
        }

        public int getColumnCount()
        {
            // subelements of this element
            return columns.getLength();
        }

        public String getColumnName(int column)
        {
            return columns.item(column).getNodeName();
        }
```

LISTING 7.5 Continued

```
    public Object getValueAt(int row, int column)
    {
        Node n = records.item(row);
        NodeList nl = n.getChildNodes();
        Node n2 = nl.item(column);
        String val = n2.getNodeValue();
        if (val == null)
        {
            // Node is an element
            // get text node
            Node n3 = n2.getFirstChild();
            if (n3 != null)
                val = n3.getNodeValue();
        }

        return val;
    }
}


public DomTable(String fileName, String recordTagName) throws Exception
{
    super(recordTagName + " Table");

    // create a SAX InputSource
    InputSource is = new
                    InputSource(new File(fileName).toURL().toString());
    // create a DOM Document
    doc = XmlDocument.createXmlDocument(is, true);
    DomUtil.normalizeDocument(doc.getDocumentElement());

    // create a DomTableModel
    DomTableModel dtm = new DomTableModel(doc, recordTagName);

    // Create a Table
    JTable tbl = new JTable(dtm);

    // Create a scroll pane
    JScrollPane scroll = new JScrollPane(tbl);

    getContentPane().add("Center", scroll);

    addWindowListener(new WindowAdapter()
                    {
```

LISTING 7.5   Continued

```java
                               public void windowClosing(WindowEvent we)
                               { System.exit(1); }
                          });

        setLocation(100,100);
        setSize(600,400);
        setVisible(true);
    }

    public static void main(String args[])
    {
        if (args.length < 2)
        {
            System.out.println("USAGE: java
➥sams.chp7.DomTable xmlfile recordTag");
            System.exit(1);
        }

        try
        {
            new DomTable(args[0], args[1]);
        } catch (Throwable t)
          {
            t.printStackTrace();
          }
    }
}
```

Note the following points about Listing 7.5:

- The main() method passes two command-line arguments (XML filename and record element) to the constructor of a DomTable object. The DomTable extends a JFrame and contains a JTable component.

- The DomTable constructor parses the XML document to create a DOM document (XmlDocument object in Sun's implementation) and then instantiates a DomTableModel. The DomTableModel constructor takes two arguments—a document reference and a string for the recordTagName (the element name representing a row). The DomTableModel is the most important object in the program and is discussed in detail in the next bullet. The DomTableModel is passed as an argument into the JTable constructor. The JTable is inserted into a JScrollpane and added to the content pane of the JFrame. Lastly, the JFrame is sized and displayed.

- The `DomTableModel` extends `AbstractTableModel`, which handles four of the nine methods in the `TableModel` interface. The `DomTableModel` class implements the other five methods of the `TableModel` interface. In general, the table model is responsible for providing the number of rows and the value of each cell (row,column) in the table. You can optionally provide a number of columns (`getColumnCount()`) and the names of those columns (`getColumnName()`). The methodology used to provide the rows and columns for the table is to get a list of the chosen elements (specified in the `recordTagName` parameter), where each element is a row. The number of children in the first element designates the columns. This is not a foolproof method to obtain the columns. A better method would be to iterate through all the elements and create a superset of all subelement names in all the records in the record list. This improvement is left to you as an exercise. The key method in the object is the `getValueAt()` method which retrieves the value of the text node for the specified row and column. Another potential improvement to the program is to allow columns to be attributes, subelements, or both.

XML in GUI Construction

Graphical user interfaces consist of graphical components laid out in a container. The creation, positioning, and connecting of these graphical components can be specified with a declarative syntax. XML is well suited to this task. This separation of an application into pluggable parts is an application-level example of Model-View-Controller. The view (graphical user object) can be separate from the application (functional operations).

In this section, we examine both a small and large implementation of this idea. The small implementation is a markup language to describe a GUI's menu. The large example is Bluestone's XwingML, which allows the creation of an entire Swing-based graphical user interface from an XML document.

The Menu Markup Language (MenuML)

The Menu Markup Language is a simple language that describes the elements and containment strategy of a menu bar. There are only three elements in the language: menubar, menu, and menu item. A menu bar must contain one or more menus. A menu must contain one or more menu items or menus (menu is a recursive definition). Menu must be a recursive concept to allow cascading menus (menu in a menu). A menu item is an empty element. A menu has a name attribute. A menu item has a name attribute and an action attribute. The action attribute allows you to assign a different action command (processed by the `ActionListener`) than the default, which is the name of the menu item. Listing 7.6 is the Document Type Definition (DTD) for the Menu Markup Language. One potential improvement to this language is to add a classname and method attribute to a menu item that would allow dynamic behavior to be loaded and linked into the Java Virtual Machine (JVM). The downside to this improvement is that it would tie the language to a Java implementation.

LISTING 7.6   Menu Markup Language DTD

```
<!ELEMENT MENUBAR (MENU)+>
<!ELEMENT MENU (MENU-ITEM|MENU)+>
<!ATTLIST MENU
          name CDATA #REQUIRED>
<!ELEMENT MENU-ITEM EMPTY>
<!ATTLIST MENU-ITEM
          name CDATA #REQUIRED
          action CDATA #IMPLIED>
```

Listing 7.7 is a document instance of the Menu Markup Language that tests all the capabilities of the language, including cascading menus and an alternate action command. The result of processing this document is shown in Figure 7.5.

LISTING 7.7   Menu Markup Language Document

```
<?xml version="1.0" ?>
<!DOCTYPE MENUBAR SYSTEM "MenuML.dtd">

<MENUBAR>
        <MENU name="File">
                <MENU-ITEM name="Open"/>
                <MENU-ITEM name="Save" action="SaveDoc"/>
                <MENU-ITEM name="Quit"/>
        </MENU>
        <MENU name="Edit">
                <MENU-ITEM name="Cut"/>
                <MENU-ITEM name="Copy"/>
                <MENU-ITEM name="Paste"/>
        </MENU>
        <MENU name="Record">
                <MENU name="New">
                        <MENU-ITEM name="database"/>
                        <MENU-ITEM name="table"/>
                        <MENU-ITEM name="row"/>
                </MENU>
                <MENU-ITEM name="Next"/>
                <MENU-ITEM name="Prev"/>
        </MENU>
        <MENU name="Help">
                <MENU-ITEM name="Contents"/>
                <MENU-ITEM name="Search"/>
        </MENU>
</MENUBAR>
```

The DomMenu Application

The DomMenu application uses a MenuML document to generate a menu bar, menus, and menu items. Figure 7.5 is a snapshot of the application that uses the menu described in Listing 7.7.

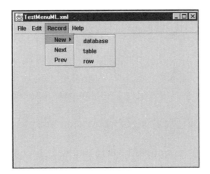

FIGURE 7.5

A menu generated from a MenuML *document.*

Listing 7.8 is the source code for the DomMenu application. The application provides a factory method to generate a menu for any Menu Markup Language document.

LISTING 7.8   DomMenu.java

```
/* DomMenu.java */
package sams.chp7;

import java.io.*;
import java.util.*;
import java.awt.*;
import java.awt.event.*;
import javax.swing.*;
import javax.swing.event.*;
import com.sun.xml.tree.XmlDocument;
import org.xml.sax.InputSource;
import org.xml.sax.SAXException;
import org.xml.sax.SAXParseException;
import org.w3c.dom.*;

public class DomMenu extends JFrame implements ActionListener
{
    XmlDocument doc;
    static final String MENU_NAME_ATTRIBUTE="name";
    static final String MENU_ACTION_ATTRIBUTE="action";
```

LISTING 7.8   Continued

```java
static final String MENU_ITEM_NAME = "MENU-ITEM";
static final String MENU_NAME = "MENU";

public Insets getInsets()
{
    return new Insets(25,5,5,5);
}

public static JMenuBar menuFactory(Document menuMLDocument,
                                   ActionListener al)
{
    JMenuBar mbar = new JMenuBar();

    Element root = menuMLDocument.getDocumentElement();
    // process top-level menus
    NodeList menus = root.getChildNodes();
    int numMenus = menus.getLength();
    for (int i=0; i < numMenus; i++)
    {
        Node menuNode = menus.item(i);
        NamedNodeMap attrs = menuNode.getAttributes();
        Node name = attrs.getNamedItem(MENU_NAME_ATTRIBUTE);
        JMenu menu = new JMenu(name.getNodeValue());
        mbar.add(menu);
        // recursively process this menu
        processMenu(menuNode, menu, al);
    }

    return mbar;
}

private static void processMenu(Node menuNode, JMenu menu,
                                ActionListener al)
{
    NodeList children = menuNode.getChildNodes();
    int len = children.getLength();
    for (int i=0; i < len; i++)
    {
        Node n = children.item(i);
        if (n.getNodeName().equals(MENU_ITEM_NAME))
        {
            NamedNodeMap attrs = n.getAttributes();
            Node action = attrs.getNamedItem(MENU_ACTION_ATTRIBUTE);
            Node name = attrs.getNamedItem(MENU_NAME_ATTRIBUTE);
```

LISTING 7.8 Continued

```
                JMenuItem item = new JMenuItem(name.getNodeValue());
                item.addActionListener(al);
                if (action != null)
                    item.setActionCommand(action.getNodeValue());
                menu.add(item);
            }
            else if (n.getNodeName().equals(MENU_NAME))
            {
                NamedNodeMap attrs = n.getAttributes();
                Node name = attrs.getNamedItem(MENU_NAME_ATTRIBUTE);
                JMenu submenu = new JMenu(name.getNodeValue());
                menu.add(submenu);
                processMenu(n, submenu, al);
            }
        }
    }
}

public void actionPerformed(ActionEvent evt)
{
    String cmd = evt.getActionCommand();
    System.out.println("Action: " + cmd);
    if (cmd.equals("Quit"))
        System.exit(0);
}

public DomMenu(String fileName) throws Exception
{
    super(fileName);

    // create a SAX InputSource
    InputSource is = new
                    InputSource(new File(fileName).toURL().toString());

    // create a DOM Document
    doc = XmlDocument.createXmlDocument(is, true);
    DomUtil.normalizeDocument(doc.getDocumentElement());

    JMenuBar mbar = menuFactory(doc, this);
    setJMenuBar(mbar);

    addWindowListener(new WindowAdapter()
                    {
                      public void windowClosing(WindowEvent we)
                      { System.exit(1); }
                    });
```

LISTING 7.8   Continued

```
        setLocation(100,100);
        setSize(600,400);
        setVisible(true);
    }

    public static void main(String args[])
    {
        if (args.length < 1)
        {
            System.out.println("USAGE: java sams.chp7.DomMenu xmlfile");
            System.exit(1);
        }

        try
        {
            new DomMenu(args[0]);
        } catch (Throwable t)
          {
            t.printStackTrace();
          }
    }
}
```

Note the following points about Listing 7.8:

- The main() method instantiates a DomMenu object and passes in the arguments received from the command line (an XML filename).

- The DomMenu constructor parses the MenuML document and then passes a reference to the XmlDocument and an ActionListener to a static method called menuFactory(). This method implements the factory pattern to instantiate a JMenuBar object from a MenuML document. The reference to the ActionListener is necessary to attach the menu items to an object that can execute the action commands specified in the MenuML document.

- The static menuFactory() method creates a menu bar, and then recurses through the MenuML document creating the associated menus and menu items described in the document. The first level of child nodes ais processed sequentially with a for loop because those are the menus that will be added to the menu bar. Then each menu is sent for further processing to a processMenu() method.

- The processMenu() method adds menu items or menus (which is why it is recursive) to the JMenu that is passed in. In addition to creating and adding the JMenuItem object, the action listener is registered using the addActionListener() method on the JMenuItem. If a name different from the name of the menu item is desired, it can be specified in an action attribute.

Summary

In this chapter we demonstrated several ways to combine XML with Swing graphical user interfaces. As a primer, we also covered the basic concepts of Swing GUIs.

The DomViewer application demonstrated how we could use the DOM API as a TreeModel delegate in order to render the DOM as a JTree.

Swing's Model-View-Controller architecture was explained. Even though MVC is used to represent widgets in Swing, we explained how it can also be used as an application architecture. XML fits into the MVC architecture as a superb model format. As a second example of this, we demonstrated the use of XML as a JTable model.

The chapter closed with a discussion and demonstration of the use of XML in graphical user interface construction. We walked through an example that renders a menu from a Menu Markup Language description file. For those familiar with the open source Mozilla project (www.mozilla.org), this is similar to the approach used to generate the browser's user interface.

Suggested for Further Study

1. In the DomViewer application, add an Open command to the file menu to open any XML file and display its DOM.

2. Change the default rendering of the DomTreeModel to only return a node name for a non-leaf node.

3. The strategy for creating the columns of the DomTableModel is flawed due to its assumption that the 0th record is the canonical model. Implement a better strategy that will account for varying numbers of subelements in the rows to be displayed.

4. Enhance the DomTable application by creating multiple views of the DomTableModel. For example, you could create various table views sorted on different fields.

5. Modify the MenuML language to allow a dynamic behavior to be associated with the menu command. This dynamic behavior will contain enough information to use reflection to load the class, instantiate the object, and invoke the specified method.

Further Reading

Graphic Java 2, Volume II, Swing. David Geary. 1999, Sun Microsystems, Inc. Extremely thorough and authoritative coverage of the Swing components and architecture.

JavaBeans, EJB, and XML

CHAPTER

8

"Though I believe little of the Java hype, I believe most of the XML hype."

—Heard on the wwwac mailing list

IN THIS CHAPTER

In previous chapters we have seen many different ways to format and manipulate XML. We've seen the SAX and DOM APIs, XSL, Collections, and Servlets. But we haven't put XML to use in a real, practical, and not-just-educational sense, although Servlets and Collections provided a great starting point. In this chapter we will examine a real-life use of XML: persisting the state of JavaBeans and Enterprise JavaBeans.

JavaBeans and XML

Just what are JavaBeans in the first place? (Those of you who are familiar with JavaBeans may want to skip forward.) JavaBeans are, in their simplest form, classes that contain certain patterns or signatures of methods. But JavaBeans are much more than simple classes; they are classes that implement the concept of a *component*. And what is a component? A component is best described by listing its characteristics:

- Components are reusable.
- Components require little effort to use on the part of the application developer.
- Components allow for rapid prototyping.
- Components often support visual programming and the drag-and-drop paradigm.

JavaBeans go a step further than simple components and have a number of additional benefits.

JavaBeans are

- Portable (written in Java, of course!)
- Object-oriented
- Dynamic
- Robust
- Simple to develop and use

Perhaps one of the best features of JavaBeans is that they scale *down* as well as up. As we shall see in the next few sections, any class can be a JavaBean as long as it follows a few simple conventions.

Specifically, the JavaBean 1.0 specification states that "A Bean is a reusable software component that can be manipulated visually by a builder."

We won't get into all aspects of JavaBeans here. There are several excellent references at the end of this chapter, but we will look at one aspect in detail: how to create and persist a JavaBean using XML.

Enterprise JavaBeans (EJBs) and XML

In a way, Enterprise JavaBeans are the big brother to JavaBeans. Enterprise JavaBeans are to server-side Java what JavaBeans are to client-side Java. However, EJBs and JavaBeans are not parents, children, or ancestors of one another. The EJB 1.0 specification describes many things about EJB, but does not require that each and every visible property have appropriate get*PropertyName* and set*PropertyName* methods, as a JavaBean must.

So what is an Enterprise JavaBean, or as they are more commonly referred to, an EJB? An EJB is a component just like a JavaBean. However, it's a *distributed* component, distributed in the sense that when you access an EJB you are accessing a remote instance of a class locally. However, that class is really living (running) on a server somewhere; you only have an instance of interface class that knows how to reference that remote object, but it's still *not* the remote object. As we shall see when we apply XML to EJBs, Enterprise JavaBeans are significantly more complex than JavaBeans and have significantly different uses. EJBs also have a lifecycle services interface used to create, delete, and otherwise manipulate the lifetime of an EJB. EJBs come in any of three separate and distinct flavors (Stateful, Stateless, and Entity), as opposed to JavaBeans' single flavor. Finally and most importantly EJBs are distributed objects!

As with JavaBeans, we won't get into an in-depth discussion of Enterprise JavaBeans, but we will look at the basics of EJBs and a special case—Bean-Managed Persistence (BMP) EJBs—and how we can develop base classes for BMP EJBs that can store and retrieve their state from XML.

JavaBeans

JavaBeans are the simpler of the two types and an excellent starting point for our foray into persistence via XML.

> **NOTE**
>
> JavaBeans and Enterprise JavaBeans are complex enough topics without involving XML. This chapter should not be considered an in-depth discussion of either topic but rather a simple introduction to the important features that facilitate persisting and restoring a bean of either type using XML.

JavaBeans Architecture

Just what is a JavaBean? A *JavaBean* is a Java class that exposes properties, methods, and events in a certain predefined fashion. JavaBeans can be either visual, in which case they must extend one of the AWT classes such as `Canvas`, or simple classes that follow a set of conventions defining what methods must exist. The only feature of JavaBeans we are really interested in are those responsible for setting and retrieving property values. Again, refer to one of the resource texts for a complete description of JavaBeans.

There are five method types defined by the JavaBeans specification:

- *Simple*—Any property that is a single instance. Can be of any primitive type as well as most provided and user-defined classes.
- *Boolean*—Similar to Simple but only supports Boolean values.
- *Indexed*—Any property that has multiple instances indexed via some index. For example, an array of integer is an Index property.
- *Bound*—Bound properties can be any of the three previous types and have similar `get` and `set` methods but are bound to zero or more event listeners that are informed whenever a value changes.
- *Constrained*—Similar to Bound properties in that the value may be Simple, Boolean, or Indexed, but event listeners may optionally veto any change, causing the property to revert back to its previous value.

JavaBeans expose their properties through one of these five method signature patterns. The five pattern types are described in Table 8.1.

TABLE 8.1 JavaBean Method Signature Patterns

Property Type	Signature
Simple	`public void set`*PropertyName*`(PropertyType newValue)` `public PropertyType get`*PropertyName*`()`
Boolean	`public boolean is`*PropertyName*`()` `public void setPropertyName( boolean newValue)`
Indexed	`public void set`*PropertyName*`(IndexType index, PropertyType newValue);` `public PropertyType get`*PropertyName*`(IndexType index)`
Bound	Any of the prior types set/get methods plus `public void addPropertyChangeListener(PropertyChangeListener listener) public void removePropertyChangeListener (PropertyChangeListener listener)`
Constrained	Any of the first three types set/get methods plus `public void addPropertyChangeListener(PropertyChangeListener listener) public void removePropertyChangeListener (PropertyChangeListener listener)`

Listing 8.1 shows an incredibly simple bean that has three simple properties. get methods, such as on line 12, allow values to be inserted into the bean. set methods, such as line 16, allow values to be returned back out of the bean. The purpose of this bean is purely to exercise several set and get methods on string float and integer properties.

LISTING 8.1   SimpleBean.java—A JavaBean with three properties

```
 1: public class SimpleBean implements java.io.Serializable {
 2:
 3:     protected String stringProperty;
 4:     protected int    intProperty;
 5:     protected float  floatProperty;
 6:     public SimpleBean()
 7:     {
 8:         stringProperty="";
 9:         intProperty=0;
10:         floatProperty = 0.0f;
11:     }
12:     public String getStringProperty()
13:     {
14:         return stringProperty;
15:     }
16:     public void setStringProperty(String newValue)
17:     {
18:         stringProperty = newValue;
19:     }
20:     public int getIntProperty()
21:     {
22:         return intProperty;
23:     }
24:     public void setIntProperty(int newValue)
25:     {
26:         intProperty = newValue;
27:     }
28:
29:     public float getFloatProperty()
30:     {
31:         return floatProperty;
32:     }
33:     public void setFloatProperty(float newValue)
34:     {
35:         floatProperty = newValue;
36:     }
37:
38:     public String toString()
39:     {
40:         return new String("stringProperty:" + stringProperty +
```

LISTING 8.1   Continued

```
41:                                    " intProperty:" + intProperty +
42:                                    " floatProperty:" + floatProperty);
43:        }
44:        public void print()
45:        {
46:            System.out.println(this.toString());
47:        }
48: }
```

A DTD for JavaBeans

Although we could just jump in and start coding, it's best to understand the problem at hand. We need a document type definition for our JavaBean; we can determine what needs to be in our DTD by examining a JavaBean at a conceptual level and seeing what it's made of. First off, we need to know what class maps to our bean. We can start our list of items with the bean's class name. Each bean must have a set of properties that describe its content. So we need some sort of hierarchy of properties. For the set of properties, we need a value for each. One interesting point to consider is whether our JavaBean can contain non-primitive properties. That is, can we have JavaBeans within JavaBeans?

With the parts of a JavaBean in mind, we can start thinking about how to translate these parts into an appropriate DTD. Listing 8.2 shows a simple DTD that defines our JavaBean.

LISTING 8.2   DTD for a JavaBean

```
1: <!DOCTYPE JavaBean [
2: <!ELEMENT JavaBean (Properties)>
3: <!ATTLIST JavaBean ClassName CDATA #REQUIRED>
4: <!ELEMENT Properties (Property*)>
5: <!ELEMENT Property (#PCDATA | JavaBean)*>
6: <!ATTLIST Property Name CDATA #REQUIRED >
7: ]>
```

We won't go through an actual description of the syntax of this DTD (see Chapter 2, "Parsing XML," for that), but we should examine the construct itself.

We defined a special document type, JavaBean, for our bean. In reality we didn't need to do this; we could have used any DTD and determined the JavaBean name from the root element of the XML document. This method was chosen because it's somewhat clearer. The JavaBean root element contains a single attribute—the ClassName of the bean; again this was done for clarity, especially when dealing with beans that are part of packages. JavaBeans contain a number of properties, so it makes sense to define a Properties (note the plural) element that contains a number of `Property` elements. Again, each `Property` element contains a single attribute, `Name`, that specifies the name the `Property` applies to. We could have used the `Element` name as the `Property` name, but using an `Attribute` seemed clearer. Interestingly enough, `Property` elements can contain data; primitive values such as long, float, and so on; or embedded `JavaBean` elements!

When we put all these elements together, we define a simple DTD that serves our purposes well. Listing 8.3 shows the XML that represents a set of values for `SimpleBean.java` (refer to Listing 8.1). Let's move on now and examine how we can actually restore the state of a JavaBean using XML and our DTD.

LISTING 8.3   `SimpleBean.xml`—XML Representing the State of SimpleBean

```
<?xml version="1.0" encoding="UTF-8" ?>
<!DOCTYPE JavaBean [
<!ELEMENT JavaBean (Properties)>
<!ATTLIST JavaBean ClassName CDATA #REQUIRED>
<!ELEMENT Properties (Property*)>
<!ELEMENT Property (#PCDATA | JavaBean)*>
<!ATTLIST Property Name CDATA #REQUIRED >
]>

<JavaBean ClassName="SimpleBean">
  <Properties>
    <Property Name="stringProperty">This is a string!</Property>
    <Property Name="intProperty">1234</Property>
    <Property Name="floatProperty">4321.0</Property>
  </Properties>
</JavaBean>
```

XML to JavaBeans

To understand how to restore a bean's content from XML, we need to understand a little more about Java Reflection and Introspection. These two Java packages allow developers to interrogate a Java class to determine information about it—such as what fields the class contains, attributes of those fields, what methods the class contains, what their method signatures are, and a slew of other information. In addition to examining a class's contents we can, using Reflection, generate parameter lists and actually call methods on-the-fly. Before I developed the code to actually restore and persist JavaBeans to XML, I developed `DumpBean.java`, which exercises a number of the interfaces required to get information about a class. In fact, `DumpBean` will dump information about any class. Listing 8.4 shows the code for `DumpBean.java`. Deep analysis of this code is left to the reader. All the method calls are well documented in the Java online documentation for the `Class` object. Simply put, Listing 8.4 takes a Java class as input; creates a `Class` object representing the methods, interfaces, variables, and so on of that class, and then, using Reflection, lists the methods, variables, interfaces, and other characteristics of the class.

LISTING 8.4   DumpBean.java—Dump a Classes Characteristics

```
 1: package sams.chp8;
 2: import java.lang.reflect.*;
 3: import java.beans.*;
 4:
 5: //
 6: // a simple class that dumps information about another class
 7: //
 8:
 9: public class DumpBean
10: {
11:
12:     public static Object DumpObject(String className)
13: s InstantiationException,IllegalAccessException
14:     {
15:         Class theClass = null;
16:         try
17:         {
18:             theClass = Class.forName(className);
19:             System.out.println("Information about:" +
20:                 theClass.getName());
21:             System.out.println("---\n");
22:
23:             Package pkg  = theClass.getPackage();
24:             System.out.println(" Package ");
25:             if (null == pkg )
26:                 System.out.println(
27:                   package:not part of a package(default)");
28:             else
29:                 System.out.println(
30:                   package:" + pkg.toString());
31:             System.out.println("---\n");
32:
33:
34:             Class[] interfaces = theClass.getInterfaces();
35:             System.out.println(
36:                 "Interfaces(" + interfaces.length + ")");
37:             for (int i = 0; i < interfaces.length; i++)
38:             {
```

LISTING 8.4   Continued

```
39:                    Class anInterface = interfaces[i];
40:                    System.out.println("    interface["+i+"]" +
41:                                    anInterface.toString());
42:                }
43:                System.out.println("---\n");
44:
45:                Constructor[] ctors = theClass.getConstructors();
46:                System.out.println(" Ctors(" + ctors.length + ")");
47:                for (int i = 0; i < ctors.length; i++)
48:                {
49:                    Constructor ctor = ctors[i];
50:                    System.out.println("    ctor["+i+"]" +
51: toString());
52:                }
53:                System.out.println("---\n");
54:
55:                Field[] fields = theClass.getDeclaredFields();
56:                System.out.println(" Fields(" + fields.length + ")");
57:                for (int i = 0; i < fields.length; i++)
58:                {
59:                    Field field = fields[i];
60:                    System.out.println("    Field["+i+"]" +
61:                                field.toString());
62:                }
63:                System.out.println("---\n");
64:
65:
66:                Method[] methods = theClass.getDeclaredMethods();
67:
68:                System.out.println(" Methods(" + methods.length + ")");
69:                for (int i = 0; i < methods.length; i++)
70:                {
71:                    Class returnType = methods[i].getReturnType();
72:                    Class[] parameterTypes =
73:                                methods[i].getParameterTypes();
74:                    System.out.println("    Method["+i+"]" +
75:                                methods[i].getName());
76:                    System.out.println("      " +
77:                                methods[i].toString());
78:                    System.out.println("      returns:"+
79:                                parameterTypes.toString());
80:                    System.out.println(
81:                      "takes "+parameterTypes.length + " parameters");
82:                    for (int j =0; j < parameterTypes.length;j++)
83:                    {
```

LISTING 8.4   Continued

```
84:                       System.out.println("        Parameter[" + j +
85:                             "]"+ parameterTypes[j].toString()
86:                       + (parameterTypes[j].isPrimitive()?"
87:                        "Primitive":" not Primitive")
88:                       );
89:                 }
90:              }
91:
92:           System.out.println("\n\n");
93:
94:        }
95:        catch (SecurityException e)
96:        {
97:            System.out.println(e);
98:        }
99:        catch (ClassNotFoundException e)
100:       {
101:           System.out.println("Class:"+className +
102:                              " not found!");
103:           System.out.println(e);
104:       }
105:
106:       return theClass!=null? theClass.newInstance():null;
107:
108:    }
109:
110:    public static void main (String argv [])
111:    {
112:        if (argv.length == 0)
113:        {
114:
115:            System.err.println(
116:              "Usage: java sams.chp9.DumpBean someClass" );
117:            System.exit(1);
118:        }
119:
120:        try
121:        {
122:            Object bean = DumpObject(argv[0]);
123:            if ( null == bean)
124:            {
125:            System.out.println("Failed to open class from " + argv[0]);
126:            System.exit(1);
127:            }
```

LISTING 8.4   Continued

```
128:           }
129:           catch (Exception e)
130:           {
131:               System.out.println(e);
132:
133:           }
134:    }
135: }
```

With the rudiments of Reflection and the `Class` object in mind, we can now detail the actual process of restoring a bean from an XML document. Listing 8.6 is an abbreviated version of `XMLBean.java` with the persist to XML portion removed. We will examine persisting to XML in the next section.

Restoring a bean's content from XML requires several steps:

1. Open the document and find the root node.
2. Find the `Properties` node and iterate over `Property` elements.
3. For each `Property` element find the `set` method.
4. Generate appropriate arguments to the `set` method.
5. Using the arguments from step 4, store into the JavaBean the value from the `Property` element.

That sounds simple enough. Let's examine the code that performs this magic. Listing 8.5, `XMLRead.java`, is fairly self-explanatory: it takes an XML file that contains an XML JavaBean and uses `XMLBean.newBeanInstance()` to create the in-memory representation of the bean. All the real work happens in Listing 8.6, `XMLBean.java`.

LISTING 8.5   XMLRead.java—Driver Application for Testing Creating XML Beans

```
1: package sams.chp8;
2: import java.lang.reflect.*;
3: class XMLRead
4: {
5:     //
6:     // Simple main for testing...
7:     //
8:     public static void main (String argv [])
9:     {
10:        if (argv.length == 0)
11:        {
```

LISTING 8.5   Continued

```
12:              System.err.println(
13:              "Usage: java sams.chp8.TestXMLRead somebean.xml" );
14:               System.exit(1);
15:
16:          }
17:          try
18:          {
19:              Object bean = XMLBean.newBeanInstance(argv[0]);
20:              if ( null == bean)
21:              {
22:                  System.out.println("Failed to create bean from "
23:                  + argv[0]);
24:                  System.exit(1);
25:              }
26:               Method toString = bean.getClass().
27:                                      getMethod("toString", null);
28:              System.out.println("Java Bean type " +
29:                                      bean.getClass().getName());
30:              String result = (String)toString.invoke(bean, null);
31:              System.out.println("toString:"+ result);
32:          }
33:          catch (Exception e)
34:          {
35:              System.out.println(e);
36:          }
37:      }
38: }
```

LISTING 8.6   XMLBean.java—Restoring from XML

```
 1: package sams.chp8;
 2: import java.lang.reflect.*;
 3: import java.beans.*;
 4: import java.io.*;
 5: import sams.chp7.*; // For XMLUtil.openDocument
 6: import org.w3c.dom.*;
 7:
 8: public class XMLBean
 9: {
10:
11:      //
12:      // Convenience method to create a new Object that
13:      // can be used as an argument to the setter method
14:      //
```

LISTING 8.6   Continued

```
15:     static Object buildSimpleArgument(Class type, String value)
16:     {
17:         Object argument = null;
18:         if (type == char.class)
19:         {
20:             char c = (char) (Integer.decode(value).intValue());
21:             argument = new Character(c);
22:         }
23:         else if ( type == java.lang.String.class)
24:         {
25:             argument = value;
26:         }
27:         else if (type == boolean.class)
28:             argument = new Boolean(value);
29:         else if (type == byte.class)
30:             argument = new Byte(value);
31:         else if (type == int.class)
32:             argument = new Integer(value);
33:         else if (type == long.class)
34:             argument = new Long(value);
35:         else if (type == short.class)
36:             argument = new Short(value);
37:         else if (type == float.class)
38:             argument = new Float(value);
39:         else if (type == double.class)
40:             argument = new Double(value);
41:         else
42:             return null;
43:         return argument;
44:     }
45:
46:     //
47:     // load a property
48:     // This method does the bulk of the work
49:     // of loading a JavaBean property
50:     //
51:     static void loadProperty(Node aProperty,Object object)
52:                 throws NoSuchMethodException,
53:                        IllFormedBeanException
54:     {
55:         if ( null == aProperty)
56:         {
57:             return; // something strange happened!
58:         }
```

LISTING 8.6 Continued

```
59:          NamedNodeMap attributes = aProperty.getAttributes();
60:          if ( null == attributes || attributes.getLength() == 0)
61:          {
62:              throw new IllFormedBeanException(
63:                          "Cannot Name attributes for "
64:                          + aProperty.getNodeName()
65:                          + " in class "
66:                          + object.getClass().getName());
67:          }
68:          String propertyName = null;
69:          for ( int i = 0; i < attributes.getLength();i++ )
70:          {
71:              Node attribute = attributes.item(i);
72:              if (attribute.getNodeName().equals("Name"))
73:              {
74:                  propertyName = attribute.getNodeValue();
75:                  break;
76:              }
77:          }
78:          if ( null == propertyName)
79:          {
80:              throw new IllFormedBeanException(
81:                      "Cannot find Name attribute for "
82:                      + propertyName + " in class "
83:                      + object.getClass().getName());
84:          }
85:
86:          //
87:          // get the class and find the method that
88:          // has the same name
89:          //
90:          // We use property descriptors to find setter
91:          // method and then use that method to
92:          // store the value into the object
93:          // We could use a hashmap to store all the
94:          // desciptors and then access them
95:          // by hash but this method, while slower,
96:          // shows more what is going on with
97:          // the property descriptors.
98:          try
99:          {
100:             Class    theClass = object.getClass();
101:             PropertyDescriptor propDescs[] =
102:                 Introspector.getBeanInfo(theClass).
```

LISTING 8.6   Continued

```
103:                       getPropertyDescriptors();
104:              PropertyDescriptor pd = null;
105:              Method setter = null;
106:              Class argumentType = null;
107:
108:              for (int i = 0;
109:                   setter == null && i < propDescs.length;
110:                   i++)
111:              {
112:                  if (propDescs[i].getName().equals(propertyName))
113:                  {
114:                      pd = propDescs[i];
115:                      setter = pd.getWriteMethod();
116:                      argumentType = pd.getPropertyType();
117:                  }
118:              }
119:              if ( null == setter )
120:              {
121:                  throw new IllFormedBeanException(
122:                      "Cannot find setter method for "
123:                      + propertyName + " in class "
124:                      + theClass.getName());
125:              }
126:              else if ( null == argumentType  )
127:              {
128:                  throw new IllFormedBeanException(
129:                      "Cannot determine argument type for "
130:                      + propertyName + " in class "
131:                      + theClass.getName());
132:              }
133:              //
134:              // Ok, one more step before we set the value.
135:              // We need to get the value of the property as
136:              // an argument that can be passed to
137:              // the setter method
138:              // there are two possiblities here:
139:              //   a: The object is a primitive type or string
140:              //      use buildSimpleArgument to create the
141:              //   b: the object is an embedded bean
142:              //      instantiate it and use the result
143:              // call the setter.
144:              //
145:
146:              Object[] args = { null };
147:              NodeList propertyChildren =
```

LISTING 8.6   Continued

```
148:                    aProperty.getChildNodes();
149:
150:            //
151:            // Is the argument a primitive type?
152:            // That is long, float, doublel etc?
153:            // Then look for the text node that represents it
154:            // and use buildSimpleArgument to
155:            // construct an appropriate object
156:            // to represent that value
157:            //
158:            if (argumentType.isPrimitive() ||
159:                argumentType == java.lang.String.class)
160:            {
161:                String value = null;
162:                for (int i = 0;
163:                     i < propertyChildren.getLength();
164:                     i++)
165:                {
166:                    Node aNode = propertyChildren.item(i);
167:                    if (aNode instanceof Text)
168:                    {
169:                        value = aNode.getNodeValue();
170:                        break;
171:                    }
172:                }
173:                if ( null == value)
174:                {
175:                    throw new IllFormedBeanException(
176:                            "Value not found in XML Bean for"
177:                            + propertyName + " in class "
178:                            + theClass.getName());
179:                }
180:                args[0] = buildSimpleArgument(argumentType,
181:                                              value);
182:            }
183:            //
184:            // If it is not a primitive type
185:            //
186:            else
187:            {
188:                //
189:                // look for a child that says it is a javabean
190:                //
191:                for (int i = 0; i < propertyChildren.getLength(); i++)
```

LISTING 8.6   Continued

```
192:                      {
193:                          Node aNode = propertyChildren.item(i);
194:                          if ( aNode.getNodeName().equals("JavaBean") )
195:                          {
196:                              args[0] = newBeanInstance(aNode);
197:                          }
198:                      }
199:                  }
200:
201:             //
202:             // At this point if args[0] is still null
203:             // we were not able to build the argument list
204:             // throw an exception
205:             //
206:             if (null == args[0])
207:             {
208:                 throw new IllFormedBeanException(
209:                 "Cannot determine parameters to set method for "
210:                     + propertyName + " in class "
211:                     + theClass.getName());
212:             }
213:             //
214:             // We found the setter method
215:             // all we need to do is call it.
216:             //
217:             setter.invoke(object, args );
218:         }
219:         catch (Exception e)
220:         {
221:             return;
222:         }
223:     }
224:
225:     //
226:     // Fill the bean based on the field names
227:     //
228:     static void loadBeanProperties(Object object,Node bean)
229:     {
230:         // get all the children of the bean
231:         // they should all be Properties children
232:         // later we will examine what we should
233:         // do if they are JavaBeans (beans within beans!)
234:         NodeList propertiesNL = bean.getChildNodes();
235:         for (int i = 0; i < propertiesNL.getLength(); i++)
```

8

JAVABEANS, EJB,
AND XML

LISTING 8.6   Continued

```
236:            {
237:                Node propertiesNode = propertiesNL.item(i);
238:                if ( propertiesNode.getNodeName()
239:                    .equals("Properties"))
240:                {
241:                    DOMArray propertiesValues
242:                        = new DOMArray(propertiesNode,"Property");
243:                    for ( int j = 0;
244:                          j < propertiesValues.size();
245:                          j++)
246:                    {
247:                        try
248:                        {
249:                            loadProperty(
250:                              propertiesValues.getAsNode(j),object
251:                              );
252:                        }
253:                        catch (NoSuchMethodException e)
254:                        {
255:                            System.out.println(
256:            "Unexpected NoSuchMethodException loading a property");
257:
258:                        }
259:                        catch(IllFormedBeanException ifbe)
260:                        {
261:                            System.out.println(
262:            "Unexpected IllFormedBeanException:" + ifbe.getMessage());
263:                        }
264:                    }
265:                }
266:            }
267:    }
268:
269:
270:    //
271:    // Create a JavaBean from a string representing
272:    // a uri to an XML file containing the JavaBean
273:     // description
274:    //
275:    public static Object newBeanInstance(String xmlJavaBean)
276:                throws InstantiationException,
277:                       IllegalAccessException,
278:                       ClassNotFoundException
279:    {
280:        Document document =
281:            XMLUtil.openDocument(xmlJavaBean,false);
282:          // create a non-validating parser
```

LISTING 8.6   Continued

```
283:            if ( null == document)
284:                return null;
285:                // Open failed cant create new instance.
286:            return newBeanInstance(document);
287:        }
288:
289:        //
290:        // Create a bean from a document
291:        // by finding the first bean instance
292:        // and returning a bean based on it.
293:        //
294:        public static Object newBeanInstance(Document document)
295:                            throws InstantiationException,
296:                                IllegalAccessException,
297:                                ClassNotFoundException
298:        {
299:            //
300:            // Find the first JavaBean node
301:            //
302:            NodeList beans =
303:                    document.getElementsByTagName( "JavaBean" );
304:            if ( beans.getLength() < 1)
305:            {
306:                return null;
307:            }
308:            return newBeanInstance(beans.item(0));
309:        }
310:
311:        //
312:        // Create a JavaBean starting from
313:        // the DOM Tree node that represents the bean
314:        // That is the <JavaBean Name=... element
315:        //
316:        public static Object newBeanInstance(Node aBean)
317:                            throws InstantiationException,
318:                                IllegalAccessException,
319:                                ClassNotFoundException
320:        {
321:            Class theClass = null;
322:            NamedNodeMap attributes = aBean.getAttributes();
323:            if ( null == attributes ||
324:                    attributes.getLength() == 0)
325:            {
326:                return null;
327:            }
```

LISTING 8.6 Continued

```
328:          String beanName = null;
329:          for ( int i = 0; i < attributes.getLength();i++ )
330:          {
331:              Node attribute = attributes.item(i);
332:              if (attribute.getNodeName().equals("ClassName"))
333:              {
334:                  beanName = attribute.getNodeValue();
335:                  break;
336:              }
337:          }
338:          if( null == beanName )
339:          {
340:              System.out.println(
341:                "Pretty weird Found a bean with no name!");
342:              return null;
343:          }
344:
345:          //
346:          // load the class
347:          //
348:          theClass = Class.forName(beanName);
349:          if ( null == theClass)
350:          {
351:              // most likely class not found
352:              return null;
353:          }
354:          //
355:          // If we are here we found the class
356:          // create a newInstance of the class
357:          // get all the properties and start setting
358:          // them one by one.
359:          //
360:          Object  object = theClass.newInstance();
361:          loadBeanProperties(object,aBean);
362:
363:          return object;
364:      }
365:
366:   . . . // Persist methods removed!
367:
368: }
```

Let's examine Listing 8.6 in terms of the numbered steps.

1. We see that in lines 275, 294, and 316 we define several versions of
   `newBeanInstance()`: one for processing XML from a file, one for processing from a
   DOM document, and one for DOM elements. We load the JavaBean dynamically using
   `Class.forName()`, much like a class loader might do, and then carry this new `Object`
   along setting its property values as we go. When we examine EJBs, we will add several
   additional `newBeanInstance()` methods that work on a user-provided bean.

2. On line 228, we see the `loadBeanProperties()` method that first finds the `Properties`
   DOM element and uses a `DOMArray` (lines 241–242) to iterate over all the `Property` elements.

3. The `loadProperty()` method begins on line 51. This method is the actual meat and pota-
   toes of creating a new bean from XML. It uses the `Property` DOM element and the
   JavaBean `Object` itself as follows:

   - Find the `Property`'s `name` attribute (lines 59–77)
   - Using the Java Introspection engine, find the `PropertyDescriptor` object that rep-
     resents the XML `Property` element we are processing (lines 100–118) and deter-
     mine the argument type information and the `setter` method.
   - Examine the argument type. If it's primitive or a `String`, we can just set it
     directly using the `buildSimpleArgument()` method. Otherwise—and here's the
     trick for handling beans within beans—call `newBeanInstance()` on the current
     JavaBean child of the `Property` element to use as an argument to the setter
     method.
   - Call the `setter` method (line 217) to store the value into the bean itself.

The `buildSimpleArgument()` method still bears some review. In general, setter methods take
arrays of `Object` elements as input. Since we are dealing with normal
`setPropertyName(Object value)` methods, we need to build a one-element array that contains a single object representing the value. For primitive arguments, it's easy:
`buildSimpleArgument()` constructs an instance of the Java class that represents the primitive
element and uses the `String`-based constructor to create an object that represents the input
`String`. For non-primitive arguments, it's a little harder, but we've already written a method to
do it: `newBeanInstance()`. We take the return value from `newBeanInstance()` or
`buildSimpleArgument()` and then pass it to the `setter` method; the method is magically
called and the XML-persisted value is inserted into the bean instance.

The remainder of the code handles other processing and legwork necessary to make the
process work, such as handling ill-formed beans, error testing, and so on.

The second half (with creating a bean from XML being the first half) of XML-based JavaBeans is persisting a JavaBean to XML. The next section examines this topic in detail and, as we shall see, uses many of the same techniques to achieve its goals.

> **NOTE**
>
> Throughout the XMLBean class, we use the getClass() method on various objects to obtain class information. Every Java object inherits the getClass() method from java.lang.Object. The class of an object is very different from an instance of an object. Instances contain an object's current state. The Class of an object contains information about the fields, method, and so forth and pertains to all objects of a given class.

JavaBean to XML

Persisting a JavaBean back to XML follows almost the exact reverse of the steps for restoring a bean's content from XML. Again, let's examine the steps first and then see how they are implemented.

1. Open a stream for writing the XML. Note that we choose a PrintStream because it is simple and straightforward. However, we could have easily generalized the code to support writing to any stream. We could easily imagine a network-based stream that serializes printing over the network or a database-based stream that persisted our XML to a database.

2. Use the Introspection engine to again examine our bean. This time, we look at the fields contained within the JavaBean so that we might save their values.

3. Examine each field and obtain a reference to the getter method for each primitive type object within the JavaBean and with that getter method obtain the field's value and type information. Note that we skip static as well as volatile fields because they don't require persisting.

4. If a given field is non-primitive, we recursively call our persistence methods to persist to XML the complex property; otherwise, we use the toString() method to obtain a string representation of the field and write it.

All of this is handled by Listing 8.8, XMLBean.java. Listing 8.7, XMLWrite.java, is a simple application that uses the XMLBean.newBeanInstance() to create a JavaBean in memory and the XMLBean.storeBeanInstance() to persist the bean back to a file.

LISTING 8.7   `XMLWrite.java`—Driver for Peristing Beans as XML

```
1: package sams.chp8;
2: import java.lang.reflect.*;
3: class XMLWrite
4: {
5:     //
6:     // Simple main for testing...
7:     //
8:     public static void main (String argv [])
9:     {
10:         if (argv.length < 1)
11:         {
12:             System.err.println(
13:           "Usage: java sams.chp8.XMLWrite frombean.xml tobean.xml" );
14:             System.exit(1);
15:         }
16:         try
17:         {
18:             // create an in-memory instance of the bean
19:             Object bean = XMLBean.newBeanInstance(argv[0]);
20:             if ( null == bean)
21:             {
22:                 System.out.println("Failed to create bean from "
23:                                     + argv[0]);
24:                 System.exit(1);
25:             }
26:             //
27:             // Now store it back
28:             //
29:             if ( argv.length == 2)
30:             {
31:                 if ( XMLBean.storeBeanInstance(argv[1],bean) != true)
32:                 {
33:                     System.out.println("Failed to export bean to"
34:                                     + argv[1]);
35:                     System.exit(1);
36:                 }
37:             }
38:             else
39:             {
40:                 if ( XMLBean.storeBeanInstance(System.out,bean)
41:                     != true)
42:                 {
43:                     System.out.println("Failed to export bean");
44:                     System.exit(1);
```

LISTING 8.7 Continued

```
45:                    }
46:                }
47:            }
48:          catch (Exception e)
49:          {
50:              System.out.println(e);
51:          }
52:      }
53: }
```

LISTING 8.8 XMLBean.java—Persist to XML

```
 1: package sams.chp8;
 2: import java.lang.reflect.*;
 3: import java.beans.*;
 4: import java.io.*;
 5: import sams.chp7.*; // For XMLUtil.openDocument
 6: import org.w3c.dom.*;
 7:
 8: public class XMLBean
 9: {
10:
11: . . . // Restore portions removed.  See CD for complete sources
12:     //
13:     // The bulk of writing a bean is done
14:     // in output properties We first find
15:     // all the fields, skipping those that
16:     // are transient, and get the associated
17:     // property descriptor.
18:     // We then use that property descriptor
19:     // to get the reader method and then
20:     // write the value.  We use each
21:     // primitive types toString method to
22:     // get a printable representation of
23:     // that object. For non-primitive
24:     // objects we simply call outputBean with the
25:     // object and recurse through the beans within beans!
26:     //
27:     static boolean outputProperties(int level,
28:                                     PrintStream ps,
29:                                     Object bean,
30:                                     Class theClass)
31:     {
```

LISTING 8.8   Continued

```
32:
33:          // go to the fields directly
34:          Field[] fields = theClass.getDeclaredFields();
35:          for (int i = 0; i < fields.length; i++)
36:          {
37:              Field field = fields[i];
38:              Method getter = null;
39:              //
40:              // Skip transient fields
41:              //
42:              int modifiers = theClass.getModifiers();
43:              if ( modifiers == java.lang.reflect.Modifier.TRANSIENT )
44:              {
45:                  continue;
46:              }
47:              Class type = null;
48:              String fieldName = field.getName();
49:              try
50:              {
51:                  PropertyDescriptor propDescs[] =
52:                    Introspector.getBeanInfo(theClass)
53:                     .getPropertyDescriptors();
54:                  PropertyDescriptor pd = null;
55:                  // find the property descriptor and
56:                  // getter for this field
57:                  for (int j = 0;
58:                          pd == null && j < propDescs.length;
59:                        j++)
60:                  {
61:                      if (propDescs[j].getName().equals(fieldName))
62:                      {
63:                          pd = propDescs[j];
64:                          getter = pd.getReadMethod();
65:                          type = pd.getPropertyType();
66:                      }
67:                  }
68:
69:              } catch ( IntrospectionException ie) {}
70:              if ( null == getter)
71:              {
72:                  System.out.println("Cannot find getter for " +
73:                                        field.getName());
74:                  continue;  // no getter skip field
75:              }
```

LISTING 8.8   Continued

```
76:              Object value = null;
77:              try {
78:                  value = getter.invoke(bean,null);
79:              } catch (Exception e) { value = null; };
80:
81:              if ( null == value ) continue;
82:                  // Couldn't get value skip it
83:              //
84:              // is it primitive or a string?
85:              //
86:              if ( type.isPrimitive() ||
87:                   type == java.lang.String.class)
88:              {
89:                  //
90:                  // just write it
91:                  //
92:                  prefix(ps,level);
93:                  ps.print("<Property Name=\""+fieldName + "\">");
94:                  try
95:                  {
96:                      Method toString =
97:                        value.getClass().getMethod
98:                        ("toString", null);
99:                      String valueAsString =
100:                        (String)toString.invoke(value, null);
101:                      ps.print(valueAsString);
102:                  } catch (Exception e)
103:                  {
104:                      System.out.println(
105:                        "toString invoke failed" + e);
106:                  }
107:                  ps.println("</Property>");
108:              }
109:              else
110:              {
111:                  prefix(ps,level);
112:                  ps.println("<Property Name=\""+
113:                          fieldName + "\">");
114:                  outputBean(level+1,ps,value);
115:                  prefix(ps,level);ps.println("</Property>");
116:              }
117:          }
118:      return true;
119:
```

LISTING 8.8 Continued

```
120:      }
121:
122:      //
123:      // Output bean is the start of writing
124:      // a bean object.  It prints the
125:      // appropriate class info and then calls
126:      // outputProperties to write the
127:      // underlying properties.
128:      //
129:      static boolean outputBean(int level,
130:                                PrintStream ps,
131:                                Object bean)
132:      {
133:          Class theClass = bean.getClass();
134:          prefix(ps,level);
135:           ps.println("<JavaBean ClassName=\"" +
136:                       theClass.getName() +
137:                        "\">");
138:          prefix(ps,level+1);
139:          ps.println("<Properties>");
140:
141:          boolean result = outputProperties(level+2,
142:                                            ps,
143:                                            bean,
144:                                            theClass);
145:
146:          prefix(ps,level+1);
147:          ps.println("</Properties>");
148:          prefix(ps,level);
149:          ps.println("</JavaBean>");
150:          return result;
151:      }
152:
153:      static void prefix(PrintStream ps,int level)
154:      {
155:          if ( level == 0) return;
156:          for ( int i = 0; i < level; i++)
157:              ps.print("    ");
158:      }
159:
160:      static void XMLBeanDTD(PrintStream ps)
161:      {
162:          ps.println("<?xml version=\"1.0\" encoding=\"UTF-8\" ?>");
163:          ps.println("<!DOCTYPE JavaBean [");
```

8

LISTING 8.8   Continued

```
164:            ps.println("<!ELEMENT JavaBean (Properties)>");
165:            ps.println("<!ATTLIST JavaBean ClassName CDATA #REQUIRED>");
166:            ps.println("<!ELEMENT Properties (Property*)>");
167:            ps.println("<!ELEMENT Property (#PCDATA)>");
168:            ps.println("<!ATTLIST Property Name CDATA #REQUIRED >");
169:            ps.println("]>\n");
170:
171:        }
172:        public static boolean storeBeanInstance(PrintStream ps, O
173:                                                 bject bean)
174:        {
175:            XMLBeanDTD(ps);
176:            return outputBean(0,ps,bean);
177:        }
178:        public static boolean storeBeanInstance(String path,
179:                                                 Object bean)
180:        {
181:            //
182:            // Open a stream to the file
183:            //
184:            boolean result = false;
185:            try
186:            {
187:                PrintStream pOut;
188:                pOut = new PrintStream (new FileOutputStream(path));
189:                result = storeBeanInstance(pOut,bean);
190:            }catch (IOException e){ }
191:
192:            return result;
193:        }
194:
```

As we did with Listing 8.6, let's examine the code and see how we handle each of the steps required to persist a JavaBean's state back to XML.

1. On lines 172 and 178, we see two versions of `XMLBean.storeBeanInstance()`. One creates a stream to which to persist the bean's contents, and the other works on an existing stream, outputs our DTD, and then calls `outputBean()` to perform the real work.

2. Our next step is to examine the bean's fields and output the non-transient/non-volatile fields to XML. The `outputBean()` method, which starts on line 129, outputs the necessary XML for the bean as a whole and then uses `outputProperties()` to do the real work of persisting the bean's underlying properties.

3. `outputProperties()`, which starts on line 27, does the real work of persisting our bean to XML. Let's examine this method closely:

- Obtain an instance of the class that represents the JavaBean we are persisting and use the `getDeclaredFields()` method of the class to get an array of all the fields in the JavaBean. See line 34.

- For each field in the bean, examine the field's modifiers, skip any fields that are transient, and so forth. See line 42.

- Use Introspection to obtain an array of the `PropertiesDescriptor` for this object and find the descriptor that describes the field we are processing. Use this descriptor to get a handle to the `getter` method and field's type information. See lines 51–66.

- Use the `getter` method and the bean itself to get the fields value. See line 78.

- Examine the field's type; for primitive types (and strings), use Introspection again to obtain a reference to the value's `toString()` method and use this method reference to obtain a string representation of the value. Then simply write the value to the output stream. See lines 86–100. If the value is not a primitive type, simply call `outputBean` using the new value recursively.

As with restoring the JavaBean's state from XML, the remainder of the code handles various legwork and housekeeping tasks to make the entire process work correctly. The complete code for `XMLBean.java` is available on the CD for your enjoyment.

Persisting and storing JavaBeans to and from XML is only half the story—the client-side Java half. What about server-side Java? In the next section, we examine Enterprise JavaBeans (EJBs), big brother or perhaps elder cousin to JavaBeans, and see how we can develop an Entity EJB that can read and write its state using Enterprise JavaBeans. In fact we'll enhance much of the code we've already written to handle persisting EJBs.

Enterprise JavaBeans

Before we can jump into reading and writing EJB states to XML, we need a better understanding of Enterprise JavaBeans and the technologies required to use them.

> **NOTE**
>
> I've tried to give a fairly complete flavor for Enterprise JavaBeans within this chapter. However, a simple chapter cannot do this topic justice. Nor can we cover all the topics necessary for a sufficient understanding of EJBs. The interested reader is encouraged to read one of the resources listed in the "Further Reading" section of this chapter for a more complete understanding of EJBs.

8

JAVABEANS, EJB, AND XML

EJB Architecture

Let's start with a refresher course in EJBs. For those readers proficient in EJBs, especially Bean-Managed Persistence Entity EJBs, feel free to skip ahead. For all others, read on as we introduce the basics of Enterprise JavaBeans.

> **NOTE**
>
> Note that the code in the following sections depends on the use of a Java Application Server such as BEA Systems WebLogic Server. A Java Application Server provides an execution environment for EJBs to run (live) in. You can download the latest version of WebLogic Server from the BEA Web site at http://www.beasys.com. For your convenience, WebLogic Server v4.51 is packaged on the CD and runs on Windows 95, 98, NT 4.0, 2000, and various UNIX platforms. See the BEA Web site for more information about WebLogic Server and all it can do.

EJBs are much like JavaBeans in that a client obtains a handle to an EJB and then uses it as if it were a regular Java object. However, that's where the similarities end. JavaBeans typically are created within the client and live out their lives there. Enterprise JavaBeans, on the other hand, live and execute on a Java Application Server, *App Server* for short, and the client has merely a reference to an object that implements a remote interface to the object. This *remoted* version of the EJB knows how to package up method call arguments, a process known as *marshalling*, and send the request over the wire to the server that then *unmarshalls* the parameters and uses Introspection to call the actual object instance. Actually there's much more to it than that: security, transactions, database support, and object lifecycle all come into the picture. Although a complete description of EJBs is beyond the scope of this chapter, we provide a number of excellent references for the interested reader. However, we will try to give enough details so that the process of persisting and restoring EJBs from XML makes some sense.

Three Types of EJBs

There are three types of EJBs:

- *Stateless session EJBs*—These are by far the simplest of the three kinds of EJBs. Stateless session EJBs normally perform simple operations that are independent of prior method calls but need to execute on a server. For example, an EJB that computes pi to a given number of decimal places or returns the exponential (!) value of a given input are both stateless session EJBs. Any method that does not need to know or use information from a prior method call is typically a stateless session EJB. Stateless session EJBs can be, and typically are, shared by multiple clients.

- *Stateful session EJBs*—These EJBs remember their conversational state from method call to method call. Stateful session EJBs are most like their JavaBeans cousins in that they remember what has happened previously. Call center EJBs, simple shopping cart EJBs, and anything where state needs to be maintained are examples of stateful session EJBs. Although stateful session EJBs can be shared, they typically are not. Anyone who has bought an item online has most likely encountered a stateful session EJB.

- *Entity EJBs*—These are by far the most complex of the EJB types. Entity EJBs are in-memory representations of the state of some persistent object such as a customer's credit card or bank balance. Entity EJBs are objects that not only store state but persist that state to some backing storage such as a file or a database. We focus on entity EJBs in this chapter.

Entity EJBs would be difficult enough, but to make matters slightly worse, they come in two distinct flavors: Container-Managed Persistence (CMP) and Bean-Managed Persistence (BMP)Beans.

Before we get into the specifics of CMP and BMP, a little more background on EJB is in order.

Java Application Server Environments

Enterprise JavaBeans live and function within what is typically called a *Java Application Server*. Java Application Servers provide an execution environment for many objects, including EJBs. Some of the most common objects supported in an App Server are

- *Servlets*—Server-side versions of client applets that can be run on the server as required to meet client need. We cover Servlets in detail in Chapter 9, "Servlets and XML."

- *Java Server Pages*—More commonly called JSPs, Java Server Pages are HTML pages that can contain Java code and are dynamic in nature. JSPs allow the developer to have the best of both Java and HTML and are compiled on-the-fly into Servlets and then executed by the App Server when called for.

- *Java Messaging Services*—More often called JMS, Java Messaging Services provide message-oriented middleware: that is, message passing between two Java applications.

- *Database Support*—Support or drivers for common databases such as Oracle, Sybase, Microsoft SQL Server and so on are often provided by an App Server.

- *Other Support Services*—In addition to the previously mentioned services, App Servers typically provide other less often used services such as startup classes, timing services, security, and so on.

- *EJB Execution Environment*—For an EJB to execute correctly, a number of additional services are provided by an App Server. We will examine each in some detail in the next section, but some of the most important are

    - *Transaction Support*—EJBs execute transactions and, as such, support for transaction commit and rollback must be provided.

- *Lifecycle Services*—EJBs come and go, and need to be created, pooled, and destroyed. App Servers provide for these features.

- *Naming and Object Lookup Services*—Since EJBs live in a remote environment, we need to be able to find a given EJB, typically via JNDI, which we will examine briefly.

- *Object Persistence*—EJBs can be persisted to secondary storage. This is one of the main differences between an EJB and a run-of-the-mill JavaBean. In fact, two forms of object persistence are provided by Application Servers: Container-Managed Persistence (CMP) and Bean-Managed Persistence (BMP).

All in all, EJB support is provided within the context of an EJB *container*. Containers wrap all the aforementioned services into a single lump defined by the EJB 1.0.1 specification. Containers provide infrastructure for all the services required by an EJB and wrap that infrastructure around the actual implementation of a bean to provide an execution environment. Many flavors of containers exist. BEA Systems WebLogic Server provides containers for persisting bean state to files and databases. Other vendors provide containers for complex database interaction, object-oriented databases, and so on.

Before we move on, let's examine the general process of EJB and App Servers. Figure 8.1 shows a big-picture view of an App Server showing how applets, Java clients, CORBA clients, and browser clients all access server services using various protocols such as HTTP, HTTPS, RMI, and IIOP. Many of these clients, particularly the Java clients, but perhaps CORBA clients as well, either directly or indirectly access JavaBeans and EJBs via Servlets, or other server-side applications. And each EJB that comes wrapped in a container can use container services such as transaction or security services support. Let's look at Remote Method Invocation, so we can better understand how EJBs are remoted.

Figure 8.2 shows what typically happens when a class calls a method on another class. Figure 8.3 shows the same class being called via Remote Method Invocation, or *RMI*. With RMI, a class is split into two parts, using a tool such as the RMIC—the RMI Compiler. The two parts are typically called the *Stub* and the *Skeleton*. The Stub represents the interface to the class as it was originally known and is used by the client to invoke methods on the remote instance. The Skeleton receives the remote calls and translates them back to local calls on the actual class instance.

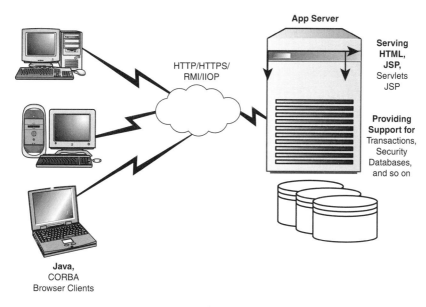

FIGURE 8.1

The big picture for Java Application Server environments.

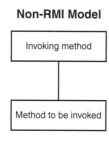

FIGURE 8.2

Normal procedure call.

EJBs are remoted in almost an identical fashion with one difference: There are two remoted interfaces for an EJB. The first handles lifecycle services (create, remove, find, and so on) for EJBs and the second interfaces to the remote instance of an EJB itself.

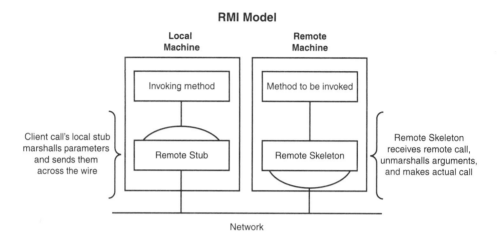

FIGURE 8.3

Remote procedure calls using RMI.

Figure 8.4 shows more of a client view of using an EJB. The client first requests a handle to the home interface of the bean, using Java Naming and Directory Interface (more on JNDI shortly). The client then uses the home interface to find an existing bean or create a new instance of a bean. The home interface then returns a remote stub that represents the bean currently being executed with the App Server. The client application then uses the bean's remote stub to call the bean's business methods normally.

Let's examine the home interface and EJB lifecycle services in more detail.

Home Interface and Lifecycle Services

The home interface of a bean provides what are typically termed *lifecycle services*. Normally developers take lifecycle services for granted, using the new operator to create new instances of objects and letting the Java Virtual Machine destroy these objects when they are no longer referenced. However, since EJBs live within a remote App Server, simply setting a reference to null or exiting enclosing scope will not delete an entity EJB. Entity EJB Objects might exist, for example, within a database and not be referenced by any running application. Or instances may need to be created or removed. All these services are provided by the Application Server and available through the home interface. In a nutshell, the home interface provides methods for

- Creating EJBs with no initial state
- Creating EJBs using specified initial values
- Finding existing instances of EJBs

- Providing meta-data about the EJB itself
- Providing methods for removing a specific instance of an EJB, or all similar instances
- Sharing by all clients using the same type of EJB
- Using a Naming Service, such as JNDI
- Extending `javax.ejb.EJBHome`

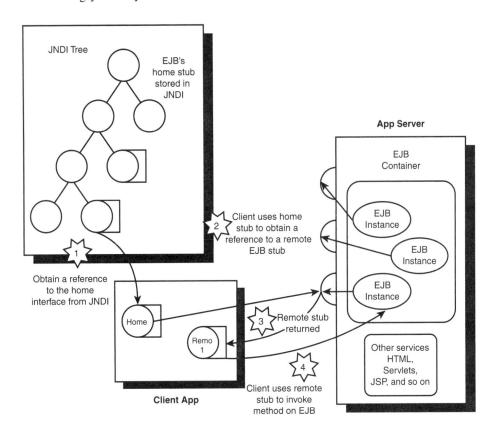

FIGURE 8.4
The client view of EJB.

Remote Interface

The second interface of interest within the EJB architecture is the *remote* interface. The remote interface, which wraps normal business methods, is the interface most clients are interested in. The remote interface provides access to the EJB's business methods and typically extends `javax.ejb.EJBObject` and `java.rmi.Remote`. The remote interface is also responsible for marshalling arguments to the remote server and unmarshalling returned results.

Trust me, we are close to an actual example of persisting an EJB to XML, but first there are a few more items we need to cover. The first is the Java Naming and Directory Interface (JNDI).

Java Naming and Directory Interface (JNDI) Basics

Before we can do anything with an EJB, we need to be able to obtain a handle to an instance of it. With regular JavaBeans this was easy; we simply created an instance of the bean and started using it, perhaps storing and retrieving state values using XML. However, since Enterprise JavaBeans live on a remote App Server, we need to obtain a handle to a remote instance of the EJB and for this we use the Java Naming and Directory Interface (JNDI). JNDI serves two functions: storing references into existing objects in a JNDI tree, typically called *binding* an object, and returning previously bound objects, typically called *object lookup*. We won't go into the process of binding an EJB into a JNDI tree. JNDI trees are hierarchical in nature and can contain complete hierarchies of objects, since binding is most often configured in a vendor specific at startup. However, we do need to understand how to perform object lookups. Listing 8.9 shows a portion of an EJB client, the portion that uses JNDI to find the home interface of an object.

> **NOTE**
>
> It should be noted that the JNDI actually specifies an interface and not an implementation. Typically, Application Server vendors such as BEA and IBM provide the necessary implementation. This is a fine distinction, but an important one. Sun now also provides a reference implementation that can be freely downloaded from http://www.javasoft.com.

LISTING 8.9   Using JNDI to Look Up an Object

```
 1:    Hashtable   env = new Hashtable();
 2:    env.put(Context.INITIAL_CONTEXT_FACTORY,
 3:            "weblogic.jndi.WLInitialContextFactory");
 4:    env.put(Context.PROVIDER_URL, "t3://localhost:7001");
 5:    try {
 6:        InitialContext   ic = new InitialContext(env);
 7:        AlarmClockHome   home =
 8:                (AlarmClockHome) ic.lookup("AlarmClock");
 9:    } catch(...)
10:    // etc
```

Lookups using JNDI start by creating a `Hashtable` object. A `Properties` object would have worked as well. You then insert values into it representing the context we want to create, in lines 1–4, and create an `InitialContext()` object. The `InitialContext()` object effectively tells JNDI where to look for objects. We then use the initial context to look up an object previously bound, most likely at boot time, by the App Server. An important thing to note is that the values placed into the `Hashtable` are dependent on the App Server. The values shown work fine for WebLogic Server version 4.5.1. Other App Servers will require other configuration values.

Once we have our context, we get handles to objects and continue on our way happily looking up objects.

What Listing 8.9 ultimately returns is a reference to the home interface for an EJB. We can then use this interface like any other object, calling its methods normally. Listing 8.10 shows a complete client that exercises JNDI to find the `AlarmClock` home interface and then creates two instances of alarms (lines 21 and 23–24). It also deletes one of the instances using the remove method (line 42). With the exception of the original lookup and performing `remove` operations, an EJB works just like any other object.

LISTING 8.10 Client.Java—Using a BMP-Managed EJB

```
 1: package sams.chp8.bmp;
 2:
 3: import java.util.*;
 4: import javax.naming.*;
 5: import javax.ejb.*;
 6: import java.rmi.*;
 7:
 8: public class Client {
 9:     public static void main(String args[]) {
10:         Hashtable    env = new Hashtable();
11:         env.put(Context.INITIAL_CONTEXT_FACTORY,
12:                 "weblogic.jndi.WLInitialContextFactory");
13:         env.put(Context.PROVIDER_URL, "t3://localhost:7001");
14:         // Now it's time to connect to the EJB Server
15:         try {
16:             InitialContext    initialContext = new InitialContext(env);
17:             AlarmClockHome    home = (AlarmClockHome)
18:                 initialContext.lookup("AlarmClock");
19:
20:             System.out.println("Peforming first insert.");
21:             AlarmClock    alarm1 = (AlarmClock) home.create();
22:             System.out.println("Peforming second insert.");
23:             AlarmClock    alarm2 = (AlarmClock) home.create("03/02/99",
```

LISTING 8.10   Continued

```
24:                    "WBCN", false);
25:
26:              System.out.println("Station1 = " + alarm1.getRadioStation());
27:              System.out.println("Time1 = " + alarm1.getAlarmTime());
28:              if (alarm1.isFmSet())
29:                  System.out.println("First alarm is FM.");
30:              else
31:                  System.out.println("First alarm is AM.");
32:              System.out.println("Station2 = " + alarm2.getRadioStation());
33:              System.out.println("Time2 = " + alarm2.getAlarmTime());
34:              if (alarm2.isFmSet())
35:                  System.out.println("Second alarm is FM.");
36:              else
37:                  System.out.println("Second alarm is AM.");
38:
39:              System.out.println("Deleting entry");
40:
41:      // Only delete a single entry to see if the data remains in the DB.
42:              home.remove(alarm1.getPrimaryKey());
43:
44:          } catch (Exception e) {
45:              System.out.println(e);
46:          }
47:      }
```

With an understanding of EJB architecture and client-side use in mind, an example is appropriate.

NOTE

Note that the code in the following sections depends on the use of a Java Application Server such as BEA Systems WebLogic Server. A Java Application Server provides an execution environment for EJBs to run (live) in. You can download the latest version of WebLogic Server from the BEA Web site at http://www.beasys.com. For your convenience WebLogic Server v4.51 is packaged on the associated CD and runs on Windows 95, 98, NT 4.0, 2000, and various UNIX platforms. See the BEA Web site for more information about WebLogic Server and all it can do.

Anatomy of a Simple Entity EJB

We now know how to object an instance of an EJB. But how was it created in the first place? We've seen part of this picture already with our discussions of the home and remote interfaces. But there are two other Java classes we need as well: the bean's actual implementation and a class representing the bean's primary key. We'll examine these two classes in detail in a moment, but before we do, let's step back and examine the home and remote interfaces for an actual example.

> **NOTE**
>
> For the remainder of this chapter we will be developing a simple Bean-Managed Persistence EJB that works as an alarm clock and stores alarm settings. Most of the files associated with this example will have names starting with `Alarm`.

We'll examine each of the required classes for an EJB in a moment, but first a short description of each is in order.

The following EJB files are required:

- *Interface class*—Defines the remote interface and business methods the client will use. Extends `javax.ejb.EJBRemote` and `java.rmi.Remote`.
- *Home interface class*—Defines the methods required for lifecycle services. Defines zero or more `create()`s that map to `ejbCreate()` methods of identical signature, methods for creating instances of the EJB, `findBy` methods, and the remove method. Extends `javax.ejb.EJBHome`.
- *Primary Key class*—Defines the fields that represent the primary key. There is a one-to-one mapping between primary key fields and EJB-persisted fields in both name and type for all fields that represent the primary key. Implements `Serializable`.
- *Bean Implementation*—Implements the business methods from the interface class and the create methods of the home interface. Also implements `javax.ejb.EntityBean` or `javax.ejb.SessionBean`.

EJB Naming Convention

A large number of files are used to represent EJBs. For entity EJBs, we need at least four Java files of our own creation plus a number of additional files that specify the container. To simplify the process, a naming convention would help. We've come up with the following with this idea in mind. Let's examine a fictitious bean, the *Jimmy Bean*.

- `Jimmy.java`—Format is `BeanName.java` and represents the remote interface and specifies the business methods of the object. Since this interface most closely resembles a normal class, its name looks like a regular Java class.

- `JimmyHome.java`—Format is `BeanNameHome.java` and contains the definition of the home interface.

- `JimmyBean.java`—Format is `BeanNameBean.java` and contains the actual implementation of the business methods as well as a number of other methods required by the EJB specification.

- `JimmyPK.java`—Format is `BeanNamePK.java` and contains the implementation of a class that represents the primary key (PK) of the bean.

A number of other files also are typically required, such as a `jar` file to hold the prepared bean, `JimmyBean.jar`, a manifest file that tells the App Server what beans are in the `jar` file, a deployment descriptor text file, typically `JimmyBean.txt`, and finally, the name the bean is bound into JNDI with, typically just `JimmyBean`, or perhaps `sams.chp8.bmp.JimmyBean`. This is a little daunting at first but is understandable enough once you get used to it.

Listing 8.11, `AlarmClock.java`, shows the first of four classes we will have to write ourselves to implement an entity EJB. Listing 8.11 represents the remote interface for our example EJB. This class defines, on lines 7–12, the business methods that our bean implements. However, we will never implement this interface exactly. Instead, the App Server manufacturer will provide a tool for generating a container class that implements this interface and delegates runtime calls to our implementation. Note that on line 6 the class is defined to extend `java.rmi.Remote` and `javax.ejb.EJBObject`. In addition, each method is defined to throw `RemoteException` as well as any user-defined business exceptions.

LISTING 8.11   `AlarmClock.java`—AlarmClock EJB Definition

```
1: package sams.chp8.bmp;
2:
3: import java.rmi.*;
4: import javax.ejb.*;
5: import java.util.*;
6: public interface AlarmClock extends Remote, EJBObject {
7:     public String getAlarmTime() throws RemoteException;
8:     public void setAlarmTime(String time) throws RemoteException;
9:     public String getRadioStation() throws RemoteException;
```

LISTING 8.11   Continued

```
10:    public void setRadioStation(String station) throws RemoteException;
11:    public boolean isFmSet() throws RemoteException;
12:    public void setFm(boolean fm) throws RemoteException;
13: }
```

Listing 8.12, `AlarmClockHome.java`, defines the home interface for our example bean. Home interfaces always extend `javax.ejb.EJBHome` and must implement at least the `findByPrimaryKey()` method and normally one or more `create` methods. If we remember that entity EJBs are a representation of some object stored persistently, it makes sense that we need a mechanism for finding existing objects. The `findByPrimaryKey()` method provides this functionality to clients so they might obtain a reference to an existing bean. In addition, zero or more `create` methods are normally defined. The reason for zero or more `create` methods is simple: Since we are dealing with potentially preexisting objects, we may not be able to create instances at all, but rather only obtain handles to existing instances. Note that for each `findBy()` method and each `create` method, we will see a similar method with a slightly different name, but a similar signature, in our bean's implementation. When we examine the bean's implementation, we'll look at each of the required methods. There are a few additional points to notice. Each create method throws both `CreateException` and `RemoteException` because we may not be able to create the instance. Any number of communications errors could occur and `findBy()` methods throw `FinderException`. After all, there is nothing that says an object must exist for a given primary key.

8

LISTING 8.12   `AlarmClockHome.java`—Home Interface for the AlarmClock EJB

```
1: package sams.chp8.bmp;
2: import java.rmi.*;
3: import javax.ejb.*;
4: import java.util.*;
5:
6: public interface AlarmClockHome extends EJBHome {
7:     AlarmClock create()
8:         throws CreateException, RemoteException;
9:     AlarmClock create(String time, String station, boolean fm)
10:         throws CreateException, RemoteException;
11:     AlarmClock findByPrimaryKey(AlarmClockPK id)
12:         throws RemoteException, FinderException;
13: }
```

Listing 8.13, `AlarmClockPK.java`, the third class required for our example, and by far the simplest, is the primary key class. This relatively simple class contains no methods and one or more public fields that, when combined, define the primary key of our entity EJB. The important point to note about this class is that it implements the `java.io.Serializable` interface and that all fields must be serializable and public.

LISTING 8.13   `AlarmClockPK.java`—AlarmClock EJB Key

```
1: package sams.chp8.bmp;
2:
3: import java.io.*;
4: public class AlarmClockPK implements Serializable {
5:     public int  id;
6: }
```

The final class required by any entity EJB is the class implementing the bean itself. Listing 8.14, `AlarmClockBean.java`, implements our example bean's business methods.

> **NOTE**
>
> The difference between an entity EJB and any other type of EJB is that entity EJBs persist. What we mean by *persist* is that these EJBs exist regardless of whether an instance exists in main memory. The EJB's data is stored somewhere at all times. The EJB itself is merely a representation of the backing stores data. Persistence can be handled in many different ways. EJBs can be persisted to files, relational databases, object databases, and, as we shall develop ourselves, XML documents.

LISTING 8.14   `AlarmClockBean.java`—AlarmClock EJB Implementation

```
 1: package sams.chp8.bmp;
 2:
 3: import java.io.Serializable;
 4: import java.rmi.RemoteException;
 5: import javax.ejb.*;
 6: import java.util.*;
 7: import java.io.*;
 8: import sams.chp8.*;
 9:
10: public class AlarmClockBean extends XMLEntityBean
11: {
12:     public                int          id;
13:     public                String       station;
14:     public                String       wakeUpTime;
15:     public                String       isFm;
```

LISTING 8.14   Continued

```
16:
17:     private void refresh(AlarmClockPK pk)
18:                throws javax.ejb.CreateException
19:     {
20:         //
21:         // The following two lines are an in-elegant
22:         // solution to the generic problem of refreshing a bean,
23:         // within generatePrimaryKte we examine the primary
24:         // key class
25:         // and get its member variables which by defn match
26:         // back to the bean class.  However, in certain instances
27:         // a wrapper class is passed instead of an actual
28:         // pk instance while the wrapper class has the same
29:         // structure as the PK class it's NOT an instance of a
30:         // PK class and so introspection and reflection return,
31:         // potentially, un-matched field names.Otherwise 33:
32:         // this method should be in the XMLEntityBean class.
33:         AlarmClockPK newPK = new AlarmClockPK();
34:         newPK.id = pk.id;
35:         String name  = generatePrimaryKey(newPK);
36:
37:         String path = System.getProperty(PERSISTPROPERTY);
38:         String separator = System.getProperty("file.separator");
39:         if( null == path )
40:         {
41:             Error("Cannot get path to persist dir!");
42:         }
43:         else
44:             Debug("Path to persist dir is " + path);
45:
46:         String fullName = path + separator + name + ".xml";
47:         Debug("Full name to bean is " + fullName);
48:         try
49:         {
50:             XMLBean.newBeanInstance(path,this);
51:         }
52:         catch (InstantiationException ie)
53:         {
54:             throw new
55:                 CreateException(
56:                 "InstantiationException:Cannot create"
57:                 + fullName);
58:         }
59:         catch (IllegalAccessException ie)
60:         {
```

LISTING 8.14   Continued

```
61:              throw new
62:                  CreateException(
63:                  "IllegalAccessException:Cannot create"
64:                  + fullName);
65:          }
66:          catch (ClassNotFoundException ie)
67:          {
68:              throw new
69:                 CreateException(
70:                   "ClassNotFoundException:Cannot create" +
71:                    fullName);
72:          }
73:      }
74:
75:      // passivate is called when a bean times out
76:      // active when it is restored.
77:      public void ejbPassivate(){ }
78:      public void ejbActivate() { }
79:
80:
81:      public AlarmClockPK ejbCreate() throws CreateException {
82:
83:          // Generate a unique ID for this EJB.
84:          // Most EJBs pass this value in.
85:
86:          Debug("Entered ejbCreate");
87:          AlarmClockPK key = new AlarmClockPK();
88:          key.id = (int) (Math.random() * 100000);
89:          this.id = key.id;
90:
91:          // we force the printstream to be garbage
92:          // collected otherwise
93:          // remove may not work later on.
94:          PrintStream pOut  = createXMLFile();
95:          XMLBean.storeBeanInstance(pOut,this);
96:          pOut = null; System.gc();
97:
98:          Debug("Exit ejbCreate");
99:          return key;
100:     }
101:     // ejbPostCreate is called when the bean
102:     // has been completely created.
103:     // signals and messages could be
104:     // sent here indicating a new bean exists.
```

LISTING 8.14   Continued

```
105:    //
106:    public void ejbPostCreate() {}
107:
108:    public AlarmClockPK ejbCreate(String time, String station,
109:                                     boolean isFm)
110:          throws CreateException
111:    {
112:        Debug("Enter ejbCreate");
113:        // Generate a unique ID for this EJB.
114:        // Most EJBs pass this value in.
115:        AlarmClockPK key = new AlarmClockPK();
116:        key.id = (int) (Math.random() * 100000);
117:        this.id = key.id;
118:
119:        this.station = station;
120:        this.isFm = new Boolean(isFm).toString();
121:
122:        PrintStream pOut  = createXMLFile();
123:        XMLBean.storeBeanInstance(pOut,this);
124:        pOut = null; System.gc();
125:
126:        Debug("Exit ejbCreate");
127:        return key;
128:    }
129:    public void ejbPostCreate(
130:      String time, String station, boolean isFm) {}
131:
132:    public AlarmClockPK ejbFindByPrimaryKey(AlarmClockPK pk)
133:        throws FinderException, RemoteException
134:    {
135:        Debug("Enter ejbFindByPrimaryKey");
136:        if (pk == null)
137:            throw new FinderException(
138:                "primary key cannot be null");
139:        try
140:        {
141:            refresh(pk);
142:        }
143:        catch (CreateException ce)
144:          {
145:            throw new FinderException(
146:                "Cannot find appropriate bean.");
147:          }
148:        Debug("Exit ejbFindByPrimaryKey");
```

8

JAVABEANS, EJB,
AND XML

LISTING 8.14   Continued

```
149:        return pk;
150:    }
151:
152:    // ejbLoad is called to tell the bean to refresh itself
153:    public void ejbLoad() throws RemoteException
154:    {
155:        Debug("Enter ejbLoad");
156:        //
157:        // load the bean from the current disk version
158:        //
159:        try
160:        {
161:            refresh((AlarmClockPK) context.getPrimaryKey());
162:        }
163:        catch (CreateException ce)
164:            {
165:              throw new RemoteException(
166:                "Cannot find appropriate bean in ejbLoad.");
167:            }
168:        Debug("Exit ejbLoad");
169:    }
170:    // ejbStore is called to tell the bean to store its state
171:    public void ejbStore() throws RemoteException
172:    {
173:        Debug("Enter ejbStore");
174:        //
175:        // update the stored xml instance of the bean
176:        // with the current bean's content.
177:        //
178:
179:        try {
180:            PrintStream pOut  = createXMLFile();
181:            XMLBean.storeBeanInstance(pOut,this);
182:            pOut = null; System.gc();
183:        }
184:        catch (CreateException  ce)
185:        {
186:            Error("AlarmClockBean:ejbStore CreateException "+ce);
187:        }
188:        Debug("Exit ejbStore");
189:    }
190:    //
191:    // business methods
192:    //
```

LISTING 8.14 Continued

```
193:      public String getAlarmTime() {
194:          return this.wakeUpTime;
195:      }
196:      public String getRadioStation() {
197:          return this.station;
198:      }
199:      public boolean isFmSet() {
200:          return new Boolean(this.isFm).booleanValue();
201:      }
202:      public void setAlarmTime(String d) {
203:          this.wakeUpTime = d;
204:      }
205:      public void setFm(boolean fm) {
206:          this.isFm = new Boolean(fm).toString();
207:      }
208:      public void setRadioStation(String station) {
209:          this.station = station;
210:      }
211: }
```

The bean implementation class is really the heart of any EJB and contains a number of required methods. As such, a close examination of Listing 8.14 is in order:

- Line 10—Each EJB must be public and implement either `javax.ejb.SessionBean` or `javax.ejb.EntityBean`. The example bean extends `XMLEntityBean`, which implements the `EntityBean` interface.

- Line 12—Shows our primary key field, which maps back to our primary key class in name, scope, and type.

- Lines 17–73—These lines implement the convenience method `refresh()`, which takes an instance of a primary key and populates the bean based on its contents. Actual population of the bean is provided by the method `XMLBean.newBeanInstance()`, which we previously developed.

- Lines 77 and 78—These lines define two methods required by the EJB specification `ejbPassivate()` and `ejbActivate()`. Since an EJB consumes resources, it may become passive due to lack of use. For example, the user may have surfed out to a site and then gone to lunch. These two methods are called after a predetermined time to tell the bean it's being written to secondary store (passivated) or returned to main memory (activated).

- Lines 81–100—For each `create()` method in the home interface, you are required to provide an accompanying `ejbCreate()`, which has the same return type and parameters as the home interface's `create`. Lines 81–100 actually create our bean instance in persistent store, which in our case is an XML document on disk somewhere.

- Line 108—The specification also requires that there be an `ejbPostCreate()`, again matching in parameters but returning `void`, for each `create` method. `ejbPostCreate()` is called when the container has finished creating the bean and all its required wrappers. The bean developer typically adds `PostCreate` functionality here such as sending messages notifying other classes of the new bean.

- Lines 152–169—These lines define the `ejbLoad()` method. Since multiple copies of the bean may exist—after all, many users may access the same instance of a database row—a method must exist for synchronizing a bean with backing store as well as loading state from backing store. `ejbLoad()` provides the bean functionality to load its state from backing store. `ejbLoad()` uses the `refresh()` method to repopulate a bean's state from backing store.

- Lines 171–189—`ejbStore()` is the companion function to `ejbLoad()`. `ejbStore()` stores a bean's state to backing store and is called after each and every business method. In this way, the persistent store version of the bean is always in sync with the in-memory representation of the bean. `ejbStore()` uses the `XMLUtil.newBeanInstance()` method to persist its contents back to XML.

- Lines 193–211—The remainder of the `AlarmClockBean.java` class is devoted to the classes' business methods.

We've examined Enterprise JavaBeans to death, but what we haven't examined is how the bean is actually persisted to XML. Listing 8.15 shows the code for the `XMLEntityBean` class that provides the required infrastructure for persisting our bean to XML.

LISTING 8.15   `XMLEntityBean.java`—An XML Persisted Entity Bean

```
 1: package sams.chp8.bmp;
 2:
 3: import java.io.Serializable;
 4: import java.rmi.RemoteException;
 5: import javax.ejb.*;
 6: import java.util.*;
 7: import java.lang.reflect.*;
 8: import java.beans.*;
 9: import java.io.*;
10:
11:
12: abstract public class XMLEntityBean implements EntityBean {
13:
14:     final static          int          debug =0;
15:     final static          int          error =0;
16:     transient protected EntityContext   context;
17:     final static   String   PERSISTPROPERTY= "sams.chp8.bmp.persistdir";
18:
19:     void Debug(String msg) {
```

LISTING 8.15   Continued

```
20:              System.out.println( msg );
21:          }
22:          void Error(String msg){
23:              System.err.println( msg );
24:          }
25:
26:          public void setEntityContext(EntityContext ctx) {
27:              this.context = ctx;
28:          }
29:          public void unsetEntityContext() throws RemoteException {
30:              this.context = null;
31:          }
32:
33:
34:          public void ejbRemove() throws RemoteException {
35:              // we need to get the primary key
36:              // from the context because
37:              // it is possible to do a remove right
38:              // after a find, and
39:              // ejbLoad may not have been called.
40:              //
41:              // use the primary key to get
42:              // the string representation of the XML
43:              // file and delete it.
44:              //
45:              Debug("Entered XMLEntityBean:ejbRemove()");
46:              try
47:              {
48:                  String key = generatePrimaryKey();
49:                  Debug("Primary key for remove="+key);
50:              }
51:              catch (CreateException ce)
52:              {
53:                  Error(
54:                      "CreateException in ejbRemove()"
55:                        +ce);
56:              }
57:              Debug("Exiting XMLEntityBean:ejbRemove()");
58:          }
59:
60:          protected String generatePrimaryKey()
61:                  throws CreateException
62:          {
63:              return generatePrimaryKey(null);
64:          }
65:          protected String generatePrimaryKey
```

LISTING 8.15   Continued

```
66:             (Object keyInstance) throws CreateException
67:     {
68:         // If we got a key use it
69:         // else go to the object itself.
70:         // on ejbCreate the key has not been created until
71:         // the class returns so
72:         // we cannot use context.getPrimaryKey
73:         // to get the key's value;
74:
75:         Method[] methods = this.getClass().
76:                     getDeclaredMethods();
77:         Class pkClass = null;
78:         if ( null != keyInstance )
79:             pkClass = keyInstance.getClass();
80:         Class EJBCreateReturnClass = null;
81:         for (int i = 0;
82:              null == EJBCreateReturnClass
83:                 && i < methods.length;
84:               i++){
85:             // EJB create is required to
86:             // return an instance of the primary key
87:             if ( methods[i].getName().equals("ejbCreate"))
88:             {
89:                 EJBCreateReturnClass =
90:                     methods[i].getReturnType();
91:             }
92:         }
93:         if ( null == pkClass)
94:             pkClass = EJBCreateReturnClass;
95:         if ( null == pkClass )
96:         {
97:             Debug("Cannot determine Primary Key fields");
98:             throw new CreateException(
99:                "Cannot determine Primary Key fields");
100:        }
101:
102:        Debug("Found primary key class" + pkClass.getName());
103:        Debug("Class of EJB Create =" +
104:                    EJBCreateReturnClass.getName());
105:
106:        //
107:        // walk the primaryKey.
108:        // get each field, then get the field
109:        // value from the object not
110:        // the primary key
111:        //
112:        String stringKey="";
```

LISTING 8.15   Continued

```
113:        Field[] fields = pkClass.getDeclaredFields();
114:        Field[] fieldsBean =
115:            this.getClass().getDeclaredFields();
116:        if ( null == fields )
117:            Debug("No fields found for "+
118:                this.getClass().getName() + "!");
119:        else
120:        {
121:            Debug("Found " + fields.length +
122:                " fields for " +
123:                    this.getClass().getName() + "!");
124:            for ( int i=0; i < fields.length; i++)
125:            {
126:                try {
127:                    Debug("Attempting get on field["+
128:                        i +"]" + fields[i].getName());
129:                    // could handle non primitive
130:                    // values recursively...
131:                    //
132:                    // find the associated field in bean
133:                    //
134:                    Field beanEqField =null;
135:                    for (int j = 0;
136:                        beanEqField == null
137:                            && j <fieldsBean.length;
138:                     j++){
139:                        if ( fieldsBean[j].getName().
140:                            equals( fields[i].getName() ) )
141:                        {
142:                            beanEqField = fieldsBean[j];
143:                        }
144:                    }
145:                    if ( null == beanEqField )
146:                    {
147:                        continue;
148:                    }
149:                    else
150:                        Debug("Found bean equiv field " +
151:                            beanEqField.toString());
152:                    Object value = beanEqField.get(this);
153:                    if ( null == value)
154:                    {
155:                        continue;
156:                    }
157:                    else {
158:                        int modifiers =
159:                            value.getClass().getModifiers();
```

8

JAVABEANS, EJB,
AND XML

LISTING 8.15   Continued

```
160:                        if ( java.lang.reflect.
161:                            Modifier.isTransient(modifiers))
162:                        {
163:                            continue;
164:                        }
165:                        if ( java.lang.reflect.
166:                            Modifier.isStatic(modifiers))
167:                        {
168:                            continue;
169:                        }
170:
171:                         Method toString =
172:                            value.getClass().
173:                            getMethod("toString", null);
174:                        if ( null != toString)
175:                        {
176:                            String valueAsString =
177:                             (String)toString.invoke(
178:                                value, null);
179:                            String tmp = stringKey +
180:                             valueAsString;
181:                            stringKey = tmp;
182:                        }
183:                    }
184:                catch (NullPointerException npe){
185:                        Error(npe.getMessage()); }
186:                catch (InvocationTargetException ive) {
187:                        Error(ive.getMessage()); }
188:                catch (NoSuchMethodException nsme) {
189:                        Error(nsme.getMessage());}
190:                catch (IllegalArgumentException iare) {
191:                        Error(iare.getMessage());}
192:                catch (IllegalAccessException iae){
193:                        Error(iae.getMessage());}
194:            }
195:        }
196:        //
197:        // got enough to make a key
198:        //
199: return stringKey;
200:    }
201:
202:    PrintStream createXMLFile() throws CreateException
203:    {
204:        String name  = generatePrimaryKey();
205:        String path = System.getProperty(PERSISTPROPERTY);
```

LISTING 8.15   Continued

```
206:            String separator =
207:                  System.getProperty("file.separator");
208:            if( null == path )
209:            {
210:                Error("Cannot get path to persist dir!");
211:            }
212:            else
213:                Debug("Path to persist dir is " + path);
214:
215:            String fullName = path + separator + name + ".xml";
216:
217:            Debug("Createing XML File with name " + fullName);
218:
219:            try
220:            {
221:                PrintStream pOut;
222:                pOut =
223:                    new PrintStream (
224:                        new FileOutputStream(fullName));
225:                return pOut;
226:            } catch (FileNotFoundException fnfe)
227:            {
228:                throw new CreateException(
229:                  "Cannot create file " +
230:                  fullName );
231:            }
232:        }
233: }
234:
```

The XMLEntityBean class supplies a number of methods required by the EJB specification but its heart is the generatePrimaryKey method, which provides information about the EJB to generate a primary key. As we have already stated, the EJB specification requires that an EJB have one or more ejbCreate() methods. In addition, for Bean-Managed Persistence beans the create methods must return an object of the primary key's type. We also know that the fields within the primary key object match in type and name their counterpart fields within the bean itself. generatePrimaryKey takes advantage of this knowledge to determine each of the primary key fields and generate a string representation of the primary keys and uses this string to create a file to persist the bean's contents into. If we examine the code, we see that the following steps are taking place:

1. If we were given a primary key object, use it. See lines 78–79.

2. Otherwise, find the ejbCreate() method. See lines 87–91. Note that we use an array of Method objects that we obtained directly from the bean using this.getClass().getDeclaredMethods().

3. We then walk the field list of the key object using the `Class.getDeclaredFields()` method on both the bean and the key. See lines 113–115.

4. Once we have the field list of both, it's a simple matter to walk the key objects fields and find the matching field within the bean object. See lines 124–196. Note that most of this code simply examines the field names using the `Field.getName()` method on both the key and the bean. For each match found, we use the `Field.get()` method to return its value and convert it to a string using its `toString()` method.

The EJB specification requires that several additional methods be implemented. They are

- `ejbRemove()`—All EJBs need to implement this method. `ejbRemove()` is called to remove a bean from backing store. If our bean was using a database as backing store we would do whatever is required to remove the database record representing the bean at this point. In the case of XML, persisted `ejbRemove` would need to remove the XML file that represents the bean. The CD-ROM version of the code has a complete implementation of this method.

- `setEntityContext()` and `unsetEntityContext()`—The `setEntityContext()` and `unsetEntityContext()` methods are used to store a reference to the container object. We don't make use of them in this exercise.

The final method of note in the `XMLEntityBean` class is the `createXMLFile()` method, lines 202–232, which uses the `getPrimaryKey()` method and a system property to create a file that will be used to either restore from or persist to.

NOTE

In our example we generated code for what is termed a Bean-Managed Persistence bean or BMP bean. In BMP beans, the developer is responsible for writing the code to persist and restore a bean's content. BMP beans are actually much more complicated than Container-Managed Persistence beans (CMP beans). In CMP, the container takes information provided when the bean is installed or deployed and generates code to persist the bean to backing store. Interested readers may want to read one of the excellent references at the end of the chapter for more information about BMP/CMP.

EJB Deployment

In this chapter, we've been examining JavaBeans and Enterprise JavaBeans. Both have their places in application development. We've also seen that EJB development is significantly more involved than simple JavaBean development. In fact, EJB development is somewhat more involved than we've seen to date. One area we haven't even touched on is EJB deployment. *Deployment* is the process of installing a bean or class into an execution environment. With simple JavaBeans, we need only have the bean available in the classpath for it to be deployed. With EJBs, which live in an App Server, deployment is move involved and requires that we generate all the container classes for the bean, package the bean into a jar file or other deployable unit, and then tell the App Server about the new deployable unit through a properties file or some other method. All this work is App Server dependent and would have taken several chapters to describe adequately. We invite the reader to delve deeper into this topic by installing any one of the excellent App Servers available online or by installing WebLogic Server v4.51 on the companion CD.

Summary

In this chapter we examined both JavaBeans and Enterprise JavaBeans. We used the Java language Reflection APIs to examine the characteristics of a Java class. We then extended these methods to develop generic mechanisms for storing and retrieving the state of JavaBeans. We also took a whirlwind tour of EJBs and saw how we could persist an EJB's state using XML. Those readers interested in adding to their understanding of JavaBeans and Enterprise JavaBeans should refer to the "Further Reading" section for several excellent references on the subjects.

8

JAVABEANS, EJB, AND XML

Suggested for Further Study

1. Examine the existing code and modify it to use the XML root object's name as the class name. What impact does this have on the DTD?

2. Discuss Reflection and Introspection. What are these two areas designed to do?

3. What were the main areas of Reflection and Introspection that were used in XML-izing beans? Give examples.

4. List four or five services of a Java Application Server. Describe what each provides.

5. List the services provided by an EJB container to a bean. Describe what each provides.

6. List the four main files required to implement an EJB. What is each used for?

7. What is the difference between bean-managed persistence and container-managed persistence?

8. What does the ejbCreate() method return? How do we use this information to interrogate a primary key object?

Further Reading

Java 2 and JavaScript for C and C++ Programmers. Michael C Daconta, Al Saganich, and Eric Monk. 1999, John Wiley and Sons. Chapter 11 contains an excellent introduction to JavaBeans and is recommended background reading.

Creating JavaBeans Components for Distributed Applications. Blake M. Watson. 1997, Morgan Kaufman. An excellent reference for those interested in more information about JavaBeans.

Enterprise Edition specification v1.2. 1999, Sun Microsystems. An intense specification covering, in a general way, all aspects of Enterprise Java.

Java Naming and Directory Service API v1.1 and 1.2. 1999, Sun Microsystems. The JNDI specification covers all aspects of Java object naming and lookup as well as describing the interfaces for developing JNDI service providers.

Enterprise JavaBeans v1.2. Mark Hapner, Vlada Matena. 1998, 1999, Sun Microsystems. A tough read but for those interested in the nitty-gritty of EJBs, these are the definitive specifications.

Servlets and XML

"Server-side XML is clearly destined to support countless practical solutions and innovations over the coming years."

—Claude Duguay, "XML Filtering with Servlets," Java Pro Guide to Middleware, Winter 1999/2000

IN THIS CHAPTER

In this chapter we will examine how servlets can generate and process XML. For those java programmers new to servlets we begin with a servlet primer. In the primer, the life cycle and API of servlets are examined in detail. After the primer, we walk through a real-world sample Web site called the Aphorisms Web site. The Aphorisms Web site processes form data, stores the result as XML, and transforms the XML with an XSLT processor to generate HTML. The site consists of two key servlets: the `ProcessAphorismsForm` servlet and the `AphorismsToHtmlTbl` servlet.

Servlet Basics

A good way to introduce servlets is to compare them to their more familiar counterparts—applets. A servlet is to a Web server what an applet is to a Web browser. An applet is a small Java program that is run by a Web browser via a simple, standard API. A servlet is a small Java program run by a Web server via simple, standard API. Table 9.1 compares the applet API to the servlet API.

TABLE 9.1   Applet API Versus Servlet API

Applet Class API	Servlet Interface API	Life Cycle
init()	init()	Called Once
start(), stop()	service()	Called Many times
Destroy()	destroy()	Called Once
getAppletInfo()	getServletInfo()	
getAppletContext	GetServletConfig()	

The applet API and servlet API are conceptually identical. Notice in the life cycle column that both have an `init()` and `destroy()` method that are called only one time. The servlet execution environment calls the `init()` method after the servlet is instantiated. The `service()` method is called to handle requests from the client. This method is called for every client request. When the Web server or servlet execution environment is being shut down it calls the servlet's `destroy()` method.

The servlet life cycle provides the framework for the execution of our small Java programs by a Web server but not the motivation for the execution. The `service()` method signifies the motivation for our server-side Java programs—to provide centralized services to multiple Web clients. A Web client for a servlet could be an applet running inside a Web browser or the browser itself via Hypertext Transfer Protocol (HTTP) requests. A client sends the servlet a request, and the servlet returns the appropriate response. Therefore, another way to view servlets is a Web-based server framework that abstracts the request/response paradigm. While

RMI uses the method call to formalize and constrain the request/response model, servlets use streams and browser-to-Web server communication.

The Servlet API

While the servlet life cycle and API are modeled after the applet's, the servlet interface API requires more parameters. Listing 9.1 shows the complete servlet API including method parameters and return types.

LISTING 9.1 The Servlet Interface API

```
package javax.servlet;
import java.io.IOException;

public interface Servlet
{
    public void init(servletConfig config) throws ServletException;
    public ServletConfig getServletConfig();
    public void service(servletRequest req, ServletResponse res)
    throws ServletException, IOException;
    public String getServletInfo();
    public void destroy();
}
```

The init() method is passed an object that implements the ServletConfig interface. ServletConfig contains a set of name/value pairs and an object that implements the ServletContext interface. The ServletConfig interface and ServletContext interface can be used to get information about the servlet execution environment, facilities such as logging, and other resources on the computer.

The service() method receives two parameters—ServletRequest and ServletResponse. A ServletRequest is an abstraction of a Multipurpose Internet Mail Extension (MIME) body request. A MIME body refers to the body of a message that contains MIME data. MIME data is specified by type and subtype, such as text/html or image/gif. A servlet request encapsulates MIME data by giving the servlet the MIME type, a binary or character stream to the data, and a set of name/value pairs that can be used to further describe the data. The servlet response is also a MIME body that is generated by the servlet for consumption by the connected client.

An abstract class, GenericServlet, implements the servlet interface. A GenericServlet defines a protocol-independent servlet meant to be subclassed with a protocol-specific implementation. Sun provides another abstract class that implements the HTTP protocol, the HttpServlet class, which extends GenericServlet. Listing 9.2 presents the HttpServlet API.

9

LISTING 9.2   The HttpServlet Class API

```
public abstract class HttpServlet extends GenericServlet
    implements java.io.Serializable
{
    public HttpServlet () { } // abstract class
    protected void doGet (HttpServletRequest req, HttpServletResponse resp)
    throws ServletException, IOException { ... }
    protected long getLastModified (HttpServletRequest req)
    { ... }

    protected void doPost (HttpServletRequest req, HttpServletResponse resp)
    throws ServletException, IOException
    { ... }

    protected void doPut (HttpServletRequest req, HttpServletResponse resp)
    throws ServletException, IOException
    { ... }

    protected void doDelete (HttpServletRequest req,
                HttpServletResponse resp)
    throws ServletException, IOException
    { ... }

    protected void doOptions (HttpServletRequest req, HttpServletResponse resp)
    throws ServletException, IOException
    { ... }

    protected void doTrace (HttpServletRequest req, HttpServletResponse resp)
    throws ServletException, IOException
    { ... }

    public void service(servletRequest req, ServletResponse res)
    throws ServletException, IOException
    { ... }
}
```

The service method of the HttpServlet is not abstract as it is in the GenericServlet. Instead, the HttpServlet's service() method dispatches the request to one of six handler methods corresponding to an appropriate HTTP request method. The six HTTP request types handled are

- Get   This method means return the data pointed to by the Uniform Resource Identifier (URI). If the URI refers to a data-producing process (such as a servlet or CGI program) the response is data from that process and not the process code. If an HTML form uses the GET method to transfer data to the Web server, the name value pairs are packaged at the end of the URI and separated by an ampersand (&). Some browsers limit the length of a URI to 256 characters.

- Post   This method sends an entity of any size as a subordinate to the resource specified in the URI. If the URI is a servlet or CGI program, the data is sent to the process on a separate stream. There is no limit on the amount of data that can be sent to the Post method. The CGI program or servlet is sent the length of the data in the request.

- Put   This method requests that the enclosed data be stored under the supplied request URI.

- Delete   This method requests that the resources referred to by the URI be deleted.

- Options   This method requests information about the capabilities and communication options of a specific resource specified by a URI or about the server.

- Trace   This method is an application-level loopback where the server echoes back what the client sent so the client can debug the application.

All of these options have a corresponding doXXX() method where XXX is replaced by the request type (for example, doPost() and doGet()). By far the most common methods you will override are doGet() and doPost().

Using the Java Server Web Development Kit (JSWDK)

To test your servlets, Sun Microsystems provides the JavaServer Web Development Kit (JSWDK), which comes with a simple Web server. In addition to a Web server, the JSWDK includes the reference implementation of servlets and Java server pages. You can download the JSWDK from http://java.sun.com/products/servlets. After selecting your target platform, you can download the distribution to your machine.

The JSWDK contains examples, JAR files of the classes in the distribution, source files of the servlet and jsp reference implementation, and Web pages including documentation. There are three JAR files: servlet.jar, jspengine.jar, and xml.jar. The files servlet.jar and xml.jar must be added to your classpath to develop servlets for the exercises in this chapter to work.

There are shell scripts and .bat files (depending on your target platform) for starting and stopping the JSWDK Web server. For windows, you double-click the startserver.bat file to start the server. Once started, you can access the server via a Web browser and the following URL:

http://localhost:8080

This will bring up the documentation Web pages and allow you to browse the sample servlet and JSP applications. The simplest way to add new servlets is to add them to the existing

9

SERVLETS AND
XML

`examples/web-inf/servlets` directory under the JSWDK home directory (wherever it was installed). For example, if JSWDK is installed directly under the C drive on Windows, we add our servlets under `c:\jswdk1.0.1\examples\web-inf\servlets`. We then access our servlet from the Web browser via a URL such as `http://localhost:8080/examples/servlet/testservlet`. For more details using the JSWDK, refer to the documentation provided with the kit.

The Aphorisms Web Site

Our real-world example to demonstrate the intersection of servlets and XML revolves around the storage (as XML) and display (as HTML) of aphorisms. An *aphorism* is a concise statement of truth or general principle. Figure 9.1 portrays the introduction page to the Aphorisms Web site.

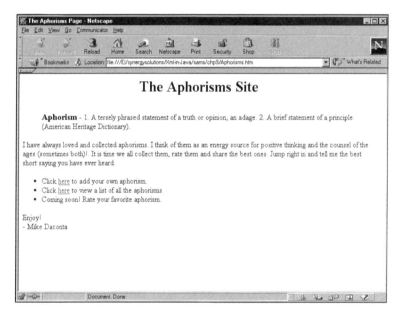

FIGURE 9.1
The Aphorisms site.

While not a complete Web site in terms of features, this site will allow us to demonstrate the key ways that XML and servlets work together. From the main page, you can select to either add an aphorism to the site or view a table of all the current aphorisms. Adding an aphorism requires us to process a form using servlets and store the data in the Aphorisms Markup Language (AML). Selecting to view all the existing aphorisms displays an HTML table that is generated using the Extensible Stylesheet Language (XSL) Tranformation processor, called XT, written by James Clark (who is also the author of the XSLT standard).

Generating XML from an HTML Form

Processing form data is one of the primary tasks performed by servlets. In our Aphorisms site, a servlet will process the Add an Aphorisms form pictured in Figure 9.2. Listing 9.3 contains the HTML source for the Add an Aphorism form. The form contains three text lines, a choice input item, and two text areas.

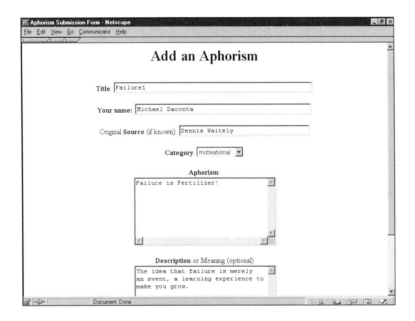

FIGURE 9.2
The Add an Aphorism HTML form.

LISTING 9.3   AddAphorismForm.htm

```
<!DOCTYPE HTML PUBLIC "-//W3C//DTD HTML 3.2//EN">
<HTML>
<HEAD>
    <TITLE> Aphorism Submission Form </TITLE>
</HEAD>
<BODY>
<FORM
ACTION="http://localhost:8080/examples/servlet/sams.chp9.ProcessAphorismForm"
➥METHOD="POST">
<P ALIGN="CENTER"><B><FONT SIZE="6">Add an Aphorism</FONT></B></P>
<P>
<CENTER>
<P><B>Title</B>: <INPUT TYPE="TEXT" NAME="Title" SIZE="52"></P>
```

LISTING 9.3   Continued

```
</CENTER>
<CENTER>
<P><B>Your name:</B> <INPUT TYPE="TEXT" NAME="Name" SIZE="46"></P>
</CENTER>
<CENTER>
<P>Original <B>Source</B> (if known):
<INPUT TYPE="TEXT" NAME="Source" SIZE="34"></P>
</CENTER>
<CENTER>
<P><B>Category</B>:
<SELECT NAME="Category">
<OPTION SELECTED>inspirational</OPTION>
<OPTION>work</OPTION>
<OPTION>motivational</OPTION>
<OPTION>discipline</OPTION>
<OPTION>education</OPTION>
<OPTION>love</OPTION>
<OPTION>humorous</OPTION>
<OPTION>other</OPTION>
</SELECT>
</P>
</CENTER>
<CENTER>
<P><B>Aphorism</B>: <BR>
<TEXTAREA NAME="Aphorism" ROWS="7" COLS="35"></TEXTAREA></P>
</CENTER>
<CENTER>
<P><B>Description</B> or Meaning (optional) <BR>
<TEXTAREA NAME="Description" ROWS="7" COLS="35"></TEXTAREA></P>
</CENTER>
<CENTER>
<P><INPUT TYPE="SUBMIT" NAME="Submit" VALUE="Submit">
<INPUT TYPE="RESET" NAME="Reset" VALUE="Reset">
</CENTER>
<P>
</FORM>
</BODY>
</HTML>
```

In the FORM tag, the action attribute specifies where to send the form data and the method attribute specifies the type of HTTP request (GET or POST). When the Submit button is clicked, the form data will be packaged into an HTTP Post request and sent to the ProcessAphorismForm servlet specified in the URI specified in the action attribute.

The `ProcessAphorismForm` Servlet

The `ProcessAphorismForm` servlet's purpose is to translate the form data received in the `Post` request into XML, save the XML, and report the completion status to the client. The result of a successful submission is displayed in Figure 9.3.

The design of this servlet requires decisions on how the form data will be translated into XML and how that XML will then be persisted. The options for translating form data into XML are to translate it into an element or into a complete document. An element lends itself to a single file strategy, which is attractive except that it requires us to insert an XML element into its containing parent element. It is cleaner and simpler to create an entire separate XML document per submission. Unfortunately, a separate document per submission would be less efficient and require assembling all the files into a single DOM to be processed by our XSLT engine (which is what is required for viewing all the aphorisms submitted at any time). Therefore, the best option would be to store an XML element to a single XML document, if we can overcome the hurdle of inserting the element before the closing tag of the parent containing element. To be specific, the Aphorisms Markup Language (AML) will have a root `APHORISM` tag and one or more child `APHORISM_RECORD` tags. The AML document will be uniform in that it will only have a single level. So, the `ProcessAphorismForm` servlet will need to insert an `APHORISM_RECORD` element before the `APHORISM` closing tag in the document. This is the strategy implemented in the `ProcessAphorismForm` servlet.

FIGURE 9.3

`ProcessAphorismForm` *response.*

9

SERVLETS AND XML

Listing 9.4 is the source code for the `ProcessAphorismForm` servlet. The solution to inserting the XML element into the single XML document was to use a `RandomAccessFile` and calculate how many bytes to "back up" into the file before inserting the new element. The servlet extends the `HttpServlet` and overrides the `doPost()` method.

LISTING 9.4   `ProcessAphorismForm.java`

```java
/* ProcessAphorismForm.java */
package sams.chp9;

import javax.servlet.*;
import javax.servlet.http.*;
import java.util.*;
import java.io.*;

public class ProcessAphorismForm extends HttpServlet
{
    RandomAccessFile raf;
    public static String [] skeleton =
                    { "<?xml version=\"1.0\" ?>",
                      "<APHORISMS>",
                      " </APHORISMS>", // extra space on purpose
                    };

    private byte [] stringArrayToBuf(String [] strs)
    {
        byte [] buf = null;
        ByteArrayOutputStream baos = new ByteArrayOutputStream();
        OutputStreamWriter osw = new OutputStreamWriter(baos);
        PrintWriter pw = new PrintWriter(osw);
        for (int i=0; i < strs.length; i++)
            pw.println(strs[i]);
        pw.flush();
        buf = baos.toByteArray();
        return buf;
    }

    private byte [] formToElement(Hashtable formvals)
    {
        byte [] buf = null;
        ByteArrayOutputStream baos = new ByteArrayOutputStream();
        OutputStreamWriter osw = new OutputStreamWriter(baos);
        PrintWriter pw = new PrintWriter(osw);
        String [] s = null;
        pw.println("<APHORISM_RECORD>");
```

LISTING 9.4 Continued

```
        pw.println("<TITLE>");
        s = (String []) formvals.get("Title");
        for (int i = 0; i < s.length; i++)
            pw.println(s[i]);
        pw.println("</TITLE>");
        pw.println("<NAME>");
        s = (String []) formvals.get("Name");
        for (int i = 0; i < s.length; i++)
            pw.println(s[i]);
        pw.println("</NAME>");
        pw.println("<SOURCE>");
        s = (String []) formvals.get("Source");
        for (int i = 0; i < s.length; i++)
            pw.println(s[i]);
        pw.println("</SOURCE>");
        pw.println("<CATEGORY>");
        s = (String []) formvals.get("Category");
        for (int i = 0; i < s.length; i++)
            pw.println(s[i]);
        pw.println("</CATEGORY>");
        pw.println("<APHORISM>");
        s = (String []) formvals.get("Aphorism");
        for (int i = 0; i < s.length; i++)
            pw.println(s[i]);
        pw.println("</APHORISM>");
        pw.println("<DESCRIPTION>");
        s = (String []) formvals.get("Description");
        for (int i = 0; i < s.length; i++)
            pw.println(s[i]);
        pw.println("</DESCRIPTION>");
        pw.println("</APHORISM_RECORD>");
        // NOTE: as the last record, include end tag
        pw.println(" </APHORISMS>");
        pw.flush();
        buf = baos.toByteArray();
        return buf;
    }

    public void init(servletConfig config)
                            throws ServletException
    {
        try
        {
            raf = new RandomAccessFile("Aphorisms.xml", "rw");
```

9

LISTING 9.4   Continued

```
        if (raf.length() == 0)
        {
            // first time
            byte [] buf = stringArrayToBuf(skeleton);
            raf.write(buf);
        }
    } catch (IOException ioe)
      {
        throw new ServletException("Reason: " + ioe);
      }
}

public void doPost(HttpServletRequest req,
                   HttpServletResponse res)
                         throws ServletException,
                                 java.io.IOException
{
    ServletInputStream sis = req.getInputStream();
    int iLength = req.getContentLength();
    String encoding = req.getCharacterEncoding();

    /* Note keys are form element names,
       vals are arrays of Strings. */
    Hashtable formvals = HttpUtils.parsePostData(iLength, sis);

    // format XML Element from Hashtable
    byte [] elem = formToElement(formvals);

    // append to XML document before End tag.
    int length = (int) raf.length();
    raf.seek(length - "  </APHORISMS>\n".length());
    raf.write(elem);

    // output confirmation
    res.setContentType("text/html");
    PrintWriter pw = res.getWriter();
    pw.println("<HTML>");
    pw.println("<HEAD>");
    pw.println("<TITLE> Processed Form </TITLE>");
    pw.println("</HEAD>");
    pw.println("<BODY>");
    pw.println("<H1> Your Aphorism has been submitted! </H1>");
    String [] s = null;
    pw.println("Title: ");
```

LISTING 9.4   Continued

```
        s = (String []) formvals.get("Title");
        for (int i = 0; i < s.length; i++)
            pw.println(s[i] + "<BR>");
        pw.println("Name: ");
        s = (String []) formvals.get("Name");
        for (int i = 0; i < s.length; i++)
            pw.println(s[i] + "<BR>");
        pw.println("Source: ");
        s = (String []) formvals.get("Source");
        for (int i = 0; i < s.length; i++)
            pw.println(s[i] + "<BR>");
        pw.println("Category: ");
        s = (String []) formvals.get("Category");
        for (int i = 0; i < s.length; i++)
            pw.println(s[i] + "<BR>");
        pw.println("Aphorism: ");
        s = (String []) formvals.get("Aphorism");
        for (int i = 0; i < s.length; i++)
            pw.println(s[i] + "<BR>");
        pw.println("Description: ");
        s = (String []) formvals.get("Description");
        for (int i = 0; i < s.length; i++)
            pw.println(s[i] + "<BR>");
        pw.println("</BODY>");
        pw.println("</HTML>");
    }

    public void destroy()
    {
        try
        {
            raf.close();
        } catch (IOException ioe) { }
    }
}
```

9

Note the following points about Listing 9.4:

- The class has two data members—a RandomAccessFile in which we store the XML elements and an array of strings with a "skeleton" XML file. The skeleton strings are written to the file if it has a zero length (such as when storing the first aphorism).

- The method formToElement() converts the hashtable returned from HttpUtils.parsePostData() into XML in the form of a byte array. This method uses the stringArrayToBuf() method described previously. The strategy the method uses is to make each form value a subelement of the APHORISMS_RECORD element. The subelements are TITLE, NAME, SOURCE, CATEGORY, APHORISMS, and DESCRIPTION. None of the subelements have attributes. Lastly, because we are always appending this new XML element as the last element in the document, we append the document closing tag (</APHORISMS>).

- The doPost() method is called from the service method in HttpServlet when it receives an HTTP post request from a client browser. First, the method uses HttpUtils.parsePostData() to parse the data from the HTTP post request. The data is stored in a hashtable where the key corresponds to the name part of the name=value pair of the Post request. The value part of each name=value pair is stored in the hashtable as an array of String objects. Second, the hashtable is converted to XML using the formToElement() method described previously. Third, we seek the position in the RandomAccessFile just before the closing document tag. At that position, the program writes the new XML element to the file. Lastly, we send HTML back to the client confirming the submission. Communicating the response to the client involves two steps: setting the content type of the response with the setContentType() method and getting a Writer object to which to output text. The content type must be a valid MIME type. The application then uses the methods in Writer to output an HTML document confirming the submission to the client.

- The destroy() method is called when the servlet is unloaded prior to shutdown of the execution engine. In this method, we close the RandomAccessFile that stores the XML.

So, the result of ProcessAphorismForm is an ever-growing XML file that can be parsed and manipulated by the tools discussed in earlier chapters. The next feature of the Web site is the ability to display all the aphorisms entered so far in the form of an HTML table.

Transforming XML to HTML

Until all browsers support processing XML and XSL in a standard and efficient manner, it is better to transform XML into HTML for presentation on the browser. Servlets, as Java programs, can use a range of XML parsers and XSL engines to transform XML to HTML. I chose to use James Clark's XSL Transformation engine, XT. You can download XT from http://www.jclark.com/xml.

James Clark's XT Program

XT is an open source Java implementation of the XSL Transformation specification. James Clark is the author of both XT and the XSL Transformation specification for the W3C. XT can be used as a standalone application to generate a result document given the names of an XML document and stylesheet on the command line. The command-line arguments for XT are as follows:

```
java -Dcom.jclark.xsl.sax.parser=your-sax-driver com.jclark.xsl.sax.Driver
➥source stylesheet_file result_file name=value...
```

To use XT on the command line, you run the class `com.jclark.xsl.sax.Driver`. XT requires a SAX parser that you specify using the `com.jclark.xsl.sax.parser` System property using the `-D` argument to the JVM. After specifying the stylesheet file and the result file, you can optionally specify any number of name=value pairs to be used as parameters in the stylesheet. However, the parameters will only be used if the stylesheet has corresponding `xsl:param` elements.

XT can also be used programmatically and exposes two types of programming interfaces—one based on SAX and the other based on DOM. It is also possible to mix both interfaces using a DOM for input and generating the result document via a SAX interface. This is the strategy demonstrated in the `AphorismsToHtmlTbl` servlet.

The previous section discussed the generation of the XML document via the `ProcessAphorismForm` servlet. To transform that XML document into HTML, we need a stylesheet with the appropriate template. Listing 9.5 presents a simple stylesheet to convert an Aphorisms Markup Language document into an HTML document with a table where each row is selected fields of the aphorism record.

LISTING 9.5   An XSL Stylesheet to Convert XML to HTML

```
<?xml version="1.0" ?>
<xsl:stylesheet xmlns:xsl="http://www.w3.org/1999/XSL/Transform">

<xsl:template match = "/">
    <html>
    <head>
        <title> Aphorisms Table </title>
    </head>

    <body>
    <CENTER> <H1> The Aphorisms List </H1> </CENTER>
    <CENTER>
    <table width="100%" border="2">
    <tr>
        <th> Title </th>
        <th> Source </th>
        <th> Aphorism </th>
    </tr>
    <xsl:for-each select="APHORISMS/APHORISM_RECORD">
    <tr>
    <td> <xsl:value-of select = "TITLE" /> </td>
    <td> <xsl:value-of select = "SOURCE" /> </td>
    <td> <xsl:value-of select = "APHORISM" /> </td>
    </tr>
    </xsl:for-each>
    </table>
```

LISTING 9.5   Continued

```
    </CENTER>
    </body>
    </html>
</xsl:template>
</xsl:stylesheet>
```

The stylesheet consists of a single template that matches the root of the document. Because the Aphorisms Markup Language is uniform with only a single set of children, I can process the document using an `xsl:for-each` element. After matching each APHORISM_RECORD, I use `xsl:value-of` to extract the XML subelements TITLE, SOURCE, and APHORISM as table date items in the table row. This stylesheet will be used by the `XSLProcessorImpl` class of the XT distribution in the `AphorismsToHtmlTbl` servlet.

The `AphorismsToHtmlTbl` Servlet

The `AphorismsToHtmlTbl` servlet generates the HTML table displayed in Figure 9.4. The HTML table will contain one row for each APHORISM_RECORD in the APHORISMS XML document.

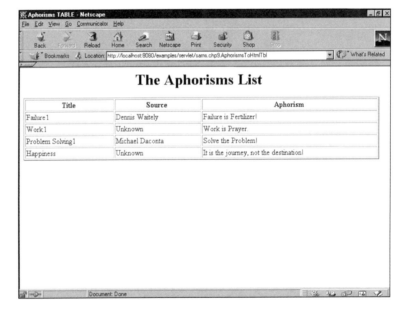

FIGURE 9.4

The Aphorisms XSL-generated HTML table.

Listing 9.6 is the source code for the AphorismsToHtmlTbl servlet. The servlet extends
HttpServlet and implements two SAX interfaces—DocumentHandler and ErrorHandler. The
servlet assumes that the XML input file and the XSL stylesheet are in the same directory as the
servlet. The servlet will fail if that is not the case. The servlet uses the XslProcessImpl class
from the XT distribution to programmatically generate a result document from the input document and the stylesheet.

LISTING 9.6   AphorismsToHtmlTbl.java

```java
/* AphorismsToHtmlTbl.java */
package sams.chp9;

import javax.servlet.*;
import javax.servlet.http.*;
import java.util.*;
import java.io.*;

import com.sun.xml.tree.XmlDocument;
import org.xml.sax.*;
import org.w3c.dom.*;

import com.jclark.xsl.sax.*;
import com.jclark.xsl.dom.*;

public class AphorismsToHtmlTbl extends HttpServlet
                                implements DocumentHandler, ErrorHandler
{
    static final String inputfile = "Aphorisms.xml";
    static final String sheetfile = "aphorismtbl.xsl";

    PrintWriter pw;

    /** Locator reference. */
    Locator loc;

    public void service(HttpServletRequest req, HttpServletResponse res)
    {
        try
        {
            res.setContentType("text/html");
            pw = res.getWriter();

            File in = new File(inputfile);
```

LISTING 9.6   Continued

```
                if (!in.exists())
                {
                    pw.println("<HTML> <HEAD> <TITLE> Aphorisms TABLE </TITLE>" +
                        "</HEAD> <BODY> <H1> No Aphorisms entered. </H1> " +
"</BODY> </HTML>");
                    return;
                }

            File sheet = new File(sheetfile);
            if (!sheet.exists())
            {
                pw.println("<HTML> <HEAD> <TITLE> Aphorisms TABLE </TITLE>" +
                    "</HEAD> <BODY> <H1> Error: No XSL Stylesheet. </H1> " +
                            "</BODY> </HTML>");
                return;
            }
            // create a SAX InputSources
            InputSource is = new InputSource(in.toURL().toString());
            InputSource sis = new InputSource(sheet.toURL().toString());

            // create a Sun DOM Xml Processor impl
            SunXMLProcessorImpl sunImpl = new SunXMLProcessorImpl();

            // create an XT XSL processor
            XSLProcessorImpl xslProcessor = new XSLProcessorImpl();

            // set the Sun impl to use a DOM as input
            xslProcessor.setParser(sunImpl);

            // load the stylesheet
            xslProcessor.loadStylesheet(sis);

            // set Document Handler
            xslProcessor.setDocumentHandler(this);

            // set Error Handler
            xslProcessor.setErrorHandler(this);

            // parse input
            xslProcessor.parse(is);
        } catch (Exception e)
          {
            e.printStackTrace();
            try
            {
                res.sendError(HttpServletResponse.SC_INTERNAL_SERVER_ERROR);
```

LISTING 9.6 Continued

```java
        } catch (IOException ioe) { }
    }
}

/** method of the DocumentHandler Interface. */
public void characters(char[] ch, int start, int length)
{
    // Receive notification of character data inside an element.
    pw.print(new String(ch,start,length));
}

/** method of the DocumentHandler Interface. */
public void endDocument()
{
    // Receive notification of the end of the document.
    pw.println("</BODY> </HTML>");
}

/** method of the DocumentHandler Interface. */
public void endElement(java.lang.String name)
{
    // Receive notification of the end of an element.
    pw.println("</" + name + ">");
}

/** method of the DocumentHandler Interface. */
public void ignorableWhitespace(char[] ch, int start, int length)
{
    // Receive notification of ignorable whitespace in element content.
}

/** method of the DocumentHandler Interface. */
public void processingInstruction(java.lang.String target,
                         java.lang.String data)
{
    // Receive notification of a processing instruction.
}

/** method of the DocumentHandler Interface. */
public void setDocumentLocator(Locator locator)
{
    // Receive a Locator object for document events.
    loc = locator;
}

/** method of the DocumentHandler Interface. */
public void startDocument()
```

9

LISTING 9.6   Continued

```
{
    // Receive notification of the beginning of the document.
    pw.println(
        "<HTML> <HEAD> <TITLE> Aphorisms TABLE </TITLE> </HEAD> <BODY>");
}

/** method of the DocumentHandler Interface. */
public void startElement(java.lang.String name, AttributeList attributes)
{
    // Receive notification of the start of an element.
    pw.print("<" + name + " ");
    for (int i = 0; i < attributes.getLength(); i++)
    {
        String attName = attributes.getName(i);
        String type = attributes.getType(i);
        String value = attributes.getValue(i);
        pw.print(attName + "=" + value + " ");
    }
    pw.println(">");
}

/** method of the ErrorHandler Interface. */
public void error(SAXParseException e)
{
    // Receive notification of a recoverable parser error.
    pw.println("Error Parsing XML! Reason:" + e + "<BR>");
    pw.println("In " + loc.getSystemId() + ",at line " +
                loc.getLineNumber() + " and col " +
                loc.getColumnNumber() + "<BR>");
}

/** method of the ErrorHandler Interface. */
public void fatalError(SAXParseException e)
{
    // Report a fatal XML parsing error.
    pw.println("FATAL Error Parsing XML! Reason:" + e + "<BR>");
    pw.println("In " + loc.getSystemId() + ",at line " +
                loc.getLineNumber() + " and col " +
                loc.getColumnNumber() + "<BR>");
}

/** method of the ErrorHandler Interface. */
public void warning(SAXParseException e)
{
    // Receive notification of a parser warning.
    pw.println("Warning Parsing XML! Reason:" + e + "<BR>");
```

LISTING 9.6 Continued

```
        pw.println("In " + loc.getSystemId() + ",at line " +
                loc.getLineNumber() + " and col " +
                loc.getColumnNumber() + "<BR>");
    }
}
```

Note the following points about Listing 9.6:

- The `service()` method is invoked when the client clicks the link from `Aphorisms.html` (displayed in Figure 9.1) to display the current list of aphorisms. The method first checks to see if the XML input file (`aphorisms.xml`) and the XSL stylesheet (`aphorismtbl.xsl`) exist in the current directory. If not, a simple HTML page is sent to the browser with an appropriate error message. If the files exist, SAX `InputSource` objects are created from the File objects. A `SunXMLProcessorImpl` object is instantiated as the parser implementation for the XSL processor. After creating an `XSLProcessorImpl` object, I set the `SunXMLProcessorImpl` as the parser using the `setParser()` method. the `SunXMLProcessorImpl` will parse an XML document and generate a DOM object from it. After the parser has been set, I load the stylesheet, set the SAX Document handler, set the SAX error handler, and parse the input. Parsing the input using the `XSLProcessorImpl` object generates a result document by firing SAX events. The object (which is set to "this") set as the `DocumentHandler` will receive those SAX events.

- The SAX handler methods simply translate the parameters passed into them into an HTML stream that is sent to the client browser. There is hardly any translation needed because the SAX Document handler methods are designed for XML documents. Also, there is no need to worry about the proper ordering of output to the browser because SAX events will be fired in the proper order.

Summary

In this chapter we covered the server-side processing of XML using Java servlets. The chapter focused the topics around a real-world sample Web site that accepted, stored, and displayed aphorisms. The chapter began by describing the basic components and API of servlets. The life cycle of a servlet is init, service, and destroy. This section also discussed the relationship between the `GenericServlet` abstract class and the `HttpServlet` class. The section ended with a walkthrough of the JavaServer Web Development Kit (JSWDK) that is used to run the examples in the chapter.

The next section examined the input side of the sample Web site. Specifically, how to generate and store XML from HTML form data. The `ProcessAphorismForm` servlet received the input from the `AddAphorismForm.html` file. The algorithm to process the data was to format a single element of a simple Aphorism markup language and append the element to the end of a single XML document. After storing the XML, the servlet returns a confirmation to the user.

The chapter ened by covering how to transform XML to HTML for display by a Web browser. When more browsers have embedded XSLT engines, you may decide to send the XML directly to the browser. In the meantime (and for large transformations), you can transform the XML on the server side and send HTML to the browser. To implement this transformation, we integrated James Clark's XSLT processor (called XT) into our servlet. The XT processor uses a stylesheet to transform the input document to a result document that is returned to the servlet via a series of SAX events.

Suggested for Further Study

1. Add error checking to the `ProcessAphorismForm` servlet. For example, return an error message if no aphorism title was entered.

2. Add links to the table generated by `AphorismsToHtmlTbl`. The link should send an HTTP `get` request to a `ViewAphorism` servlet.

3. Create a `ViewAphorism` servlet to display a filled-in Aphorism form that contains all the fields in the `APHORISM_RECORD`.

Further Reading

Developing Java Servlets. James Goodwill. 1999, Sams Publishing, Inc. This book provides a detailed explanation of all the aspects of servlets and includes several real-world examples. It also briefly examines areas related to servlets, such as JDBC and distributed objects.

XML and Database Access

"There is no question that XML Queries will be required in the future. The real question is whose query language will be accepted."

—Heard on the XML mailing list

IN THIS CHAPTER

XML is a great tool for integrating various disjointed data sets into a cohesive whole. When using XML and databases and automatic generation of schemas to define format and content, there are a number of progressive activities from which to choose . Using a database to produce XML documents has two major facets: selection and output. In this chapter, we will examine some of the tools currently available for producing XML using a relational database, including DB2XML and Oracle tools, and see how each deals with the different aspects of database access. We will also examine XML queries and the Java Database Connectivity (JDBC) APIs to see how we can manipulate a database to produce XML.

Mapping XML to a Relational Database

Currently there are a small number of vendors offering XML extensions to their database products. Both Oracle and Microsoft support SQL-like queries that return XML documents. Microsoft's implementation is completely proprietary and requires both Microsoft Internet Information Server and Microsoft SQL server and will not be discussed here. Oracle's implementation only requires the Oracle database server and we will examine it later in this chapter.

One thing is clear: We need to map relational data to XML. On the surface, this appears somewhat difficult as the structure of XML documents and relational database tables differs. XML documents are completely tree based, containing elements within elements within elements. Database products traditionally contain databases (and views) containing tables, and tables containing fields. However, close examination shows that a relational database is an example of a limited tree and can be mapped as such.

In general, there is a broad spectrum of possible mappings from a relational database to XML. At one end of the spectrum is a completely customized mapping, which requires a large investment in time and resources to develop. On the other end of the spectrum is raw output from a *data dumper,* which does nothing more then read a table and output its data. In fact, we provide a simple example of such a dumper when we review JDBC and how we can use it to access database.

Let's look at a table that represents a set of real estate listings. Such a table might be created with SQL syntax similar to that which follows.

NOTE

Note that the "SQL" here is really a just a convenient representation for presentation purposes and does not exactly match the syntax of any given database product. It is meant purely as a guide for demonstration purposes.

```
CREATE DATABASE RELISTINGS;

CREATE TABLE RELISTING (
      KEY INT PRIMARY KEY,
      BROKER INT,
      TYPE CHAR(20) ,
      LISTPRICE INT ,
      ADDR CHAR(50) ,
      DESCRIPTION CHAR(100) );

CREATE TABLE BROKERS (
      BROKERKEY INT PRIMARY KEY FOREIGN KEY,
      NAME CHAR(30)
      ADDR CHAR(124));
```

The XML representation of this might look something like this:

```
<REListings>
    <REListing ID="1">
        <BROKER ID="1000">
            <NAME>RE is Us</NAME>
            <ADDR>200 Some Street, Anytown, USA</ADDR>
        </BROKER>
        <TYPE>Residential</TYPE>
        <LISTPRICE>100000</LISTPRICE>
        <ADDR>100 farm lane</ADDR>
        <DESCRIPTION>A Wonderful 4 bedroom farm</DESCRIPTION>
    </REListing>
. . .
    <REListing ID="43214">
        <BROKER ID="012">
            <NAME>Better Homes Inc</NAME>
            <ADDR>12 Pleasant Lane, Somewhere, USA</ADDR>
        </BROKER>
        <TYPE>Commercial</TYPE>
        <LISTPRICE>1000000</LISTPRICE>
        <ADDR>1 Ind. Way</ADDR>
        <DESCRIPTION>100000sq warehouse!</DESCRIPTION>
    </REListing>
</REListings>
```

However, the generation of such an XML document is not trivial. You will notice that we embedded into the list the broker information where key/foreign key information was stored in the database. Embedding the broker information into a listing followed the rules of XML, but such a mapping from a set of database tables might not always be possible. We also left out a fair amount of information, some of which might have been important. For example, we might have wanted to include

- Data type and precision
- Primary key information, which we loosely encoded using an ID
- Foreign key information
- Other information specific to a table such as column headers

In fact, what we defined might not even always be possible. Null foreign keys, missing data, malformed tables and so on all combine to make such a mapping difficult and problematic.

Although we will not duplicate the work going on in the XML schema group, we can see that under normal circumstances the following rules hold true:

- Tables map to <!ELEMENTS...>, which contain fields as subelements.
- Field information such as database, precision, column headers, and be mapped as attributes.
- A primary key can be mapped to an attribute of the parent as a required element.
- A Foreign key can be mapped to the appropriate key element as an optional attribute.
- Model data type, using a fixed list of attributes, map to simple values such as float, double, string, int, date, and so on.
- The precision of a model is defined by its attribute.

For example, we might have created the following DTD snippet to simulate this:

```
<!ELEMENT RELISTING (BROKER, TYPE, LISTPRICE,ADDR,DESCRIPTION)>
<!ATTRLIST RELISTING pkey ID #required>
<!ELEMENT BROKER (NAME,ADDR)>
<!ATTRLIST BROKER pkey ID #REQUIRED>
. . .
```

Our purpose in describing this simple relational-to-XML mapping is to show how complex it can be to translate from one format to another. In the next section, we examine another aspect of XML and databases, *XML Queries*.

XML Queries

Another aspect of database access is the ability to formulate queries or questions that can be posed to the database engine to generate a result, which is then presented to the requestor. An XML Query Language (XQL) would make it easy to process a large number of documents or document fragments and extract appropriate elements for return to the requestor. XML queries are loosely defined as the ability to query an XML document or documents using a standard query language, much like SQL 92, and return DOM documents or XML snippets that define the result. One of the key benefits of an XML Query Language would be the ability to take advantage of the document's structure, improving the precision of the query. Such a language would be a great improvement over current approaches, which search the entire text of a document without regard to markup.

NOTE

As of this writing there was significant work in progress to define the requirements of an XML Query Language. The World Wide Web Consortium (W3C) has been working on a set of requirements for an XML query language and has released, in draft format, the XML Query Requirements specification. See the www.w3.org/WD-xmlquery-req-20000131.html for the complete text of this specification.

Requirements for an XML Query Language

Although there is no current W3C-sanctioned XML Query Language, there are a number of features such a language would need to have:

* The language must be able to perform queries on XML documents, XML document fragments, and repositories of XML documents and produce results that are the aggregate of the original set.

* Queries must not implicitly alter and must make available the original document sequence and hierarchy. However, queries should be able to specify the result order in a fashion similar to an SQL sort by modifier.

* Queries must take into account NULL values and must be able to represent NULL values in a query as well as identify NULL values in a result.

* Queries must be able to make structural changes to the resulting data—that is take input data and reformat it much like XSL does. Queries must also be able to generate new structure.

* Queries must be environment independent—that is such a query must not require or prevent the use of a given operating system.

* Queries must be language independent. All queries must be expressed as XML and be able to be embedded in C, C++, Java, or any other language developed in the future.

* Queries must be protocol independent.

* Queries must be based on the information provided by an XML document whether represented as a DOM tree or a text file. No outside information may be required.

Properties of Relational Database Queries

To better understand what is provided by some of the currently available XML query languages, it would be helpful to understand what database query languages provide today. Database query languages typically have the following features:

- Queries consist of three distinct parts: a *pattern,* which represents what we want to select based on; a *filter* which removes unwanted results from the original query; and a *construction* clause which defines how the end result is created from the result of the query.

- Additionally, a construction clause can have *ordering* subclauses that change the presentation order of the resulting data. Such ordering functions can be used to index, reorder, or perform nested queries on the results of the original query.

- Database queries have the ability to perform *joins* across multiple input sets. Such a join results in a new set of data that is aggregated from the original input data.

- Database queries have the ability to generate intermediate variables or path expressions to uniquely identify portions of the result making the construction of the result, easier.

XML Query Languages

A number of query languages exist today. All were developed to solve one problem or another. None solve all the problems or fit all the requirements previously discussed. In fact, there are a number of competing mechanisms for processing queries. In the remainder of this section, we will look at several different query languages and see how they attempt to achieve the goals and fit the previously mentioned requirements.

XML-QL

XML-QL, or the XML Query Language, is a query language submitted to the W3C by Microsoft, Texcel, and webMethod. At its simplest, XML-QL is seen as a superset of XSL. XML-QL query statements always take the form

```
WHERE XML-QL pattern CONSTRUCT output
```

pattern matches a given portion of an XML document and *output* specifies the resulting constructed output.

For example, consider the following XML snippet, adapted from the XML-QL submission:

```
<bib>
    <book year="1995">
        <title>An Introduction to Database Systems</title>
        <author><lastname>Date</lastname></author>
```

```
      <publisher><name>Addison-Wesley</name></publisher>
   </book>
   <book year="1998">
      <title>Foundation for Object/Relational Databases </title>
      <author><lastname>Date</lastname></author>
      <author><lastname>Darwen</lastname></author>
      <publisher><name>Addison-Wesley</name></publisher>
   </book>
   <book year="1999">
      <title>Java 2 and Javascript for C/C++ Programmers</title>
      <author><lastname>Daconta</lastname></author>
      <author><lastname>Saganich</lastname></author>
      <publisher><name>J. Wiley and Sons</name></publisher>
   </book>
</bib>
```

An example query against the sample might then be

```
WHERE <author><lastname>Saganich</lastname></author><book>$a</book>
➡ CONSTRUCT $a
```

This query is based on the original input structure, and matches exactly a portion of the original data.

This query might then produce

```
   <book year="1999">
      <title>Java 2 and Javascript for C/C++ Programmers</title>
      <author><lastname>Daconta</lastname></author>
      <author><lastname>Saganich</lastname></author>
      <publisher><name>J. Wiley and Sons</name></publisher>
   </book>
```

In this example, the variable $a contains the resultset of the query.

In general, patterns and filters appear in the XML-QL WHERE clause and constructors in the CONSTRUCT clause. Let's look at a slightly more complex example:

```
CONSTRUCT <bib> {
    WHERE
        <bib>
            <book year=$y><title>$t</title></book>
            <publisher></name>J. Wiley and Sons</name></publisher>
            </book>
        </bib> IN "www.booksonline.com/bib.xml", $y > 1998
    CONSTRUCT <book year=$y><title>$t</title></book>
} </bib>
```

In this example of a nested where clause, we construct <bib>...</bib> entries from any <book> element in the specified URL with a year value of > 1998. We specifically bind the title to $t and the year to $y for each element that matches. As a result, any entries thatmatch the given pattern and have a year greater than 1998 are formatted with the end CONSTRUCT element. Basically, the query returned a set of $y and $t pairs, which are used to generate the resulting output.

We could join multiple data sources with XML-QL. For example, assume a second XML document, structured like this:

```
<reviews>
    <entry>
        <title>Java 2 and Javascript for C/C++ Programmers</title>
        <price>54.99</price>
        <review>An excellent book for C/C++ programmers looking to
➥learn Java!</review>
</entry>
. . .
</reviews>
```

We can then structure a query that joins the two data sources:

```
CONSTRUCT <priced-books> {
    WHERE
        <bib>
            <book>
                <title>$t</title>
                <price>$p</price>
            </book>
        </bib> IN "www.booksonline.com/bib.xml"
        <reviews>
                <entry>
                    <title>$t</title>
                    <review>$r</review>
                </entry>
        </review> IN www.reviewsonline.com/review.xml
        ORDERBY $p
    CONSTRUCT
        <priced-book>
            <title>$t</title>
            <price>$p</price>
            <review>$r</review>
        </priced-book>
} </priced-books>
```

In this example, we specified that the title ($t) and the price ($p) be bound from the first database and the matching review ($r) be bound from the second database. Additionally, for spice, we specified that the result be ordered by price.

As we can see, this query satisfies all our early requirements; it joins two data sets, uses intermediate variables to store the result, and sorts the given result.

Let's look now at two products currently available: DB2XML(a free set of JDBC wrapper classes for querying XML from a database) and the Oracle database system.

DB2XML

DB2XML is a tool for transforming database tables into XML documents. DB2XML is freely available for download from http://www.informatik.fh-wiesbaden.de/~turau/DB2XML. DB2XML is 100% pure Java and contains a number of servlets as well as a Java programming API. DB2XML uses JDBC to access any given database to automatically generate XML from tables supporting many of the features discussed in previous sections.

DB2XML provides support for three major areas:

- Transforming database tables into XML
- Generating DTDs from the meta-data provided via JDBC
- Transforming XML documents via XSL stylesheets

DB2XML works by generating, for each table and field, a single element. For example, in our fictional database of real estate listings we have a REListing table containing a number of fields, one of which is price. DB2XML would generate a mapping of <!ELEMENT REListing.price> for the price field. The benefit of such a mapping is that it voids the problem of name clash within an XML document. Since XML is a flat name space—that is, each element is defined only once, although it can be used any number of times—two elements can have the same name and be differentiated by context. An automated mapping from a database table to a <!ELEMENT> element could very well generate the same name twice, resulting in an error.

When a query is executed, all records resulting from that query are grouped into a single result element. The user can choose the name of the element, or else it defaults to the table name. Additionally, primary keys and foreign keys are supported via the special keywords PKEY and FORKEY. Typically, the values of these two elements are a comma-separated list of data with the element's name representing the table's primary key columns.

Records are represented as elements within a top-level table element and DB2XML contains a number of default settings so that NULL values and the like still produce valid XML.

DB2XML supports simple queries against a database. For example

```
[tablePrefix] select * from orders when ORDERID >1000
```

generates an XML document that contains the result of the given select. Within that document, *tablePrefix* is used as the root element with the underlying child elements being represented by the fields in the *orders* table.

10

XML AND DATABASE ACCESS

DB2XML does not support joins across tables, other than those supported by standard SQL. Nor does DB2XML support data transformations beyond those allowed by XSLT.

Even with these limitations, DB2XML has been tested and put to use on a number of operating systems, including several UNIX variants as well as Windows NT. DB2XML has also been tested with Oracle, SQL Server, MySQL, and Access. Because it's based on JDBC, DB2XML should be able to take advantage of just about any database that has a JDBC driver.

Output from DB2XML can come as,a file, a Java Stream–based object, or a DOM document, making DB2XML an easy addition to any development effort. Future versions of DB2XML promise support for database updates as well, although this feature is not available in version 1.3.

Programming with DB2XML

DB2XML provides an entire package for developing Java-based DB2XML applications. The main class of interest when developing with DB2XML is the `db2xml.xml.JDBCXML` class. JDBCXML has five constructors, all of which generate an XML representation of a database query into one of several forms. The five most common versions of the constructor are

- `public JDBCXML(Database db, JDBCXMLProperties props) throws DB2XMLException`

    Generates a `JDBCXML` object from a database query and a `JDBCXMLProperties` object(more on this in a moment). Overrides defaults with the properties from `props`.

- `public JDBCXML(Database db, JDBCXMLProperties props, org.w3c.dom.Document empty) throws DB2XMLException`

    Generates an XML DOM `Document` that represents the database query. Override defaults with the properties from `props`. Standard DOM `Document` methods can be performed on the result.

- `public JDBCXML(JDBCXMLProperties props, org.w3c.dom.Document empty)throws DB2XMLException`

    The same as the previous constructor except use all default property values. Overrides defaults with the properties from `props`.

- `public JDBCXML(Database db, JDBCXMLProperties props, db2xml.xml.XMLDocument empty) throws DB2XMLException`

    Generates a DB2XML `XMLDocument` that represents the database query. DB2XML provides a limited version of the W3C DOM API. Overrides defaults with the properties from `props`. Standard DOM `Document` methods can be performed on the result.

- `public JDBCXML(JDBCXMLProperties props) throws DB2XMLException.`

    Generates a JDBCXML object overriding any default with those provided in `props`.

The JDBCXML class uses the JDBCXMLProperties helper class, which simply wraps a standard properties object and provides some convenient methods for setting, getting, and querying properties.

Listing 10.1, adapted from one of the original sources provided with DB2XML, shows a simple servlet that generates an XML document from a database using the DB2XML classes. Listing 10.2 shows the resulting XML document.

LISTING 10.1 db2xmlservlet.java—Simple Application to Dump Table Contents Using DB2XML

```
 1: package sams.chp10;
 2: import db2xml.xml.*;
 3: import db2xml.util.*;
 4: import db2xml.jdbc.*;
 5: import javax.servlet.http.*;
 6: import javax.servlet.*;
 7: import java.io.*;
 8: import java.util.*;
 9:
10: public class DB2XMLServlet extends HttpServlet
11: {
12:     private JDBCXMLProperties map;
13:     public void setProperty(String key, String value)
14:     {
15:         map.setProperty(key, value);
16:     }
17:     public void init(ServletConfig config) throws ServletException
18:     {
19:         super.init(config);
20:         try
21:         {
22:             map = new JDBCXMLProperties();
23:         }
24:         catch (DB2XMLException e)
25:         {
26:             throw new ServletException(e.getMessage());
27:         }
28:     }
29:
30:     public void doGet(HttpServletRequest req, HttpServletResponse res)
31:       throws IOException, ServletException
32:     {
33:         setProperty("out", "stream");
34:         setProperty("el.binfields", "ignore");
```

LISTING 10.1   Continued

```
35:          map.setBooleanProperty("el.protectStrings", true);
36:          setProperty("genDTD", "intern");
37:
38:          res.setContentType("text/xml");
39:          PrintWriter out = res.getWriter();
40:
41:          res.setStatus(HttpServletResponse.SC_OK);
42:          try
43:          {
44:            JDBCXML jx = new JDBCXML(map);
45:            jx.generateXML();
46:            XMLOutput outServ = new XMLOutput(map,out,jx.getXMLDocument());
47:            outServ.writeToOutput();
48:            out.flush();
49:            jx.closeDatabase();
50:          }
51:          catch(Exception e)
52:          {
53:            out.println("DB2XMLServlet exception: " + e);
54:            e.printStackTrace(out);
55:            out.flush();
56:          }
57:      }
58: }
59:
```

LISTING 10.2   XML Document Produced by db2xmlservlet.java

```
<?xml version="1.0" encoding="UTF-8"?>
<!--
   Generated with DB2XML version 1.3
   http://www.informatik.fh-wiesbaden.de/~turau/DB2XML/index.html
   Database: jdbc:cloudscape:D://Personal//book//sams//chp10//xmldb
   Date: Mon Mar 13 14:53:32 EST 2000
   Driver: Cloudscape Embedded JDBC Driver 2.0
   Database system: DBMS:cloudscape  2.0.1
-->
<!DOCTYPE database [
  <!ELEMENT database (relistings)>
    <!ATTLIST database URL CDATA #REQUIRED>
  <!ELEMENT relistings (relistings_rec)*>
    <!ATTLIST relistings
            QUERY CDATA #REQUIRED
    >
```

LISTING 10.2 Continued

```
<!ELEMENT relistings_rec (LISTINGBROKER, TYPE, LISTPRICE, ADDR, DESCRIPTION)>
<!ELEMENT LISTINGBROKER (#PCDATA)>
  <!ATTLIST LISTINGBROKER
          TYPE CDATA #FIXED "CHAR"
          NAME CDATA #FIXED "LISTINGBROKER"
          ISNULL (true|false) #IMPLIED
>
<!ELEMENT TYPE (#PCDATA)>
  <!ATTLIST TYPE
          TYPE CDATA #FIXED "CHAR"
          NAME CDATA #FIXED "TYPE"
          ISNULL (true|false) #IMPLIED
>
<!ELEMENT LISTPRICE (#PCDATA)>
  <!ATTLIST LISTPRICE
          TYPE CDATA #FIXED "INT"
          NAME CDATA #FIXED "LISTPRICE"
          ISNULL (true|false) #IMPLIED
>
<!ELEMENT ADDR (#PCDATA)>
  <!ATTLIST ADDR
          TYPE CDATA #FIXED "CHAR"
          NAME CDATA #FIXED "ADDR"
          ISNULL (true|false) #IMPLIED
>
<!ELEMENT DESCRIPTION (#PCDATA)>
  <!ATTLIST DESCRIPTION
          TYPE CDATA #FIXED "CHAR"
          NAME CDATA #FIXED "DESCRIPTION"
          ISNULL (true|false) #IMPLIED
>

]>
<database URL="jdbc:cloudscape:D://Personal//book//sams//chp10//xmldb">
 <relistings QUERY="select * from relisting"
>
  <relistings_rec>
   <LISTINGBROKER><![CDATA[Broker 1]]></LISTINGBROKER>
   <TYPE><![CDATA[land]]></TYPE>
   <LISTPRICE>10000</LISTPRICE>
   <ADDR><![CDATA[1 cheap land way]]></ADDR>
   <DESCRIPTION><![CDATA[a way cheap piece of land!]]></DESCRIPTION>
  </relistings_rec>
 </relistings>
</database>
```

Using DB2XML in a servlet is a relatively simple process.

First, choose whichever representation best fits your needs. In our example, we just present the generated XML to the client, so the simplest version of the JDBCXML constructor is appropriate (lines 44 and 45). Line 46 uses the db2xml.util.XMLOutput object to write the generated content to the normal output PrintWriter. XMLOutput has a number of interesting methods, so see the DB2XML documentation for a complete list. And that is all! We could have done something much more complex by obtaining an instance of a Document or XMLDocument and then using DOM methods on either to perform whatever processing was required.

> **NOTE**
>
> Installing DB2XML only requires making sure the DB2XML.jar file is in your class path. Get the most recent source and then unpack or unzip it to d:\db2xml or a similar directory. After it's unpacked, install DB2XML by adding *PATHTODB2XML*\db2xml.jar to CLASSPATH.
>
> V1.3 of DB2XML is provided on the companion CD-ROM in the DB2XML directory; both tar.gz and .zip versions are provided. A complete set of source code, samples, and online documentation is available in the file db2xmlsrc.zip.

DB2XML depends on a number of properties, which are loaded from a default db2xml.properties file. The DB2XML properties defaults file needs to reside in the top-level directory of your application server. If you install WebLogic Server into d:\weblogic, you need to place the properties file into d:\weblogic\db2xml.properties. Other application servers will have a different root but will behave similarly.

DB2XML uses a number of properties to control how it functions. You may choose all or none or some of the defaults by setting name=value pairs into the properties map using JDBCXMLProperties.setProperty(String name, String value). Some of the most common properties are listed in Table 10.1. See the DB2XML Web site for an exhaustive list of all properties. Example uses of properties are shown in Listing 10.1, lines 33–36.

TABLE 10.1   DB2XML Properties

Property	*Description*
driverClass	Driver class for JDBC access. For example, COM.cloudscape.core.JDBCDriver for the Cloudscape database.
dbURL	URL for the database. For example, dbc:cloudscape:D://Personal//book//sams//chp10//xmldb. See the "JDBC Refresher" section later in this chapterfor more on database URLs.

TABLE 10.1   Continued

Property	Description
dbQuery	This is perhaps the most important property and defines the database query that will be used to generate the result. Separate queries with the | character.
stylesheetURL	The URL of a stylesheet to apply to the generated XML.
applyStylesheet	True/false value controlling whether to apply a stylesheet.
defaultStyleSheet	URL of a default stylesheet to apply in the absence of stylesheetURL.

DB2XML is a rudimentary but functional tool for generating XML from a JDBC database. Its strength lies in the fact that it can automatically apply a stylesheet as well as use any database that has a JDBC-compliant driver.

Using Oracle and XML

DB2XML is a publicly available free database access tool. On the other hand is the Oracle Database. Oracle is an industrial-strength database running on a large number of platforms from low-end Windows NT servers to the highest-end Sun/Sparc machines. Oracle is fast, robust, and expensive.

Oracle queries are defined by creating an XML document that looks something like this snippet:

```
<?xml version="1.0">
<?xml-stylesheet type="text/xml" href="somestylesheet.xsl"?>
<datapage connection="xml" cat="anyCatagory">
    <query doc-element="elementName" row-element="some row">
        select tableElements from tableName
        where whereClause
        order by orderClause
    </query>
. . .
    <query doc-elemement="anotherElement" row-element="subElement">
        another select statement...
    </query>
</datapage>
```

Oracle typically processes such a query via the XSQL Servlet. The processesing takes five steps:

1. The query is submitted from a browser via a form, or in a similar fashion, to the XSQL servlet.

2. The servlet parses the XML and passes the queries to the Oracle XML query processor.

3. The query processor generates a result.

4. The result is optionally passed through an XSL processor and a stylesheet is applied.

5. The resulting XML, or transformed HTML, is returned to the browser.

Assuming that we have appropriate database tables, we could write a query to generate complete pages using this XML:

```
<?xml version="1.0">
<datapage connection="someConnection" >
    <query>
        select * from RELListings
        where BrokerName like '%{@find}%'
        order by {@sort}
    </query>
</datapage>
```

Assuming that the RELListings table contains elements brokerName, description, and price, the XSQL servlet would generate an XML document that might look something like this:

```
<?xml version="1.0">
<datapage>
<relistings>
    <brokerName>A Broker</brokerName>
    <description>This is where the description should be</description>
    <price>1000000</price>
</relistings>
. . .
</datapage>
```

If we had specified a stylesheet, that stylesheet would have been applied by the servlet and we could have transformed the result into an HTML page or performed another appropriate transformation.

The XSQL servlet takes several possible parameters. If specified, the find='finderClause' is dynamically inserted into the where clause. Likewise, the sort='sortClause' can by used to sort the result.

The Oracle XML query language actually allows for quite sophisticated processing. A more general example follows:

```
<?xml version="1.0">
<?xml-stylesheet type="text/xsl" hreg="myStylesheet.xsl">
<datapage connection="someConnection" variable="value" ... variableN="valueN">
    <query doc-element="parent" row-element="child">
    <!--query to select the data
```

```
      The query could use any of the variables above
      By inserting @variableName strings into the query.
      Each of which would be run time replaced by the correct value
      as the query is processed.
      -->
   </query>
</datapage>
```

The Oracle database provides the following features that pertain to working with XML:

- *XML-enabled object views over standard relational data*—The previous examples show how existing relational data can be queried at runtime to produce well-formed XML.

- *Intermediate XML searching*—Oracle also supports indexing and searching XML documents and XML fragments and provides full search capabilities based on the underlying document structure using XSL-like queries.

- *XML SQL utilities*—Oracle provides a number of extensions to standard JDBC for inserting, deleting, updating, and querying XML from JDBC.

- *Oracle XDK (developers kit)*—Oracle provides a full suite of tools for developing XML-based applications such as an XML parser for C/C++, Java, and other languages. The developers kit also contains a robust XSLT transformation engine, a class generator, and a number of other tools all geared towards developing XML-enabled applications.

For a complete list of offerings, see the Oracle Web site at `www.oracle.com`.

JDBC Refresher

Both Oracle and DB2XML use Java Database Connectivity. For those with limited database background, the Java Database Connectivity API, or JDBC, is an API that performs database access from Java applications. JDBC accomplishes most of what it does through a native API that translates Java methods to native calls. One key feature of JDBC is that it is platform independent. A JDBC-based application can run virtually unchanged from one JVM to another, from one database to another, making it a perfect vehicle for accessing XML information. In the remainder of this section, we will introduce the basics of JDBC so that new developers can get up to speed with JDBC quickly.

> **NOTE**
>
> Those developers familiar with JDBC might want to skip this section.

Over time, JDBC has evolved into an API for accessing any form of tabular data—that is, spreadsheets and flat files, as well as databases. JDBC is also an alternative to using CGI programs to retrieve data from databases and display them in Web-based applications. It's only natural that Java developers would want to use JDBC to manage XML data.

Historically, JDBC was modeled after the Microsoft ODBC de facto standard. Interestingly enough, ODBC itself was based on the X/Open CLI specification. Although Open Database Connectivity (ODBC) is simply a C-level API, JDBC represents a fully object-oriented database access layer. Since JDBC closely follows the functionality of ODBC, a JDBC driver can be implemented on top of an ODBC driver (a JDBC-ODBC "bridge"). In fact, numerous JDBC-ODBC bridge drivers exist.

Driver Types and the JDBC Architecture

Figure 10.1 shows the JDBC architecture. The top of the architecture is the Java application that accesses a database via the JDBC API, defined in the `java.sql` package. The JDBC API then calls one of four different types of JDBC drivers, depending on the data source.

The four driver types are

- Type 1 drivers, often called bridge drivers, show a JDBC face but call into an ODBC driver, which itself is normally implemented on top of a native driver written in C, C++, or another language.

- Type 2 drivers are implemented directly against the underlying native driver, eliminating the ODBC layer. Native drivers are still required.

- Type 3 drivers interface over the network to a remote database. Type 3 drivers are typically written in Java.

- Type 4 drivers are completely written in Java and access a database directly without the need for any intervening layers. From a pure performance perspective, type 4 drivers are best because they have the least overhead. In addition, since they are written completely in Java, type 4 drivers can run virtually unchanged on any platform.

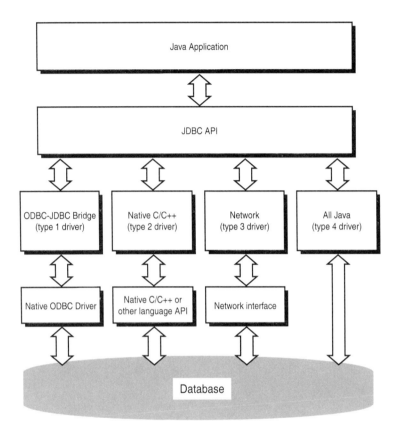

FIGURE 10.1
The JDBC architecture.

A Simple JDBC Application

Listing 10.3 shows a simple JDBC application, but one that shows many of the useful features of JDBC.

LISTING 10.3   dumpDB.Java—Simple Application to Dump Table Contents

```
1:   package sams.chp10;
2:   import java.sql.*;
3:   public class dumpDB
4:   {
5:       public static void main(String args[])
6:       {
```

LISTING 10.3   Continued

```
 7:          try
 8:          {
 9:              if (args.length<2)
10:              {
11:                  System.out.println("Usage:");
12:                  System.out.println("
                     ➥ sams.chp10.dumpDB dbName tableName");
13:                  System.exit(1);
14:              }
15:              Class.forName("COM.cloudscape.core.JDBCDriver");
16:              Connection   connection =
17:                  DriverManager.getConnection("jdbc:cloudscape:"+ args[0]);
18:              Statement   statement = connection.createStatement();
19:              ResultSet   resultSet;
20:              String      sql;
21:              // printout entire database
22:              sql = "SELECT * FROM "+args[1];
23:              resultSet = statement.executeQuery(sql);
24:              ResultSetMetaData md = resultSet.getMetaData();
25:              int colCt = md.getColumnCount();
26:              while (resultSet.next())
27:              {
28:                  for ( int i = 1; i<= colCt; i++)
29:                  {
30:                      String value  = resultSet.getString(i);
31:                      if ( i > 1)
32:                          System.out.print(" ");
33:                      System.out.print(value.trim());
34:                  }
35:                  System.out.println(" ");
36:              }
37:              statement.close();
38:              resultSet.close();
39:              connection.close();
40:          }
41:          catch (Exception e)
42:          {
43:              System.out.println("Error:" + e);
44:          }
45:      }
46:  }
```

Examining a few key lines of the listing, we see

- Line 1—All JDBC-based applications must import `java.sql.*`.

- Line 15—We force the class loader to load an appropriate driver. For this example we are using the Cloudscape database available from `www.cloudscape.com` and also on the CD-ROM. The actual driver name is database dependent; the name `COM.cloudscape.core.JDBCDriver` was defined by Cloudscape.

- Lines 16–17—After we have loaded the driver, we can use the JDBC driver manager to create a connection to the database on our behalf using the driver. The driver URL is also driver dependent. The URL `jdbc:cloudscape:dbName` was also specified by Cloudscape. The format of the URL is always `jdbc:subprotocol:subname` where `subprotocol` is typically the database provider and `subname` is data necessary to make the database connection. What the driver manager does is work as a class factory object, returning objects that implement the connection interface.

- Line 18—We obtain a `Statement` object from the connection. Later we use this statement object to execute an SQL statement such as `select * from...` or something similar. The `Statement` class is the most basic of the three classes representing SQL statements. We could have also used a prepared statement or a callable statement. Examination of these two classes is left to the reader.

- Line 19—JDBC returns results into a `ResultSet` object, which can be used like `Enumeration` objects. Resultsets represent rows of data returned. We then use the `ResultSet.type ResultSet.type get(int columnNumber)` or `type get(String columnName)` to get the actual data.

- Line 23—Executing a statement results in our resultset, which we walk on line 30, getting each value back as a string. We could have used `statement.executeUpdate("sql...")` to update the table. Insert and delete functionality is also provided.

- Lines 37–39—These lines clean up any mess we have made, freeing objects in the reverse order of their creation. We should `.close()` any statements and connections we made to free up resources.

Meta-data

One of the cool things about JDBC is that we can use it to gather meta-data, or data about the data. From an XML standpoint, this is very useful because we can create, on-the-fly, XML data and DTDs with nothing more then a table name. The class that makes this possible is `java.sql.ResultSetMetaData`. The meta-data class contains information such as

- How many columns are in the resultset?
- What are the column names and are they case sensitive?

- Is NULL a valid value for a field?
- Do the columns have display labels?
- Which table did the results come from?
- What is the data type of a given field?

Listing 10.4 makes use of the resultset meta-data and outputs an XML document, including its DTD, from the contents of the table.

LISTING 10.4   dumpAsXML.Java—Export a Table as XML

```
 1: package sams.chp10;
 2: import java.sql.*;
 3:
 4: public class dumpAsXML
 5: {
 6:     public static void OutputData(ResultSetMetaData md, ResultSet rs)
 7:     {
 8:         try
 9:         {
10:             System.out.println("<" + md.getTableName(1)+"s>");
11:             while (rs.next())
12:             {
13:                 System.out.println("\t<"+ md.getTableName(1)+">");
14:                 for ( int i = 1; i<= md.getColumnCount(); i++)
15:                 {
16:                     System.out.print("\t\t<" + md.getColumnName(i)+">");
17:                     String value  = rs.getString(i);
18:                     System.out.print(value.trim());
19:                     System.out.println("</" + md.getColumnName(i) +">");
20:                 }
21:                 System.out.println("\t</" +md.getTableName(1)+">");
22:                 System.out.println(" ");
23:             }
24:             System.out.println("</" + md.getTableName(1)+"s>");
25:         }
26:         catch (SQLException sqle) {}
27:     }
28:
29:     public static void OutputDTD(ResultSetMetaData md)
30:     {
31:         try
32:         {
33:             System.out.println("<?xml version=\"1.0\"
                ➥encoding=\"UTF-8\" ?>");
```

LISTING 10.4   Continued

```
34:              // make the rather simplistic choice that the table
                 ➥name of column 1
35:              // is the name of the results
36:              System.out.println("<!DOCTYPE " + md.getTableName(1) + "s [");
37:              System.out.println("<!ELEMENT " +
38:                                     md.getTableName(1) + "s (" +
39:                                     md.getTableName(1) + "*)> ");
40:              System.out.println("<!ELEMENT " + md.getTableName(1) + " (");
41:              for ( int i = 1; i<= md.getColumnCount(); i++)
42:              {
43:                  System.out.print("\t"+ md.getColumnName(i));
44:                  if ( 1 == md.isNullable(i) )
45:                      System.out.print("?");
46:                  if ( i < md.getColumnCount())
47:                      System.out.println(",");
48:              }
49:              System.out.println("\t)>");
50:              for ( int i = 1; i<= md.getColumnCount(); i++)
51:              {
52:                  System.out.println("\t<!ELEMENT " +
53:                                     md.getColumnName(i) +
54:                                     " (#PCDATA)>");
55:              }
56:              System.out.println("]>");
57:          }
58:      catch (SQLException sqle) {};
59:  }
60:  public static void main(String args[])
61:  {
62:      try
63:      {
64:          if (args.length<2)
65:          {
66:              System.out.println("Usage:");
67:              System.out.println("
                 ➥sams.chp10.dumpAsXML dbName tableName");
68:              System.exit(1);
69:          }
70:          Class.forName("COM.cloudscape.core.JDBCDriver");
71:          Connection   connection =
72:              DriverManager.getConnection("jdbc:cloudscape:"+ args[0]);
73:          Statement   statement = connection.createStatement();
74:          ResultSet   resultSet;
75:          String      sql;
```

LISTING 10.4   Continued

```
76:            // printout entire database
77:            statement = connection.createStatement();
78:            sql = "SELECT * FROM "+args[1];
79:            resultSet = statement.executeQuery(sql);
80:            ResultSetMetaData md = resultSet.getMetaData();
81:            OutputDTD(md);
82:            OutputData(md,resultSet);
83:            statement.close();
84:            resultSet.close();
85:            connection.close();
86:        } catch (Exception e) {};
87:    }
88: }
```

A close examination of this listing shows how outputting the data and DTD is achieved. Line 80 exercises the `ResultSet.getMetaData()` method and returns a `ResultSetMetaData` object, which is then used as input to outputting a DTD. Lines 36 and 41 use the meta-data to get the table name associated with the data as well as the column names and generate a DTD from the table.

> **NOTE**
>
> IBM has a proprietary product known as XLE, the *XML Lightweight Extractor*, which maps databases to a given DTD using JDBC. XLE allows developers, using special DTD constructs, to map database fields and views to a given DTD. At runtime the user specifies one or more selection constraints and XLE produces an XML document that matches the original mapping and the runtime constraints. For more information about XLE, surf to www.alphaworks.ibm.com and search for XLE.

Even without special database extensions, we can take advantage of JDBC to generate SQL.

Summary

Seventy-five percent of all Web applications today access databases. It's clear that XML will be stored and returned from database products, whether they be simple products such as DB2XML or full-featured databases such as those provided by Oracle. There are still a number of outstanding issues concerning XML and how it will be queried. Many interesting proposals are still being debated and it will be some time before a clear winner emerges. Once thing is certain: XML, XML queries, and databases will be part of future Web-enabled applications.

Further Reading

The XML Query Specification. 1999, www.W3C.org.

XML-QL: A Query Language for XML. Microsoft, Texcel, and webMethods. 1999, www.w3c.org/TR/NOTE-xml-ql.

Java 2 and JavaScript for C and C++ Programmers. Michael C. Daconta, Al Saganich, and Eric Monk. 1999, John Wiley and Sons.

Java Unleashed, 2nd Edition. George Reese. 1997, Sams Publishing.

Advanced Java Networking. Prashant Sridharan. 1997, Prentice-Hall.

JDBC Developer's Resource. Art Taylor. 1997, Informix Press.

Database Programming with JDBC and Java. George Reese. 1997, O'Reilly.

XML Tools

IN THIS APPENDIX

The information provided in this appendix is the name of each tool; whether it is a commercial, shareware, free, or open-source product; and a Web site you can visit to get more information.

Editors/Authoring Tools

Table A.1 provides a list of both commercial and free products to create and edit XML documents. I recommend first experimenting with the free editors before buying a commercial product. The free tools are quite robust and getting better all the time.

TABLE A.1   Editors and Authoring Tools

Product Name	Type	Web Site
FrameMaker+SGML	Commercial product	www.adobe.com
ADEPT Editor	Commercial product	www.arbortext.com
XMetal	Commercial product	www.sq.com
XML Spy	Commercial product	www.xml-spy.com
XML Pro	Commercial product	www.vervet.com
VisualXML	Open source	www.pierlou.com
XED	Freeware	www.ltg.ed.ac.uk/~ht/xed.html
XEENA	Freeware	www.ibm.com/xml
XML Notepad	Freeware	www.microsoft.com/xml

Parsers/XSL Processors

Table A.2 lists the numerous parsers and XSL processors available. Special attention should be given to the Apache XML contributions as they are gaining prominence and support of the key players (specifically Sun and IBM).

TABLE A.2   Parsers and XSL Processors

Product Name	Type	Web Site
Sun's Java API for XML Parsing	Parser. Community source license. Will ship with JDK.	java.sun.com/xml
IBM's XML for Java, XML for C++	Java parser. C++ XML Parser. Freeware/Open source.	www.ibm.com/xml

TABLE A.2 Continued

Product Name	Type	Web Site
James Clark's Tools	XP (Java parser),expat (C parser), XT (Java implementation of XSLT). Open source.	www.jclark.com
Aelfred	Small Java parser. Free for commercial use. Source available.	www.microstar.com
Lotus XSL	XSLT processor, freeware.	www.ibm.com/xml
Apache's Xerces	Java XML parser. Open source.	xml.apache.org
Apache's Cocoon	Java XSL processor.	xml.apache.org
James Tauber's FOP	XSL FO implementation.	www.jtauber.com

XML Storage/Servers

Table A.3 provides a list of cutting-edge products entering this new arena of XML storage and query. As the XML Schema and XML Query standards mature, more players will move into this area.

TABLE A.3 XML Storage and Servers

Product Name	Type	Web Site
Poet	Commercial product	www.poet.com
HotMetal Application Server	Commercial product	www.sq.com
EXcelon	Commercial product	www.objectdesign.com
Bluestone's XML Server	Commercial product	www.bluestone.com

XML Tutorials

Here is a list of tutorials available on the Web. More are being added each week.

- Microsoft XML Tutorial

  http://www.microsoft.com/xml/tutorial/default.asp

- 20 Questions on XML

  http://builder.cnet.com/authoring/xml20/index.html

- IBM Tutorials: Overview of XML

  http://www.software.ibm.com/xml/education/tutorialprog/overview.htm

- Writing XML Documents

  `http://www.software.ibm.com/xml/education/tutorialprog/writing.html`
- XSL Tutorial

  `http://nwalsh.com/tutorials/xml98/xsl/slides.html`

Web Sites

Here is a list of key XML information sites on the Web. These sites also have links to further resources.

- The World Wide Web Consortium (standards)

  `http://www.w3c.org`
- XML information/articles/resources

  `http://www.xml.com`
- IBM's XML home

  `http://www.ibm.com/xml`
- Sun's Java XML home

  `http://java.sun.com/xml`
- IBM's online laboratory

  `http://www.alphaworks.ibm.com`
- Microsoft's XML home

  `http://www.microsoft.com/xml`
- XML university (training, news, articles)

  `http://www.xmlu.com`
- SGML/XML Web page

  `http://www.oasis-open.org/cover`
- XML FAQ

  `http://www.ucc.ie/xml`
- XML Resources page

  `http://www.jclark.com/xml`
- Simple API for XML (SAX)

  `http://www.megginson.com/SAX/index.html`
- Apache's XML tools

  `http://xml.apache.org`
- XML Repository (run by OASIS)

  `http://www.xml.org`

INDEX

SYMBOLS

L

What's on the CD-ROM

The companion CD-ROM contains the source code from the book and several useful evaluation software packages, including Apache Software Foundation's Cocoon, FOP, SOAP, Xalan, and Xerces; BEA Systems' WebLogic Server; Extensibility's XML Authority; Icon Information Systems' XML Spy; Microsoft Corporation's XML Notepad; Tek Tools' Kawa; and Vervet Logic's XML Pro.

Windows 95, Windows 98, Windows Millennium Edition, Windows NT 4, and Windows 2000 Installation Instructions

1. Insert the CD-ROM disc into your CD-ROM drive.
2. From the desktop, double-click on the My Computer icon.
3. Double-click on the icon representing your CD-ROM drive.
4. Double-click on the icon titled AUTOPLAY.EXE to run the installation program.
5. Follow the on-screen prompts to finish the installation.

> **NOTE**
>
> If Windows 95, Windows 98, Windows Millennium Edition, Windows NT 4 or Windows 2000 is installed on your computer and you have the AutoPlay feature enabled, the AUTOPLAY.EXE program starts automatically when you insert the disc into your CD-ROM drive.

Solaris and Linux Installation Instructions

1. Insert the CD-ROM disc into your CD-ROM drive.
2. If your volume manager is running, the CD-ROM will be mounted automatically. If the CD-ROM is not mounted automatically, you need to issue the mount command. From a shell prompt, type **mount *your_cdrom_device your_mount_point*** where *your_cdrom_device* is the device that represents your CD-ROM drive and *your_mount_point* is the mount directory.
3. Use your text editor to view the readme.txt file.

Technical Support from Sams Publishing

We cannot help you with computer problems, operating system problems, or third-party application problems, but we can assist you with any problems you might have with the book or the CD-ROM. Problems with other companies' programs on the disc must be resolved with the company that produced the program or demo.

If you need assistance with the information provided in this product, please feel free to access our Web site at http://www.mcp.com/sams/detail_sams.cfm?item=0672316536

Related Titles

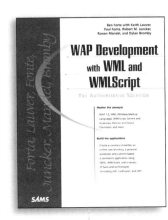

WAP Development with WML and WMLScript

Ben Forta, et al.
0-672-31946-2
$54.99

Pure JSP: Java Server Pages
James Goodwill
0-672-31902-0
$34.99

Pure Java 2
Kenneth Litwak
0-672-31654-4
$24.99

Pure JFC Swing
Dr. Satyaraj Pantham
0-672-31423-1
$19.99

XML Unleashed
Michael Morrison
0-672-31514-9
$49.99

Applied XML Solutions
Benoit Marchal
0-672-32054-1
$49.99

Java 2 Unleashed, Second Edition
Michael Morrison
0-672-31992-6
$49.99

Developing Java Servlets
James Goodwill
0-672-31600-5
$29.99

JavaServer Pages Application Development
Ben Forta, David Aden, Roger Kerr, Larry Kim, Andre Lei, Edwin Smith, Scott M. Stirling
0-672-31939-X
$39.99

Java Security Handbook

Jamie Jaworski and Paul Perrone
0-672-31602-1
$49.99

Building Java Enterprise Systems with J2EE

Paul Perrone and Krishna Chaganti
0-672-31795-8
$59.99

SAMS

www.samspublishing.com

All prices are subject to change.

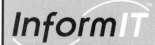

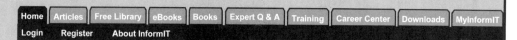